Contemporary Parenting and Parenthood

Contemporary Parenting and Parenthood

From News Headlines to New Research

Michelle Y. Janning, Editor

PRAEGER™

An Imprint of ABC-CLIO, LLC

Santa Barbara, California • Denver, Colorado

Library of Congress Cataloging-in-Publication Data

Names: Janning, Michelle Yvonne, editor.
Title: Contemporary parenting and parenthood : from news headlines to new
    research / Michelle Y. Janning, editor.
Description: Santa Barbara, California : Praeger, [2019] | Includes
    bibliographical references and index.
Identifiers: LCCN 2018028195 (print) | LCCN 2018033976 (ebook) | ISBN
    9781440855931 (eBook) | ISBN 9781440855924 (hardcopy : alk. paper)
Subjects: LCSH: Parenthood—United States. | Parenting—United States. |
    Child rearing—United States.
Classification: LCC HQ755.8 (ebook) | LCC HQ755.8 .C6557 2019 (print) |
    DDC 306.874—dc23
LC record available at https://lccn.loc.gov/2018028195

ISBN: 978-1-4408-5592-4 (print)
        978-1-4408-5593-1 (ebook)

23 22 21 20 19   1 2 3 4 5

This book is also available as an eBook.

Praeger
An Imprint of ABC-CLIO, LLC

ABC-CLIO, LLC
130 Cremona Drive, P.O. Box 1911
Santa Barbara, California 93116-1911
www.abc-clio.com

This book is printed on acid-free paper ∞

Manufactured in the United States of America

For my mom, Yvonne Atkinson Janning, MA, CFLE, an inspiration in the big and small worlds of parent education

Contents

Acknowledgments

My gratitude jar is filled with thanks to the authors whose words make up this volume. This project is the result of their hard work and passion, and I am honored to have been given the gift of organizing this book to showcase their voices. I am thankful for the support, wisdom, and kindness from Jessica Gribble at Praeger, who approached me about this project early on and who patiently awaited its completion while cheering for me.

Thanks to my friends and family, especially those who work tirelessly to support parents from all walks of life and who work tirelessly in their own parenting.

Thanks to my students and colleagues at Whitman College who motivate me to ask complex questions and to present sophisticated answers and follow-up questions in an accessible way.

I am grateful to my partner, Neal Christopherson, whose version of parenting is, in no uncertain terms, the model of patience and kindness. I'm also grateful to my exchange student daughters, Louisa and Anna, who called me their host mom as they stayed in our home. And thanks to my son, Aaron, the child whose existence most defines me as a parent. I am constantly in awe of you, I learn from you, and I love you. And in about five minutes, you're going to be bigger than I am.

I hold in high esteem my own parents. Dad's no longer alive, but I'm so glad I am the beneficiary of his lifelong dedication to teaching all of us—his kids and his students—to be kind, smart, funny, grateful, and just weird enough to make life interesting. The music helped, too. My mom's life work serves as the inspiration for mine. I say this both as a daughter who has learned from a loving and brilliant mother and as a scholar whose aim—like hers—is to share good information about how parents and children actually live their lives and how we can participate in improving the lives of all parents.

Mom, you started this. Thanks for letting me continue your work.

Introduction

Michelle Janning

From News Headlines to New Research

News and social media headlines abound with contradictory stories about parents—from tales of neglect to fear of helicopter parenting, from woes of social inequalities to concern about screen time. Journalists cover great stories, but sometimes these stories and their spinoffs and commentary can make parents feel as if the world is judging them at every turn, and they can make people who are in professions that help parents or conduct research about them feel conflicted about what is actually going on. What readers think they know and understand about parenting and parenthood can stem from misinformation and oversimplification. This edited volume of new and sophisticated research and writing from top and up-and-coming social science scholars on topics ripped from the headlines helps to clarify the debates and demystify hyperbolic headlines and social media frenzy. The book offers much needed clarity for students, practitioners, scholars, and parents.

This book is meant to bridge the gap between the reality for families today and the news headlines about families that may shock and awe us. The authors of each chapter take timely and often contradictory headlines from news and social media and offer accurate and nuanced research-based views of the actual experiences of parents and the cultural construction of parenthood in contemporary society.

While the news items cited in this book may be outdated as soon as you start reading, the gap between how we see news about parenting and parenthood and the actual experiences of today's parents and children is always worth scrutinizing. The scrutiny of this gap is offered in each chapter in a sophisticated way. Social scientists are interested in people's realities, to be sure. But we are particularly intrigued when our perceptions of reality are shaped by powerful media sources, peers, and politicians. And there's no guarantee that these sources actually capture the reality of parents' lives. As a parent and as a social scientist, I find it challenging to navigate the news and figure out which new research I should trust. Turns out, I'm not alone in this challenge; the authors of each chapter in this book offer their own inspired and rigorous research-based responses to the headlines. I hope you find inspiration in their offerings.

In the remainder of this introduction, I define terms, point out overlaps and divergences between the academic disciplines represented by this volume's authors, and note the overarching themes that weave the chapters together.

Defining Parenthood and Parenting

I am a parent.

I parent.

As you read the chapters in this volume, you may notice that the word "parent" is used as a noun, a verb, and sometimes as both. My interest is in both uses of the term. As a noun, "parent" is the collection of characteristics we associate with raising a younger person—the state or identity of being a parent—as in, "I am a parent." It is a set of traits that we can see present in individual families and in our larger cultural milieu, meaning that we can see patterns among many parents in a particular time and place that suggest there could be such a thing as the state of being parents *here and now.* I refer to this as "parenthood." Scholars who are interested in parenthood may ask questions that get at large social forces that define the characteristics of being a parent, characteristics that play out in individual families and in discourse about larger cultural values. For example, some may say that contemporary parenthood consists of the expectation that parents are the protectors of children, who are supposed to be kept away from potential harm.

Necessarily, some of these parenthood traits include what parents are doing—as in the active verb "to parent." The actions of parents are worth investigating in addition to the state of parenthood today. What do parents do? Or, as some media sources emphasize, what are they *supposed* to do? This active part of being a parent can be seen in individual parents' daily lives, and it can be viewed as a larger set of actions that are culturally scripted. I call this "parenting." For example, some may say that contemporary parenting consists of actions such as monitoring computer screen time in an effort to protect children from potential harm.

The chapters in this book, in different ways, present the latest rigorous research on both the state of contemporary parenthood—what we say parents are—and the ways that people actually fulfill their parenting roles—what parents actually do. As you read, you may wish to seek out the news articles referenced and see if your interpretation of the stories changes after you read the chapter presenting research on what's actually going on in contemporary families.

How Academic Discipline Shapes Research

The authors of the chapters in this book present their research through the lenses of a variety of academic disciplines, including psychology, sociology, economics, demography, and some interdisciplinary work in anthropology, human-computer interaction studies, cultural studies, and family social science. The authors whose work is contained in this volume fulfill different professional roles—working as professors at colleges and universities, researchers funded by public and private donors, and practitioners whose work is centered in clinical or counseling settings. This disciplinary and professional variety manifests not only in terms of the types of questions asked in our research and writing, but also in terms of the methods we use (some of us do quantitative analyses, some qualitative; some do surveys or analyze online data; others do more ethnographic research or use in-depth interviews), the population level we're interested in (some of us focus on small groups and within-family dynamics, while others examine traits found in large groups or even nation-states), and even our writing styles (some use first person and include personal stories; others write more formally). I think this is wonderful and have left the variety in place so you may see how different voices and academic lenses shape the questions that matter about and for parents in contemporary society. You may wish to read the book with an eye toward epistemological frames and writing voice to see in which direction your own research and writing may lean.

This Book

While topics and findings and connections to news stories overlap throughout the book, and while the scholarship contained in this volume could have been arranged in numerous ways, I have chosen to cluster the chapters into three themes. Early chapters, under the heading "Changing Patterns in Contemporary Parenting and Parenthood," are dedicated to general introductions to the patterns that indicate what life is like for U.S. parents today. Middle chapters, under the heading "Work, Family, and Leisure for Parents," focus on the significance of time, cultural values, and social policy in different areas of parents' lives. Later chapters, under the heading "Inequalities," are dedicated to the explicit investigation of how demographic characteristics and group inequalities may matter in parents' and children's experiences, and in our conception of what constitutes modern U.S. parenthood. The themes and chapter overviews are introduced before each of the three sections.

The authors whose work is featured in this volume discuss demographic patterns and large historical changes in family structures and values. All of the patterns mentioned are impacted by the near-ubiquitous availability and consumption of digital information and communication technologies. The relationships between parents and children represented by the research in these chapters are impacted by whether parents are able to care for children in their homes, whether certain things available to children are culturally defined as dangerous or desirable, and whether parents are impacted by the large volume of news media sources discussing the latest ways that they ought to fear unlikely things.

The role of state- and nation-level policies impacting parents is covered as well, including a focus on how policy may be differentially experienced by people in different social locations based on race, age, social class, citizenship status, occupation, gender, sexual orientation, and geographic location. Often, the ability to benefit from a policy that is meant to help parents is affected by family circumstances and larger cultural forces. For policies that may negatively affect families, such as those that separate parents and children based on citizenship, the inequalities among parents are built into the policies themselves. So, while general historical overviews, definitions, policies, and culturally prescribed parenting roles are covered in this volume, inequality is at the crux of the questions that are asked. This is because structural inequality and group status affect both practice and outcomes related to parents' desire and ability to care for children. But how that plays out depends on which aspect of parents' experiences are studied, and which groups are at the center of the research focus. As you read each chapter, you will see how these themes and threads play out.

I wish for you to read these chapters with an eye toward the specific topics covered, absorbing new ideas and new ways to look at older ideas. There are plenty of topics here, and the breadth of topics is impressive. But, of course, not all topics are covered. I hope you are inspired to ask questions about topics that matter to you that may not be covered here, perhaps nudged by the methods, questions, or recommendations offered by the authors in this volume. I hope you read the chapters with an eye toward how research questions are asked, and how flashy news headlines are dissected, myths dispelled, and claims complicated. That process—separating out the news headlines from the new (and accurate) research—is a process that is not specific to one topic, one book, or even one academic discipline. We are in constant need of understanding how information is processed and disseminated. One of the most important parts of this understanding is to engage directly with good research done by people who are invested, first and foremost, in understanding what's really going on in families today. Only after we know what's really going on can we figure out how best to remedy any challenges families may face. As I discuss in my book *The Stuff of Family Life: How Our Homes Reflect Our Lives* (2017), we cling to the allure of nostalgia when we think about families. But if we do this, we fail to understand that many aspects of family life that are defined as "normal" have only been mythologized to be that way. We need to understand that "there has never been such a thing as a normative perfect white picket fence suburban family with no problems. We realize that . . . inequalities have meant that ideals are just that—idealized images of what is desired, but likely not what is achieved by many families" (152). If we want to know what's best for today's parents, we first need to know what parents are really experiencing, not just what is presented in sensationalized news headlines that purvey fear, judgment, or inaccuracies about parents and families from different walks of life.

This book is meant to be read by multiple audiences, including students and practitioners in professions focusing on parent-child relations, scholars who want a single place to look for the best new research in the field of parenting and parenthood, and parents who want to understand the larger context in which they're operating on a daily basis (and who have a desire to delve into some academic research on the subject). I hope that the breadth of topics, the variety of disciplinary voices, and the rigor with which the scholarship is presented will offer you a go-to source for important and timely questions that matter both in the everyday lives of parents and in the work that scholars pursue. While I would not classify this a "self-help" book, the chapters can help anyone have a more thorough and sophisticated understanding of parenting and parenthood.

As a sociologist, my primary goal is to help people gain understandings of how family life *actually* is so that we don't base our assumptions, practices, or recommendations about policy and practice on myths or oversimplifications that we come across as we scroll through sensationalized headlines in our media feeds.

PART 1

Changing Patterns in Contemporary Parenting and Parenthood

Introduction: Changing Patterns in Contemporary Parenting and Parenthood

What do we need to know to start our journey into understanding parents' experiences today? How can we contextualize oft-cited terms such as "helicopter parent" or oversimplified news stories about what's good or bad for children? What does research really say about what's going on in families these days? What should we be worried about, what can we celebrate, and what myths might be dispelled or complicated by examining new research?

We begin, in chapter 1, with research from sociologist Margaret Nelson, who captures the overarching theme of this book—the explicit connection between news headlines and new research. Nelson questions whether news items about helicopter parents in recent years constitute a "moral panic." Many moral panics concern youth (e.g., drug users, obese children, or teen mothers), and especially those "disadvantaged" youth who are viewed as inadequately supervised by parents and other authority figures while being unable to make good decisions on their own. Recently, however, the media has been concerned with the children of the elite—youth who are subject to the hypervigilance of what is known as helicopter parenting. Through a content analysis of media stories about helicopter parents (and the public commentary on those stories), this chapter concludes that helicopter parenting, though criticized, is reconfirmed as a practice that is necessary if the elite is going to reproduce itself.

Intensive parenting (along with helicopter parenting) has been presented in our news media (and in some research) as the predominant parenting style over the past 30 years, and in chapter 2, sociologist Valerie Adrian shares interview findings that complicate this. Although mainstream press and bloggers write concerned articles about helicopter parents, these parents seem to be a small but vocal minority. By citing interview data, this chapter introduces a new type of parenting style—adaptive management parenting—that captures how parents are actually navigating a balance between "hovering" and allowing freedom for their children.

Parenting occurs throughout the life course, and in chapter 3, psychologist Joshua Coleman offers an analysis of parents and their adult children, with an emphasis on changing values. Values that were once prioritized in the family, such as obligation, responsibility, loyalty, and even love, have been radically reconfigured to emphasize the happiness and well-being of the individual. Many parents enter the phase of parenting adult children with an expectation of continued closeness but lack the tools sufficient to ensure that. This chapter discusses these historical changes (including changes that have come about with communication technology) and makes observations about the dilemmas facing many of today's parents as well as recommendations for solving this common conflict.

In chapter 4, I offer a sociological analysis of my and others' current social scientific research findings on the role of technology in parents' and children's lives. I cover research findings on how the "digital divide" creates inequalities for parents and children (especially in their access to information). I also take an overview of current research on how technology impacts family communication, work-family boundaries for working parents, and surveillance and screen time relating to topics including online sexual predation, violence, cyberbullying, and obesity. Woven throughout the chapter is reference to the ubiquitous presence of parenting advice columns and stories that are sometimes challenging for parents to navigate, suggesting that technology matters not only in the ways that parents parent, but also in the ways that our society evaluates that parenting.

In chapter 5, sociologist Robin Simon delves into a common topic covered in the news: parental happiness. More explicitly, she covers past and present research on parental well-being and mental health, noting that parents experience greater symptoms of emotional distress and depression, more anger, and less happiness and life satisfaction than childless adults. This chapter describes long-held cultural beliefs about the effect of parenthood on adults' happiness and health in the United States and then reviews empirical findings on parental status differences in well-being—findings that contradict these widespread beliefs. The chapter then delves into theoretical explanations of why parents do not derive the promised benefits, and it reviews research on gender, marital status, and employment status variations in well-being among parents.

CHAPTER ONE

Helicopter Parents: A New Moral Panic?[1]

Margaret K. Nelson

According to an article in *Parents* magazine (Bayless 2013), the term "helicopter parenting" was first used in 1969 in Dr. Haim Ginott's book (1969) by "teens who said their parents would hover over them like a helicopter." Look the phrase up in Google, and the very first item is an unattributed definition (complete with a tacked-on identification of victims and harm), a definition that segues into a quote that curiously fails to define the object (an explicit type of behavior) to which it refers: "helicopter parent: a parent who takes an overprotective or excessive interest in the life of their child or children. 'Some college officials see all this as the behavior of an overindulged generation, raised by helicopter parents and lacking in resilience.'" This same definition is exemplary in another way in that it makes explicit the link between a specific kind of parental behavior and a specific social class location. Another one from the Urban Dictionary (see Appendix A) does the same: a helicopter parent is the "bane of the dean's existence. The parent who hovers and flaps his wings while the kid lives in his shadow. Particularly prevalent at *high-priced* colleges, where parents feel obliged (or entitled) to intervene on issues down to the candlepower of the lightbulbs" (emphasis added).

According to Google News archives, the term remained in relative obscurity for almost four decades after its invention; by 2007, however, it was appearing, on average, twice a week in standard news outlets (Figure 1.1). References to helicopter parents in a broader set of media (including blogs, online magazines, and Web sites) took off somewhat earlier, shooting up

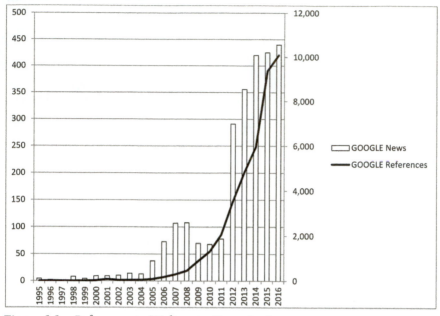

Figure 1.1 References to "Helicopter Parenting"

from 19 references in 2000 to 77 in 2001; by 2016, over 10,000 new references had appeared (around 200 a week). Put the term into Google today, and almost instantaneously you will be told that there are "about" 1,350,000 results. As Figure 1.1 shows, the number of references to this term continues to grow yearly; in any case, no clear diminution is in sight. These media discussions of helicopter parenting constitute the data for this analysis. I argue here that a particular kind of attention to a particular style of parenting—and the linkage between that style of parenting and more privileged parents—constitutes a new and unusual kind of moral panic.

In his 1972 study of the "Mods and Rockers," in *Folk Devils and Moral Panics*, Stanley Cohen offers a frequently quoted definition of a moral panic that includes the notion of a "threat to societal values and interests" presented in a stylized manner by experts (moral entrepreneurs).[2] Aiming for even more precision, Goode and Ben-Yehuda (1994) identify "five key features of the phenomenon":

(i) *concern* (some reported conduct or event sparks anxiety); (ii) *hostility* (the perpetrators are portrayed as folk devils); (iii) *consensus* (the negative social reaction is broad and unified); (iv) *disproportionality* (the extent of the conduct, or the threat it poses, are exaggerated); [and] (v) *volatility* (the media's reporting and the associated panic emerge suddenly, but can dissipate quickly too).

Garland (2008) adds to this two additional elements that he believes must be present for there to be a true moral panic: "(i) the *moral dimension* of the social reaction . . . and (ii) the idea that the deviant conduct in question is somehow *symptomatic*."[3]

As I show below, public discussions of "helicopter parenting" have many of these same elements. What is unusual is that, rather than focusing on a stigmatized group and a clearly delineated behavior—as is the case for many moral panics—discussions of helicopter parenting focus on an elite group and rarely draw a distinct line between acceptable and unacceptable behavior. I suggest as well that the moral entrepreneurs raising the hue and cry about helicopter parents are quite different from the "editors, bishops, politicians and other right-thinking people" who, Cohen (2003) suggested, most often launch moral panics. Moreover, I show that, rather than punishment or legislation, these moral entrepreneurs propose accommodation and opportunities for self-improvement. Finally, I consider what it is that this moral panic is diverting us from and what, in isolating some behaviors as reprehensible, ultimately comes to be defined as acceptable behavior.

Methods

Because I wanted a broad range of discussions of helicopter parenting, I worked with the linked references that came up when I simply put the term "helicopter parent" into Google's search engine. In late December 2016, I downloaded the links until I had achieved 100 discrete items (after deleting repetitions and items that were simply lists of other items; see Appendix A). Then, two research assistants and I coded them on several categories, including the date on which they first appeared, type of material, author's attitude toward helicopter parenting, the nature of perceived harms and benefits, mention of a "golden age," and the experts cited in the discussion. The research assistants and I worked together to devise and refine the codes; by discussing our decisions and double coding, we made certain that we all understood the codes and were applying them in the same way.[4] After an initial round of coding, we found that we were seeking to make distinctions that were too fine (e.g., among different attitudes toward helicopter parenting and among the different kinds of harm that helicopter parenting might produce). When we broadened our categories, we achieved far greater consistency among the several coders.

In an article relying on a somewhat similar methodology, Colomb and Damphousse (2004, 152) drew on a sample of references to the moral panic they were studying—in this case hate crimes—as they appeared in the "U.S. News" domain of LexisNexis. I based my decision to rely instead on Google on two reasons: 1) I wanted to broaden my investigation to include blogs, commentary, and Web sites rather than rely on traditional press alone; and

2) I wanted some measure of "popularity" to ensure that I was tapping into discussions that were widely read. Items in LexisNexis are not ranked in terms of popularity; Google, however, uses an algorithm to rank sites.

Table 1.1 presents an overview of some of the characteristics of these items. The bulk of the articles (40 percent of all; 62 percent of those with dates) were produced in 2016; the oldest were from 2005 (1.1A). Those with no dates included sites that update frequently, such as online dictionaries. The most common "form" for these items was a personal blog (24 percent); among those that were not blogs, the most common source was magazines that offered parenting advice (1.1B). Half of the discussions (49 percent) are about helicopter parents in general, describing and characterizing their behavior. Among those that focus on a specific age range, 55 percent focus on issues involving children before college, 27 percent focus on issues arising for children in college, and 18 percent focus on what happens after college (1.1C).

Table 1.1   General Overview of Items

TABLE 1.1A: Year of Publication	Frequency	Percent of all	Percent of those with dates
2005	2	2%	3%
2006	1	1%	2%
2009	2	2%	3%
2010	1	1%	2%
2011	2	2%	3%
2012	2	2%	3%
2013	4	4%	6%
2014	4	4%	6%
2015	7	7%	11%
2016	40	40%	62%
No date	35	35%	
Total	100	100%	100%

TABLE 1.1B: Source	Frequency	Percent of all	Percent of those with clear type	Percent of those that are not blogs
Blog	24	24%	25%	
Parenting magazine	9	9%	9%	12%

Table 1.1 *(continued)*

TABLE 1.1B: Source	Frequency	Percent of all	Percent of those with clear type	Percent of those that are not blogs
Newspaper	8	8%	8%	11%
General magazine	8	8%	8%	11%
Business magazine	8	8%	8%	11%
College magazine/ Web site	8	8%	8%	11%
Online news	7	7%	7%	10%
Dictionary	7	7%	7%	10%
Other	7	7%	7%	10%
Health or psychology magazine	5	5%	5%	7%
Religious magazine	4	4%	4%	5%
Wikipedia	2	2%	2%	3%
Unclear	3	3%		
Total	100	100%	100%	100%

TABLE 1.1C: Age of Children	Frequency	Percent of all	Percent of those with specific age
General or unclear	49	49%	
Before college	28	28%	55%
College	14	14%	27%
Post college	9	9%	18%
	100	100%	100%

Helicopter Parenting as a Moral Panic

Consensus and Concern

The authors of the 100 items we coded largely agree that helicopter parenting is a problem. Almost two-thirds (71 percent) view helicopter parenting negatively; another fifth are mixed or neutral. Almost none (3 percent) express a positive view of what they believe that practice to be (Table 1.2A).

Table 1.2 Helicopter Parenting as a Moral Panic

TABLE 1.2A: Point of View	Frequency	Percent of all	Percent of those with clear point of view
Clearly negative	71	71%	76%
Mixed/Neutral	20	20%	21%
Clearly positive	3	3%	3%
Unclear	6	6%	
Total	100	100%	100%

TABLE 1.2B	Frequency	Percent of all	Percent of all with perceived harm
No harm	23	12%	
Maturity	68	35%	40%
Mental health	39	20%	23%
Entitlement and moral/ ethical concerns	19	10%	11%
No childhood	18	9%	11%
Other harm	18	9%	11%
Bad behavior	8	4%	5%
	193	100%	100%

TABLE 1.2C: Benefits	Frequency	Percent of all	Percent of those with perceived benefits
Helicopter parent has no benefits	60	55%	
Engaged parenting has benefits	16	15%	33%
Helicopter parenting creates advantage	13	12%	27%
Helicopter parenting provides security	11	10%	22%
Helicopter parents are happier parents	8	7%	16%
Other benefits	1	1%	2%
Total	109	100%	100%

TABLE 1.2D: Moral Entrepreneurs	Frequency	Percent of all	Percent of those with experts
Teachers	24	15%	21%
Psychologists and counselors	24	15%	21%

Table 1.2   (*continued*)

TABLE 1.2D: Moral Entrepreneurs	Frequency	Percent of all	Percent of those with experts
Others	27	17%	23%
Students	6	4%	5%
Doctors	5	3%	4%
"Studies"	29	19%	25%
No one	41	26%	
	156	100%	100%

These accounts indicate a variety of harms caused by helicopter parents (Table 1.2B). The greatest harm (or at least the one most frequently cited) is that children will to fail to develop properly into independent, self-reliant, autonomous adults. Along these lines, several items raise the concern that the children of helicopter parents will return home after college rather than setting out on their own; the implication here is not that these emerging adults are short of resources but that they lack sufficient backbone to live independently.[5] Commentators argue also that the children of helicopter parents show poor mental health (23 percent). Combining these two concerns and putting them into neurological language, a Stanford dean worries that these children will lack "executive function" [32]. As these data suggest, one aspect of the *moral* element of the helicopter parent panic has to do with the specific harm perceived as being done to those subject to this particular form of parenting. Commentators worry not just about creating dysfunctional young adults but specifically about creating dependency rather than the ability to fulfill the uniquely American social ideals of independence, autonomy, and self-reliance.

Other items raise additional concerns. Some of these items suggest that the harm being done is more or less in the realm of ethical behavior, including the notion that youth raised by helicopter parents will have an undue sense of entitlement: "They expect the world to take care of them because they are so much more 'special' than other people [59]." Still others fear that children will demonstrate other forms of bad behavior (e.g., being rebellious later). The involvement of religious communities indicates that some observers find helicopter parenting to be un-Christian: the Gospel Coalition suggests that Christians "recognize a problem that's even worse than the loss of independence: [helicopter parents] inadvertently model for our children that God's faithfulness isn't dependable"; "[helicopter parents] reason with faulty logic, instead of learning to trust God for our children's growth so they, too, may one day learn to lean on Him" [19].

More simply, some commentators worry that helicopter parents put their children into too many organized activities and thus deny them the pleasures of an unstructured childhood. When advocating for childhood play, however, these same commentators are quick to reassure parents that play itself may be more conducive to success than constant study: "An hour at the playground helps them unwind and is just as good for their intellectual growth in the long run" [55].

While evidence of some harm is mentioned in all but 12 percent of the items, evidence of benefits crop up as well in almost half (45 percent) of them (Table 1.2C): these benefits include a greater sense of security for children along with the material advantages and psychological advantages that result from having engaged parents. Some note that this engagement is good for the parents too, because they will be less prone to worry and will have more fulfilling relationships with their children.

Five issues about these claims of harm (and of benefits) stand out. First, to a large extent they depend on measures that are necessarily relative (although the commentators suggest that those measures are unchanging). The issue of maturity is one such changing standard: what is considered immature behavior in one time or place might be seen as age appropriate in another. Second, normative terms are treated as if they are absolute: for example, [30] offers you a "well-adjusted college student" if you "stop helicopter parenting" without defining precisely just what that quality of being might mean.

Third, the cited studies rely on correlations and therefore cannot prove causation. This problem is noted by Reed et al. (2016, 3,145), who are frequently cited scholars on the subject of harm done: "Due to the cross-sectional nature of the data causal direction of the relationships cannot be determined." Yet this study is widely interpreted as if the association between "hovering and intrusive parental behaviors" and both "low autonomy" and low "competence" can be taken as sufficient proof of the damage that helicopter parents can do.

Fourth, the commentators frequently juxtapose sentences to create the illusion of a meaningful connection. An article by EdSurge [83] (self-defined as "independent information resource and community for everyone involved in education technology"), for example, discusses helicopter parents as an item of concern because they have a "deleterious effect on emerging adult college students' mental health." The next sentence in the article, by its placement, links these "deleterious" effects to a monumental rise in psychological problems among college students:

> In a recent report from the National Survey of College Counseling Centers, 89% of directors reported an increase in student anxiety disorders, 58% reported an increase in student clinical depression, and 35% reported an increase in self-injury issues, over the past 5 years.

Finally, this same example illustrates another kind of sleight of hand. Not only are separate points juxtaposed to create the appearance of linkage, but no baseline information is provided for percentage increases. An increase in, for example, "student anxiety disorders" could mean one more student presenting that problem, or it could mean thousands.

Hostility and Disproportionality: Folk Devils Are Everywhere

The discussions of helicopter parenting transform helicopter parents into folk devils by use of a variety of common images. Over a third (36 percent) of the 61 items that are accompanied by a visual image portray some version of a helicopter: some include the caricature of an adult with helicopter blades attached to the head or back and suspended over a seemingly defenseless child. Other, albeit less common images, include a child enclosed in bubble wrap, a child entirely within a bubble, or a child covered with sticky notes. These images both mock and disdain. They evoke the hostility that scholars view as a key component of a moral panic.

Commentators suggest as well that these folk devils are commonplace, that helicopter parenting has "taken over America" and now affects "half the parents in the playground." EdSurge reports, "one in five college students are in touch with their parents three or more times a day, and 41 percent are in touch every day." Of course, rather than suggesting that this is a good thing—an indication of positive parental involvement in a child's life—the context implies the reverse.

A Vanished Golden Age

As McRobbie and Thornton (1995) note, "moral panics often entail looking back to a 'golden age' where social stability and strong moral discipline acted as a deterrent to delinquency and disorder." About a fifth (18 percent) of the discussions of helicopter parenting do the same by focusing on some aspect of the past, such as the freedom, autonomy, and independence of earlier genera-tions in contrast with the coddling of today. These discussions ignore con-crete dangers in a long-lost past, including them as part of a reverie:

When I think back to my own childhood, some of my happiest memories were playing outdoors, generally without restraints, such as balancing on the front handlebars of my dad's bike as he circled the parking lot behind our house and climbing trees behind my friend's house while our parents sat indoors drinking wine, oblivious to our antics or roller-blading up and down our street without a helmet or protective pads. Those were carefree days, for sure. [30]

. . . at night, we were free. And we did many dangerous things. Mothers were not yet against drunk driving; cheerful ladies did not give you con-doms at school. It wasn't an arcadia, and many times things went terribly wrong. But most of us survived. [13]

Look Who's Talking: Moral Entrepreneurs

Some moral panics focus on an obvious event. For example, a vicious assault on a jogger in Manhattan's Central Park in 1989 touched off a moral panic about what were called "wilding" teens (Anonymous 2014). The moral panic surrounding helicopter parenting is different. It refers to a perceived pattern of *ongoing* behavior that "experts" define as problematic.[6] Moreover, the experts are happy to do so. The experts—or, in the language of social problems, the moral entrepreneurs—who discuss helicopter parenting in the media include teachers (21 percent), psychologists (21 percent), and social science "studies" (25 percent), some of which are named and others of which are not (Table 1.2D).

We Have Met the Enemy and It Is "Us"

Moral panics are usually directed at "folk devils" who are not "us." Othering is involved. For example, Campos (2005, 58) notes that the moral panic about obesity is "serving to reinforce moral boundaries against minorities and the poor." However, the panic about helicopter parenting differs in four ways: in who is addressed, in who is described as being the problem, in the sympathetic understanding of why helicopter parenting occurs, and in how the pieces are written.

Addressing the Elite

Articles on helicopter parenting appear in sites focused at an elite population: e.g., alumni newsletters of elite institutions (e.g., Grinnell College), *Business Insider*; BenefitsPRO (which "covers everything top agents and benefits brokers need to help your business be more successful"); Harvard Health publications; the Cambridge Nanny Group (which promotes itself as the "*first and only* agency to offer Nanny View Virtual Interviews"); Sittercity.com (which advertises advice about "how to handle tough conversations with your nanny.") Other items refer to elite institutions:

> The average middle-class kid (as we were called back then, meaning: a white kid whose parents owned a house and whose father was steadily employed) was not burnishing dreams of Princeton [13].

This same article describes an approach it calls "Get-Real Parents" who make accommodations to student drinking; these accommodations assume a hefty wallet: "On the nights of big high-school events, Get-Real Parents pay for limos, party buses, Ubers—whatever it takes to ensure that their kids are safe. What is an Uber except a new kind of bike helmet?" Moreover, this article assumes that the parents are among the elite themselves: "What 80-hour-a-week executive doesn't drop her handbag on the console table and head to the wine fridge the second she gets home?"

Elite Experiences

These discussions feature elite experiences. For example, parents are offered ways to identify themselves as helicopter parents with situations that arise only among those with advantages. One item [87] asks, "Do you say things like 'We're on the travel soccer team' 'We're applying to college'?" Like the examples itself, a solution—"skipping [your child's] soccer practice to go for a run"—implies both financial resources to underwrite traveling to play a sport *and* that the only constraints in parents' lives derive from their obligations to their children. Another item suggests that you "make your [three-year-old] a résumé" and reward accomplishments with a gold star. That way, the child will "be much less apt to ask you to wait on her, since she'll be so proud." Parents also will have "evidence that [they] don't need to provide *concierge* service after all" (emphasis added).

Parents are reminded that making these changes is urgent: as one mother says in an example, if she does not make her child a more autonomous decision maker, she will not be able to "get out of the house to meet clients." In case they remain ambivalent, parents are soothed by the reminder that nothing terrible will happen if they "back off" and let their children flounder. In a site dedicated to finding child care (Sittercity.com), parents are told that if they allow children to make their own choices, the worst that can happen is a *single* bad grade; handled well, it will be a one-time event:

> When children are allowed to make choices, they sometimes make bad ones. These experiences contribute to the growth of their decision-making abilities mentioned above. Did your child skip studying and get a bad grade on a test? Don't scold them—and don't scold yourself either. Talk it over and use it as a learning experience to prevent it from happening again.

Why They (and We) Do It

All but 16 percent of the items under consideration identify causes for helicopter parenting, and many articles refer to more than one reason. Most frequent is that parents are concerned about a child's success in school or the workplace. Others (23 percent) point to the "culture of fear" that has predominated since the media attention to the disappearance of Etan Patz and Adam Walsh (Glassner 1999). Less commonly, an item suggests that parents would not engage in this practice were it not for the pressure they received from *other* parents (Table 1.3A). An occasional article will suggest the full range of "common triggers" [1]:

> *Fear of dire consequences*: A low grade, not making the team, or not getting a certain job can appear disastrous to a parent, especially if it seems it could be avoided with parental involvement. . . . *Feelings of anxiety*: Worries about the economy, the job market, and the world in general can push parents toward taking more control over their child's life in an attempt to protect them. . . . *Overcompensation*: Adults who felt unloved, neglected, or ignored as children can overcompensate with their own children. . . . *Peer pressure from other parents*: When parents see other overinvolved parents, it can trigger a similar response.

We Confess; We Are You

The "confessions" of a helicopter parent and the writer's identification with the helicopter parent (even if not *confessing*) are common tropes. In fact, in 17 percent of the items, the author suggests that she is an ally of helicopter parents; in another 17 percent, the author acknowledges that he is himself a helicopter parent (Table 1.3B). Tim Elmore, writing for Focus on the Family, "a global Christian ministry dedicated to helping families thrive," provides

Table 1.3   We Have Met the Enemy

TABLE 1.3A: Reasons for Helicopter Parenting	Frequency	Percent of reasons
Concern about kids' success	54	34%
Presence of a culture of fear	31	19%
Other	22	14%
Peer pressure	18	11%
Parent's economic issues	11	7%
	161	100%

TABLE 1.3B: Does Author Identify as Helicopter Parent	Frequency	Percent of all
Yes, as ally	16	16%
Yes, as confession	16	16%
No	62	62%
Unclear/missing	6	6%
Total	100	100%

an example of confession. He admits to having slipped into helicopter parenting when his children were young: "In the name of our children's safety and self-esteem, we've hovered over them, desiring to prevent any negative experience that might damage their esteem or hinder their safety. Now that my own kids are grown adults, I can see how, at times, my wife and I did a better job *protecting* our kids from the world than *preparing* them to live in it." Having learned from the error of his ways, he suggests acting more like a lighthouse: "A lighthouse stays in one location, and it's a beacon that has ongoing communication with passing ships. A lighthouse reveals its location; it warns mariners of danger and provides wise guidance—but it won't chase down the ships." The inclusiveness of this style of writing invites parents to self-identify as a helicopter parent. The acknowledgment of the benefits of a parenting policy that is wrongheaded further encourages parents to align themselves with the author's perspective. The advice discussed below suggests what they should do with that self-identification.

The Response to "Misbehavior" by the Elite

Moral panics are "successful" when they have met their clear goals of prohibition through legislation or punishment aimed at stopping the offending behavior. For example, we could consider the moral panic attached to alcohol use during pregnancy. Once alcohol use became associated with birth defects, a campaign was launched that allowed no drinking at all during pregnancy, because women as a group were viewed as unable to decide what level of drinking is too much (Armstrong and Abel 2000). Signs in bars and restaurants, labels on alcoholic beverages, and admonitions by physicians (and lay folk) testify to the effectiveness of this campaign. The moral panic surrounding helicopter parenting differs. In the panic under consideration here, the "elite" are treated with a measure of respect rather than punishment: they are accommodated and are invited to participate in ethical self-formation (Critcher 2009). Women more often than men are the targets here, but women are not told to stay home and watch their children more closely; rather, they are invited to *loosen* the reins of control.

Accommodations

When commentators address directly those who have to deal with "helicopter parents," they suggest making accommodations. A piece from the National Education Association (NEA) advises teachers [47], "the best way to handle this type of parent, and all parents, is to treat them as allies and experts on their children." Indeed, recognizing the elite nature of this class of parents, the NEA suggests that teachers can draw on their skills and thus kill two birds with one stone: "Some of the most heavily involved parents are driven and successful in their fields. Take advantage of that drive and tap into their expertise."

EdSurge [83] offers personnel in higher education technical solutions for handling the arrival of helicopter parents. Fully accepting that parents want to be informed of what their children are doing, EdSurge introduces Colleg-eESP, which it describes as a platform that allows access to "the student's academic and financial information, such as midterm grades or financial aid details" if the student grants permission. A site like this, EdSurge claims, gives "helicopter parents a place to land." It is a win-win situation: parents get what they want; at the same time, the platform "helps college admissions and financial aid departments cut down on the number of phone calls and requests they receive from parents."

If CampusESP is not for you or your institution, EdSurge offers alternatives. It describes NextTier education as an "easy-to-use technology for families to stay connected, informed, and educated" by allowing family members to "keep up-to-date with student activities and progress in order to champion their success." And of course, colleges themselves have their own parent portals; EdSurge directs its readers to the examples available at two elite private institutions: St. Olaf College and Colby College.

A "leading staffing agency" [48] offers a Web page: "When Helicopter Parents Hover: A Guide for Hiring Managers." Robert Half, the company CEO, advises his readers that they don't want to alienate anyone who might say bad things about their businesses: "In the age of social media, you don't want to give anyone cause to complain about you or your company." He suggests that managers should, instead, find a way to dismiss politely parents who become involved in their children's job searches.

Ethical Self-Formation

Commentators invite parents to engage in ethical self-formation through the choice of alternative behaviors designed to slow down and divert their energy. Indeed, these discussions do not usually contrast helicopter parents with absent or neglectful parents; they do not characterize helicopter parents as being inadequately attentive to their children's care (as might be the case with a critique of some parents); rather, parents are accused of being "too involved."

Some sites give lists of actions that qualify someone as a "helicopter parent"; others offer quizzes to parents to help them identify which behaviors are appropriate and which are not. The quiz from the College Board [92] asked questions such as how often a parent communicated with college-age children on the phone or by e-mail and what parents might do if their college-age child had been found responsible for "a minor conduct violation."

Four response options were given for each question; they were both graduated and graded: those indicating a minimal response (e.g., sympathetic listening) were given an A; those indicating full, head-on engagement (e.g.,
"Call Alan Dershowitz and print up 'Free Jenny' T-shirts.") were given a D.
The parents were told what their scores meant: "All A's:—You're on the Distinguished Honor Roll. Great job!"; "Mostly D's—We know you mean well,
but you've just learned that hovering can be detrimental to your student."

The quiz offered by the College Board leaves room for parents to sometimes deviate from appropriate distance and still be on the "Honor Roll."
Other discussions suggest the existence of a borderline which, when over-
stepped, transforms an appropriately concerned parent into something else:

> There's a fine line between being a helpful parent and a suffocating one to
> undergrads [83].
>   . . . hey, where do you draw the line between letting your kids make
> their own decisions at an untested and inexperienced young age and exert-
> ing your parental prerogative to help them make the right choices, based
> on their expressed and implied preferences? [79]

And lest one believe oneself to be outside the characterization, in an article in *Slate*, Katie Roiphe helps parents self-identify as overly intrusive: "Do
you not allow your children to watch television? Do you allow them any time
on the Internet unsupervised? Are you keeping very close track of what they
eat? Do you get a little too involved in homework? Do you barely ever hire
baby sitters at night?" Roiphe provides no age range for her questions, thus
lumping together, for example, a parent who does not allow screen time for a
six-month-old and one who refuses to allow the same for an adolescent.
Moreover, she is not only inclusive in her definition, but she also denies the
escape hatch of excluding oneself from this category: "I know parents who
think of themselves as very unhelicoptery but who are just helicoptering in
different ways."

Commentators then suggest that parents have to change themselves from
within. Helpfully, WikiHow [42] offers thirteen steps that can be taken to
transform oneself. Other sites offer alternatives. One article that labels its
alternative "submarine parenting" [38] teases with the notion that you should
keep "a hidden eye on your child's progress" so that you can "pop up when
needed" as if the definition of "when needed" is not precisely the problem.
Other alternatives include "lighthouse" parents who, unlike helicopter parents, do not "hover and control"; rather, they "check in and communicate."

Of course, parents who try these alternatives can be caught between a
rock and a hard place. At best, they are subject to the scolding of others:
Melanie Thernstrom [43] finds Lanza, a self-defined "anti-helicopter parent"
to be as "insufferable" as the helicopter parent because he "lets his children

play on the roof of their house and then rubs it in the face of his neighbors—thereby forcing the other parents to become imagination-quashing killjoys, AKA people who try to keep their kids from potentially breaking their necks." At worst, parents who try these alternatives are subject to arrest. For example, in Florida, a 34-year-old white woman was arrested when she allowed her seven-year-old son to walk from their home to play in a park less than a half mile away; she faced up to five years in jail for child neglect (CNN 2015). Similarly, a 46-year-old black woman in South Carolina was arrested for letting her daughter play alone in a nearby park while she worked her shift at McDonalds; not only was the mother arrested, but the child was placed temporarily in foster care (Friedersdorf 2014).

Putting Women in Their Place?

Because helicopter parenting is about parents, it might seem that all of this is yet another attack on women as mothers. Anti-helicopter-parent articles might be viewed as joining society's long history of holding mothers responsible for the well-being of their children and of blaming them for any perceived problems. And, indeed, there is some evidence in these articles that this is mostly about the female parent: 40 percent of the items have a visual image portraying a mother and child; only 3 percent have a father and child, and 28 percent have both parents with a child (Table 1.4). Even so, I am not convinced that these diatribes have the goal of putting women in their place—or, at least, in the home. In fact, the commentators do not suggest

Table 1.4   Images

Image	Frequency	Percent of all	Percent of those with photo
Mother and child	29	29%	40%
Both parents and child	20	20%	28%
Child alone	9	9%	13%
Father and child	2	2%	3%
Father alone	1	1%	1%
Mother alone	1	1%	1%
Both parents alone	1	1%	1%
Other	9	9%	13%
Unclear	1	1%	1%
No photo	27	27%	
Total	100	100%	100%

that women would be better off staying at home (as is the case in so many antiwomen campaigns), but they suggest that less rather than more attention from the parents is the goal. Moreover, even if this is in part about women, I think there is more to the story.

Discussion

As noted, the moral panic that defines helicopter parenting as a problem has two components: it addresses what is assumed to be a widespread new style of behavior (i.e., parenting that involves intervention on a child's behalf), and it suggests that that behavior is more common among one group of parents (i.e., the elite). (Interestingly, these two components are sometimes in conflict: if *most* parents engage in these activities, they cannot be the province of the elite alone.)

Many scholars agree with these commentators that a new style of parenting is afoot, and they offer reasons why this is so. Sharon Hays (1996) calls this style "intensive" mothering, and she identified the causes in a deep cultural ambivalence about the pursuit of self-interest. Others (including many of the discussions under consideration here) point to the "culture of fear." Some note that this culture has been reinvigorated by repeated moral panics about pedophiles, the dangers of the Internet, and campus rape (Bennett, Maton, and Kervin 2008; Potter and Potter 2001; Stewart 2016). Scholars point as well to the withdrawal of the state. Noting that in a neoliberal society the task of raising children has moved back on to families, scholars suggest that it is not surprising that contemporary parents feel alone in attempts to handle the significant tasks of raising and protecting their children (Katz 2001; Nelson 2010).

Some scholars explain why those in the middle and upper-middle classes are the people most likely to engage in some form of intensive parenting. They identify the social norms that make this a preferred style among a narrow group of parents; they demonstrate the material resources and cultural capital that make this style of parenting possible (Hays 1996; Lareau 2003; Nelson 2010). They focus on how increased competition among children of boomer parents for elite spots at elite institutions has heightened the stakes of the parent game even as the hollowing out of the middle class has made the risks of failing considerably greater. They acknowledge also that in this new era, it makes sense for parents to do all they can to ensure the success of their children (Armstrong and Hamilton 2015; Hamilton 2016; Smith and Sun 2016).

By way of contrast, some scholars do the opposite and suggest that the rise in some form of more intensive parenting is more widespread, reflecting broad, rather than narrow, sources of anxiety (Villalobos 2014). And there is at least some reason to believe that this latter group of scholars has a point.

The Pew Research Center (2015) reports that parents are divided about assessments of their own involvement in their children's education: "About half (53 percent) of those with school-age children say they are satisfied with their level of engagement, but a substantial share (46 percent) wish they could be doing more." Even more interesting are findings about who believes that involvement is good or bad—findings that indicate that elite parents are more bothered by parental engagement than are those with fewer advantages: "While majorities of parents with a postgraduate (65 percent) or a bachelor's (57 percent) degree say that too much involvement could have negative consequences, just 38 percent of those with some college and 28 percent with no college experience say the same."

It could be that the elite parents are more worried about parental engagement because they do so much more of it. However, the Pew Research Center finds that parents' "level of engagement . . . is fairly consistent across income groups." And lest one think that these findings indicate different starting points among different groups of parents, the data specify concrete actions that are quite widespread:

> A majority of parents are involved—at least to some extent—in their children's education. Among parents with school-age children, 85% say they have talked to a teacher about their children's progress in school over the 12 months leading up to the survey. Roughly two-thirds (64%) say they have attended a PTA meeting or other special school meeting. And 60% have helped out with a special project or class trip at their children's school.

Of course, these data—like those offered by the commentators discussed above—are subject to critique. Like the commentators, different scholars use quite different measures of parental involvement in the lives of their children. The issue here, however, is not whether helicopter parenting really exists as a phenomenon unique to the elite, but what this moral panic—with its assertion that the elite are especially engaged in these actions—accomplishes. Why does this high level of concern about the elite get expressed so frequently?

I suggest that one major thing these discussions accomplish is the protection of a social order that allows for a vast array of privileges for the elite. The elite are *not* told *not* to secure the well-being of their children; they are *not* told *not* to provide them with privileges. The awkward double negative here is intentional. I mean that these practices that are available only to the elite (e.g., a traveling soccer team, "classes every day of the week," "burnishing dreams of Princeton") are never fully interrogated. The child can still go to the traveling soccer game; she just will not have a parent on the sidelines *this time*. The child still can take classes; he just probably should not take them without a break to "play." Another Ivy League school or a smaller elite college might suit the child better than Princeton.

In an ironic exception, the author [43] scolding Lanza (the "anti-helicopter parent") points out that the play Lanza proposes constitutes the great "privilege" in today's society, and that at least some of what helicopter parents do is necessitated by the decline of social support for families (as noted above). However, this author still assumes a certain amount of privilege when s/he describes parents paying for afterschool activities "on their own" and then worrying "about chauffeuring their children around town to access these same programs." The author thus normalizes and justifies elite parenting experiences such as the capacity to pay for private classes or take time off in the middle of a school day to drive a child from place to place; the material resources that underlie the provision of *these* advantages are utterly ignored.

Moreover, these commentators do not turn their attention to the practices that most challenge meritocracy—e.g., purchasing private education, hiring tutors, residential segregation by class and race, editing and revising student work even after the children are in college, securing internships, or social networking to get children jobs. Rather, they focus on screen time and minor conduct violations. Thus we might conclude that this particular moral panic—like other moral panics—acts as a diversion (Anderson and Andrijasevic 2008), shifting attention from the stark causes of rising social inequality to its incidental manifestations. The stark causes remain untouched; the incidental manifestations are demonized, and the problem is viewed entirely as one that arises as individual actions within private families.

Viewing the diatribes against helicopter parenting as a moral panic that diverts also invites us to consider how differently the elite are treated—even when lambasted in popular and elite news outlets—from other groups who are viewed as disrupting the social/moral order. No legislation challenges them. No punishment is proposed. Indeed, even colleges and universities are loath to indicate just which behavior "crosses the line." Middlebury College, where I worked for over four decades, has an honor code that defines plagiarism: "Plagiarism is passing off another person's work as one's own. It is taking and presenting as one's own the ideas, research, writings, creations, or inventions of another" (Middlebury College 2017). This statement does not say just how much support in writing or editing someone else might provide. Data from a decade ago show that 19 percent of students reported that their parents proofread their papers, and 14 percent reported that their parents actually edited their work (Hofer et al. 2009, 286). However, a parent who wondered whether what he or she was doing crossed the line and made a child guilty of plagiarism in all likelihood would enter the Web site through the "parent" tab; nothing there would provide the answer either.

Decades of discussions about helicopter parents appear to have achieved little. For all the critical commentary, the elite (like the parents of Middlebury

College students) can—and probably do—continue to do (almost) everything in their power to secure success for their children. No one places them under arrest or takes their children away from them. But perhaps they don't get off entirely scot-free. As the commentators just suggest they should, they might be left with a feeling of shame about some (but not all) of what they do.

Notes

1. I thank Rebecca Tiger for her support for this project for over a decade. I thank also my two extraordinary research assistants—Emily French and Sarah Koch. Finally, I thank Michelle Janning and Jessica Gribble for their helpful commentary along the way.

2. For a thorough review of the concept, see Krinsky (2012).

3. Many subsequent scholars draw on some combination of these original definitions as they work to distinguish moral panics from social problems that fail to "launch" (Jenkins 2009): moral regulation (Critcher 2009), moral language in general (Hunt 1997), concerns about risk (Hier 2002, 2008; Ungar 2001), culture wars (Irvine 2000), mediatized rituals (Cottle 2006), and urban myths (Potter and Potter 2001).

4. I might add that my research assistants noted that many of the articles they were coding were not *really* about helicopter parenting. The term itself was used as a hook to draw in readers and to discuss a wide range of issues of concern. These included God, binge drinking, technology, and the scars of one's own childhood.

5. For evidence that this pattern is more common among those without a college education, see Sussman (2015).

6. This is what Critcher (2009) refers to as moral regulation (like obesity and others having to do with behavior).

References

Anderson, Bridget, and Rutvica Andrijasevic. 2008. "Sex, Slaves and Citizens: The Politics of Anti-Trafficking." *Soundings* 40: 135–45.

Anonymous. 2014. "How Our Fear of 'Wilding' Colored the Central Park Five Case." *Grist*. Retrieved December 10, 2016. http://grist.org/cities/how-our -fear-of-wilding-colored-the-central-park-five-case/.

Armstrong, Elizabeth A., and Laura T. Hamilton. 2015. *Paying for the Party: How College Maintains Inequality*. Reissue edition. Cambridge, MA: Harvard University Press.

Armstrong, Elizabeth M., and Ernest L. Abel. 2000. "Fetal Alcohol Syndrome: The Origins of a Moral Panic." *Alcohol & Alcoholism* 35: 276–82.

Bayless, Karen. 2013. "What Is Helicopter Parenting?" *Parents*. Retrieved December 4, 2016. http://www.parents.com/parenting/better-parenting/what-is -helicopter-parenting/.

Bennett, Sue, Karl Maton, and Lisa Kervin. 2008. "The 'Digital Natives' Debate: A Critical Review of the Evidence." *British Journal of Educational Technology* 39: 775–86.

Campos, P. 2005. "The Epidemiology of Overweight and Obesity: Public Health Crisis or Moral Panic?" *International Journal of Epidemiology* 35 (1): 55–60.

CNN. 2015. "Mom Arrested for Letting 7-Year-Old Walk to the Park." Retrieved April 10, 2015. http://www.cnn.com/2014/07/31/living/florida-mom-arrested-son-park/index.html.

Cohen, Stanley. 2003. *Folk Devils and Moral Panics: 30th Anniversary Edition*. New York: Routledge.

Colomb, Wendy, and Kelly Damphousse. 2004. "Examination of Newspaper Coverage of Hate Crimes: A Moral Panic Perspective." *American Journal of Criminal Justice* 28 (2): 147–163.

Cottle, Simon. 2006. "Mediatized Rituals: Beyond Manufacturing Consent." *Media, Culture & Society* 28: 411–432.

Critcher, Chas. 2009. "Widening the Focus: Moral Panics as Moral Regulation." *British Journal of Criminology* 49: 17–34.

Friedersdorf, Conor. 2014. "Working Mom Arrested for Letting Her 9-Year-Old Play Alone at Park." *The Atlantic*. Retrieved April 10, 2015. http://www.theatlantic.com/national/archive/2014/07/arrested-for-letting-a-9-year-old-play-at-the-park-alone/374436/.

Garland, David. 2008. "On the Concept of Moral Panic." *Crime, Media, Culture* 4: 9–30.

Ginott, Haim G. 1969. *Between Parent and Child: The Bestselling Classic That Revolutionized Parent-Child Communication*. New York: Harmony.

Glassner, Barry. 1999. *The Culture of Fear: Why Americans Are Afraid of the Wrong Thing*. New York: Basic Books.

Goode, Erich, and Nachman Ben-Yehuda. 1994. "Moral Panics: Culture, Politics, and Social Construction." *Annual Review of Sociology* 20: 149–71.

Google. n.d. "Algorithms—Inside Search—Google." Retrieved December 7, 2016. https://www.google.com/insidesearch/howsearchworks/algorithms.html.

Hamilton, Laura T. 2016. *Parenting to a Degree: How Family Matters for College Women's Success*. Chicago, IL: University of Chicago Press.

Hays, Sharon. 1996. *The Cultural Contradictions of Motherhood*. New Haven, CT: Yale University Press.

Hier, Sean P. 2002. "Raves, Risks and the Ecstasy Panic: A Case Study in the Subversive Nature of Moral Regulation." *The Canadian Journal of Sociology* 27: 33–57.

Hier, Sean P. 2008. "Thinking beyond Moral Panic: Risk, Responsibility, and the Politics of Moralization." *Theoretical Criminology* 12: 173–190.

Hofer, B. K., C. Souder, E. K. Kennedy, N. Fullman, and K. Hurd. 2009. "The Electronic Tether: Communication and Parental Monitoring During the College Years." In *Who's Watching: Daily Practices of Surveillance Among Contemporary Families*, edited by Margaret K. Nelson and Anita Ilta Garey, 277–94. Nashville, TN: Vanderbilt University Press.

Hunt, Arnold. 1997. "Moral Panic' and Moral Language in the Media." *British Journal of Sociology* 48: 629–48.

Irvine, Janice M. 2000. "Doing It with Words: Discourse and the Sex Education Culture Wars." *Critical Inquiry* 27: 58–76.

Jenkins, Philip. 2009. "Failure to Launch: Why Do Some Social Issues Fail to Detonate Moral Panics?" *British Journal of Criminology* 49: 35–46.

Katz, Cindi. 2001. "The State Goes Home: Local Hyper-Vigilance of Children and the Global Retreat from Social Reproduction." *Social Justice* 28: 47–56.

Krinsky, Charles. 2012. *The Ashgate Research Companion to Moral Panics.* Farnham: Routledge. Retrieved December 4, 2016.

Lareau, Annette. 2003. *Unequal Childhoods: Class, Race, and Family Life.* Berkeley: University of California Press.

McRobbie, Angela, and Sarah L. Thornton. 1995. "Rethinking 'Moral Panic' for Multi-Mediated Social Worlds." *The British Journal of Sociology* 46: 559–74.

Middlebury College. 2017. "Honor Code." *Middlebury.* Retrieved June 26, 2017. http://www.middlebury.edu/academics/administration/newfaculty/handbook/honorcode.

Nelson, Margaret K. 2010. *Parenting Out of Control: Anxious Families in Uncertain Times.* New York: New York University Press.

Pew Research Center. 2015. "Parenting in America." *Pew Research Center's Social & Demographic Trends Project.* Retrieved December 6, 2016. http://www.pewsocialtrends.org/2015/12/17/parenting-in-america/.

Potter, Roberto Hugh, and Lyndy A. Potter. 2001. "The Internet, Cyberporn, and Sexual Exploitation of Children: Media Moral Panics and Urban Myths for Middle-Class Parents." *Sexuality & Culture* 5: 31–48.

Reed, Kayla, James M. Duncan, Mallory Lucier-Greer, Courtney Fixelle, and Anthony J. Ferraro. 2016. "Helicopter Parenting and Emerging Adult Self-Efficacy: Implications for Mental and Physical Health." *Journal of Child and Family Studies* 25 (10): 3136–49.

Smith, Jill M., and Ken Chih-Yan Sun. 2016. "Privileged American Families and Independent Academic Consultants They Employ." *Sociological Forum* 31 (1): 159–80.

Stewart, Matthew. 2016. "The Campus 'Rape Crisis' as Moral Panic." *Academic Questions* 29 (2): 177–87.

Sussman, Anna Louie. 2015. "'Boomerang' Millennials Get Cozy at Home." *WSJ.* Retrieved December 7, 2016. http://blogs.wsj.com/economics/2015/07/29/boomerang-millennials-get-cozy-at-home/.

Ungar, Sheldon. 2001. "Moral Panic versus the Risk Society: The Implications of the Changing Sites of Social Anxiety." *British Journal of Sociology* 52: 271–91.

Villalobos, Ana. 2014. *Motherload: Making It All Better in Insecure Times.* University of California Press.

APPENDIX A: List of Sites

(NOTE; this list extends beyond 100; repetitions and irrelevant sites were removed; the numbers refer to this original list.)

1. What does helicopter parenting mean?—Parents www.parents.com › Parenting › Better Parenting › What Is Helicopter Parenting?

2. Helicopter parent—Wikipedia https://en.wikipedia.org/wiki/Helicopter_parent

3. 5 Signs You Were Raised By Helicopter Parents | Huffington Post www.huffingtonpost.com/.../5-ways-to-tell-you-were-raised-by-helicopter-parents_56...

4. Helicopter parent | Define Helicopter parent at Dictionary.com www.dictionary.com/browse/helicopter--parent

5. The Anti-Helicopter Parent's Plea: Let Kids Play!—The New York Times www.nytimes.com/2016/10/23/.../the-anti-helicopter-parents-plea-let-kids-play.html

6. 10 Warning Signs That You Might Be a Helicopter Parent (And How to . . . afineparent.com/be-positive/helicopter-parent.html

7. How to Stop Worrying and Avoid Helicopter Parenting: Don't Do These . . . https://www.empoweringparents.com › . . . › Accountability & Responsibility

9. The message of 'Moana': Don't be a helicopter parent | New York Postnypost.com/2016/11/28/the-message-of-moana-dont-be-a-helicopter-parent/

10. Helicopter Parent | Definition of Helicopter Parent by Merriam-Webster www.merriam-webster.com/dictionary/helicopter%20parent

11. 20 Signs You're a Helicopter Parent | The Stir thestir.cafemom.com/being_a_mom/157835/20_signs_youre_a_helicopter

13. How Helicopter Parenting Can Cause Binge Drinking—The Atlantic www.theatlantic.com/magazine/archive/2016/09/how-helicopter-parents.../492722/

14. How helicopter parents are ruining college students—The Washington . . . https://www.washingtonpost.com/.../parenting/.../how-helicopter-parents-are-ruining-coll...

15. Five ways to avoid becoming a helicopter parent—The Washington Post https://www.washingtonpost.com/.../parenting/.../five-ways-to-avoid-becoming-a-helico...

17. Helicopter Parenting—It's Worse Than You Think | Psychology Todayhttps://www.psychologytoday.com/blog/.../helicopter-parenting-its-worse-you-think

18. Move over, helicopter parents: Here come the lawnmower parents . . . www.treehugger.com › Living › Family

19. Are You a Helicopter Parent? | Education.com www.education.com/slideshow/helicopter-parenting/

21. Helicopter Parenting—Statistics Show You Need To Let Your Child Be . . . https://www.davidwolfe.com/the-damaging-effects-of-helicopter-parenting/

22. helicopter parent—Word Spy www.wordspy.com/words/helicopter parent.asp

23. Here's a Helpful Infographic on the Many Risks of Helicopter Parenting . . . bigthink.com/ideafeed/helpful-helicopter-parenting-infographic

24. How 'helicopter parenting' is ruining America's children—LA Times www.latimes.com/opinion/op.../la-oe-morrison-lythcott-haims-20151028-column.htm...

25. The NYC Playground That's Opposite of Helicopter Parenting ...nymag.com/.../2016/.../the-nyc-playground-thats-opposite-of-helicopter-parenting.ht...

26. How to Stop Helicopter Parenting | Parenting www.parenting.com/article/helicopter-parenting

27. Helicopter Mom (2014)—IMDb www.imdb.com/title/tt3094236/

28. From '80s latchkey kid to helicopter parent today—CNN.com www.cnn.com/2016/03/30/health/the-80s-latchkey-kid-helicopter-parent/

30. Anti-helicopter parent playground comes with a large dose of slur and . . . www.sheknows.com › PARENTING › K-12

32. Stanford Dean Says Parents are Ruining Their Kids By . . .—Daily Crackle www.dailycrackle.com/helicopter-parenting/

33. The rise of the helicopter parent—Business Insider www.businessinsider.com/the-rise-of-the-helicopter-parent-2016-7

34. Parenting Styles | Helicopter Tiger Attachment Parenting . . . https://www.familyeducation.com › Mom's Life › Parenting Style

35. Helicopter Parents—The NHHEAF Network Organizations www.nhheaf.org/index.asp?page=pl_helicopter

36. Helicopter parents: Hovering may have effect as kids transition to . . . https://www.sciencedaily.com/releases/2016/06/160628110215.htm

38. Forget helicopter parenting. It's all about submarine parenting. The . . . https://www.bostonglobe.com/lifestyle/...helicopter-parenting-all...parenting/.../story.htm...

39. helicopter parent—definition of helicopter parent in English | Oxford ... https://en.oxforddictionaries.com/definition/helicopter_parent

40. Helicopter Parenting—Slate www.slate.com/.../madeline_levine_s_teach_your_children_well_we_are_all_helicopt...

41. Urban Dictionary: helicopter parent www.urbandictionary.com/define.php?term=helicopter%20parent

42. How to Stop Being a Helicopter Mom or Dad: 13 Steps www.wikihow.com › . . . › You and Your Parents › Improving Relations with Parents

43. The 'Anti-Helicopter Parent' Is Just as Insufferable as the Helicopter . . . https://blog.longreads.com/.../the-anti-helicopter-parent-is-just-as-insufferable-as-the-...

44. Want A Well-Adjusted College Student? Stop Helicopter Parenting www.forbes.com/.../want-a-well-adjusted-college-student-stop-helicopter-parenting/

45. Your Helicopter Parent is Ruining Things for You—Black Enterprise www.blackenterprise.com/career/helicopter-parent-ruining-things/

46. Helicopter Parents—University Counseling and Testing Center counseling.uoregon.edu › Topics & Resources › Parents & Family › Helpful Articles

47. NEA—The 'Helicopter Parent' www.nea.org › ... › NEA Today Magazine › 2006-2011 Archives › September 2007

48. How to Handle Helicopter Parents | Robert Half https://www.roberthalf.com/.../when-helicopter-parents-hover-a-guide-for-hiring-man...

49. Helicopter Parenting Articles, Photos, and Videos—Chicago Tribune www.chicagotribune.com/.../parenting/helicopter-parenting/140060011255-topic.htm...

50. MOMAHOLIC: Confessions of a Helicopter Parent: Dena Higley . . . https://www.amazon.com/MOMAHOLIC-Confessions-Helicopter-Dena.../084994736...

52. helicopter parent Definition in the Cambridge English Dictionary dictionary.cambridge.org/us/dictionary/english/helicopter-parent

53. Helicopter parents face off against stealth bombers, mowers and . . . www.startribune.com/stealth-bombers-lawn...and...helicopter-parents.../384885881/

54. I Can't Help But Be a Helicopter Parent—The Kids Tips & Advice | mom . . . https://mom.me/kids/33912-i-cant-help-but-be-helicopter-parent/

55. Helicopter parenting—News, Research and Analysis—The . . . https://theconversation.com/us/topics/helicopter-parenting-12807

56. The anti-helicopter parent—Jane Green www.janegreen.com/2016/10/helicopter-parent/

57. The Anti-Helicopter Parent's Plea: Let Kids Play | Hacker News https://news.ycombinator.com/item?id=12742853

58. FSU researchers link "helicopter parenting" to young adult well-being www.wctv.tv/.../FSU-Researchers-make-connection-between-helicopter-parents-and-...

60. Are YOU a helicopter parent? | Rewire Me https://www.rewireme.com › Relationships › Parenting

61. [PDF]Confessions of a Helicopter Parent—Grinnell College https://www.grinnell.edu/sites/default/files/documents/helicopter_0.pdf

62. Helicopter Parents—Reddit https://www.reddit.com/r/helicopterparents/

63. Helicopter Parents and Overparenting: Truths and Traits www.positive -parenting-ally.com/helicopter-parents.html

65. A Generation Tethered to their Helicopter Parents | Aspen Education . . . aspeneducation.crchealth.com/articles/article-helicopter-parents/

66. Are You a Helicopter Parent? 7 Signs You Shouldn't Ignore—WebMD www .webmd.com/parenting/ss/slideshow-helicopter-parent

67. What is a helicopter parent? | Reference.com https://www.reference.com › Vehicles › Airplanes & Helicopters

68. Why Helicopter Parents Produce Boomerang Kids—Tim Elmore https:// growingleaders.com/blog/helicopters-and-boomerangs/

69. In Defense of Helicopter Parents (Like Me)—Momtastic www.momtastic .com/parenting/405381-in-defense-of-the-helicopter-parent/

70. "What Was Your Worst Experience as the Child of Helicopter Parents . . . www.freerangekids.com/what-was-your-worst-experience-as-the-child -of-helicopter-...

71. A Helicopter Mom—A Blog About Parenting, Recipes, Crafts, DIY . . . ahelicoptermom.com/

72. Three Types of Parents—Which Parenting Style Is Yours?—Love & Logic https://www.loveandlogic.com/.../three-types-of-parents-which-parenting -style-is-you...

73. Dear Helicopter Moms, You're Ruining It For Everyone Else—Scary . . . www.scarymommy.com/helicopter-moms-ruining-it/

74. If you want kids to soar, ground helicopter parenting | Miami Herald www .miamiherald.com/news/local/education/article94120732.html

75. Helicopter parents are the new HR challenge | BenefitsPRO www.benefitspro .com/2016/08/23/helicopter-parents-are-the-new-hr-challenge

76. 5 Ways to Tell if You're an ADHD Helicopter Parent—Blocked to . . . margitcrane.com/5-ways-to-tell-if-youre-a-helicopter-parent/

77. 6 Signs You've Become Helicopter Parents—Care.com Community https:// www.care.com/c/stories/4698/6-signs-youve-become-helicopter-parents/

78. Are You A Helicopter Parent? How to Give Your Kids Wings https://health .clevelandclinic.org/.../are-you-a-helicopter-parent-how-to-give-your-kid...

79. Are You A Helicopter Parent?—Admit This!—College Confidential www .collegeconfidential.com › Read & Learn › Admit This!

80. 15 of the Worst Helicopter Parents Ever—Effects and Stories of . . . www .womansday.com/life/a56299/helicopter-parenting-stories/

81. The Effects of Helicopter Parenting | KindredBond https://kindredbond.com › Parenting

82. Helicopter Parenting: When Too Much Help Is No Help—Harvard Health www.health.harvard.edu/parenting.../helicopter-parenting-when-too-much-help-is-no...

83. Helicopter Parents Have Landed on Campus. Here's How to Handle . . . https://www.edsurge.com › News › Higher Education › Postsecondary Learning

84. Helicopter Parenting: Are you overprotecting or constantly rescuing . . . www.theravive.com/.../Helicopter-Parenting%3A-Are-you-overprotecting-or-constant...

85. Helicopter Parents—When Helping Hurts—Cambridge Nanny Group www.cambridgenannygroup.com/blog/helicopter-parents-when-helping-hurts/

86. 11 Signs You Are A Helicopter Parent—Romper https://www.romper.com/p/11-signs-you-are-a-helicopter-parent-13352

87. Tips for grounding your own helicopter-parenting behaviors scouting magazine.org/2016/04/tips-grounding-helicopter-parent-behaviors/

88. The Remedy for Our Helicopter Parenting https://www.thegospelcoalition.org/article/the-remedy-for-our-helicopter-parenting

89. I Am a Helicopter Parent—And I Don't Apologize | TIME time.com/3528619/in-defense-of-helicopter-parents/

90. Are You a Helicopter Parent?—Sittercity.com. https://www.sittercity.com › Posts › Parents › More parenting resources

91. How the Government Became the Worst Helicopter Parent—Acculturated acculturated.com/no-child-left-alone/

92. [DOC]Are You a Helicopter Parent—The College Board www.collegeboard.com/prod_downloads/.../forum06_helicopter-parent-quiz.doc

93. Don't Worry, You are NOT a Helicopter Parent—Grown and Flown grownandflown.com/you-are-not-helicopter-parent/

94. New book shows pros and cons of 'helicopter parenting' | University of . . . https://www.universityofcalifornia.edu/.../new-book-shows-pros-and-cons-helicopter-...

95. Heard of helicopter parents? Watch for drones, stealth bombers www.freep.com/story/life/2016/07/03/heard-helicopter-parents-watch.../86608592/

96. Helicopter Parents—Dreamreader Dreamreader—Dreamreader.net dreamreader.net/lesson/helicopter-parents/

98. Helping or Hurting: Helicopter Parenting—Winter Springs Pediatrician . . . www.familyfirstpeds.com/helping-or-hurting-helicopter-parenting/

99. A Helicopter Parent Lands in Israel—Kveller www.kveller.com/article/a-helicopter-parent-lands-in-israel/

100. Helicopter Parents « Power to Change https://powertochange.com /experience/family/helicopterparents/

101. Kids With Helicopter Parents May Be More Prone to Anxiety and . . . news .health.com/2016/06/27/hovering-parents-may-harm-kids/

102. The risks of being a helicopter parent—Kidspot www.kidspot.com.au /parenting/parenthood/parenting.../the-risks-of-being-a-helicopte...

104. Involved Parent vs. Helicopter Parent—Shmoop www.shmoop.com › Teachers › Parents › Parents and Children

107. what's wrong with Helicopter Parenting http://childmind.org/article/whats -wrong-with-helicopter-parenting/

108. 4 Ways to avoid being a Helicopter Parent http://www.imom.com/4-ways -to-avoid-being-a-helicopter-parent/#.WEQKp330-LQ

109. 11 Things All Helicopter Parents Do http://www.popsugar.com/moms /What-Helicopter-Parent-40506273

111. Are you sure you're a 'helicopter' parent? —Florida Todaywww.floridatoday .com/story/life/family/2016/01/27/helicopter...parent/79410588/

112. The Perils and Perks of Helicopter Parents | Education | US Newshttps:// www.usnews.com/education/.../12/.../the-perils-and-perks-of-helicopter -parents

113. Sociologist studies helicopter parents in higher education

114. Dear Helicopter Parents: You Are Ruining Your Child's Life—And . . . https://www.theodysseyonline.com/dear-helicopter-parents-ruining -childs-life

115. Helicopter Parents: Hovering May Have Effect as Kids Transition to neurosciencenews.com/neurodevelopment-helicopter-parenting-4592/

CHAPTER TWO

World's Okayest Mom: The Adaptive Management Parent

Valerie Adrian

In April 2014, Hanna Rosin wrote an article for *The Atlantic* entitled "The Overprotected Kid." In it, she expounds on the brief history of overprotective parenting on the playground. Rosin suggests that child injury lawsuits brought against local parks departments in the late 1970s and subsequent safety modifications made to parks to reflect the hazards brought up in the lawsuits have led to parents who are more risk-averse with their children. She notes the connection between childhood abduction awareness campaigns in the late 1970s and early 1980s and a decrease in childhood freedom as parents began insisting that children walk to school in groups or with an adult. However, it is healthy for children to take risks, and Rosin points to potential solutions in new parks that have opportunities for risky behaviors but are under the distant but watchful eye of park monitors (Rosin 2014).

Rosin's article carries the same tone as many contemporary articles and advice columns on "helicopter" parenting: there is a sociological reason that explains the existence of helicopter parenting, but such parents are often too extreme, and the behaviors have consequences for children, parents, and society at large. There is some truth to this well-trodden argument. However, the concept of helicopter parenting is often oversimplified or taken for granted as a monolithic category of experience for parents and children. I share research here that uncovers a parenting style that is far more nuanced and leaves space for children to make healthy choices and take mild risks while growing up.

In this chapter, I discuss findings from interviews with 31 parents of recent college graduates. I interviewed these parents to learn about their relationships with their children throughout their lifetimes. Throughout these interviews a theme emerged, one that highlighted a previously undiscovered intensive parenting style I call "adaptive management parenting" (AMP), a parenting style that is present throughout the child's life. Intensive parenting (Hays 1996) is based on the notion that children are inherently precious and pure, and that it is the parents' role to investment large amounts of resources during childhood to ensure the most optimal outcomes. Sometimes, but not always, this results in parents "hovering" over their children, resulting in the label of helicopter parenting. AMP is an unconscious style of parenting that focuses on the need of the individual child in any given situation. Parents are not deliberately practicing the specific parenting style I refer to as AMP; nor are they labeling it as such. Rather, they are responding to their children's needs as they arise, including approaching discipline in a fluid way. With AMP, the same parents will use different methods with different children or even with the same child on different days. This finding adds nuance to the current parenting literature because it allows for change over time and between different parent-child interactions.

Background

There are many historical reasons for intensive parenting (See Hays 1996; Warner 2006; Nelson 2012 for examples of the anxieties facing parents that have led to the type of parenting popular today). Some of those reasons include the perception of risk to children, parental guilt, and an aggressive expert-led push toward more parental involvement. A shift to smaller families and later marriage and childbirth gave parents reasons to consider intensive parenting while also facilitating these new parenting styles.

Safety concerns helped foster a parenting style that was more watchful. In the 1980s, Tylenol bottles were tampered with, causing the deaths of seven people (Markel 2014) and creating public panic. Television brought shows like *America's Most Wanted* into the living rooms of millions of Americans, and the 24-hour news cycle created more competition and sensationalism (Fritz and Altheide 1987; Fass 1997; Rivers 2008). While shows like these helped reunite families and catch criminals, they also heightened a sense of unease—the erroneous idea that danger lurks in every neighborhood.

The shifts in parenting are one way in which the early 1980s and 1990s were a period of "unsettled lives" (Swidler 1986, 278). When people are in periods of transformation, they will form habits that may eventually become doctrine, which stems from both new and existing practices (Swidler 1986). In this way, parenting has been transforming from the parent-centric strategies of the midcentury into a more collaborative, child-centric style (Hays 1996). In other words, the focus has shifted from a paradigm where parents establish house rules and expect the children to abide by them to a standard that prioritizes children's wants and needs over those of the parents (Hays 1996). Parents have had to sift through their own role models, the advice of experts, and what fits into their family life in order to raise their children (Hays 1996; Nelson 2012).

Parents have turned to spending more time with their children because childrearing experts have advised them to do so. The top-selling child-rearing books of the 1980s suggested that parents should practice intensive parenting—an expensive, child-centric, labor-intensive, maternal approach to parenting—because children are priceless and sacred, not a commodity (Hays 1996). Smaller families mean that parents have been able to invest more time and money into each child. If the payoff is a healthy, financially solvent adult, the investment risk and need for success is greater with a small family, since fewer children mean fewer chances of success.

Not only are U.S. families smaller, but parents are older (Bianchi 2011). The first wave of millennials was born in the early 1980s and early 1990s, and their parents were likely to be older and more educated than parents of earlier generations (Howe and Strauss 2007). The mean age of first pregnancy was 21.4 in 1970 and 24.2 in 1990 (Matthews and Hamilton 2009), and the percentage of women who were over 30 during their first pregnancy rose from 4.1 percent in 1969 to 21.2 percent in 1994 (Heck et al. 1997). Powell and colleagues (2006) found that older parents tend to bestow more material and cultural resources on their adolescent offspring. And so, intensive parenting increased alongside an increase in focus (and quantity) of child-centric advice and changing demographics.

Hays suggests that intensive mothering is an ideology that espouses the best child-rearing practices are "child-centered, expert-guided, emotionally absorbing, labor-intensive, and financially expensive" (1996, 8).[1] I posit that two distinct kinds of intensive parenting are "helicopter parenting" and "concerted cultivation." Each parenting style requires significant parental investment, and there is overlap between the two styles, but the popularity, methods of engagement, and outcomes are different.

"Helicopter parenting" is a commonly derided form of intensive parenting. The term "helicopter parent" was introduced decades ago and used in the 1990 book *Parenting with Love and Logic* (Cline and Fay 1990). These authors defined "helicopter parents" as those who hover around their children and "drill sergeant" parents as those who bark orders at their kids. Helicopter parents micromanage their children's lives, starting in infancy and potentially continuing into adulthood. Helicopter parents try to manipulate their children's environment (Cline and Fay 1990). They try to negotiate favorable outcomes for their children, and they remain in a position to help smooth out difficult encounters well into the child's adulthood (Hamilton 2016). There has been backlash against helicopter parenting, with concerns that this parenting style negatively affects young adults' ability to function in academics, business, and life in general (Begley 2013; Bradley-Geist and Olson-Buchanan 2014; Cassling et al. n.d.; Gray 2015; Ludden 2012; Reed et al. 2016; Stahl 2015). This backlash may lead to parents distancing themselves from the helicopter moniker.

"Concerted cultivation" was a term coined in the early 2000s, referring to involved, intensive parents who manage their children's lives in a way that reproduces middle-class social norms and values (Lareau 2003). Middle-class parents enroll their children in many sports and activities, stay involved in their children's schools, and encourage children to negotiate with elders and people in authority. In this way, middle-class children become primed for a life working in collaborative settings with some level of autonomy.

Lareau (2003) described another type of parenting and associated it with working-class and poor families. She labeled it the "accomplishment of natural growth." Parents who practice this parenting style are largely hands-off, are more likely to give their children directives than engage in negotiations, and rely on the expertise of their children's teachers even though the parents may have trust issues with authority figures (Lareau 2003).

To sum up, intensive parenting is an ideology that encompasses concerted cultivation, helicopter parenting, and adaptive-management parenting. Therefore, I do not use it as a separate concept in this chapter but rather an umbrella term for any parenting that falls into Hays's definition. Concerted cultivation is a type of intensive parenting. Lareau lists the key components of concerted cultivation as parental involvement in the development of a child's skills and talents from inception through mastery, adult oversight in children's activities, fostering the art of negotiation, and active advocacy on the child's behalf, all in a culturally rich environment with the expectation of a transmission of middle-class advantages onto the child (2003). Helicopter parenting is the most involved version of intensive parenting. In this iteration, parents actively insert themselves into their children's lives and affairs, even into adulthood (Cline and Fay 1990; Fingerman et al. 2012). I did not find evidence of helicopter parenting in the activities I discuss in this chapter. Helicopter parenting is so stigmatized that parents may have actively avoided practicing it, or the parents interviewed may have avoided discussing helicopter behaviors. In fact, I found that middle-class parents can also take a hands-off approach to parenting. Sometimes AMP looks like helicopter parenting, sometimes it resembles concerted cultivation, and sometimes it is the accomplishment of natural growth. Heavy interventions were used when parents deemed them necessary, while at other times, parents would be hands-off after ensuring that a situation was a safe environment for exploration and independence. This customized approach to parenting was used by parents of all social classes (see Table 2.1).

Table 2.1 Interview Demographics

Pseudonym	Approximate SES	Parent marital status	Region
Lydia	Middle class	Divorced	Midwest
Eleanor	Middle class	Married	West
Paige	Middle class	Married	West
Maya	Working class	Divorced when son was in high school	South
Doris	Middle class	Divorced at 13	Northeast
Lindsey	Working class	Married	Northeast
Mark/Sienna	Working class	Married	West
Simone	Middle class	Married	Northeast
Georgia	Upper middle class	Married	West
Jayda	Middle class	Married	West
Erica	Middle class	Divorced, remarried	West
Natasha	Working class	Divorced, remarried	South
Nicole	Working class	Divorced, remarried	West
Melissa	Middle class	Single mom	West
Sydney	Middle class	Married	Northeast
Katherine	Middle class	Divorced	South
Anastasia	Middle class	Married	Northeast
Natalie	Middle class	Married	Midwest
Stella	Middle class	Single mom	West
Linda	Middle class	Married	West
Maggie	Upper middle class	Married	West
Jillian	Upper middle class	Married	West
Quinn	Working class	Married	West
Peyton	Middle class	Married	West
Ruth	Upper middle class	Married	West
Elise	Middle class	Divorced	West
Caitlyn	Middle class	Divorced	Midwest
Lauryn	Middle class	Married	West
Kristen	Working class	Married	West
Elaine	Upper middle class	Married	West
Cristina	Middle class	Married	West

Methods: Tapping into Parenting Behaviors

I interviewed 31 parents that I found through social media and personal contacts. The parents had a total of 42 children who had graduated college between the years 2007 and 2014. The interviews took place in the last half of 2014 and into 2015, giving 2014 graduates time in the job market. The median age of the children of the parents I interviewed was 27 at the time of the interviews. The youngest was 20, and the oldest was 46. The data was collected during semi-structured interviews that took place by phone or face-to-face. Four interviews took place in person, and 27 interviews were done over the telephone. I recorded the interviews on an Olympus 6000 digital recorder and recorded through the note-taking application on Microsoft Word as a backup. For phone interviews, I used the speakerphone option to capture the voice of my respondents. Interviews lasted about an hour. The range was 20 minutes for a mother of an older, nontraditional student to two hours for a mother with several children. After I completed my interviews, the data was transcribed using professional transcriptionists and then reviewed by me. Interviews were then coded using MaxQDA qualitative software to organize and categorize data. The interviews were reviewed and coded for emerging themes such as childhood experiences and parenting styles using a modified grounded-theory style (Bulawa 2014). I used an online random name generator to give each respondent a pseudonym and omitted specific identifying information such as cities, colleges, and company names.

I defined social class by parent education and profession. Exact social class definitions were difficult in some cases because people would shift over the course of their children's lifetimes. For instance, Stella was a teenage mother who had a low social status when her child was small and the mother was still in high school and college, but the mother went through college at the traditional age and was able to move into a middle-class lifestyle with a medical career that pays middle-class wages. Divorce and remarriage would also affect a person's social class standing over a lifetime. If at least one parent had a college degree and a professional, white-collar job, the family was listed as middle-class. If one or both parents had a high-paying career such as doctor, lawyer, engineer, or college professor, they were labeled upper-middle class. Again, divorce can affect this metric. Families that did not have a college degree and were working manual blue- or pink-collar jobs were considered working class. Thirty percent (N=9) of my sample was working-class, 53 percent (N=16) were middle-class, and 17 percent (N=5) were upper-middle-class. These numbers are comparable to the 2015 national averages reported by Pew Research of 29 percent, 50 percent, and 21 percent respectively (Pew Research Center 2015).

I explore the dinnertime, extracurricular activities, and homework routines of the families interviewed. These rituals helped me explore whether intensive parenting practices were present, and if so, what type. To understand this part of family life, I asked the following questions:

What was dinner time like when your child was in elementary school? In high
school?

What activities did your child participate in in elementary school? What was
your level of involvement?

What was homework time like in your house? (Probe for scheduled times, parental help, child mood during homework).

Dinner Rituals

Frequent family dinners have benefits for children, including emotional
well-being, reduced incidence of risky behaviors in adolescents, and better
academic outcomes (Eisenberg et al. 2004; Fulkerson et al. 2006; Musick
and Meier 2012; Offer 2013; Sen 2010; Snow and Beals 2006). Due to the
length and complexity of conversation, family dinnertime is frequently a site
of concerted cultivation (Lareau 2003; Snow and Beals 2006). Parents use
mealtime as an opportunity to pass on language, manners, cultural customs,
and even literacy strategies (Snow and Beals 2006).

Between the ages of 5 and 18, a child will eat more than 4,700 dinners.
Given that it is one of the few family events that occurs daily and has an interactive component, I used it as a touchstone because it was likely to be an occasion
that parents remembered while also allowing a glimpse into family relations to
learn whether parents practiced concerted cultivation with their children. Lareau notes that some middle-class families use this time as an opportunity to
build their children's language and negotiation skills. While it is not a perfect
metric, it is suggestive of parenting styles during elementary and high school.

I asked respondents about their family's dinner routine because it can be
used as a time to pass on cultural literacy. Parents in my study tended to prioritize family dinners, especially when their children were in elementary
school. Fifteen parents commented on dinner. Most said they ate dinner
together as a family while their children were growing up. Through these
dinner examples, the parents demonstrated the discussion-heavy style of
concerted cultivation and the independence-encouraging practices found in
AMP. Helicopter parenting was not evident in descriptions of past dinners.

Caitlyn the Cultivator

Caitlyn,[2] a middle-class working mother of three boys, describes dinner
when her children were young:

Interviewer: What was dinner time like?
Caitlyn: Dinner time, we all ate together. There were periods where
[sighs] the boys would want me to read books to them at dinner. We certainly would sit and discuss what was going on. I didn't get back from
work till shortly before dinner, so dinner was my time to at least figure out

what was going on with the kids and what else we had to do with homework or whatever. And then I always had one-on-one time. . . . If there
were problems, they often got dragged to a room . . . with me, and then we
would just sit, talk about what they were feeling, and that it was okay, and
how to handle it, and how to just deal with the things that were going on
in their life. After the divorce, it did take quite a while for me to get them
stabilized again.

Caitlyn practiced concerted cultivation during and after dinner. She would
use dinner to check in with her children, and then after dinner, she would
give each child individual attention, complete with problem solving. These
concerted cultivation techniques served her family well. She and her husband divorced when her children were in elementary school, and she continued to use her dinnertime rituals and one-on-one meetings to help the
boys work through their feelings and give them a sense of normalcy.

Laid-Back Linda

Linda is a middle-class mother who homeschooled her children and practiced a child-centric philosophy. This parenting and educational philosophy
means that homeschool lessons are determined by a child's interest. Linda
viewed food the same way she viewed education: the child was given as
much freedom of choice as possible. Although she prepared a meal every
night, her children could eat what she made or prepare their own food. She
did not insist that the children sit and eat.

Linda's quotation will illustrate two phenomena. First, she demonstrates
adaptive management parenting. As mentioned earlier, AMP parents adapt
their parenting style to fit the needs of a child in any given situation. Specifically, Linda puts the child first and prioritizes the child's desires while also
fostering independence and personal responsibility. Second, she is a good
example of the role conflict parents sometimes feel due to the mixed messages they receive about good parenting:

> Just like with education where I let people choose, I let them choose the
> eating. All of it. I mean I wouldn't let them choose—"we're going to have
> Tootsie Rolls for dinner, and call it good!" But I did let them choose . . .
>
> My husband and I might be having salmon and salad, and the kids
> might—I mean—they would not be eating the same way that we were eat-
> ing. I would tell them they couldn't eat garbage, and I'm not going to cook
> four different meals, so you either need to learn to cook what you like, eat
> what I cook, or you know, I was very flexible.

Linda was practicing a style of intensive parenting that looks quite different from concerted cultivation or helicopter parenting. Linda's brand of

adaptive management parenting places a premium on a child's autonomy and promotes independence. To the casual observer, her method may look like negligent parenting, but Linda devoted a significant portion of her life to child rearing. Homeschooling required a significant commitment; Linda did not work outside the home in favor of staying home and facilitating their education. Each year necessitated a negotiation between Linda and each child. At the beginning of each year throughout K-12, Linda would ask each child if he or she wanted to go to public school, homeschool, or do a hybrid of both. Linda had a broad idea of subjects to study for the year, but she would leave the specifics up to the child. In the same way, Linda was deliberate about how mealtimes would work. She treated meal choices like she treated educational choices, which meant that the child was given a range of safe choices and then had self-guidance within those choices. Linda may not have made her children's dinners, but she put a lot of time and thought into the preparation that allowed them to make their own. She had to keep food on hand that her children liked, that was healthy, and that was easy enough for a child to prepare.

Perhaps because she practiced an unconventional form of homeschooling for so many years, Linda seemed to anticipate criticism for her decisions. She knew that by not insisting on the family meal, she violated a contemporary parenting norm. She also projected some guilt, noting that her decisions were "probably . . . bad." At the same time, Linda practiced child-centric parenting because she saw it as good parenting. Linda seemed to feel tension between the norm that espouses the superiority of family meals and the guidelines of child-centric learning, which honor child autonomy above almost all else.

As these two stories demonstrate, dinner was a time for parents to transmit their family's cultural values in ways that made sense for their parenting styles and family needs. While some parents could do this in a way that complied with expert advice, others found their own paths. By varying their responses to the often-stressful dinner hour, parents showed the adaptive management parenting mindset.

Homework Help

Homework can be a big part of a child's after-school routine and can be a site of adaptive management parenting. Teachers encourage parents to stay involved with the homework process (Walker et al. 2004), and parents who practice concerted cultivation are more likely to give their children academic help outside the classroom (Lareau 2003). About half the parents interviewed gave little or no help with homework when their children were in school. Six parents said they did not give help, and ten parents said they gave very little help. One common theme among parents who said they did not help was that the children were self-directed and did not require help. The parents who gave very little help would ask if the children had homework and would have a set homework time or would provide reminders. Parents were also available for occasional answers or to review the homework. Eight parents gave their children some help. In this group, parents would have a certain subject or two in which they helped their children. Four parents gave their children more extensive help. While there is not a clear class distinction in types of help, all upper-middle-class parents gave some homework help, and no lower-middle-class parents gave extensive home help (see Figure 2.1).

Some parents asserted that they had a hands-off approach to homework help. Lauryn noted that she did not give her children very much help and described the help she gave:

> I had more of a hands-off kind of parenting style. You know, I know that the helicopter parent that is kind of really up in the kids, fussing about what their homework and everything is. But we're not that type, we're kind of just "want them, you know, [to] fly on their own." Of course, if you had a paper early, we would read it over and give them some tips, advice, you know, especially for writing, you know, if they wanted us to read something that, you know, math they're on their own. Many of the core subjects, social studies or science, they're on their own.

While Lauryn seemed to retreat from science and math subjects, she and her spouse were willing to give hands-on help in writing. Given her use of the term "helicopter parent," it seems that she viewed that form of parenting

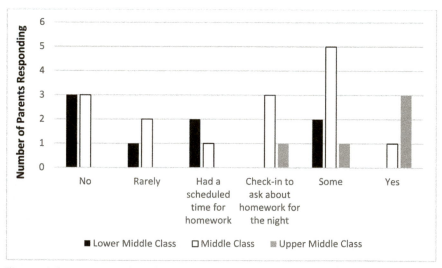

Figure 2.1   Homework Help

as undesirable and felt the need to distinguish herself from it. Lauryn's act of distancing of her parenting practices from those of helicopter parents lends evidence to the earlier speculation that the stigma surrounding helicopter parenting is leading to parents who either eschew the practice or will not admit to using it.

Earlier, I spoke of Linda's parenting conflict. On one hand, she wanted to allow her children the freedom of choice that she admired in the child-centric homeschooling ideology. However, she felt deviant because parenting in accordance with those beliefs meant she violated the good parenting norms that call for cohesive family dinners. Lauryn also seems to suffer from some role conflict. She wanted her children to succeed and wanted to give them help if she could. However, she also thought that helicopter parenting is not a good parenting strategy, so she wanted to thread the needle between being involved but not too involved.

Maggie is an upper-middle-class parent; both she and her husband have advanced degrees and work in the education field. She described being more involved in helping with her children's homework. Although she said that her children were self-directed, she and her spouse helped their children come up with writing topics and sometimes edited papers. It seemed important that she not identify as an overinvolved parent, but she also did have clear memories of ample homework help when she was young. Nelson (2012) noted that this "tightrope" is common for modern parents who struggle to find the balance between being permissive and protective, or firm but fair, or engaged but not overbearing. This balancing act may be a motivating factor behind adaptive management parenting as parents try to navigate the very crowded paths indicated by child-rearing advice.

Adaptive management parents delegate responsibilities when they deem it the right path. For example, Mark and Sienna explained that they did not understand their children's homework as it became more advanced. They would send the younger children to the older children and ask the older children to help. Jillian's children received homework help from their grandmother, which surprised Jillian because her mother had not been a help to her when she was in school. These parents were able to outsource homework help to trusted relatives.

Another way that parents can help their children succeed is by intervening at school when the child is having an issue there (Lareau 2003). Parents who practice concerted cultivation speak to the school early and often (Lareau 2003). They do this to guide their children's education as much as possible. Although many parents I interviewed had memories of intervening on behalf of their child when the child was in K-12, that intervention was not frequent. Some of the parents said they did not intervene, and it was because their children did not have any issues that needed addressing (see Table 2.2).

Table 2.2   Teacher Intervention

Name	Social Class	Issue	Parent Response	Resolution
Nicole	Working class	Teacher in wrong	Went to principal	Resolved in child's favor
Lindsey	Working class	Teacher in wrong	Went to principal	Resolved in child's favor eventually
Maya*	Working class	Child in wrong, teacher in wrong	Went to school, mom offered alternate discipline for child	Resolved in child's favor eventually
Maya*	Working class	Teacher in wrong	Asked teacher to challenge sons	Switched schools
Natasha	Working class	Teacher in wrong	Got child moved	Switched classes
Kristen	Working class	Teacher in wrong	Mom met with teacher several times	Resolved in child's favor eventually
Eleanor	Middle class	Teacher in wrong	Went to principal over child's objections	Child didn't want mom to step in/ not resolved
Jayda	Middle class	Child in wrong	Just to talk, not to ask for special treatment	Mom worked with school
Lauryn	Middle class	ADHD testing	Met with teacher	Good resolution
Linda	Middle class	Values mismatch	Removed child from school	Switched schools
Doris	Middle class	Child acting bored in class	Asked teacher to test for giftedness	Good resolution
Natalie	Middle class	Teacher in wrong	Called to schedule an appointment with teacher	Resolved in child's favor
Simone	Middle class	Teacher in wrong	Asked for help so child would know how to work with teacher	Good resolution

Table 2.2 (*continued*)

Name	Social Class	Issue	Parent Response	Resolution
Erica**	Middle class	Teacher in wrong	Mom coached child in confrontation, then mom wrote a letter threatening action	Resolved in child's favor
Jillian*	Upper middle class	Academic issues	Homeschooled son, worked with the school, reenrolled	Good resolution
Jillian*	Upper middle class	Academic issues	Worked with teacher to clarify expectations	Good resolution
Maggie	Upper middle class	Child wrongfully accused	Met with school	Resolved in child's favor

*Same parent for 2 separate interventions

**Parent intervened on behalf of Generation X child

The most common reasons for parent intervention were if the child was having behavioral issues or academic issues. Working-class and middle-class parents remembered intervening at times, and there was no class-based difference in outcomes. One set of working-class parents did specify that they would ask their children to try to work it out on their own, and then if that failed, the parents would step in. In other words, in contrast to earlier studies where working-class parents were more deferential and compliant than middle-class parents when interacting with the professionals who were in their children's lives (e.g., Hays 2004; Lareau 2003), the working-class parents I spoke to were as likely to fight for a favorable resolution to the issue as more affluent parents. The manner of intervention suggests an adaptive management approach. Parents did not interfere unnecessarily and did not call the teachers often. Instead, if their child needed them at school, they would go. It seems that the parents allowed their children the freedom to build relationships with classmates and faculty without excessive parental hovering. Most studies have found that middle-class parents are more likely to intervene than working-class families and that parents hover around their children's academic progress, ready to leap in at a moment's notice (Albright 2013; Bodovski and Farkas 2008; Hunt 2008; Lareau 2003). My findings stray from the typical narrative surrounding parent interventions at school.

The parents' actions in the current study suggest that there is more nuance in terms of social class and parental involvement in the classroom.

Fostering Self-Sufficiency on the Way to Adulthood

One of the main concerns expressed about the millennial generation is that it has been coddled by helicopter parents and will not be able to function well in adulthood (Ferdman 2016). Contrary to these claims, many of my interview subjects used helicopter parenting sparingly and gave their children more autonomy as their children got older. Seventeen parents talked about ways in which they taught their children to be self-sufficient adults.

Parents tended to give their children more freedom in high school to prepare them for adulthood. For two households, parents allowed their children a chance to live on their own. Peyton and her spouse practiced an 18th birthday rite of passage, for example. The parents would take a two- or three-week vacation and leave the 18-year-old at home alone. The new adult practiced independent living in a safe setting. This type of freedom is quite different from the hand-holding by helicopter parents showcased in anxious media stories.

Elaine is an upper-middle-class woman who adapted her parenting strategies for different times in her children's lives. Elaine could be described as a very hands-on parent, at least in academics. She gave feedback on papers throughout high school and college for her three older children. When her son was in college, she drove over four hours each way to tutor him, because he was at risk of failing a course. However, Elaine also allowed each of her daughters to live away from home when the girls were in high school. Here she speaks of her oldest daughter's early college credits:

> Alexandra was a good student in high school but was a little bit restless and bored and she was very difficult to get along with at that time in her life. She completed her junior year of high school and we encouraged her to test the waters of college by her and one of her good friends, we rented them a little house and the two of them went over to a small town in Arizona. And those two girls took classes at [the community college], for the summer after their junior year of high school. And they did very well, both of them. And they had a great time because they were 17 and yet they were living in a house and taking college classes in this little town.

Elaine continued to encourage Alexandra on this advanced academic track. Alexandra stayed at the community college and lived in the dorms for the fall of her senior year. In the spring, she transferred to the large state university in her hometown. Elaine helped her navigate the application process. Due to summer and fall coursework and some equivalency testing, Alexandra entered the university in her senior year of high school as a college sophomore.

Elaine's younger daughter Elizabeth lived with Alexandra during Elizabeth's ninth and tenth grade years. Elaine took a job out of state, and Elizabeth had academic reasons for wanting to complete those two years in their old city. Elaine rented an apartment for the girls and moved 1,000 miles away to her new city. She spoke with Elizabeth weekly and visited often. But for the day-to-day living, Elizabeth was on her own. Elaine felt that Alexandra, who was a junior and senior in college during this time, was mature enough to take care of herself but not to take care of a teenager. However, she thought of Elizabeth as a very responsible teenager who would do well on her own with some small amount of support from Alexandra.

Other parents also encouraged self-sufficiency through childhood independence. Linda homeschooled her children, and each child was largely in charge of his or her own education. Her oldest daughter, Tiffany, began attending a state-sponsored college program while she was still a junior in high school. Linda left the interactions with college staff to Tiffany to encourage maturity in her approach to bureaucracy. Lauren is a middle-class mother to Jacob, her son who spent many hours at the skate park starting at the age of five. Older teens and young adults would mentor him and teach him new tricks. Skateboarding turned into his passion, and after college, he found ways to combine this passion with travel and career. Lauren thought the support he received at the skate park was instrumental in Jacob's maturity.

Four of the parents noted that their children were very responsible without any extra reinforcements. Instead of being coddled, these children picked up the need for self-sufficiency at such a young age that their parents seem to think the quality is inherent. For instance, Natasha was a working-class mother. Robert, her only child, would do his homework and go to bed without any reminders. In high school, he secured a professional job working in the field of his choice. According to Natasha:

> He was very focused and he'd always say, "I don't know why my friends are so worried about having girlfriends, I got a job and I got school and I've got to do this and I've got to do that." So, he's always very focused and I didn't have to give him more responsibility, he was kind of responsible for himself early on.

Stella's daughter had a similar maturity. Stella had gotten pregnant with Rachel while she was still in high school, and this had seemed to foster a close friendship between mother and daughter. Stella and Rachel did meal planning and grocery shopping together when Rachel was young. Stella does not remember doing much to prepare Rachel for college, because Rachel was "literally just the most responsible person you'll ever meet."

There are multiple parenting strategies that foster independence, resiliency, and competence in children. The parents in my sample tailored their response to their children's transition to adulthood based on their family's culture, the children's needs, the parent's needs, and the parent's priorities. In each family, the parents were striving to do what was best for their children while balancing myriad and sometimes competing wants and needs.

Although there was strong evidence of AMP in my sample, I did not perform a comparison study. A study of parents of millennials who have not achieved a college diploma could provide insight into the scope of this parenting style. It may be widespread as parents try to balance competition with parenting behaviors formed in their own childhoods.

This finding is important because it accounts for more of the variability in parenting than the broad categories of "intensive parenting," "helicopter parenting," and "concerted cultivation" allow. It demonstrates the agency parents have been practicing within the larger structure of American parenting practices.

Contrary to concerns that helicopter parenting remains into adulthood (Bradley-Geist and Olson-Buchanan 2014; Fingerman et al. 2012; Gray 2015; Hunt 2008), many of the parents in my study viewed high school as a first step toward independence. Parents began the process of letting go, giving more responsibility and autonomy as their children demonstrated competence. In this way, the parents gave both the "safety nets" and "scaffolding" into adulthood that allowed for a gradual transition to adulthood (Swartz et al. 2011).

Conclusion

In her article about overprotective parenting, Rosin notes that she spends her entire weekends with her children (2014). But perhaps the link between increased closeness and overprotection is not as strong as Rosin fears. Lareau (2003) predicted that intensive parenting would help create competent adults who know how to advocate for themselves and that one residual effect of the practice is that parents interact with their children often, which one might assume would result in continued closeness throughout the life course. My study suggests that a close parent-child relationship does not equate to helicopter parenting by default, and that parents who practice adaptive management parenting can foster independence in adulthood while also maintaining close emotional connections with their children.

The parents I interviewed practiced AMP, which was a combination of concerted cultivation, helicopter parenting, and, at times, benign neglect parenting. The main difference between the practices described in my interviews and what scholars have defined as intensive parenting was that the parents I interviewed did not demonstrate solely high levels of intervention.

Although parents practiced archetypal intensive parenting at times, they also employed a more hands-off parenting throughout the childrearing process as needed. For instance, parents remembered being actively involved in their children's lives when their children were young, pulling back as the children got older, and introducing self-sufficiency before college.

Parents who practice AMP can be very involved with their children's lives in one scenario and completely hands-off in another, and different parents have different levels of intervention. For example, one parent remembered heart-to-heart talks during dinner, while another allowed her children to plan and prepare their own dinners on their timetable. My exploratory study suggests that AMP may highlight the role that agency plays in parenting. This parenting style makes sense when seen through the lens of Swidler's concept of the cultural tool kit (1986). Parenting has undergone a drastic shift in the past 40 years, and this shift left many parents with what Swidler refers to as "unsettled lives," trying to navigate old parenting styles and new ones to create enduring habits and doctrine. In this time of unsettledness, the adaptive management parent pulls from her cultural tool kit the wisdom of her own parents, her experiences growing up, her friends, parenting books, and childhood experts to find the method of parenting that works best.

These findings complicate the current literature that looks at parenting differences through the lens of social class. While my findings do not negate earlier research, they do complicate the ideal types. Perhaps parenting has more in common with Swidler's cultural tool kit than has been accounted for (1986). In other words, all parents have tool kits that they use in their parenting journeys. The parents in my study were parenting at an unsettled time when goals and outcomes were radically shifting from the more hands-off, parent-centric methodology common through the middle of the 20th century to a more child-centric style that saw children as precious commodities and centered a parent's success as an individual on his or her child's successes throughout life (Hays 1996; Nelson 2012; Warner 2006).

Notes

1. In this chapter, I will rely Sharon Hays's definition of intensive mothering. All but one of my respondents were women, and my examples of intensive parenting are almost exclusively intensive *mothering*, but I did not have a father comparison group to help me determine that it is solely the domain of mothers. I cannot say that the style was exclusively used by mothers as opposed to fathers, so I will continue to use the term "intensive *parenting*" instead of "intensive *mothering*," and I will apply it to parenting in general instead of just mothers even though I acknowledge that there are important gendered dynamics that make this concept especially salient for mothers.

2. All respondent names are pseudonyms.

References

Albright, Matthew. 2013. "Online Grade Access Can Lead to 'Helicopter Parents.'" *USA Today*. Retrieved May 22, 2017. https://www.usatoday.com/story/news/nation/2013/09/24/education-online-grades-helicopter-parents/2862105/.

Begley, Sara. 2013. "'Helicopter Parents' Crash Kids' Job Interviews: What's An Employer To Do?" *Forbes*. Retrieved March 12, 2017. http://www.forbes.com/sites/theemploymentbeat/2013/09/20/helicopter-parents-crash-kids-job-interviews-whats-an-employer-to-do/.

Bianchi, Suzanne. 2011. "Family Change and Time Allocation in American Families." *The Annals of the American Academy of Political and Social Science* 638 (1): 21–44.

Bodovski, Katerina, and George Farkas. 2008. "'Concerted Cultivation' and Unequal Achievement in Elementary School." *Social Science Research* 37 (3): 903–19.

Bradley-Geist, Jill, and Julie Olson-Buchanan. 2014. "Helicopter Parents: An Examination of the Correlates of Over-Parenting of College Students." *Education + Training* 56 (4): 314–28.

Bulawa, Philip. 2014. "Adapting Grounded Theory in Qualitative Research: Reflections from Person Experience." *International Research in Education* 2 (1): 145–168.

Cassling, Kyle, Justine Frederick, Ingrid Olson, William Totimeh, and Matthew Venker. n.d. "Helicopter Parenting?: Parental Involvement In the Workplace." Retrieved April 30, 2013. http://www.stolaf.edu/depts/sociology/major/371/2011/Paper%20-%20Helicopter%20parents.docx.

Cline, Foster, and Jim Fay. 1990. *Parenting with Love and Logic: Teaching Children Responsibility*. Colorado Springs, CO: NavPress.

Eisenberg, Marla, Rachel Olson, Dianne Neumark-Sztainer, Mary Story, and Linda H. Bearinger. 2004. "Correlations Between Family Meals and Psychosocial Well-Being Among Adolescents." *Archives of Pediatrics & Adolescent Medicine* 158 (8): 792–796.

Fass, Paula S. 1997. *Kidnapped: Child Abduction in America*. New York: Oxford University Press.

Ferdman, Roberto. 2016. "The Baffling Reason Many Millennials Don't Eat Cereal." *The Washington Post*, February 23. https://www.washingtonpost.com/news/wonk/wp/2016/02/23/this-is-the-height-of-laziness/.

Fingerman, Karen L., Yen-Pi Cheng, Eric D. Wesselmann, Steven Zarit, Frank Furstenberg, and Kira S. Birditt. 2012. "Helicopter Parents and Landing Pad Kids: Intense Parental Support of Grown Children." *Journal of Marriage and Family* 74 (4): 880–96.

Fritz, Noah J., and David L. Altheide. 1987. "The Mass Media and the Social Construction of the Missing Children Problem." *The Sociological Quarterly* 28 (4): 473–92.

Fulkerson, Jayne A., Mary Story, Alison Mellin, Nancy Leffert, Dianne Neumark-Sztainer, and Simone A. French. 2006. "Family Dinner Meal Frequency and Adolescent Development: Relationships with Developmental Assets and High-Risk Behaviors." *Journal of Adolescent Health* 39 (3): 337–45.

Gray, Peter. 2015. "Helicopter Parenting & College Students' Increased Neediness." *Psychology Today*. Retrieved October 24, 2016. https://www.psychologytoday.com/blog/freedom-learn/201510/helicopter-parenting-college-students-increased-neediness.

Hamilton, Laura T. 2016. *Parenting to a Degree: How Family Matters for College Women's Success*. Chicago: University of Chicago Press.

Hays, Sharon. 1996. *The Cultural Contradictions of Motherhood*. New Haven: Yale University Press.

Heck, K. E., K. C. Schoendorf, S. J. Ventura, and J. L. Kiely. 1997. "Delayed Childbearing by Education Level in the United States, 1969–1994." *Maternal and Child Health Journal* 1 (2): 81–88.

Howe, Neil, and William Strauss. 2007. "Helicopter Parents in the Workplace." *Syndicated Research Project*. Retrieved April 29, 2013. http://www.wikinomics.com/blog/uploads/helicopter-parents-in-the-workplace.pdf.

Hunt, Judith. 2008. "Make Room for Daddy . . . and Mommy: Helicopter Parents Are Here." *The Journal of Academic Administration in Higher Education* 4 (1): 9–11.

Lareau, Annette. 2003. *Unequal Childhoods: Class, Race, and Family Life*. Berkeley: University of California Press.

Ludden, Jennifer. 2012. "Helicopter Parents Hover in the Workplace." *NPR*. Retrieved November 30, 2012. http://www.npr.org/2012/02/06/146464665/helicopter-parents-hover-in-the-workplace.

Markel, Howard. 2014. "How the Tylenol Murders of 1982 Changed the Way We Consume Medication." *PBS NewsHour*. Retrieved February 28, 2016. http://www.pbs.org/newshour/updates/tylenol-murders-1982/.

Matthews, T. J., and Brady Hamilton. 2009. *Delayed Childbearing: More Women Are Having Their First Child Later in Life*. U.S. Department of Health and Human Services Centers for Disease Control and Prevention National Center for Health Statistics. https://www.cdc.gov/nchs/data/databriefs/db21.pdf.

Musick, Kelly, and Ann Meier. 2012. "Assessing Causality and Persistence in Associations Between Family Dinners and Adolescent Well-Being." *Journal of Marriage and Family* 74 (3): 476–93.

Nelson, Margaret. 2012. *Parenting Out of Control: Anxious Parents in Uncertain Times*. New York: New York University Press.

Offer, Shira. 2013. "Family Time Activities and Adolescents' Emotional Well-Being." *Journal of Marriage and Family* 75 (1): 26–41.

Pew Research Center. 2015. *The American Middle Class Is Losing Ground: No Longer the Majority and Falling Behind Financially*. Washington, D.C.: Pew Research Center.

Powell, Brian, Lala Carr Steelman, and Robert M. Carini. 2006. "Advancing Age, Advantaged Youth: Parental Age and the Transmission of Resources to Children." *Social Forces* 84 (3): 1359–90.

Reed, Kayla, James M. Duncan, Mallory Lucier-Greer, Courtney Fixelle, and Anthony J. Ferraro. 2016. "Helicopter Parenting and Emerging Adult

Self-Efficacy: Implications for Mental and Physical Health." *Journal of Child and Family Studies* 25 (10): 3136–49.

Rivers, Caryl. 2008. *Selling Anxiety: How the News Media Scare Women.* Hanover, NH: University Press of New England.

Rosin, Hanna. 2014. "The Overprotected Kid." *The Atlantic*, April. https://www .theatlantic.com/magazine/archive/2014/04/hey-parents-leave-those -kids-alone/358631/.

Sen, Bisakha. 2010. "The Relationship between Frequency of Family Dinner and Adolescent Problem Behaviors After Adjusting for Other Family Charac- teristics." *Journal of Adolescence* 33 (1): 187–96.

Snow, Catherine, and Diane Beals. 2006. "Mealtime Talk That Supports Literacy Development." *New Directions for Child and Adolescent Development* 2006 (111): 51–66.

Stahl, Ashley. 2015. "Five Reasons Why Helicopter Parents Are Sabotaging Their Child's Career." *Forbes.* Retrieved March 12, 2017. http://www.forbes .com/sites/ashleystahl/2015/05/27/5-reasons-why-helicopter-parents -are-sabotaging-their-childs-career/.

Swartz, Teresa Toguchi. 2009. "Intergenerational Family Relations in Adulthood: Patterns, Variations, and Implications in the Contemporary United States." *Annual Review of Sociology* 35: 191–212.

Swartz, Tersa Toguchi, Minzee Kim, Mayumi Uno, Jeylan Mortimer, and Kirsten Bengtson O'Briend. 2011. "Safety Nets and Scaffolds: Parental Support in the Transition to Adulthood." *Journal of Marriage and Family* 73 (2): 414–429.

Swidler, Ann. 1986. "Culture in Action: Symbols and Strategies." *American Socio- logical Review* 51 (2): 273–86.

Walker, Joan, Kathleen Hoover-Dempsey, Darlene Whetsel, and Christa Green. 2004. *Parental Involvement in Homework: A Review of Current Research and Its Implications for Teachers, After School Program Staff, and Parent Leaders.* The Harvard Family Research Project: Harvard University. http://www.hfrp .org/publications-resources/browse-our-publications/parental-involvement -in-homework-a-review-of-current-research-and-its-implications -for-teachers-after-school-program-staff-and-parent-leaders.

Warner, Judith. 2006. *Perfect Madness: Motherhood in the Age of Anxiety.* New York: Riverhead Books.

CHAPTER THREE

The Changing Landscape of Parent–Adult Child Relations

Joshua Coleman

Advice for parents is plentiful in our news media, but also present is advice for adult children about their older parents. For example, a recent *Huffington Post* Lifestyle piece (Wong 2017) offers suggestions to adults for how and why to "break up" with a narcissistic parent. But what do we really know about the relationships between parents and their adult children, and how might perceptions of adult children and their parents be shaped by larger familial and societal forces? There's a good news/bad news story to changes in parent–adult child relations over the past few decades. As a psychologist specializing in parental estrangement, I live in the bad news: sitting with parents every day, whose adult children want nothing to do with them (Parker-Pope 2010; Coleman 2007). However, if recent research is reliable, many parents and their adult children appear to be getting along better than ever (Fingerman, Sechrist and Birditt 2013; Furstenberg and Fingerman 2012; Furstenberg 2015). For example, in 1986, only half of adult children said that they'd spoken to a parent in the past week, while in 2008, that number shot up to 87 percent (Furstenberg and Fingerman 2012). According to a Pew survey (2009), most parents report feeling closer to their adult children than they believe their parents felt to them at a similar age, and adult children report feeling closer to their parents than those in prior generations. Sociologists Frank Furstenberg and Karen Fingerman observed that these trends have accelerated over the past decade (Furstenberg and Fingerman 2012).

Some of this can be explained by parenting ideologies that have moved away from authoritarian, parent-centered perspectives and toward those that are more egalitarian, democratic, and child-centered. As historian Stephanie Coontz noted (Bahrampour 2016),

> There's been a trend . . . where you really allowed the child to explore their own interests rather than expect them to become a clone of you, and the result is that young people, they like their parents more than our generation did. There's been an increase in respect for kids, and as a result, an increase in kids seeing their parents as people they can confide in and show weakness to.

They also have more in common with their parents than did prior generations who were more likely to be divided around tastes in clothing, music, and even the use of drugs or alcohol (Furstenberg 2015).

In many ways, this new level of contact with adult children is the realization of a desire expressed by the bulk of today's parents raising children. According to a recent survey published by the Culture of American Families Project (Bowman 2012), a majority of today's parents say that they want to be friends with their children for life. Almost three-quarters of parents of school-age children state that they eventually want to be their children's best friends; only 17 percent disagree. According to recent data, while 70 percent of parents provide practical help on a monthly basis to an adult child, a whopping 90 percent report giving advice on a monthly basis. This also doesn't appear to be restricted to one gender over the other, as young men and young women appear to be equally involved with a parent (Fingerman and Furstenberg 2012).

Today's more intimate parent–adult child relations are also the product of smaller family sizes and more time with children. According to a briefing report for the Council on Contemporary Families, sociologists Orielle Sullivan and Scott Coltrane report that between 1965 and 2003, men tripled the amount of time they spent with their children, and mothers—including working mothers—doubled theirs (Sullivan and Coltrane 2008). Women created this time by giving up hours for housework, leisure, sleep, and sometimes time with their marital partners. Today's fathers now report more work-family conflict than do working mothers (Aumann, Galinsky, and Matos 2011).

In fact, for the past few decades, working mothers spent more time with their children than did stay-at-home mothers in the supposedly halcyon days of the 1960s (e.g., Bianchi, Robinson, and Milkie 2005). Part of this historic shift toward children is due to the fact that many Americans believe that their relationship with their child or children may be the only long-term relationship on which they can count (Ehrensaft 1999; Silva 2013). More parental involvement is also animated by increased parental worry and guilt about the safety and well-being of children. According to the *Culture of American Families Survey* (Bowman 2015), 80 percent of today's parents say that children are very vulnerable and must be protected. Their greatest fears are that their children might be snatched away, preyed upon sexually by other adults, or injured in a serious accident. The watchful eye of the Internet broadcasts dangers from every corner, causing today's parents to believe that peril is constantly lurking. The ever-changing advice from parenting experts (LeVine and LeVine 2016) leads today's parents to worry about doing the *wrong thing* and creating a child with low self-esteem, depression, anxiety, or addiction. Getting children into decent colleges and into decent jobs also preoccupies and worries parents of all classes both during the child-rearing years and well into adulthood (Cooper 2014; Silva 2013).

The Downside

On the other hand, high expectations of closeness and collaboration between parent and adult child can create problems, especially when the rules for family engagement are built upon the ever-shifting sands of affection and personal fulfillment, rather than obligation or duty. A recent example from my practice illustrates this (note: to protect the confidentiality of my clients, all case examples cited in this chapter are formed from composites of cases rather than identifiable individuals):

24-year-old DAUGHTER: "When you were my age, did you call Grandma every day because you wanted to or because that's what she wanted you to do?"

MOTHER: "I guess because she wanted me to. I wasn't that close to her, but I felt like it was the right thing to do."

DAUGHTER: "Yeah, I don't want that kind of relationship with you."

THERAPIST: "What kind of a relationship would you like with your mother at this point?"

DAUGHTER: "If I want to call her, I'll call her. If I don't, then I don't want to be made to feel guilty about it."

As this interaction demonstrates, the daughter believes that calling her mother out of obligation goes against her values of honesty and integrity. She believes that setting some general guidelines about the rules of engagement is a healthy expression of her adulthood and individuality. She also believes she's giving her mother a useful and arguably loving perspective for how to have a better relationship with her, a perspective the mother would be wise to heed.

While Mom was hurt and resentful that her daughter felt burdened by any obligation to her, she also recognized that her daughter was behaving exactly how she had raised her to behave: to be true to oneself and not do things out of guilt or convention, because that gets in the way of happiness and success; and honesty, even if it hurts, is preferable to a false presentation of self.

The mother had raised her daughter with those values because, as a woman growing up in the 1960s, she had strongly disliked her own inclinations toward compliance, dutifulness, and guilt. She had worked most of her life to feel more immune to those pressures and wanted to make sure that her daughter didn't have to struggle in the same way.

While the mother in my practice was glad she had succeeded in inoculating her daughter against those constraints, she resented, and not that quietly, that her daughter wasn't more responsive and sensitive to her needs, since she had also provided her with a life far richer than that provided by her parents: one that included foreign travel; private schools; tutors; full college tuition; and a kind of loving, dedicated parenting only seen in the bland TV family dramas or sitcoms of her generation. The mother had also undergone years of her own therapy so that she could be a better mother to her daughter than hers had been to her. This comparison was sometimes spoken: "You have no idea how good you have it compared to what I grew up with." This was a source of conflict between the mother and daughter, since the mom had been raised to respect authority and to be responsive to the demands of family obligation, while the daughter had been raised to see both as constraints on her happiness and independence.

The American Parent

The previous example illustrates that, however positive current relations are between parents and adult children, in many homes, there's still quite a bit of conflict. A large international study of nearly 2,700 parents over the age of 65 found that parents in the United States have almost *twice* as much conflict with their adult children compared with parents in Israel, Germany, the United Kingdom, and Spain (Silverstein, Gans, Giarrusso, and Bengtson 2010). Merril Silverstein, a social gerontologist at the University of Southern California, summarized his findings by stating that "American families can be characterized by greater strain" (Span 2010).

The difference between American families and families of other countries may stem from a style of individualism that's unique to the United States. Sociologist Amy Schalet has observed that American parenting practices are based on the idea that children learn to become adults by pushing hard against parents' limits around authority, sex, and alcohol consumption (Schalet 2011). She terms this "adversarial individualism" and contrasts it with Dutch parenting practices where teens are brought into adulthood by having sleepovers in the parents' home with their boyfriends or girlfriends starting at around the age of 16, as well as drinking moderately with the family.

While American parents believe that rebellion against the parental order is a normal, even expectable set of behaviors on the path to adulthood, Dutch parents believe that teens should be eased into the world of adulthood with the parents' knowledge and collaboration, a process she calls "interpersonal individualism." These differences, Schalet notes, stem from contrasting national values—*freedom* in the United States and *gezelligheid* (cozy togetherness) in the Netherlands. Whereas children in the United States struggle to escape the chains of parental constraint, Dutch children expect that they'll rely on their parents even as they move into adulthood.

To return to the example of the 24-year-old, a desire to feel separate from her mother stems from a need to see herself as charting her own course, sometimes in opposition to the desires and needs of her mother and with an expressed desire to feel free from the emotional limitations imposed by guilt or worry about the mother's feelings. In contrast, a Dutch parent's involvement would more commonly be seen as a collaborative effort where identity and adulthood are cocreated without an inherent threat to that young adult's individuality.

Conflict in Today's Families

If a parent's role is to raise individuals who are assertive and uncompromising in their pursuit of happiness and individuality, then family conflict takes on a very different meaning: conflict stops being seen as an unavoidable and instead even as a *necessary* component of family life and rather like a referendum on each member's potential to limit or enhance the other's pursuit of growth, happiness, and individuality. The investment in a parent's happiness becomes based not on a presumed sense of obligation or duty, however problematic those may also be, but rather upon the way that the relationship makes the adult child *feel* about himself or herself.

When obligation, respect for authority, guilt, and shame are reduced or removed from the family equation, each developmental step taken by a child or parent provides a potential for greater intimacy than in earlier generations but also greater conflict with the parent. As a result, relationships that were once close can quickly become mired in discord when the child goes off to college, gets married, becomes a parent, gets divorced, moves back home, or simply wants less contact with the parent than the parent wants.

Boundaries and Enmeshment

In my practice, a surprisingly large number of estrangements can be explained by the adult child wanting more distance and privacy. And contrary to what they be might be telling their therapists, it's not always because the parent was so troubled or toxic. It is more because the parent was once so *involved*.

Maintaining one's boundaries is very important if becoming an individual is a goal, and Americans care very much about being individuals. According to the Hofestede cultural dimensions model (Hofstede 2011), Americans rank higher on scores of individualism than members of any other culture. One of the negative consequences of recent changes in parenting is that many, if not most, children know quite a bit about the interior lives of their parents: their dreams, their frustrations, their failures, and their successes. All the careful communication that parents have been doing with children over the past few decades has created a lot of information about who we all are. Many parents and adult children feel closer because they know each other, arguably more intimately than did prior generations of parents and adult children.

But more knowledge can also create more guilt, worry, strain, and feelings of obligation. If an adult child is trying to focus on a career, a relationship, a move, college, marriage, or raising a family, then thinking about a parent's well-being or needs may be more distracting than productive. Some of the conflict between parents and grown children can be explained by changing generational views of what constitutes adulthood. Overall, today's adult children attain all the prior markers of adulthood far later than did their parents and in a much less clear-cut sequence (Arnett and Schwab 2012; Benson and Furstenberg 2006; Furstenberg 2015; Silva 2013).

As other markers of adulthood, such as financial independence or marriage, have become less certain, *feeling* like an adult might become more important than ever to a young adult's developing sense of identity and self-esteem. This means, among other things, that the teenage rebellions of previous generations may get extended well into the mid-to-late twenties. Some adult children may be distant from or contemptuous of their parents because they need to prove to themselves that they can function without them.

This may be especially true for those raised by single mothers, since these children may have not had another parent to whom to become attached, and the parent may not have had another adult who could help meet their needs. As I often see in my practice, an adult child may later in life kick Mom to the curb in favor of Dad—not because she was such a terrible mother but because that child doesn't know any other way to feel separate from her.

While prior generations of parents may have made the mistake of being insufficiently involved, at least according to current standards, today's parents are more likely to be "too" involved with their children (Arnett and Schwab 2012). Fewer children per family; more fluid lines of authority; greater sensitivity and psychological-mindedness on the part of the parent; more parental guilt, worry, and time; and more communication all provide a much more emotionally intensive family environment than may have existed in prior generations—where children were seen and not heard, the lines of authority were much clearer, and parents were less concerned with what their children thought about the quality of their parenting.

In addition, because of the ways that today's parents have invested far more in their children, both financially and emotionally, they may feel entitled to a kind of availability that is at odds with what their adult child can reasonably or sanely provide. This entitlement may cause them to communicate in ways that work against them and may cause the adult child to push back in ways that are more distressful to the parent.

The difficulty in defining adulthood according to more traditionally sanctioned ways, plus the high degree of dependence that so many children have on their parents, may lead today's young adults to define it in more internal, personal, or idiosyncratic ways.

"My Therapist Thinks You Suck": Psychotherapy and the Curated Childhood

The U.S. Census Bureau reports that in 1975, more adults ages 18 to 34 lived with a spouse than with their parents; by 2016, more young adults lived with their parents than with a husband or wife (Cummings 2017). As markers of adulthood, such as financial independence or marriage, have become less certain, *feeling* like an adult might become more important than ever to a young adult's developing sense of identity and self-esteem. Some adult children may be distant from or contemptuous of their parents because they need to prove to themselves that they can function without them.

Others may blame their parents as a way to defend against the shame they feel about not feeling more successful or accomplished in their lives. In a meritocracy, you have no one to blame but yourself if you don't succeed in life. But according to the ideology of contemporary psychotherapy, your ability to become successful depends more upon the quality of parenting you received. Therefore, blaming parents for one's lack of success allows the individual to insulate themselves from the toxic effects of shame by locating the cause in the parent rather than the self.

People in the United States, seemingly more than in any other country, feel passionately about the therapeutic promise of self-actualization (Aubry and Tryst 2015; Ilouz 2008; Silva 2013). If guilt and obligation are today's obstacles to happiness, then psychotherapists are the high priests dedicated to its exorcism. In my practice, I've observed that many estrangements begin as a result of the adult child entering psychotherapy.

Part of our success as therapists comes from our ability to help our clients feel less guilty, shameful, or defective. In so doing, we often look to what they did or didn't get from their parents as a way to help them make sense of their conflicts, increase their feelings of self-awareness, and develop a healthy entitlement to better treatment from others.

Helping individuals to understand how their families affected them is indeed important. Parents can powerfully shape identity, self-esteem, feelings of trust or safety in the world, and, later, one's ability to parent. Psychotherapists can be efficacious teachers about the connection between the adult child's difficulties as an adult and the parent's contribution to those inadequacies, deficits, or conflicts.

However, the liability of our historically recent preoccupation with parents is that it assumes that: (a) they're more responsible than they, in fact, are in adult outcomes (LeVine and LeVine 2016); and (b) the deficits in parenting are something to feel mad about rather than have some degree of compassion for (Coleman, Cowan and Cowan 2014). While parenting is indeed important, many problems in adulthood can be more powerfully explained by genetics; neighborhood; relations with peers, siblings, and other adults; and socioeconomic level (Trzaskowski, Maciej, Harlaar, Arden, Kraphol, Rimfeld, McMillan, Dale, and Plomin 2014; Coontz 1992, Keating 2017, Sapolsky 2017).

Many of today's parents have worked hard to create assertive, empowered people who are uncompromising in the pursuit of their dreams. In so doing, they've created an environment where they're expected to comport themselves much like soul mates: sensitive but not intrusive, tolerant but not neglectful, supportive but not smothering. Those who fail in this endeavor are tempted, often in the therapy office, to criticize the parent for failing them.

But the other reason so many adult children are comfortable criticizing their parents is that they're doing exactly what they were raised to do. Sociologist Annette Lareau noted how common it is for middle-class children, in contrast with working-class children, to make demands of their parents and insist that they prioritize the child's needs over theirs (Lareau 2011). A follow-up study of the same children 10 years later found that young adult children of the middle class felt far less grateful to their parents than did the children of the working class. They also valued extended family less than did the working-class young adults. Her study shows how class, in the same way as culture, can curate a young adult's evaluation of a parent and what he or she may owe to that parent.

However, more recent research by sociologist Jennifer Silva (2013) finds that young adult children of the working class are also increasingly critical of their families as they struggle to find identity and meaning now that once taken-for-granted pathways to adulthood have become far less certain. In her book *Coming Up Short: Working-Class Adulthood in an Age of Uncertainty*, Silva writes,

> ...at the center of the therapeutic coming of age narrative are not more traditional sources of identity such as work, religion, or gender, but instead the family—as the source of one's individuality, the source of the self, and the

source of the neuroses from which one must liberate oneself...the more the market renders the future unimaginable and the present unmanageable, the more hyper symbolized the family past becomes. (Silva 2013, 125)

As Silva and others have argued (Ilouz 2008), psychotherapy and its language can create division between parents and adult children because it locates adult dysfunction in the family and not in other important causes of difficulty or failure such as the lack of decent-paying jobs, affordable colleges, or accessible health care.

This isn't to say that an adult child's complaints or criticisms of a parent are always rooted in attempts at individuation or a displacement of blame. Not infrequently, conflict arises or is perpetuated for no other reason than that the parent is unable to address the adult child's reasonable complaints or criticisms in a way that moves the conflict toward resolution.

Aging Parents, Gray Divorces, Later Remarriages

Aging parents can also be a point of division in families. When an older parent remarries, the event may bring new people into the lives of adult children with whom they may have to compete for emotional or financial resources. Concerns about an estate potentially being shared with new family members, in this case unrelated by blood, may cause tensions all around. Guilt toward the other parent (alive or deceased, single or unhappily remarried) may also strain relationships between a parent and adult child. The child may feel torn by guilt, worry, or disloyalty with regard to one or both of the parents.

A significantly high number of parents over 50 are getting divorced, and this is also changing the landscape of parent–adult child relations. Between 1990 and 2010, the divorce rate among adults age 50 and older doubled (Brown and Lin 2012). On one hand, a later divorce can provide a sense of relief to adult children who wish their parents had done it when they were younger and saved everyone a lot of headaches. On the other hand, a later divorce may cause the parent to become more dependent on the adult child for meaning, emotional support, and, in some cases, financial help (Silverstein et al. 2010).

Expectations of closeness can unduly burden an adult child who is more weighed down with raising her own children, developing her career, or working on her own romantic relationship without having to provide the parent with emotional support. While adult children are very much on the minds of parents, parents are not necessarily very much on the minds of their adult children, at least not in the same way (Fingerman, Sechrist, and Birditt 2013).

Recent studies show that parents' provision of support to grown children is associated with positive mood on the part of the parent, whereas it doesn't necessarily work in the other direction. Overall, adult children providing emotional support to parents is associated with a more negative mood (Fingerman, Kim, Tennant, Birdit and Zarit 2016).

Of course, giving help is associated with better mood for parents when the child is doing well or when it's in the context of an overall positive relationship. When an adult child is faring poorly or in active conflict with the parent, then the parent suffers considerably. Research shows that the saying "A parent is only as happy as their least happy child" has some truth to it (Fingerman, Chang, Birditt and Zarit 2012, 184).

The Role of Technology

One of the benefits of technology has been an increase in the means available to families for staying in touch (Louis 2012). While families once had to wait weeks, sometimes months, for letters to arrive, contact is now available from almost any part of the world at any time. This not only allows more opportunities to feel included, connected, and involved but also more chance to give and provide support, assess others' needs, determine their states of mind, and work to resolve conflicts. Video chatting now allows contact with family members who are not only too far away for regular contact but also may be restricted due to financial or health limitations.

However, availability for contact isn't always a good thing. For example, it used to be that estrangements between parents and their adult children were done far more privately. Prior to the existence of social media or the rapid transmission of the Internet, one could be estranged from a child or parent, and the only people who would hear about it might be whomever the parents wanted to tell and the close circle of confidants of the estranged adult child. For all the anguish it caused, an estrangement could mean a fairly clean break, however painful, for both the parent and the child. People would cut off contact and perhaps never be heard from again, unless or until they reconciled.

Social-media communications have stood all that on its head. In my practice, where I specialize in parental estrangement, I've seen how commonly social media is used by adult children to:

- publicize their estrangement, eliciting the feedback of known others and perfect strangers;
- shame and humiliate the parent in a very public way;
- hurt the parent by posting photos of the estranged child, their children, or other nonestranged family members, stepparents, or family friends;
- end access to the adult child by unfriending the parent;
- list stepmothers or stepfathers, but not the biological parent, as family members;

- in the case of adoptive parents, list only the birth mother and not the adoptive mother as the mother;
- isolate the parent by announcing such critical events as births, parties, or weddings through social media while not letting the parent know directly; and
- provide other motivated friends or family members with information to hurt or malign the estranged parent.

In many ways, social media radically increases the suffering of an estranged parent, as it multiplies the vehicles and modes of rejection. It's one thing not to get a letter; it's another to be blocked on Facebook, Twitter, and Instagram and have your e-mail address and phone number blocked. However, social media also allows a motivated parent to hurt or punish an adult child through the same means, such as involving other family members in criticizing or isolating the adult child. In other words, at the same time that social media provides numerous formats for feeling included by a parent or an adult child, it generates an equally high number of ways for family members to feel hurt or excluded.

This suffering is exacerbated by the constant opportunity for comparison that social media creates (Vogel, Rose, Roberts, and Eckles 2014). Family members can feel hurt or humiliated not only by lack of contact but also by the many ways in which they can compare themselves negatively to more fortunate peers or family members, some of whom are still active with the adult child on Facebook or other forms of social media. In fact, many of the estranged parents in my practice learn of such important events as upcoming weddings, births, college acceptances, or graduations from nonestranged family members or friends. In those cases, the parent not only has the sadness of feeling excluded but also the humiliation of learning of these events from those closer to the adult child than the parents themselves.

E-mail, Texting, and the Presentation of Self in the Family

E-mail and texting also provide a vehicle for the adult child to try on different aspects of the self that might be too threatening to do in a face-to-face environment with the parent. In the same way that online avatars create the potential to try on novel ways of experiencing in relation to others, the safe removal of the Internet creates the ability to try on behaviors in a family that might have been impossible prior to its invention. For example, a young adult who suffers from severe social anxiety might be able to complain to or criticize a problematic or hurtful parent over text or e-mail in ways that he or she could never do up close, either because of the adult child's anxiety or because the parent is too self-absorbed, psychologically uninformed, or unwell for the adult child to safely relate to. Similarly, e-mail or texting may allow parents or adult children to have a safe distance within which to communicate thoughts or feelings without the potential dysregulation that may be triggered in one or both through face-to-face contact.

New Rules

In the same way that individuals are no longer obligated to stay in marriages that are romantically unfulfilling (Carson, Miller, Sassler, and Hanson 2016), today's adult children are not obliged to stay in contact with parents with whom they don't feel close or whom they believe will threaten their feelings of happiness or well-being. From that perspective, little ties an adult child to a parent today beyond his or her desire to have a relationship with the parent.

While it used to be the child's job to earn and maintain the parent's love, today it's the parent who needs to earn and maintain that of the adult child. This means that parents fare better if they can acknowledge the adult child's right to set the terms of the relationship from a perspective of happiness, not one of obligation or duty. This is especially important, however fraught, when the adult child wants to share their view of the parent-as-parent in a not-so-flattering light. Here, parents are required to view the interaction not from the resentful platform of how lucky the adult child has it in comparison to the parent's own childhood, or even of what can be reasonably expected from any parent, but more from whether or not the parent helped the adult child to become an individual in harmony with their ideals of who or what they could be.

For adult children, it can be helpful to consider that parenting over the past few decades has required much more psychological heavy lifting than that done by prior generations (Bowman 2015), where parents were less stressed, less worried, and more confident that their efforts were sufficient to launch a child into adulthood. In addition, in the same way that couples expect their partners to provide much more to sustain a long-term commitment (Keating 2017), so too do today's adult children expect that their parents satisfy a longer and more demanding list of roles to justify staying connected to them.

***

It's an interesting time for families in United States. On one hand, positive, greater hopes for closeness with children over the life course, greater solicitation of parental advice or emotional support, and a decreased emphasis on duty or compliance with parental authority all characterize the dream (and its realization) for perhaps most parents with adult children today. On the other hand, delayed transitions to adulthood, parental divorce, longer lives across the generations, decreased boundaries between parent and adult child, and an increased need for family to be a source of personal growth and fulfillment may create more anxiety, uncertainty, conflict, or even estrangement between parent and adult child.

Historian Stephanie Coontz observed that marriage has changed more in the past 30 years than it did in the prior 3000 (Coontz 2007). The same could be said of parenting. Throughout most of our history, family life was governed by neighborhood, church, and an impulse to conform. Historical social norms that kept families in contact and, in many ways, reduced conflict have been replaced by personal choice and self-development as the engines that determine decisions about relationships with family. Today, little compels adult children to maintain a relationship with a parent beyond the desires of that adult child.

It's incumbent on today's parents to learn how to communicate in ways that maximize the probability of maintaining that relationship while acknowledging that the highly individualistic culture of the United States may exert a powerful pull away from the parent, as adult children seek to define themselves in ways that allow them to feel independent and in charge of their own lives. Parents who are able to develop this perspective have a better chance of realizing their dreams of a close relationship with their adult children over the life course. And adult children who are able to empathize with the ways their parents are traveling uncharted territory are the most likely to create a relationship that provides them with the kind of intimacy and guidance that's most in line with their ideals of family involvement.

References

Arnett, Jeffery, and Joseph Schwab. 2012. "The Clark University Poll of Emerging Adults: Thriving, Struggling, and Hopeful." http://www2.clarku.edu/clark-poll-emerging-adults/pdfs/clark-university-poll-emerging-adults-findings.pdf.

Aubry, T., and Travis Tryst, eds. 2015. *Rethinking Therapeutic Culture*. Chicago: University of Chicago Press.

Aumann, K., E. Galinsky, and K. Matos. 2011. *The New Male Mystique*. http://familiesandwork.org/site/research/reports/newmalemystique.pdf.

Bahrampour, Tara. 2016. "A Joy or a Drag? Parents Whose Adult Children Live with Them Say It Can Be Both." https://www.washingtonpost.com/local/social-issues/a-joy-or-a-drag-parents-whose-adult-children-live-with-them-say-it-can-be-both/2016/05/31/5bed055c-2444-11e6-aa84-42391ba52c91_story.html?utm_term=.e63957ebbf9c.

Benson, J., and F. Furstenberg. 2006. "Entry into Adulthood: Are Adult Role Transitions Meaningful Markers of Adult Identity?" *Advances in Life Course Research* 11: 199–224.

Bianchi, Suzanne, and Melissa Milkie. 2010. "Work and Family Research in the First Decade of the 21st Century." *Journal of Marriage and Family* 72 (3): 705–725.

Bianchi, Suzanne M., John P. Robinson, and Melissa A. Milkie. 2006. *Changing Rhythms of American Family Life* (Rose Series in Sociology). New York: Russell Sage Foundation.

Bowan, C. J. 2013. "Holding Them Closer." *The Hedgehog Review: Critical Reflections on Contemporary Culture* 15 (3) 8–23.

Bowman, Carl Desportes. 2012. *Culture of American Families: A National Survey.* Charlottesville, VA: Institute for Advanced Studies in Culture.

Brown, Susan L., and I-Fen Lin. 2012. "The Gray Divorce Revolution: Rising Divorce Among Middle-Aged and Older Adults, 1990–2010." *The Journals of Gerontology, Series B, Psychological Sciences and Social Sciences* 67 (6): 731–741.

Carson, Daniel, Amanda Miller, Sharon Sassler, and Sarah Hanson. 2016. "The Gendered Division of Housework and Couples' Sexual Relationships: A Reexamination." *Journal of Marriage and Family* 78 (4): 975–995.

Coleman, Joshua. 2007. *When Parents Hurt: Compassionate Strategies When You and Your Grown Child Don't Get Along.* New York: HarperCollins.

Coleman, Joshua, Philip Cowan, and Carolyn Pape Cowan. 2014. "The Cost of Blaming Parents." *Greater Good Magazine.* https://greatergood.berkeley.edu/article/item/the_cost_of_blaming_parents

Coltrane, Scott. 1996. *Family Man: Fatherhood, Housework and Gender Equity.* New York: Oxford University Press.

Coontz, Stephanie. 2007. "The Family Revolution." *Greater Good Magazine.* September.

Coontz, Stephanie. 2007. *Marriage, a History: How Love Conquered Marriage.* New York: Penguin.

Cooper, Laura Fitzgerald. 2014. "Parents: We Need to Get a Grip on Our Own College Application Anxiety." https://www.washingtonpost.com/news/parenting/wp/2014/11/17/parents-we-need-to-get-a-grip-on-our-own-college-application-anxiety/?noredirect=on&utm_term=.5635a2ed6171.

Cummings, W. 2007. "Millennials Differ from Other Generations in Almost Every Regard. Here's the Data." https://www.usatoday.com/story/news/nation/2017/04/19/young-americans-census-report-millenials/100640966/.

Ehrensaft, Diane. 1999. *Spoiling Childhood: How Well-Meaning Parents Are Giving Children Too Much—But Not What They Need.* New York: Guilford.

Fingerman, Karen, Yen-Pi Cheng, Kira Birditt, and Steven Zarit. 2012. "Only as Happy as the Least Happy Child: Multiple Grown Children's Problems and Successes and Middle-aged Parents' Well-being." *The Journals of Gerontology, Series B, Psychological Sciences and Social Sciences* 2: 184–193.

Fingerman, Karen, and Frank Furstenberg. 2012. "You Can Go Home Again." *New York Times,* May 30.

Fingerman, Karen, Kyungmin Kim, Patrick S. Tennant, Kira S. Birditt, and Steven Zarit. 2016. "Intergenerational Support in a Daily Context." *Gerontologist* 56 (5): 896–908.

Fingerman, Karen, Jori Sechrist, and Kira Birditt. 2013. "Changing Views on Intergenerational Ties." *Gerontology* 59 (1): 64–70.

Furstenberg, Frank. 2015. "Becoming Adults: Challenges in the Transition to Adult Roles." *American Journal of Orthopsychiatry* 85 (5, Supplement): S14–S21.

Hays, Sharon. 1988. *The Cultural Contradictions of Motherhood*. New Haven: Yale University Press.

Illouz, Eva. 2007. *Cold Intimacies: The Making of Emotional Capitalism*. Cambridge: Polity Press.

Keating, Daniel P. 2017. *Born Anxious: The Lifelong Impact of Early Life Adversity and How to Break the Cycle*. New York: St. Martin's Press.

Lareau, Annette. 2011. *Unequal Childhoods: Class, Race, and Family Life, 2nd Edition with an Update a Decade Later*. CA: University of California Press.

Levine, R. A., and Sarah Levine. 2016. *Do Parents Matter? Why Japanese Babies Sleep Soundly, Mexican Siblings Don't Fight, and American Families Should Just Relax*. Berkeley: Public Affairs.

Louis, Catherine Saint. 2012. "In the Facebook Era, Reminders of Loss After Families Fracture." *New York Times*, June 14.

Parker-Pope, Tara. 2010. "When the Ties That Bind Unravel." *New York Times*, May 3.

Quart, Alissa. 2006. *Hothouse Kids*. New York: Arrow Press.

Sapolsky, Robert M. 2017. *Behave: The Biology of Humans at Our Best and Worst*. New York: Penguin.

Schalet, Amy. 2011. *Not Under My Roof: Parents, Teens and the Culture of Sex*. Chicago: University of Chicago Press.

Silva, Jennifer. 2015. *Coming Up Short: Working-Class Adulthood in an Age of Uncertainty*. Oxford: Oxford University Press.

Silverstein, Merril, Daphna Gans, Ariela Lowenstein, Roseann Giarrusso, and Vern L. Bengtson. 2010. "Older Parent-Child Relationships in Six Developed Nations: Comparisons at the Intersection of Affection and Conflict." *Journal of Marriage and Family* 72 (4): 1006–1021.

Span, Laura. 2010. "Family Relations: An International Comparison." https://newoldage.blogs.nytimes.com/2010/07/30/family-relations-a-worldwide-comparison/?_r=0.

Sullivan, Orielle, and Scott Coltrane. 2008. "Men's Changing Contribution to Housework and Childcare." https://contemporaryfamilies.org/mens-changing-contribution-to-housework-and-childcare-brief-report/.

Trzaskowski, Maciej, Nicole Harlaar, Rosalind Arden, Eva Kraphol, Kaili Rimfeld, Andrew McMillan, Philip S. Dale, and Robert Plomin. 2014. "Genetic Influence on Family Socioeconomic Status and Children's Intelligence." *Intelligence* 42 (1): 83–88.

Vogel, Erin. A., Jason P. Rose, Lindsay R. Roberts, and Katheryn Eckles. 2014. "Social Comparison, Social Media, and Self-Esteem." *Psychology of Popular Media Culture* 3 (4): 206–222.

Wong, Brittany. 2017. "How to 'Break Up' with a Narcissistic Parent." https://www.huffingtonpost.com/entry/what-its-like-to-break-up-with-your-narcissistic-parent_us_5a1f1d16e4b037b8ea1f3f0f.

CHAPTER FOUR

Parenthood in the Age of Apps and Mommy Blogs: Technology and Digital Culture in Parent–Child Relations

Michelle Y. Janning

I have a teenage son, and this sometimes requires an ability to decide what the best parenting course of action may be in the face of changing hormones, mounting homework, and easy access to a small screen that he uses for texting, watching videos, playing video games, and occasionally talking on the phone. Influenced by news pieces with titles such as "Young Children Are Spending Much More Time in Front of Small Screens" (Kamenetz 2017), I wonder whether he may be spending too much time staring at a screen and not enough time talking to others in person. I also spend time thinking about how different his childhood is compared to mine, in large part due to the vast amount of digital information he has at his fingertips. In many ways, the most salient part of parenting for me has become teaching him how to navigate the digital world and discern what counts as a reputable source of information and what is defined as a good use of his time.

As a seeker of all types of information, including that which I'm using in this chapter, I recently conducted separate Internet searches for the terms "parenting advice" and "technology." These pulled up thousands of articles, images, and advice columns that would take years to read. Upon scrolling through the countless results (and giving up trying to identify the best advice), I realized that there's huge overlap in the search results on these two topics. From the subjects of cyberbullying to screen time, from online privacy to robot toys, our online ether is filled with advice about parenting, trends relating to technology, and ideas about how parenting and technology are intimately connected. In addition, for every online source that says something is wrong with today's parents, children, or parent-child relations as they relate to technology, there's another that complicates the location of the problem, suggests it has become exaggerated, or offers alternative explanations.

Setting the Stage: Competing News Headlines

In late summer 2017, a series of articles were published in varying news outlets covering new research on the impact of smartphones on children. First came psychologist Jean Twenge's warning in *The Atlantic* that young people like their phones more than they like other people, triggering a decline in the desire (perhaps counterintuitively) to be both independent and social and an uptick in teen depression and suicide. In her article "Have Smartphones Destroyed a Generation?" that accompanied the publication of her book, Twenge labeled the generation of teens born between 1995 and 2012 "iGen," with 2012 as the fulcrum in a seesaw that now leans toward heavy dependence on smartphones and social media among young people. Alongside Twenge's warning came a contrasting one from technology writer Alexandra Samuel, who claimed in a *JStor Daily* article that the iGen message not only overblows the claim that teens are unhappy (Samuel looked at the same data and came up with a different interpretation), it also ignores the fact that it may, in fact, be parents who are the problem. In "Yes, Smartphones Are Destroying a Generation, but Not of Kids," Samuel notes that teens are not, in fact, more unhappy, and that it is parents whose social media use skyrocketed after the appearance of smartphones. And with increased smartphone use, Samuel says, comes a greater likelihood to tune out kids. Scholars who have begun to study this phenomenon have labeled it "technoference" (McDaniel and Radesky 2017), whereby increased use of digital technology by parents is associated with problematic behaviors in children such as tantrums and crying. Observation studies (e.g., Radesky et al. 2014) have reported greater likelihood of parents to respond impatiently or harshly to children if the parents are absorbed in their tech devices. Lebo (2017) reports that nearly two-thirds (64 percent) of mobile phone users say they were ignored because someone in their household spent too much time on a mobile device. Technology and paying attention to children thus have become competing activities for parents, made increasingly worrisome to some scholars because smartphone use can become a rein-forced habit more than watching television can (McDaniel and Radesky 2017). As countless studies across numerous social scientific disciplines attest, families are primary socializing agents. And so, when it comes to the possibility of smartphones causing antisocial behavior and unhappiness, kids learn from their parents.

Not to be outdone by these competing claims, *New York Magazine* writer Malcolm Harris in "Are Smartphones Destroying a Generation, or Are Consultants?" paints a picture in which the problem is not necessarily the deleterious effects of smartphones on parents and/or children, but the way that academics who write books—like Twenge's *iGen*—use magazine and news articles as promotional tools for getting onto mainstream bookshelves. Harris claims that these books are based on vetted social scientific analysis of issues such as technology use in families but also says that they lack sophisticated interrogation or in-depth criticism of market structures. His critique, then, is not of the state of affairs for parents and children but of research that lacks rigor in its unsophisticated presentation and lacks respectability in its for-profit production. Given the ubiquitous presence of social media feeds of news articles next to fake news next to parenting stories next to links to research, it is easy to claim that the news headlines *are* the new research. But, just as I teach students (and my son) how to discern real news from fake news when writing reports about anything from politics to climate change—more than ever before—I also need to be careful about which research I believe is valid as I navigate my role as a parent.

So, what are parents to do amid not only competing claims about what's good for kids in terms of technology, but also when the experts on whom they rely may merely be aiming to coin catchy phrases and using allegedly less-than-rigorous evidence to fill their bank accounts? And what are children to do when they make up the bulk of the population being studied for presumed problems? There are many conflicting ideas about whether technology is harmful or helpful for parents and children; this chapter offers an overview of widely discussed topics that contextualizes some of these conflicting ideas. And it sifts through myriad sources to uncover what social scientists currently deem most worth studying and sharing with parents.

There is no shortage of online parenting advice columns, confusing "what not to do" lists, and comments in social media feeds lamenting the woes of parenting and the problems with problem parents—especially as these woes relate to technology use and abuse. But despite this deluge of information, and despite arguments among scholars and pundits about the best way to communicate it, there is also a plethora of online platforms where parents find support on all sorts of topics. And there is good research to back all of it up, good locations for dialogue among those scholars who may disagree, and good ways for academic researchers to use these platforms to understand how parenthood and childhood are being defined in contemporary society. Parents find research-backed help online on topics that include how to care for special-needs kids using innovative learning technologies, how to monitor kids' technology use, how to discern whether a child's illness requires medical attention, how to think about their own technology use, and how to deal with cyberbullying and other online activities that carry risk for children, among other things. Scholars can see what matters to parents by analyzing what parents are seeking in online support. Admittedly, the presence of problems and support can include disagreement among casual observers, as well as among scholars, about where problems and support may lie in contemporary parent-child relations as they relate to technology use, as the above news headlines illustrate. But there has never been an easier way to access information to help get good parenting ideas and to share parenting stories. Technology thus infiltrates the ways that parents parent and the ways that our society evaluates that parenting.

What Counts as Technology?

Certainly the term "technology" includes items and practices found in the daily doses of our digital worlds: smartphones, tablets, social media apps, computers, and other items classified under the oft-referenced umbrella of information and communication technologies (ICT). But technology also infiltrates parts of our lives that we may think of less often or only when we use it, and that may or may not be categorized under the heading of "digital": birth control and infertility procedures that are sometimes referred to as reproductive technology, equipment used for children with special physical or cognitive needs, GPS used in cars on family road trips and in shuttling kids to and from soccer practice, and even cooking devices that speed up dinner prep for working parents. Even the pencils kids use to do homework and the beds parents sleep in after a grueling evening of homework help count as technology, especially if there is some kind of mechanical device involved that has moving parts (think Sleep Numbers!). Given all of the things that can count as technology, this topic is broader than one chapter (or even one book) can cover. To remain focused, I've chosen to outline the current key themes on parenthood and childhood as they relate primarily to information and communication technology (ICT), acknowledging that some themes and some technology types may be left out.

In the next section, I detail what scholars currently know, and what some of my own research suggests, with emphasis on the following themes: demographic trends, inequalities, and the digital divide; technology in family communication; the use of technology in work-family boundaries for working parents; and surveillance and "screen time" for children and parents.

I conclude with a reminder of the complexity of the issues presented in this chapter and a note about future directions for research and reporting.

Demographic Trends, Inequalities, and the Digital Divide

Parents, while sharing in common with each other the need to care for dependents, hardly represent a monolithic group. And children also represent a diverse group of people. When it comes to resources, roles, and everyday experiences as they relate to ICT, there are differences among parents and children along key demographics that include, among other characteristics, age, class, and race. Social scientists often point out that differences translate into inequalities when access to valuable resources such as information and wealth are not equal across groups. When it comes to access to digital technologies that matter for parents and children along these demographic lines, we see inequalities in terms of access to technology, roles associated with technology use, and outcomes for children—inequalities that I introduce in this section and thread through the rest of the chapter as I discuss other topics.

But first, some statistics about ICT use in families (statistics that will likely be outdated by the time this book is published): use of digital technology is increasing in the United States. Survey results from individuals in more than 2,000 households across the country conducted by scholars working on the Digital Future Project at USC Annenberg (Lebo 2017) show that more than nine out of every ten Americans (92 percent) use the Internet, spending on average nearly twenty-four hours per week online. More than eight out of ten (82 percent) go online using a mobile phone, and most of these phone users are online daily (Lebo 2017). As Kamenetz (2017) reports in a fall 2017 *Morning Edition* on National Public Radio, "98 percent of homes with children now have a mobile device such as a tablet or smartphone." More than half of children ages 6–12 have cell phones, mostly used for texting, downloading apps, playing games, accessing Web sites, and video calling. Among those who get service plans (usually on a parent's plan) and cell phones, most do so at age 10. More boys than girls get cell phones. As of 2017, nearly two-thirds (65 percent) of student Internet users go online for school-related work, a proportion that has doubled in the last decade (Lebo 2017). Nearly three-quarters of kids with cell phones have voice, messaging, and data on their phones ("Mobile Kids" 2017). Clearly, childhood today, as measured by access to ICT, looks strikingly different from childhood even ten years ago.

Children are not the only ones increasing their ICT use. More than 8 out of every 10 American households have a computer, and over 7 in 10 have an Internet connection in the home (Rainie and Cohn 2014). American adults report increasing use of online platforms, even in the last year. As evidence of this, Americans have increased their likelihood to get news online to almost the same rate as getting news on television (Gottfried and Shearer 2017). And over 60 percent of young adults ages 18 to 29 primarily use online streaming to watch TV (Rainie 2017). While there are differences in the use of digital technology by age, there has been significant growth in its use by Americans age 65 and older. According to the Pew Research Center (Anderson and Perrin 2017), smartphone use among seniors has almost quadrupled in the last few years, though use of the Internet and broadband services is still lower among this population compared to younger groups. And, most of the growth in use has been among seniors whose annual household income is at least $75,000 a year. So, whether by webcam or texting, children are increasingly likely to connect with geographically distant grandparents in ways that differ from the infrequent intergenerational phone call from just a decade or two ago. And adult children are more able to connect with their own parents to report on the goings-on of the grandchildren. But it's easier to do this if the family has a higher socioeconomic status.

Social class makes up a big part of the discussion in what scholars have labeled "the digital divide"—defined by Merriam-Webster as "the economic, educational, and social inequalities between those who have computers and online access and those who do not." The Internet has been around for nearly thirty years, and the digital divide has narrowed in terms of people's use of Internet, broadband, and smartphones. But, as recent data from Anderson (2017) reveals, "the digital lives of lower- and higher-income Americans remain markedly different." More specifically, the more money a family has, the more devices its members have that allow them to go online. Lower-income families rely more on smartphones than do higher-income families for everything from job searches for parents to homework for children, though more than a third of adults in households with incomes of less than $30,000 a year do not have one. In terms of comfort with using ICT, often required for obtaining high-paying jobs and helpful for completing sophisticated school projects, lower-income Americans report less use of the Internet (including for work tasks) and have a greater likelihood to be classified as "digitally unprepared" (Horrigan 2016). This means that technology itself can play a role in the reproduction of class inequality across generations, as parents and children of lower socioeconomic statuses have less access to valuable ICT that may help afford better jobs, better information about parenting, and better information that kids can use for schoolwork.

Other social inequalities persist in terms of access to, and use of, ICT. Disabled people are less likely to use technology (Anderson and Perrin 2017), as are rural Americans (Perrin 2017). In terms of race, the digital divide is lessening, evidenced by similar rates of Internet use (all between 85–88 percent) and social media use (all between 63–74 percent) among whites, blacks, and Hispanics ("Internet Use by Race" 2017; "Social Media Use by Race"

2017). But there are still gaps, especially between Hispanics, blacks, and whites in their use of smartphones. Mobile devices—owned at similar rates across racial-ethnic groups—are more likely to be used by blacks and Hispanics than whites for online access to such things as looking for work and looking up health information. Blacks and Hispanics are more likely than whites to have to cut off Internet service because of the expense. This yields greater use of public library Internet services for blacks in particular (Perrin 2017).

In sum, while ICT access and use has expanded greatly in the last decade across all social groups, there remain differences between groups, especially socioeconomically, that can translate into less access to valuable resources for both parents and children. Despite these differences, all parents and children must navigate a world where ICT is increasingly used in communication, increasingly blurs the lines between work and family for working parents, and increasingly requires parents to understand how best to monitor their children's online access.

Technology in Family Communication

How parents talk to kids is not only a topic of conversation among parents themselves; it also makes up a large body of research among family scholars. In fact, there is an entire academic journal devoted to this topic—the *Journal of Family Communication*. Many of the most-cited articles in this journal refer to information and communication technologies—the digital side of family communication—in their titles. For example, they may refer to the Internet (Mesch 2006), Facebook (Child and Westermann 2013), and children's television viewing (Warren 2001).

Parents and children not only talk about the role of ICT in their own communication practices; they use the technology to communicate with each other. For parents—especially mothers—of teenagers, the role of information and communication technologies is now a normal topic of everyday conversation, even though discussions about offline behavior are more frequent. Pew Research Center survey data (Anderson 2016) on parents' communication with teens shows that talking about acceptable online behavior is more common than not, and more common among families with teens under 15 years old. More specifically, in addition to checking their teen's social media profiles or friending/following them on Facebook, Twitter, or other social media platforms, most American parents (90 percent) talk at least occasionally with their teens about what is appropriate in terms of sharing, viewing, and behaving toward others online. Kids tend to accept Facebook friend requests from parents, especially if they have preexisting trust, a high-quality relationship, and do not perceive the request as a privacy invasion. In addition, interaction via social media between parents and children can give the children easy ways to maintain family connections without a lot of effort. Of course, since parents hold authority over children, a parental friend request may feel more like an obligation than an option (Child and Westermann 2013).

For everyday interactions—and even though the amount of face-to-face time that people spend with their family members has remained constant over the last decade (Lebo 2017 reports around 17 hours per week)—the cell phone has become the preferred method of parents and teens for quickly getting in touch, with about half of all parents reporting they most often use text messaging (parents whose household income is at least $75,000 a year report slightly higher frequency than lower-income parents [Anderson 2016]). Kids and parents alike see texting as important for maintaining social relationships (Lebo 2017). Parents cite being able to get hold of kids, reach out to them, or track their location easily as reasons that they get their children wireless service, especially if the kids are under 13 years old ("Mobile Kids" 2017). If children are involved in sports or other extracurricular activities, parents increasingly use digital means to download schedules, communicate with coaches and teachers, and even view games and events with smartphone apps if they can't be physically present (Kennedy 2017). So, digital devices are increasingly used not only for parents and children to communicate, but also for parents to manage and view what children are doing even if they are not present. This serves to enhance communication and connectedness at the same time that it gives parents more platforms to use to monitor their children, a topic that I return to later in the chapter.

Class and racial-ethnic groups matter in family communication about technology and in family communication practices using ICT. Parents with lower levels of education and lower household income are more likely than more educated and affluent parents to talk regularly with their teens about appropriate behaviors, both online and offline. This is true in terms of online content, sharing, and behavior toward others. In terms of racial-ethnic groups, Hispanic parents are more likely than black parents to have these kinds of talks, and both groups are more likely than whites to do so. Some of this may be attributed to minority teens reporting that they go online more often than whites (Anderson 2016).

So, what are the outcomes of these patterns of parent-child communication using ICT? What does the latest research reveal? The results are mixed. Critics such as media scholar Sherry Turkle lament the fact that superficial connection via digital communication leads us to sacrifice meaningful conversation, leaving people to rely too heavily on tech devices. They lose both connection with others and any in-depth sense of self that may develop from introspection and in-person conversation (Turkle 2015). On the other hand, research and writing on the use of ICT to help long-distance family members stay in touch offers a less pessimistic interpretation (for a great example of this research, see Beck and Beck-Gernsheim's *Distant Love* [2014], a book dedicated to showing how webcams and other digital communication devices foster connection between long-distance family members who, sometimes by choice and sometimes out of necessity, live in different places across the globe from each other). Additionally, recent research shows how kids who leave home for college or study abroad during college are able to keep connected with families at home via ICT more easily than in the past, fostering not only closer ties but also quicker access to family news and travel schedule changes.

Importantly, though, the use of ICT, while it can enhance social relationships, can also increase feelings of isolation that may result from not interacting face-to-face with friends and family (and some research suggests that too much ICT can displace face-to-face interactions, leading to a decline in attachment to parents and peers [Lepp, Li, and Barkley 2016]). Finally, parents report that they see ICT as useful for their kids in order to navigate an increasingly complex world. Among those who get their children wireless service and a cell phone before the child is 13 years old, more than two-thirds say they do it to get their child familiar with mobile technology ("Mobile Kids" 2017).

In my research (Janning 2017) with young adults whose parents have divorced, the role of ICT matters for family communication in two ways that highlight both benefits and drawbacks. First, because children whose parents have separated or divorced spend time in two homes, the communication between family members needs to traverse geographic distance. Often this comes in the form of texting or calling when one parent comes to the other parent's home to pick up the kids. This, according to the kids who participated in my interview research, can help make transportation, scheduling, and custody arrangements work more smoothly. It can also mean that parents who may not get along do not need to meet face-to-face and kids may gain independence in negotiating the logistics directly with a parent. But the downside is that this may fail to "foster the opportunity for parents to productively interact with each other face-to-face" (140).

The second way that ICT matters for kids in separated families is by serving as a material representation of similarity or difference between parents' homes and thus, for some kids, as a way to demonstrate preference of one home over the other. Put another way, technology matters to young people, and lack of access to it through slower Internet, an older computer, or inadequate cell phone service can make a space less desirable. When parents separate or divorce, the parent-child relationship for each parent changes such that parents are now seen as representing different households, perhaps in competition with each other. Children are more willing to go to a parent's house because it has better ICT, which means that researchers and those who work with divorcing parents need to take into consideration the access each parent has to the digital world. This is not to say that the latest tech gadgets make kids get along better with their parents after a divorce or automatically enhance parent-child communication. It merely suggests that ICT (and its affordability for parents) matters in the minds of kids who spend time in two homes (Janning 2017).

Technology and Work-Family Boundaries for Working Parents

Our work worlds are changing, seemingly by the minute. While this matters for workers of all occupations and parents of kids of all ages, I see it firsthand and vividly in my profession as a college professor and researcher with a son still living at home. I'm typing this chapter, for example, on a laptop that has sat in my office, my dining room, my backyard, and in various coffee shops and restaurants. At times while I write, I hear my phone calendar notify me that it's time to pick up my son from his athletic practice or to pick up some veggies for dinner. While I sit in my car waiting for my son to stroll to the car before we stop by the grocery store, I check my e-mail to see if my upcoming flight for a research trip is on time. And while I'm on the airplane, headed out to do research, I pull out my laptop and glance back at what I wrote in the coffee shop to see if it makes as much sense as what I wrote in the restaurant, all while looking at the picture of my son and husband in the background on my laptop's home screen.

In that sequence of events, there are several distinct moments when paid work and parenting roles meet up. It is in these moments when social researchers pay attention to how boundaries between the roles we play in different life realms matter. And sometimes, the roles of parent and worker conflict—evident in working parents' use of ICT.

Here's what we know about working parents in the United States today, especially in terms of the role of technology in the boundary between work and home. For many professions and for most American workers, at least some portions of paid work can be done anywhere and at any time (Chesley and Johnson 2010). Whether it's texting a client to schedule a plumbing appointment, responding to an e-mail about a work trip itinerary, checking on a request for a shift change on a smartphone app, or posting an advertisement for a business on social media, working parents in the United States are increasingly networked. While the ability to perform work using ICT may increase productivity on the job, it can also increase stress and workload, sometimes spilling that work into home life (Casey 2012). And, while increased ICT use at home can enhance family connectedness and make logistical maneuvers easier, adding work e-mails or texts to the mix can create a spillover of job stress into family life.

In my research on work and family roles for working parents, especially as they may relate to technology, I have found that ICT is most useful in navigating calendars. Parents and children need to manage busy schedules where work roles and family events intersect, especially since there are more mothers working and since childhood activities are increasingly likely to be structured and managed by parents (Janning 2017). Households have numerous calendars to navigate, from sports schedules to doctor appointments, from school pickup times to work travels. By using shared online calendars, some parents and children are able to manage complex work and family roles and events more easily than by looking at five different calendars during three different conversations over a hectic dinner. But, as with other topics I've already mentioned, there exists differential access not only to online tools to manage schedules but also to the types of paid work that allow (or do not) a parent to have flexibility, autonomy, time, and space to use the tools in the first place.

Surveillance and "Screen Time" for Parents and Children

How much time children should spend online depends on how parents perceive the purpose of the online activities. Around 40 percent of adults say that children in their households spend too much time online; yet just under half of adults (49 percent) say that using the Internet helps children get better grades. While adults are still more likely than not (55 percent) to report that children in their households spend the right amount of time online, this number has declined from over 70 percent a decade ago (Lebo 2017). The more access to technology we have, the more parents are concerned that their kids are spending too much time with it.

As the headlines at the beginning of this chapter illustrate, the amount of time that parents and children dedicate to looking at digital screens can compete with time they could spend with each other in person. And, if parents can't be present, we have even seen the development of (and mixed response to) artificial intelligence objects such as talking devices that can respond to crying babies by automatically playing a lullaby (see Aubrey 2017 for a discussion of Mattel's failed Aristotle device that some feared would cause babies to become too attached to a piece of technology at the same time that the device collects private information about a child).

But the question of "screen time" extends beyond interpersonal communication into two areas: surveillance of children's lives and chronicling their development. Take, for example, parents "friending" their children on Facebook. Child and Westermann (2013) note that parent-child communication can be fostered via social media, but that platforms such as Facebook can also be used by parents to chronicle their child's development with photos and commentary. When children are young, parents control the privacy. But as children mature, they develop a desire to control their own "privacy management decisions." As my own research on the management of digital family photographs (Janning 2017) suggests, sometimes the preservation and display of these images is more about demonstrating good parenting (especially for mothers) among an audience of other parents than it is about doing something for the child. As the next decade of social science research questions are proposed, it will be important to focus on the impact of a lifelong digital footprint for children born since the beginning of Facebook, including the footprint's impact on their views on privacy, their job prospects, and their likelihood to share photos and commentary about their own children.

In the meantime, paying attention to screens for both parents and children calls to mind current social scientific research and theorizing about surveillance, privacy, and risk, as well as the display of parenting beyond the family, as I elaborate below.

In the *Technology in Family Communication* section, I highlighted research that suggests that kids tend to accept their parents' Facebook friend requests. But the likelihood of this depends on the level of parent-child trust, the quality of the relationship, the communication norms within a family, and the family's privacy norms. Whether kids should have privacy, when they should be entitled to it, and who should be able to control it are all issues at play in social science research on technology use in families. From baby monitors to cell phone monitor apps, parents have countless technological tools at their disposal to keep track of their kids. Parents can use these tools to keep track of their children via frequent communication—which has increased to multiple times a day. This can become problematic, as evidenced by reports of parents demanding daily cell phone check-ins and updates from kids at summer camps where cell phones are banned so that kids can disconnect from the wired world (Kamenetz 2017). Interestingly, then, at least according to those who find this kind of parental behavior troubling in the context of summer camps for kids, the desire of parents to ensure their children's well-being by staying connected via digital devices is thwarting efforts to enhance children's well-being that may result from by disconnecting them from technology.

Parental participation in surveillance—"keeping track" of kids by watching out for them and by watching them, sometimes without their knowing—stems from a cultural norm that encourages parents to do so. The use of digital devices to do this not only has increased in recent years but also calls attention to the ways that technology is used to enact the monitoring of children by parents even in places where parental involvement is not acceptable (such as summer camp). Importantly, though, there are numerous research studies that uncover ways that ICT is used in efforts by parents and others to ensure children's well-being and safety.

ICT and the Innocence of Children

Why do parents keep track of kids? This seems like a silly question, but it should be answered in light of shifting cultural norms about children's independence, the construction of fear and risk in contemporary society, and changing views about when childhood ends and adulthood begins. Childhood is a category that has become collectively defined as a time of innocence, a life stage requiring management by adults, and a place of shelter from the marketplace and adult themes such as sex and violence (Buckingham 2011). Our 24-hour-news society is filled with scary stories of abduction and mistrust of strangers. In terms of technology, this means that parents in the United States today are cautioned to protect their children from online sex and violence, predators who prey on children, social media bullying, and the materialism and gluttony that can be heightened by either too much devotion to the newest tech gadgets or too much exposure to advertisements on online platforms.

Recent news items reporting on current research from the aforementioned Jean Twenge (referenced in Bret Stetka's 2017 article in *Scientific American* entitled "Extended Adolescence: When 25 is the New 18") suggest that the age at which children become adults may be increasing in some ways (delayed sex, lower rates of alcohol use as compared to teens from past generations, less likelihood to drive, delayed dating, and decreased likelihood to have an after-school job) at the same time that younger and younger children have smartphones and are exposed to racy photos on Snapchat. This is especially true for kids from affluent families, where increased years of schooling and career are deemed important in the steps toward growing up. And so, it seems as if childhood is being extended at the same time that fears surrounding online dangers for children have increased.

Despite the overwhelming presence of fear, concern, and tips to avoid danger that parents see in online advice columns, the classification of children as needing protection from adults is not universal, is not applied to all ages evenly, and has not been around forever (Buckingham 2011). In fact, this protection can be negative. Technology expert danah boyd, in recounting evidence from interviews and fieldwork in her book *It's Complicated: The Social Lives of Networked Teens*, offers that adults too often hinder young people's ability to become independent and thoughtful citizens by (over) protecting them from what they perceive as online dangers. Teens are able to use ICT not only to be informed about the world but also to develop a sense of identity and develop skills that allow them to navigate issues of privacy, bullying, and safety from harmful others.

The monitoring of children, in part, stems from the cultural view that children need monitoring to protect them from aspects of our world that have been labeled as dangerous or only appropriate for adults to handle. And the life stage of childhood, at least in some ways, is being elongated into extended adolescence at the same time that younger kids have more and more access to "adult" things online. This is why every year, numerous tech devices are marketed to parents who want their children to be trackable.

For example, phone watches with GPS tracking allow parents to set geographical boundaries for their kids that, if crossed, send notifications to the kids to stay in bounds. Some even track kids' physical activity and sleep habits (Kenney 2015). The question of how long childhood lasts, as well as what things are appropriate for children to see and do, is evident in current research on the role of ICT in sexual predation, exposure to media and video game violence, cyberbullying, obesity, and other everyday practices.

Online Sexual Predation

Online sexual predation of children has been a focus of research and reporting for over a decade (Lebo reports that 16 percent of children under age 18 received unwanted sexual attention online in 2016), but the claims of it are not necessarily uniform. The popular impression of sexual predators is that they are deceptive, manipulative, violent, and uniquely dangerous for children because online communication is anonymous and therefore disinhibiting. They are seen as seeking young people in online venues and planning in-person meetups that ultimately lead to statutory rape and other violence. However, research indicates that online and offline offenses are more similar than different—and also that most of these predators' crimes are not violent. They do not involve deception but rather target adolescents online and lead to "nonforcible crimes involving illegal sexual contact with youth who are too young to consent to sexual activity" (Wolak and Finkelhor 2013, 737).

Violent Media and Video Games

Under half of adults (41 percent) report that children in their households are spending too much time playing video games, while 52 percent report that the amount of time children play video games is just right—a number that has decreased slightly over the last five years. Most research on the effects of violent media, including video games, on children is conducted in experimental settings, most often with college students taking psychology courses. This renders their ICT use at least somewhat artificial. Nonetheless, important findings about the role that video games may play in children's lives have emerged from these studies. However, the findings sometimes conflict with each other. Short-term effects of violent video games are not necessarily causally attributable to the games themselves. That is, people who play violent video games and demonstrate violent attitudes or tendencies afterward may be predisposed to such tendencies rather than having the games directly cause their behaviors (Saleem, Anderson, and Gentile 2012). Other research fails to provide compelling evidence for violent effects from video games (Ferguson and Konijn 2015). However, some research suggests that the more exposure people have to violence, the more likely they are to become numb to it, thus not seeing its potentially deleterious effects. Importantly, this suggests that there are contextual risk factors for aggression and violence—what Bushman (2016) calls "situational variables"—that accompany personal variables that precede an individual's exposure to violent media.

Some meta-analytic studies (those that take an overview of findings from numerous studies at the same time) show that "violent media increase aggressive thoughts, angry feelings, and physiological arousal" and decrease empathy (Bushman 2016: 193). On the other hand, other meta-analyses fail to show this (Ferguson and Konijn 2015). In terms of other outcomes, those who view a lot of violent media are more likely to fear being victims of violence and see the world as dangerous and full of untrustworthy people, a phenomenon that Gerbner and Gross (1976) call the "mean world syndrome." Video games that are designed to be prosocial (meant to create social acceptance) can increase helpful behaviors and decrease hurtful ones in kids who play them (Saleem, Anderson, and Gentile 2012). Important to add to this collection of research findings, however, is the notion that the outcomes being defined as harmful need to be situated in our cultural context. It is difficult to draw a causal arrow from video games to violent behavior, especially since the research methods used to collect data on the subject are limited and may only capture temporary attitudes and behaviors. What may be important for further research, as the debate continues, is threefold: first, readers need to understand that research on children and violent media always includes multiple variables, is challenged by how best to measure both exposure to media and aggressiveness, and rarely includes claims that the *only* cause for aggressive behavior is playing video games; second, it may be beneficial for researchers to examine how the content of some video games (and other media) that is defined as morally objectionable may impact children's likelihood to treat other people with compassion and kindness rather than focusing just on violence and aggression; and third, people need to understand that social scientists do not always agree on what "counts" as evidence to make claims about the effect of violent media on children (Ferguson and Konijn 2015).

Cyberbullying

Lebo (2017) notes that children (27 percent) are more likely than adults (between 6 percent and 9 percent) to report being harassed or bullied online in the last year. Children in schools are increasingly learning about bullying and ways to deal with it. Now, with increased social media use, including images and words that disappear after a short time (e.g., with Snapchat), among young people, the question of whether bullying occurs differently online has been taken up by parents, schools, and academic researchers. Olweus (2016), a Swedish scholar who has been writing about bullying since the concept was first introduced in the 1970s, provides a critical overview of what scholars know about cyberbullying—when children are bullied using online platforms such as social media, photo sharing, and texting. The field of research on this topic is still relatively new, and the results are still tentative. From the studies that do exist, it is safe to define cyberbullying as similar to verbal, physical, and relational bullying. There are a few important ways that cyberbullying may differ from these other forms, though. First, despite large numbers of news reports about it, the prevalence of cyberbullying is hard to capture, with increases shown between 1 and 50 percent, depending on the report. This is due in part to how prevalence is reported. Sometimes the periods in which bullying may have occurred is not clear in reports. Researchers make different decisions about cutoff periods for counting incidents of bullying (is it two or three times a month? More? Less? Such a distinction was not made in the statistics I shared at the beginning of this paragraph). And sometimes, cyberbullying is singled out in research studies (perhaps because of the media hype), thus isolating it as somehow different from other types of bullying and potentially exaggerating its prevalence. Second, the types of bullying that occur online can be especially hurtful, especially if they include degrading pictures or videos, but these instances are quite rare. Third, intervention programs that work best to prevent bullying target all its forms, not just cyberbullying. Fourth, cyberbullying, like other forms of bullying, often includes an imbalance of power—but this imbalance may be due to differences in technological understanding in addition to social status or number of friends. Fifth, since bullying is often defined as repetitive, cyberbullying may occur differently than other forms of bullying yet still have damaging effects. That is, since a negative message about a person can reach many individuals simultaneously through social media and other online sharing platforms, the effects may be just as damaging as repeated instances of bullying done in person.

Obesity and Health

One last area of concern about technology and children—obesity—carries with it just as much complexity and contradiction as online sexual predation, violent media, and cyberbullying. In particular, plenty of news and research report a growing concern over childhood obesity—see for example former First Lady Michelle Obama's healthy eating and exercise campaigns; or the ongoing debate on the role of sedentary activities such as video game playing, computer and cell phone use, and TV watching in maintaining children's healthy energy levels, healthy social lives, sleep and eye health, and overall mental and physical health (Shochat 2012). But media and information and communication technology can also play a role in shaping societal perceptions of obesity and healthy body sizes. According to Frederick, Saguy, and Gruys (2016), the more exposure people have to online articles about obesity as a public health crisis and the notion of overcoming obesity as a personal responsibility, the greater their prejudice against people labeled as fat. Thus, current research considers the effects of ICT use on children but also the effects of representing obesity in media and ICT venues that shape people's attitudes about fatness.

Everyday Monitoring

Around two-thirds of adults (65 percent) monitor the social networking activities of children in their households, and 53 percent have password access to their children's social networking accounts; those who do not monitor their kids' social networking activities trust their children (Lebo 2017). Not all monitoring of kids online stems from parents' fear of danger invading their children's lives. Adults also manage online what we define as good for kids—doing homework, expanding opportunities, and making friends. Parents now have ongoing access to children's grades online. There are online education and tutoring programs that parents can use to help their kids do better in school. Even news about children's friends in their own parents' social media posts can be shared so that kids are in the loop about each other's lives.

Some of the surveillance that parents do of their children is regarding technology use itself. Parents monitor their kids' tech use in varying ways, though this is usually done through personal interaction rather than via software, and it is more common when kids are 13 and 14 rather than 15–17 (Anderson 2016). Parents monitor their kids' online and social media use several ways up to age 17. Anderson (2016), who reports that parents are figuring out ways to balance oversight with children's independence, notes that taking away technological devices or Internet privileges—"digitally grounding" misbehaving kids—is more common than not, with two-thirds of American parents reporting that they have done this. But parent-child interactions regarding tech are more complex than just these problematic moments. Over half (55 percent) of parents report limiting their teens' online time—in terms of either amount or the time of day when it is allowed—not as punishment but as an everyday practice. Additionally, 61 percent of parents check Web sites that their teen has visited, 60 percent report checking their teen's social media profile, 48 percent look at their teen's phone calls or messages, 39 percent use parental controls for online activities, 16 percent use parental controls to restrict cell phone use, and 16 percent use tracking tools to monitor their teen's location. Nearly half of parents know the password to their teens' e-mail accounts and cell phones, and just over a third know the password to at least one of their teen's social media accounts. Finally, the age of parents matters: parents under the age of 45 are more likely than older parents to limit their teens' online time or frequency and to take away a cell phone or Internet privileges as punishment (Anderson 2016).

Parenting Displays

Much of this chapter has been devoted to whether and how parents may be concerned about their children's online experiences and exposure. But parents themselves are part of the "screen time" picture, too. Watching out for kids or monitoring them, whether it's deemed "helicoptering" or just being a good parent, is easy to define when it takes the form of actual monitoring. But the chronicling of children's lives online by parents can constitute an important, yet often overlooked, area of focus for those interested in understanding the surveillance and protection of children. This is because surveillance extends to parents, too. Consider the increasing presence of "mommy blogs"—online locations where parents may seek advice but also disclose their own stories about parenting (usually mothering) for others to see. Initially viewed as a way for parents to collectively sort through the challenges of parenthood, now many have become monetized via advertising and product endorsements (Hunter 2016) and have thousands of followers. These are locations where parents seek and find support but also where they may judge each other or present their parenting stories so that they may be evaluated in (hopefully) favorable ways. Sometimes the judgment is about the content of what's shared, and sometimes it's about the connections the blog may have to products in the marketplace. In either case, the process of sharing about parenting carries with it the emotional work of assessing the potential judgment from others. Relatedly, my own research on the management of family photographs, often shared informally via online social media venues, suggests that putting a picture of a child on Facebook may not just be about chronicling the child's developments or accomplishments for the child's own sake; it may also be about displaying proper parenting (again, usually mothering) (Janning 2017). While sharing photos on Facebook and mommy blogging are different actions, the project of parenting now contains not only deliberations about how much ICT is appropriate to use around children, as discussed in the introduction to this chapter, but also the emotional work of deciding whether and how to showcase that parenting to others.

Conclusions

As the back-and-forth discussion of research findings in this chapter shows, there is not a simple yes-or-no answer to any question about whether ICT is harmful or helpful for parents and children. When social scientists consider what may constitute a social problem, they usually combine some sort of objective reality (kids are more likely to have cell phones as compared to five years ago) along with a subjective interpretation of that reality (it may be a problem that more kids have smartphones than five years ago). Whether one sees a societal pattern as problematic depends not only on his or her personal experience with it (my kid stares at his cell phone too much), but also on how one may interpret evidence for the problem (are we sure that a tendency toward violence is the best variable to examine when wondering about the possible negative effects of increased cell phone use on children?). Add to this complexity that many of the topics discussed here may be defined as problems differently depending on the age group of the children in question. After all, a cell phone for a five-year-old somehow seems different than one for a seventeen-year-old. I highly recommend looking more in depth at the myriad studies and reports I mentioned in this chapter with respect to children's ages.

Socialization—the process whereby we learn our culture—happens in two directions: from parent to child and from child to parent. Children learn how to behave around technology from their parents and other adults. But parents sometimes learn about the latest ICT gadgets from their children. Socialization also happens to parents and children simultaneously from other social forces, especially when it's about learning how to navigate the complex and ever-changing world of ICT. As new rituals, roles, and family rules emerge (should we allow texting at the dinner table?) and new norms about childhood arise (is 25 really the new 18?), both parents and children are faced with the task of sorting out how things should be in their own homes. Ubiquitous online information from experts (and from those claiming to be experts) offers increased support at the same time that it necessitates the overwhelming tasks of sorting, seeking, and studying by parents. Researchers have a responsibility to study topics as they relate to technology and parent-child relations ethically and rigorously, and now they also have a great responsibility in figuring out how best to communicate this to others not necessarily well versed in research design, theoretical tenets, or disciplinary terminology. It's not that research needs to be dumbed down. It's that researchers need to understand the world in which their findings are being communicated and participate in it responsibly. The emerging research of social scientists increasingly makes the news. This means that researchers are also being socialized, along with parents and children, into a complex world of information and communication technologies that disseminate "what's best for kids" in a matter of nanoseconds.

What it means to be a child varies with time and place. The same goes for what it means to be a parent. The platforms, norms, and accessibility of ICT change even more rapidly than the definitions of childhood and parenthood. By the time of this writing, the social media platforms and demographic patterns I've mentioned will likely be outdated. Both researchers and those who report on the research have a difficult task ahead when it comes to the role that technology plays for contemporary American children and their parents, in terms of both the content of the research and the way it is communicated.

References

Anderson, Monica. 2016. "Parents, Teens and Digital Monitoring." Pew Research Center. January 7. http://www.pewinternet.org/2016/01/07/parents-teens-and-digital-monitoring/.

Anderson, Monica. 2017. "Digital Divide Persists Even as Lower-Income Americans Make Gains in Tech Adoption." Pew Research Center. March 22. http://www.pewresearch.org/fact-tank/2017/03/22/digital-divide-persists-even-as-lower-income-americans-make-gains-in-tech-adoption/.

Anderson, Monica, and Andrew Perrin. 2017. "Disabled Americans Are Less Likely to Use Technology." Pew Research Center. April 7. http://www.pewresearch.org/fact-tank/2017/04/07/disabled-americans-are-less-likely-to-use-technology/.

Anderson, Monica, and Andrew Perrin. 2017. "Tech Adoption Climbs Among Older Adults." Pew Research Center. May 17. http://www.pewinternet.org/2017/05/17/tech-adoption-climbs-among-older-adults/.

Aubrey, Allison. 2017. "Amid Privacy Concerns, Mattel Shelved Planned Device for Kids." *NPR Morning Edition*. October 30. https://www.npr.org/2017/10/30/560767502/mattel-shelved-its-aristotle-device-for-kids-over-privacy-concerns.

Beck, Ulrich, and Elisabeth Beck-Gernsheim. 2014. *Distant Love*. Cambridge: Polity.

boyd, danah. 2015. *It's Complicated: The Social Lives of Networked Teens*. New Haven: Yale University Press.

Buckingham, David. 2011. *The Material Child: Growing Up in Consumer Culture*. Cambridge: Polity.

Bushman, Brad J. 2016. "Aggressive Cues: Weapons and Violent Media." In *Aggression and Violence: A Social Psychological Perspective*, edited by Brad J. Bushman, 184–98. Hove, UK: Psychology Press.

Casey, Judi. 2012. "The Impact of Technology on our Work and Family Lives." Huffington Post. December 2. http://www.huffingtonpost.com/judi-casey/the-impact-of-technology-_b_1932974.html.

Chesley, Noelle, and Britta E. Johnson. 2010. "Information and Communication Technology, Work and Family (2010)." Sloan Network Encyclopedia. Sloan Work and Family Research Network. https://workfamily.sas.upenn.edu/wfrn-repo/object/ej08hr00at6ew6q3.

Child, Jeffrey T., and David A. Westermann. 2013. "Let's Be Facebook Friends: Exploring Parental Facebook Friend Requests from a Communication

Privacy Management (CPM) Perspective." *Journal of Family Communication* 13 (1): 45–59.

Ferguson, Christopher J., and Elly A. Konijn. 2015. "She Said/He Said: A Peaceful Debate on Video Game Violence." *Psychology of Popular Media Culture* 4 (4): 397–411.

Frederick, David A., Abigail C. Saguy, and Kjerstin Gruys. 2016. "Culture, Health, and Bigotry: How Exposure to Cultural Accounts of Fatness Shape Attitudes about Health Risk, Health Policies, and Weight-Based Prejudice." *Social Science & Medicine* 165: 271–79.

Gerbner, George, and Larry Gross. 1976. "Living with Television: The Violence Profile." *Journal of Communication* 26(2): 172–99.

Gottfried, Jeffrey, and Elisa Shearer. 2017. "Americans' Online News Use Is Closing In on TV News Use." Pew Research Center. September 7. http://www.pewresearch.org/fact-tank/2017/09/07/americans-online-news-use-vs-tv-news-use/.

Harris, Malcolm. 2017. "Are Smartphones Destroying a Generation, or Are Consultants?" *New York Magazine*. August 28. http://nymag.com/selectall/2017/08/jean-m-twenges-igen-review.html.

Horrigan, John B. 2016. "Appendix: Detail on Digital Readiness and Other Metrics Across Groups." Pew Research Center. September 20. http://www.pewinternet.org/2016/09/20/appendix-detail-on-digital-readiness-and-other-metrics-across-groups/.

Hunter, Andrea. 2016. "Monetizing the Mommy: Mommy Blogs and the Audience Commodity." *Information, Communication & Society* 19 (9): 1306–20.

Janning, Michelle. 2017. *The Stuff of Family Life: How Our Homes Reflect Our Lives.* Lanham, MD: Rowman & Littlefield.

Kamenetz, Anya. 2017. "Are Helicopter Parents Ruining Summer Camp?" *NPR All Things Considered.* July 24. https://www.npr.org/sections/ed/2017/07/24/533059271/are-helicopter-parents-ruining-summer-camp?utm_campaign=storyshare&utm_source=facebook.com&utm_medium=social.

Kamenetz, Anya. 2017. "Young Children Are Spending Much More Time in Front of Small Screens." *NPR Morning Edition*. October 19. https://www.npr.org/sections/ed/2017/10/19/558178851/young-children-are-spending-much-more-time-in-front-of-small-screens.

Kennedy, Kristy. 2017. "Can't Make It to Your Kid's Game? There's an App for That." *Chicago Tribune*. June 22. http://www.chicagotribune.com/lifestyles/parenting/sc-game-apps-parents-family-0627-20170619-story.html.

Kenney, Briley. "The GPS Tracking Watches for Kids: Updated February, 2017!" Smartwatches.org. https://smartwatches.org/learn/here-are-the-best-gps-tracking-watches-for-kids/.

Lebo, Harlan. 2017. *Surveying the Digital Future: The 15th Annual Study on the Impact of Digital Technology on Americans.* Los Angeles: Center for the Digital Future at USC Annenberg. http://www.digitalcenter.org/wp-content/uploads/2013/10/2017-Digital-Future-Report.pdf.

Lepp, Andrew, Jian Li, and Jacob E. Barkley. 2016. "College Students' Cell Phone Use and Attachment to Parents and Peers." *Computers in Human Behavior* 64: 401–8.

McDaniel, Brandon T., and Jenny S. Radesky. 2017. "Technoference: Parent Distraction with Technology and Associations with Child Behavior Outcomes." *Child Development* 89 (1): 100–9.

Mesch, Gustavo S. 2006. "Family Relations and the Internet: Exploring a Family Boundaries Approach." *Journal of Family Communication* 6 (2): 119–38.

Nielsen. 2017. "Mobile Kids: The Parent, the Child and the Smartphone." February 28. http://www.nielsen.com/us/en/insights/news/2017/mobile-kids --the-parent-the-child-and-the-smartphone.html.

Olweus, Dan. 2016. "Cyber Bullying: A Critical Overview." In *Aggression and Violence: A Social Psychological Perspective*, edited by Brad J. Bushman, 225–40. Hove, UK: Psychology Press.

Perrin, Andrew. 2017. "Digital Gap between Rural and Nonrural American Persists." Pew Research Center. May 19. http://www.pewresearch.org/fact -tank/2017/05/19/digital-gap-between-rural-and-nonrural-america -persists/.

Pew Research Center. 2017. "Social Media Use by Race." January 11. http://www .pewinternet.org/chart/social-media-use-by-race/.

Pew Research Center. 2017. "Internet Use by Race." January 11. http://www .pewinternet.org/chart/internet-use-by-race/.

Radesky, Jenny S., Caroline J. Kistin, Barry Zuckerman, Katie Nitzberg, Jamie Gross, Margot Kaplan-Sanoff, Marilyn Augustyn, and Michael Silverstein. 2014. "Patterns of Mobile Device Use by Caregivers and Children During Meals in Fast Food Restaurants." *Pediatrics* 133 (4): e843–49.

Rainie, Lee. 2017. "About 6 in 10 Young Adults in U.S. Primarily Use Online Streaming to Watch TV." Pew Research Center. September 13. http:// www.pewresearch.org/fact-tank/2017/09/13/about-6-in-10-young -adults-in-u-s-primarily-use-online-streaming-to-watch-tv/.

Rainie, Lee, and D'Vera Cohn. 2014. "Census: Computer Ownership, Internet Connection Varies Widely Across U.S." Pew Research Center. September 19. http://www.pewresearch.org/fact-tank/2014/09/19/census-computer -ownership-internet-connection-varies-widely-across-u-s/.

Saleem, Muniba, Craig A. Anderson, and Douglas A. Gentile. 2012. "Effects of Prosocial, Neutral, and Violent Video Games on Children's Helpful and Hurtful Behaviors." *Aggressive Behavior* 38 (4): 281–87.

Samuel, Alexandra. 2017. "Yes, Smartphones Are Destroying a Generation, but Not of Kids." *JStor Daily*. August 8. https://daily.jstor.org/yes-smartphones -are-destroying-a-generation-but-not-of-kids/.

Shochat, Tamar. 2012. "Impact of Lifestyle and Technology Developments on Sleep." *Nature and Science of Sleep* 4: 19–31.

Stetka, Bret. "Extended Adolescence: When 25 Is the New 18." *Scientific American*. September 19. https://www.scientificamerican.com/article/extended -adolescence-when-25-is-the-new-18/.

Turkle, Sherry. 2015. *Reclaiming Conversation: The Power of Talk in a Digital Age.* New York: Penguin Press.

Twenge, Jean. 2017. "Have Smartphones Destroyed a Generation?" *The Atlantic.* September. https://www.theatlantic.com/magazine/archive/2017/09/has -the-smartphone-destroyed-a-generation/534198/.

Warren, Ron. 2001. "In Words and Deeds: Parental Involvement and Mediation of Children's Television Viewing." *Journal of Family Communication* 1 (4): 211–31.

Wolak, Janis, and David Finkelhor. 2013. "Are Crimes by Online Predators Different from Crimes by Sex Offenders Who Know Youth In-Person?" *Journal of Adolescent Health* 53: 736–41. https://www.merriam-webster.com /dictionary/digital%20divide.

CHAPTER FIVE

Parenthood and Mental Health in the United States: Why Don't Children Improve Adults' Emotional Well-Being?

Robin W. Simon

In 2010, Jennifer Senior published an article in *New York Magazine* about why parents hate parenting. She presented an example of her own parenting experiences, informal interviews with other parents of minor children, and some findings of social science research which indicate that parents report less happiness and more depression than nonparents in the United States. One of Senior's most insightful points is that, despite their often challenging experiences raising children, parents have a hard time accepting these findings, because they violate their deepest intuitions about the advantages of parenthood for emotional well-being.

In this chapter, I first review decades of sociological research on disparities in mental health between parents and nonparents in the United States, and the current explanation of these disparities. I then review studies of sociodemographic variations in mental health among parents as well as some important knowledge gaps. I conclude with a discussion of recent cross-national research which points to specific public policies that would help improve American parents' mental health. However, before turning to my review of this research, I first discuss *why* parents have a hard time accepting research findings that parenthood does not increase adults' emotional well-being.

Background

Our Cultural Belief That Parenthood Increases Adults' Emotional Well-Being

One of the most long-standing, widespread, and deeply held cultural beliefs in the United States is that parenthood increases adults' emotional well-being (Hansen 2012; Margolis and Myrskyla 2011; Simon 2008). Concrete manifestations of this cultural belief can be found in all corners of social life—from greeting cards and baby showers celebrating impending parenthood and flowers, cigars, and birth announcements marking the arrival of new parents' "bundle of joy" to everyday social interactions with family members and friends. Our cultural preoccupation with the importance of parenthood for achieving an emotionally rich, fulfilling, and meaningful life extends to both women and men, who, by the time they reach a certain age, find that they are the targets of other peoples' prodding about when they intend to have children (Blackstone 2014). While Americans increasingly recognize that parenthood is "hard work," particularly when children are young (e.g., during the "terrible twos") and in the turbulent teenage years—as the recent popular TV show *Parenthood*, dozens of *films* (e.g., "Ladybird" and "Eighth Grade"), and countless parenting advice books portray—most assume that in the long run, the advantages of having children for emotional well-being far outweigh the challenges associated with parenting.

Indeed, the taken-for-granted assumption that parenthood increases emotional well-being undoubtedly contributes to why parenthood is nearly universal in the United States. Although attitudes about the disadvantages of childlessness have been declining since the 1970s (Blackstone 2014; Koropeckyj-Cox and Pendell 2007; Thornton and DeMarco 2001) and the average age when men and women become parents has been rising (U.S. Census Bureau 2012), sooner or later, most Americans have their own biological children or subject themselves to the time-consuming, intrusive, and expensive adoption process in order to become parents (Fisher 2003). While recent cohorts of adults in their childbearing years—particularly men and women with a college education—are delaying parenthood until their mid-to-late twenties and having fewer children than in the past, the most recent estimate is that 85 percent eventually become parents and have an average of two children (National Center for Health Statistics 2015). Although these estimates conceal variations in both fertility rates and the timing of parenthood across different socioeconomic (SES) and racial/ethnic groups (including both documented and nondocumented immigrants, for whom fertility rates tend to be higher than among native-born adults), there is no indication that parenthood is going out of style anytime in the foreseeable future for any social group in the United States.

In fact, recent developments in reproductive medicine such as the availability of sperm banks, egg repositories, in-vitro fertilization, and gestational surrogacy—as well as corresponding changes in social norms about who is entitled to become a parent—have made parenthood available not only to reproductively challenged heterosexual couples but also to same-sex couples and nonpartnered individuals who want to have their own genetic offspring (Almeling 2011; Jacobson 2016; Hertz 2008). Although these procedures are only available to people who can afford them or have medical insurance that helps cover their very high cost (Bell 2014), the increasing number of Americans who use these alternative, "high tech" paths to parenthood testify to the persistence of the cultural belief that parenthood increases emotional well-being.

The dramatic rise in rates of nonmarital childbearing over the past few decades provides further evidence of the perceived importance of parenthood for emotional well-being. It is estimated that 40 percent of all births in the United States today are to nonmarried women, and the estimate for African American women is as high as 70 percent (Centers for Disease Control 2017). The decoupling of marriage and parenthood represents an important social change in the life course of a few different social groups—which can include not only African Americans but other socially disadvantaged men and women of all racial/ethnic groups, highly educated professional women, and gay and lesbian couples for whom legal marriage has only recently become available.

The members of these disparate social groups have children outside of marriage for different reasons. Sociologist Katherine Edin and her colleagues' ethnographic research reveals that poor unmarried men and women have children because parenthood is one of the few available paths for them to achieve adult status in their communities (Edin and Kefalis 2011; Edin and Nelson 2013). While they often enter cohabiting relationships with their children's biological parent, the many problems associated with living in poverty make these unions unstable and short-lived. At the other end of the SES continuum, highly educated professional women who find themselves single at "a certain age" have children before their "biological clocks" run out (Hertz 2008). However, like their married counterparts, the core belief motivating members of these different social groups' desire to become parents is that having children will enhance their emotional well-being. While policy analysts, politicians, and the public are alarmed by this trend in the United States, rates of nonmarital childbearing are even higher in many other advanced industrialized countries in North America and Europe, where there is greater public acceptance of both nonmarital cohabitation and nonmarital parenthood (Centers for Disease Control 2017).

The Historic Roots of Our Cultural Belief

It is important to note that the emotional significance we currently attach to parenthood is neither an historical constant nor a cultural pattern that is unique to the United States. Social historians document that a nascent version of our contemporary belief that parenthood increases emotional well-being emerged in the late 19th and early 20th centuries in North America and Europe when the transition from a home-based, agrarian economy to a market-based, capitalist economy was complete (Aries 1965; Gordon 1978; Mintz 2006; Shorter 1977). While children had had economic value to parents as laborers in agrarian societies, the new economic system provided fertile ground for the development of a new cultural paradigm of modern parenthood and childhood that emphasized the emotional value of children who needed tender, loving care. Making creative use of data on life insurance policies for children from the late 1800s to the 1930s in the United States, sociologist Vivian Zelizer (1994) showed that as children went from economic assets to economic liabilities for parents, they became viewed as emotionally "priceless."

The cultural shift in the meaning of both parenthood and childhood in the United States and other industrializing countries in Europe coincided with the development of elaborate and highly gendered parenting ideologies and practices, a physical and psychological separation between the worlds of paid work and home, and an intensification of motherhood in which raising children became viewed as a full-time "job" for women (Aries 1965; Degler 1980; Gordon 1978; Lasch 1995; Shorter 1977; Welter 1966; Vandenberg-Daves 2014). At the same time, sole responsibility for the provision of the family's material needs fell on men, who earned a "family" wage (Griswold 1993). Although these ideological and behavioral changes first occurred among the upper and middle classes, they ultimately spread to the working class—many members of whom were recent immigrants from Europe and targets of the social reform movement during this period in the United States (Bodnar 1985; Hareven 1991). By the end of the first quarter of the 20th century, both mothers and minor children had been excluded from the industrial labor force, fathers had a limited role in child rearing, and parenthood was perceived as essential for achieving a full and meaningful life for both women and men throughout much of the industrialized world.

Incidentally, the increased emotional importance of children, the intensification of motherhood as well as the rise in the financial cost of raising children to adulthood in the United States and other countries are among the many social factors that contributed to the historic decline in the number of children per family during industrialization (Aries 1965; Shorter 1975). Referred to as the "demographic revolution" (Thompson 1949), smaller families allowed parents to invest more time, energy, and economic resources in each child to prepare them for future adult roles in society. Except for the increase in fertility in the United States. during the 1950s, which resulted in the large baby-boom birth cohort (Coontz 2016; Easterlin 1980), the overall historical trend of smaller families persisted during the 20th and early 21st centuries. However, while the overall fertility rate has been below the replacement level of 2.1 children per woman in the United States since 1971 (National Center for Health Statistics 2015), fertility rates are even lower in many other economically advanced countries (Balbo et al. 2012; OECD Factbook 2015–2016). Referred to as the "second demographic revolution" (Lesthaeghe 2010), this further decline in fertility is a result of the continued rise in the cost of raising children, the decline in men's wages, the increase in women's labor force participation and divorce as well as shifts in cultural beliefs—including a decline in the importance of religion and an increase in support for gender equality. The decline in fertility to below replacement is partially responsible for the development of State-provided social policies for families in wealthy countries except the United States—a point to which I will return.

The Evidence from Decades of Sociological Research

Parental Status Disparities in Mental Health in the United States

What is the evidence with respect to parental status disparities in mental health in the United States? In sharp contrast to our long-held cultural belief that having children increases adults' emotional well-being, decades of sociological research based on cross-sectional analyses of survey data from nationally representative samples of adults indicate that parenthood is associated with significantly poorer mental health—typically measured with symptoms of emotional distress and depression. The higher levels of psychological distress and depression experienced by parents compared to nonparents was first documented in the 1970s—a period marked by major social and economic changes in gender and family life that I referred to earlier such as a decline in men's wages, the increase in women's employment and divorce as well as the rise of both dual-earner and single-parent families. However, dozens of studies based on more recent national data continue to find that parents report significantly poorer mental health (including more anger) than childless adults when sociodemographic differences between parents and nonparents are held constant (Evenson and Simon 2005; Hansen 2012; McLanahan and Adams 1989; Ross and Van Willigen 1996; Simon 2008; Simon and Caputo 2017; Umberson and Gove 1989; Umberson et al. 2010).

Most earlier studies focused on disparities in mental health between nonparents and parents of minor children (i.e., children under 18 years), when the time, energy, and financial demands of parenthood are greatest. However, an accumulating body of evidence indicates that parents of adult offspring do not enjoy better mental health than their childless counterparts. Like "full-nest" parents, "empty-nest" parents report more symptoms of emotional distress and depression than adults who never had children (Bures et al. 2009; Koropeckyj-Cox 2002; Zhang and Hayward 2001). This finding belies another cultural belief, which is that the advantage of having children for emotional well-being is greatest when children are grown and independent.

Moreover, dozens of studies across social science disciplines indicate that parents report significantly less happiness and life satisfaction than childless adults (see Hansen 2012 and Pollman-Schult 2014 for reviews). The one dimension of mental health in which parents have an advantage over nonparents is alcohol abuse; studies find that parents of minor children are significantly less likely to abuse alcohol than their childless peers (Simon and Caputo 2017; Umberson 1987; Wolfe 2009). Sociologist Debra Umberson and others argue that minor children inadvertently serve as social control agents for parents with respect to this dimension of mental health. That is, parents of minor children are less likely to abuse alcohol because of their responsibility for attending to children's nonnegotiable everyday needs.

Furthermore, although most studies focus on differences in symptoms of emotional distress and depression between nonparents and parents of *either* minor *or* adult children, Jennifer Caputo's and my recent study examined parental status disparities in eight measures of mental *and* physical health across four distinct parenting stages (Simon and Caputo 2018). These stages included parents whose youngest child is: (1) under 13, (2) 13–17, (3) 18–29, and (4) 30 years and older. Our analyses indicate that except for the lower level of alcohol abuse among parents whose youngest child is under 13 years and greater life satisfaction among parents whose youngest child is 30 years and older, there are few advantages of parenthood for mental and physical health. Another one of my papers, with Ranae Evenson (Evenson and Simon 2005), indicates that parenthood is also depressing for noncustodial parents of minor children who are disproportionately men, and that stepchildren do not enhance adults' mental health.

In sum, the results of decades of sociological research provide little evidence for our cultural belief that parenthood increases adults' emotional well-being; except for parents of minor children's lower levels of alcohol abuse, parents in the United States experience more symptoms of emotional distress and depression, greater anger as well as less happiness and life satisfaction than their childless counterparts. While the negative association between parenthood and mental health varies in size depending on parents' personal and household characteristics as well as their stage of parenthood, it is evident among both mothers and fathers; in households containing married, cohabiting, and single parents; and across several dimensions of mental health. Because these results are consistent across many nationally representative samples, they are highly reliable; in fact, there is no study based on a national sample in which parents report better mental health than nonparents. These paradoxical findings not only contradict our cultural belief about the emotional advantages of parenthood but are an anomaly in research documenting that marriage and employment—two other major adult social roles—increase adults' mental health (Durkheim 2013; House et al. 1988; Tausig 2013; Thoits 1983; Umberson et al. 2013).

The Current Explanation of Parental Status Disparities in Mental Health

The Stress Associated with Parenthood in the United States

Why does parenthood not have its presumed positive effect on Americans' emotional well-being? The dominant sociological explanation of these findings is based on the "stress process perspective" (Pearlin 1989) and posits that parenthood is stressful in the United States, which undermines parents' mental health. Also referred to as the "costs and benefits hypothesis," several scholars argue that the costs associated with having children for emotional well-being cancel out or exceed the presumed benefits (Evenson and Simon 2005; Nomaguchi and Milkie 2003; Liefbroer 2005; Simon and Caputo 2017; Woo and Raley 2005; Umberson and Gove 1989). To evaluate this hypothesis, researchers have identified several stressors to which parents are uniquely exposed that help explain disparities in mental health between parents and childless adults.

A major stressor for contemporary parents of minor children is the high and steadily increasing financial cost of raising children to adulthood (Bird 1997; Glass et al. 2016; Meadows et al. 2008; Simon 1998). The U.S. Department of Agriculture estimates that today's families spend an average of between $134,370 to $269,520 raising a child from birth through age 17, which does not include the astronomical cost of providing the child a college education. Indeed, the unprecedented cost of raising children, along with the decline in men's wages since the 1970s, are among the many complex social factors that propelled mothers into the labor force in the third quarter of the 20th century (England and Farkus 1986, Glass 2000); demographers estimate that 70 percent of American children are currently being raised in households in which all adults work outside the home (Kreider and Ellis 2011).

However, while employment reduces the financial stress of raising children (Bird 1997; Simon 1998), numerous studies find that employed parents of minor children experience role conflict and overload as well as a lack of leisure time from combining paid work and parental responsibilities, which are stressful and emotionally distressing (Hochschild 1989, 2001; Glass and Fugimoto 1994; Lennon and Rosenfield 1994; Offer and Scheider 2011; Simon 1995, 1998). Securing affordable, high quality child- and after-school care for children is another stressor contributing to employed parents' poorer mental health relative to their childless peers (Crouter and Booth 2004; Nomaguchi et al. 2005; Ross and Mirowsky 1988). Employed parents also report stress from not having time with their children (Milkie et al. 2004; Nomaguchi et al. 2005; Simon 1995). Not surprisingly, disparities in emotional distress are even greater between nonparents and parents who have a child with behavioral and/or health problems (Simon 1992).

Research also indicates that parents of adult children are exposed to other stressors that contribute to their poorer mental health relative to persons who never had children—the most significant one being strain in their relationships with their adult offspring (Knoester 2003; Koropeckyi-Cox 2002; Pudrovska 2009). Given their "linked lives," parents' mental health is also influenced by their adult offspring's own stressful life circumstances and events, such as divorce and/or employment and financial problems (Greenfield and Marks 2006; Milkie et al. 2008). On the other hand, studies show that having an emotionally close and supportive relationship with adult offspring reduces parental depression in mid-to-later life (Knoester 2003).

Although this issue has surprisingly not received attention from sociologists, it is highly likely that the high cost of health care in the United States is another chronic stressor for parents of both minor and adult children, particularly for parents who have a child with mental and/or physical health problems. While federally funded health care covers dependent children in families living in or near poverty through the Children's Health Insurance Program (CHIP), this coverage is not available to working-class parents who often struggle to make ends meet. However, by making health insurance premiums more affordable, preventing health insurance companies from discriminating against individuals with preexisting health conditions, and allowing young adults to remain on their parents' health insurance until they reach 27 years of age, it is likely that the 2010 Affordable Care Act (i.e., the ACA, or "Obamacare") has reduced this potential source of stress for millions of parents who do not receive insurance benefits through their employment. At the same time, threats to reduce or discontinue funding for CHIP and continued promises to repeal the ACA under the current administration would surely add to the stress burden placed on parents. Even if these federal policies survive, it is unlikely that the United States will provide universal health care coverage for its citizens at any time in the foreseeable future. If it did, that would further reduce this source of chronic stress for parents of both minor and adult offspring (Glass et al. 2016).

Overall, sociological research documents that parenthood is stressful in the United States, which helps explain disparities in mental health between nonparents and parents of minor and adult children. Given the multitude of chronic stressors to which American parents are exposed, it is no wonder that parents experience lower levels of emotional well-being than childless adults. However, above and beyond identifying these stressors, sociologists have also elucidated some of the social conditions under which parenthood is more or less stressful and emotionally distressing. Most of this research focuses on marital status and gender variations in depression *among* parents.

Variations in Stress and Mental Health among Parents in the United States

Marital Status

Motivated by rising rates of divorce, single parenthood, and both non-marital cohabitation and childbearing that began during the last quarter of the 20th century, sociologists have examined the extent to which marital status moderates the association between parenthood and mental health. Not surprisingly, this research finds that single parents of minor children report significantly more depressive symptoms than their married peers (e.g., Avison, Ali, Walters. 2007; Evenson and Simon 2005; McLanahan 1983; Pearlin and Johnson 1977; Simon 1998). This finding is attributed to single parents' greater exposure to financial stress, conflict between employment and parental obligations as well as role overload due to lower levels of social (particularly household) support relative to their married counterparts. The stress of arranging child care, which is greater among unmarried than married parents, contributes to their higher level of distress as well (Nomaguchi et al. 2005; Ross and Mirowsky 1988).

Since women are more likely than men to be custodial parents in the event of divorce or relationship dissolution, the stress associated with single parenthood is disproportionately experienced by mothers (Avison, Ali, and Walters 2007; Simon 1998). In fact, because women continue to earn lower wages than men (the current gender wage gap reveals that full-time U.S. women are paid 80 percent of what men are paid), the increase in single parenthood has resulted in the "feminization of poverty," in which mothers of minor children now make up a large portion of the impoverished population in the United States (McLanahan and Kelly 1999; Christopher et al. 2001). Marital status also moderates the association between having adult children and mental health; the impact of strain in relationships with adult children on depression is greater for nonmarried than married parents (Greenfield and Marks 2006).

Gender

In light of persistent gender inequality in both the family and the workplace (Hochschild 1989; Budig and England 2001), researchers have also investigated the degree to which gender moderates the parenthood-depression association. Although women report more depression than men irrespective of parental status (e.g., Kessler et al. 1994), the association between parenthood and depressive symptoms does not significantly differ for mothers and fathers of minor or adult children in general (Evenson and Simon 2005; Simon and Caputo 2017). Parenthood is, however, associated with greater emotional distress, depression, and anger among employed married mothers than among employed married fathers of minor children due to their greater exposure to the stress of balancing the demands of paid work and parenting (Hochschild 1989; Lennon and Rosenfield 1994; Offer and Schneider 2011; Ross et al. 1985; Ross and Mirowsky 1988; Simon 1995, 1998; Thoits 1986). Indeed, the gender gap in depression among parents in dual-earner marriages is smaller when husbands help with child care and when affordable, high-quality child care is available (Kessler and McRae 1982; Ross and Mirowsky 1988). Moreover, although recent studies find that the gender gap in time spent in domestic work and child care in dual-earner, married-couple households has narrowed over the past few decades (Bianchi et al. 2006), mothers are still more likely than fathers to "multitask," which is depressing (Offer and Schneider 2011). The one source of stress that is greater for married fathers than for married mothers of minor children is financial, which reflects the persistence of men's traditional breadwinner responsibilities in dual-earner, married-couple households (Bird 1997; Simon 1998).

The Long Reach of Women's Age and Marital Status at First Birth on Mental Health in Mid- and Later- Life

In addition to identifying marital status and gender variations in emotional well-being among parents at a single point in time, scholars have utilized longitudinal survey data to investigate the extent to which women's age at first birth affects their mental health over time. Drawing on theoretical insights from both the stress process and life-course perspectives, studies show that mothers who had their first child at a younger age report significantly greater depression in mid- and later life than mothers who had their first child at an older age (Henretta 2007; Mirowsky 2002; Spence 2008). These findings are attributed to older mothers' greater financial and psychosocial resources during the early parenting years, which allowed them to more effectively cope with the stress of raising children than women who have children at younger ages.

Given the current high rates of nonmarital childbearing in the United States, researchers have also examined the consequences of women's marital status at first birth and marital history for their health at midlife. One study finds that nonmarital childbearing is negatively associated with self-rated health in midlife for white and black but not Hispanic mothers (Williams et al. 2011). However, this study also revealed that a subsequent and enduring marriage to their child's biological father mitigates this association for white and Hispanic but not for black women when compared to their counterparts who remained nonpartnered. In other words, nonmarital childbearing does not adversely affect some racial/ethnic groups of women's health in midlife as long as they eventually marry and remain married to their child's biological father.

Taken together, these studies suggest that women's other social characteristics, such as their level of education when they became mothers, may also influence the impact of parenthood on their subsequent mental health. For example, because educated professional women who have children outside of marriage had more financial and psychosocial resources to cope with the stress of raising children (Hertz 2008), they may enjoy better mental health in mid- and later life than their less educated counterparts. Men's age, marital status, and level of education when they became fathers may also influence their mental health in mid- and later life. Longitudinal studies examining the intersections of men's and women's social statuses at first birth would shed additional light on variations in the long-term impact of parenthood on emotional well-being.

In short, sociologists have documented marital status and gender variations in mental health among parents as well as the influence of women's age and marital status when they became mothers on their emotional well-being in mid- and later life. Thus, in addition to elucidating the stressors to which parents are exposed—which help explain their poorer mental health relative to nonparents—sociologists have elucidated some social conditions under which parenthood is more or less stressful and emotionally distressing. These findings provide compelling evidence for the argument that the *social context* of parenthood is *crucial* for understanding the impact of having children on adults' emotional well-being. However, there are also some important gaps in our knowledge about other potential variations in mental health among parents in the United States.

Current Gaps in Knowledge about Variations in Mental Health among Parents in the United States

Race, Ethnicity, and Socioeconomic Status

Despite sociodemographic differences in rates of fertility, the timing of parenthood, and nonmarital childbearing in the United States that I referred to earlier (Centers for Disease Control 2017), there are surprisingly no quantitative studies to my knowledge that have investigated racial, ethnic, and SES variations in mental health among parents. The paucity of research on the impact of these social statuses on parents' emotional well-being constitutes an important gap in knowledge about the ways in which the social context of parenthood influence mental health in the United States. There is, however, reason to expect that parenthood is even more stressful and emotionally distressing for minority and low-SES parents than for their nonminority and higher-SES peers.

An abundance of research documents profound racial, ethnic, and SES disparities in mental health in the United States—with minorities and lower-SES individuals reporting significantly poorer mental health than their nonminority and higher-SES counterparts (see Schnittker and McLeod 2005 for a review). Scholars have identified several social factors that contribute to these groups' lower levels of emotional well-being, which not only include their limited access to mental health care but also their greater exposure and vulnerability to acute and chronic stress (e.g., Turner, Lloyd, and Wheaton 1995). It is, therefore, highly likely that parenthood takes an even greater toll on minorities' and socially disadvantaged persons' mental health than their nonminority and socially advantaged peers. Although there have been no studies comparing the mental health of parents across these different social groups, research provides insight into how the experiences of minority and low-SES parents may influence their emotional well-being.

For example, ethnographic research finds that economically disadvantaged parents are exposed to additional sources of stress, including the stress of raising children in fragile families residing in unsafe neighborhoods with under-resourced schools and insufficient green spaces, grocery stores, and health care facilities (Edin and Kefalis 2005; Edin and Nelson 2013). These stressors, coupled with insufficient financial resources to cover children's most basic needs as well as the chronic threat of eviction from their homes (Desmond 2012), may erode poor parents' mental health. Moreover, because racial and ethnic minorities of all SES backgrounds are exposed to discrimination stress (Williams and Mohammed 2009), it is likely that an unrelenting stressor for minority parents is their children's interaction with teachers, law enforcement, and other authorities in their communities. For example, African American children are subjected to the "soft bigotry" of teachers' low expectations (Downey and Pribesh 2004) and are perceived as "dangerous" by the police—as the recent rash of media coverage on police brutality against them vividly illustrates.

Furthermore, in a recent article, sociologist David Williams and his colleagues (Williams et al. 2017) document that events linked to the 2016 presidential campaign and election have increased fear and anxiety among many Americans who are targets of what they perceive as hostility and discrimination. It is likely that the increase in hostility toward these stigmatized and marginalized racial/ethnic and religious groups—including the threat of mass deportation of undocumented immigrants under the current administration—is even more stressful and distressing for minority and immigrant parents. However, while these findings suggest that minority and immigrant parents (including black, Hispanic, Asian, and Muslim parents) experience poorer mental health than their more privileged white peers, conclusions about racial/ethnic as well as SES variations in mental health among parents awaits future research.

The Culture of Intensive Parenting among the Middle Class

While socially advantaged parents are not exposed to the stressors to which disadvantaged parents are exposed such as those that I discussed above, and have greater financial and psychosocial resources to more effectively cope with the everyday demands of raising children than their less advantaged peers, they are nevertheless exposed to other sources of stress that may take a toll on their mental health. A number of social, economic, and cultural forces have come together over the past two decades that have resulted in a further intensification of parenthood among the middle class in the United States. Contemporary middle-class parenting culture, which Hays (1998) first coined as "intensive parenting," includes unprecedented expectations for parents to invest an inordinate amount of time, energy, and emotional and financial resources in their children from birth through early adulthood. The ultimate goal of intensive parenting (also known as "concerted cultivation") is to produce children with an abundance of cultural capital who will be well positioned to successfully compete in the increasingly competitive college admissions process and reproduce their parents' advantaged SES in adulthood (Hays 1998; Lareau 2011; Milkie and Warner 2014).

There is evidence that a cultural shift in parenting practices has occurred over the past two decades to an even more time-intensive and child-centered model of parenthood (Bianchi et al. 2006; Nomaguchi et al. 2005). Believing that children need to be "cultivated" to prepare them for "successful" adulthood (Lareau 2011, 2012), white and black middle-class parents now go to extraordinary lengths to provide their children with not only the "best" schools but also often expensive supplemental enrichment experiences (e.g., private sports clubs, art and music lessons, tutors to prepare them for advanced placement and college admissions exams, and "meaningful" volunteer activities) to give them a leg up in the college admissions process (Lareau 2011, Milkie and Warner 2014). Although there is no sociological research on racial and ethnic variations in commitment to intensive parenting beliefs and practices among the middle class, it is likely that the recent popular book on "tiger moms" (Chua 2011) has contributed to the perception that Asian American parents, particularly Asian mothers, are even more intense in their approach to raising children than their non-Asian middle-class counterparts.

Not surprisingly, intensive parenting disproportionately falls on women; today's mothers are spending even more time *with* children as well as *facilitating* their numerous activities than they did in previous decades, which has created a time squeeze for employed middle-class mothers (Bianchi et al. 2006; Blair-Loy 2005; Hays 1998; Jacobs and Gerson 2005; Hochschild 1989, 2001; Lois 2012; Stone 2008). In fact, the further intensification of parenting among the middle class has resulted in an increase of married professional women leaving lucrative jobs to spend more time with their children (Hays 1998; Stone 2008). While most families with minor children depend on women's wages to make ends meet, the retreat to full-time motherhood for those who can afford it harkens back to an earlier period in our nation's history when most mothers, especially white, middle-class married mothers, did not work outside the home.

Although the ideology of intensive parenthood has its roots in the late 19th and early 20th centuries, the further intensification of parenting among the middle class in the United States today appears to be a response to the uptick in college applications from students in both the States and abroad over the past two decades (Simon 2017). It is also likely to be a response to the recent downturn in the economy, which has made it difficult for young adults, including those with a college education, to find stable, well-compensated, and meaningful employment (Furstenberg et al. 2004). However, while sociologists have documented the overwhelming demands of intensive parenting among the middle class, we currently do not know if parents perceive the culture of intensive parenting as stressful or whether it takes a toll on their mental health.

To examine these issues, I recently conducted a study on an ethnically diverse sample of upper-middle-class mothers and fathers residing in an affluent town in the Northeast who had a child at the local public high school. Although I am still in the process of analyzing the data, my in-depth interviews with parents, supplemental interviews with school administrators as well as ethnographic observations of parent meetings at the high school indicate that the culture of intensive parenting is indeed highly stressful, anxiety provoking, and emotionally distressing for women *and* men (Simon 2017). My data also reveal that an unexpected stressor for most of the parents I interviewed is their worry about the effect of the culture of intensive parenting on their *children's* mental health. Although one can argue that these highly privileged parents have brought this source of stress on themselves—and are part of the group that medical sociologists refer to as the "worried well"—this ramped-up parenting culture nevertheless appears to have negative consequences for both mothers' and fathers' stress and mental health.

LGBT

Although LGBT families were largely "invisible" in both their communities and social science research, there has been some exciting new qualitative sociological research elucidating the experiences of gay and lesbian parents (Lewin 2009; Moore 2011). Not surprisingly, this research finds that LGBT parents confront some of the same stressors to which heterosexual parents of minor children are exposed, such as financial stress as well as the stress of combining employment and parental obligations. Similar to their heterosexual counterparts, gay and lesbian parents also negotiate the division of household labor including child care, as sociologist Mignon Moore's insightful research on black lesbians demonstrates (2011). Because they cannot fall back on well-established and taken-for-granted gendered parenting norms and scripts, the division of labor tends to be more fluid when both parents are the same sex. Moore nevertheless finds that while mothers who had their children together share parental responsibilities, mothers who brought children into the relationship from a prior heterosexual relationship (i.e., birth mothers) tend to assume primary responsibility for their upbringing and care.

However, while we know more about these families than we did in the past, it is unclear whether LGBT parents of minor and adult children experience higher or lower levels of emotional well-being than their heterosexual counterparts. Since parenthood was not an option for LGBT people in the not-too-distant past, it is possible that they enjoy greater mental health than their heterosexual peers. At the same time, because they constitute another social group that is exposed to discrimination stress, parenthood may be even more stressful and distressing for LGBT parents than for heterosexual parents, as Moore's study suggests. An empirical examination of these two competing hypotheses would provide much-needed knowledge about the mental health of gay, lesbian, and transgender parents compared to their heterosexual and gender-conforming peers. Researchers should also consider whether the region of the country and neighborhood in which they reside affect LGBT parents' mental health; those residing in more supportive states and inclusive neighborhoods may experience less stress and emotional distress than their less supported counterparts. A consideration of these contextual factors is crucial if we are to understand the impact of parenthood on LGBT and other minority parents' mental health.

In sum, despite decades of sociological research documenting disparities in mental health *between* parents and nonparents as well as marital status and gender variations in mental health *among* parents, we still do not know the extent to which parents' race, ethnicity, SES, and sexual status influence their emotional well-being. The vast body of scholarship on the everyday lived experiences of members of various racial, ethnic, SES, and LGBT groups behooves sociologists to systematically compare the stress and mental health of parents across these sociodemographic groups in the United States. However, while this research would provide much-needed additional insight into the importance of the immediate social context of parenthood for understanding the impact children on mental health, there are broader, institutional-level contextual factors that help explain why American parents report lower levels of emotional well-being than childless adults.

Conclusions

Parenthood in a Larger Social Context: Cross-National Variation in Parental Status Disparities in Happiness

Are the well-documented disparities in mental health between parents and nonparents in the United States evident in other economically advanced countries? Although I have focused on the results of research on the United States, I will conclude with a discussion of findings from cross-national studies of parental status disparities in happiness. In contrast to research in the United States, which tends to focus on parental status disparities in symptoms of emotional distress and depression, most comparative studies focus on happiness because it is a global measure of mental health that is available in data sets on individuals residing in many countries. Indeed, a recent study of parental status disparities in happiness across 22 economically advanced countries provides additional insight into why parenthood does not increase Americans' emotional well-being.

I noted earlier that over the past several decades, fertility rates have declined to below replacement levels in most economically advanced countries. Recall that this decline in fertility (referred to as the "second demographic revolution") corresponded with other major social and economic changes that have swept through the developed world since the 1970s—including the decline in men's wages, the increase in women's employment and divorce as well as the rise of both dual-earner, married-couple and single-parent families (Lesthaeghe 2010; Kohler et al. 2006). These profound changes in families and gender roles have resulted in a proliferation of cross-national research on parental status disparities in happiness in advanced industrial nations.

Interestingly, despite considerable differences between these countries' social and economic histories (Misra et al. 2011), gross domestic product, (Ono and Lee 2013), level of social inclusion and inequality (Mandel and Semyonov 2005), population health (Pickett and Wilkinson 2015), and languages and cultures—including emotional cultures, which include social norms about appropriate emotional experience and expression (Hochschild

1979; Veenhovan 2010)—dozens of studies based on international survey data from individuals residing in developed countries throughout North America, Europe, and Asia indicate that parents report significantly less happiness than childless adults (Hansen 2012; Savolainen et al. 2001; Kahneman et al. 2010, Ono and Lee 2013). Researchers attribute these findings to the demands associated with raising children in economically advanced countries, including the financial stress of raising children and the stress of balancing employment and family life. It thus appears that disparities in emotional well-being between parents and nonparents in the United States are echoed in similarly developed nations.

However, while informative, these studies do not provide insight into cross-national variation in the *relative gap* in happiness between parents and nonparents *within* countries or whether this gap is greater in some nations than in others. Nor do they tell us whether differences in the social policy context between countries contribute to cross-national variation in the magnitude of the parenthood happiness gap. It is likely that variations in the larger social policy context of countries contribute to variations in parental status disparities in happiness across wealthy countries, as one comparative study of two developed nations suggests (Kahneman et al. 2010).

The Importance of Social Policies for Improving the Mental Health of Parents

Over the past couple of decades, most economically advanced nations have implemented social welfare policies that provide a variety of benefits for their citizens (Budig et al., 2016; Misra et al., 2011; Savolainen et al. 2001; Kahneman et al. 2010). These policies not only include universal health care coverage but also work-family balance policies such as paid parental leave and workplace flexibility; the United States is the single outlier among developed nations, having yet to provide these institutional resources and supports to parents. These policies are intended to improve the quality of life for individuals and families as well as encourage parenthood by alleviating the stress associated with raising children; they also tend to be available to parents residing in *all* types of households, including those composed of married, cohabiting, and nonpartnered adults.

The social and economic factors that have given rise to social welfare policies in some developed countries but not others are highly complex and beyond the scope of this chapter. It does, however, appear that the decline in fertility to below replacement as well as a commitment to gender equality in the workplace and family are two of the reasons why many wealthy nations have implemented these institutional resources and supports (Thévenon and Gauthier 2011). Regardless of the underlying factors that gave rise to these social policies, cross-national research on population health documents that individuals residing in countries with more generous social welfare policies enjoy greater happiness and health than those residing in countries with weaker policy provisions such as the United States (Bambra 2016; Wilkinson and Pickett 2009). Another benefit of these policies is that they have reduced inequality in happiness and health within these countries (Pickett and Wilkinson 2015). It is, therefore, possible that by alleviating the stress associated with parenthood, disparities in happiness between parents and nonparents are also smaller in nations with stronger rather than weaker social policies for families.

To examine this issue, Jennifer Glass, Mathew Andersson, and I examined variations in the happiness gap between parents and nonparents across 22 Organisation for Economic Co-operation and Development countries, and their possible contextual determinants. Our study (Glass et al. 2016) revealed considerable variation in the magnitude of the happiness gap between parents and nonparents across these countries, with the United States showing the largest disadvantage of parenthood. We also found that the gap in happiness between parents and nonparents is smaller in countries that have more generous family policies—including paid parental leave, flexible work time and schedule, paid vacation days as well as child care subsidies—than in countries that provide minimal assistance to parents such as the United States. Our study further showed that both mothers and fathers benefit from these family policies and that, while they increase parental happiness, they do not reduce nonparents' happiness. In other words, the advantage of supportive social welfare policies for individuals' happiness is not a zero-sum game as some researchers claim (Ono and Lee 2013) but improve parents' as well as nonparents' happiness.

Overall, these findings indicate that the absence of supportive public policies for parents in the United States is a major contextual factor that helps explain why they report less happiness than nonparents. Because happiness is a global measure of emotional well-being, it is likely that the lack of work-family balance policies also help explain why American parents experience more symptoms of emotional distress, depression, and anger as well as less life satisfaction than nonparents. While research on parental status disparities in mental health tends to focus on the proximate sources of stress to which parents are exposed, the larger social policy context is a distal yet crucial source of stress for contemporary American parents that contributes to their lower levels of emotional well-being. Since parental stress and emotional distress may inadvertently negatively affect the quality of relationships with children, it is possible that cross-national variation in the policy context of countries also contributes to variations in *children's* emotional well-being across economically advanced nations—a topic that my colleagues and I are currently exploring.

In conclusion, despite the cultural belief that children increase adults' emotional well-being—a cultural belief that first emerged in the United

States and other industrial countries during the late 19th and early 20th centuries—there is no evidence that parenthood enhances Americans' mental health. On the contrary, parents experience greater symptoms of emotional distress, depression and anger as well as less happiness and life satisfaction than childless adults. The stressors to which American parents are exposed help explain their lower levels of emotional well-being relative to nonparents. There are, however, important lessons to be learned from other economically advanced nations with regard to concrete ways in which we could reduce parental status disparities in mental health. Although it is highly unlikely that the United States will implement supportive family policies for all parents in the foreseeable future, I am optimistic that we will eventually catch up with the rest of the developed world and provide institutional resources and supports to alleviate the stress of having children for future generations of American mothers and fathers.

References

Almeling, Ranae. 2011. *Sex Cells: The Medical Market for Eggs and Sperm*. Berkeley: University of California Press.

Aries, Phillippe. 1965. *Centuries of Childhood: A Social History*. New York: Vintage.

Avison, William, Jennifer Ali, and David Walters. 2007. "Family Structure, Stress, and Psychological Distress: A Demonstration of the Impact of Differential Exposure." *Journal of Health and Social Behavior* 48 (3): 301–17.

Balbo, Nicoletta, Francesco C. Billari, and Melinda Mills. 2012. "Fertility in Advanced Societies: A Review of Research." *European Journal of Population* 29: 1–38.

Bambra, Clare. 2016. *Health Divides: Where You Live Can Kill You*. Bristol: Policy Press.

Bell, Ann V. 2014. *Misconception: Social Class and Infertility in America*. New Brunswick: Rutgers University Press.

Bianchi, Suzanne M., John P. Robinson, and Melissa Milkie. 2006. *The Changing Rhythms of American Family Life*. New York: Russell Sage.

Bird, Chloe. 1997. "Gender Differences in the Social and Economic Burdens of Parenting and Psychological Distress." *Journal of Marriage and the Family* 59: 809–23.Blackstone, Amy. 2014. "Childless or Child-Free?" *Contexts* 13: 68–70.

Blair-Loy, Mary. 2005. *Competing Devotions: Career and Family among Women Executives*. Cambridge, MA: Harvard University Press.

Bodnar, John. 1985. *The Transplanted: A History of Immigrants in Urban America*. Bloomington: Indiana University Press.

Budig, Michelle, and Paula England. 2001. "The Wage Penalty of Motherhood." *American Sociological Review* 66: 204–25.

Bures, Regina M., Tanya Koropeckyj-Cox, and Michael Loree. 2009. "Childlessness, Parenthood, and Depressive Symptoms Among Middle-Aged and Older Adults." *Journal of Family Issues* 30 (5): 670–87.

Centers for Disease Control. 2017. https://www.cdc.gov/nchs/fastats/unmarried-childbearing.htm.

Christopher, Karen, Paula England, Sara McLanahan, Katherine Ross, and Tim Smeeding. 2001. "Gender Inequality and Poverty in Affluent Nations: The Role of Single Motherhood and the State." In *Child Well-Being, Child Poverty, and Child Policy in Modern Nations,* edited by K. Vleminckx and T. Smeeding, 199–220. Bristol: Policy Press.

Chua, Amy. 2011. *Battle Hymn of the Tiger Mother.* New York: Penguin.

Coontz, Stephanie. 2013. *The Way We Never Were: American Families and the Nostalgia Trap.* New York: Basic Books.

Crouter, Ann C., and Allen Booth. 2004. *Work-Family Challenges for Low-Income Parents and their Children.* Mahwah, NJ: Erlbaum.

Degler, Carl N. 1980. *At Odds: Women and the Family in America from the Revolution to the Present.* Oxford: Oxford University Press.

Desmond, Matthew. 2016. *Evicted: Poverty and Profit in the American City.* New York: Crown.

Downey, Douglas, and Shana Pribesh. 2004. "When Race Matters: Teachers' Evaluations of Students' Classroom Behavior." *Sociology of Education* 77: 267–82.

Durkheim, Emile. 2013. *Suicide: A Study in Sociology.* Snowball Publishing.

Easterlin, Richard A. 1980. *Birth and Fortune: The Impact of Numbers on Personal Welfare.* New York: Basic Books.

Edin, Kathryn, and Maria J. Kefalis. 2011. *Promises I Can Keep: Why Poor Women Put Motherhood Before Marriage.* Berkeley: University of California Press.

Edin, Kathryn, and Timothy J. Nelson. 2013. *Doing the Best I Can: Fatherhood in the Inner City.* Berkeley: University of California Press.

England, Paula, and George Farkas. 1986. *Households, Employment, and Gender: A Social, Economic, and Demographic View.* Piscataway, New Jersey: Aldine.

Evenson, Ranae J., and Robin W. Simon. 2005. "Clarifying the Relationship Between Parenthood and Depression." *Journal of Health and Social Behavior* 46 (4): 341–58.

Fisher, Allen. 2003. "Still 'Not Quite as Good as Having Your Own'? Towards a Sociology of Adoption." *Annual Review of Sociology* 29: 335–61.

Friedman, Stewart. 2013. *Baby Bust: New Choices for Men and Women in Work and Family.* Philadelphia, PA: Wharton Press.

Furstenberg, Frank F. Jr., Sheela Kennedy, Vonnie C. McLoyd, Ruben G. Rumbaut, and Ruchard A. Settersten Jr. 2004. "Growing Up Is Harder to Do." *Contexts* 3 (3): 33–41.

Glass, Jennifer. 2000. "Towards a Kinder, Gentler Workplace: Envisioning the Integration of Family and Work." *Contemporary Sociology* 29: 129–43.

Glass, Jennifer, and Tetsushi Fugimoto. 1994. "Housework, Paid Work, and Depression Among Husbands and Wives." *Journal of Health and Social Behavior* 35: 179–91.

Glass, Jennifer, Robin W. Simon, and Mathew A. Andersson. 2016. "Parenthood and Happiness: Effects of Work-Family Reconciliation Policies in 22 OECD Countries." *American Journal of Sociology* 122: 886–929.

Gordon, Michael. 1978. *The American Family: Past, Present, Future.* New York: Random House.

Greenfield, Emily A., and Nadine F. Marks. 2006. "Linked Lives: Adult Children's Problems and Their Parents' Psychological and Relational Well-Being." *Journal of Marriage and Family* 68 (2): 442–54.

Griswold, Robert L. 1993. *Fatherhood in America: A History.* New York: Basic Books.

Hansen, Thomas. 2012. "Parenthood and Happiness: A Review of Folk Theories Versus Empirical Evidence." *Social Indicators Research* 108 (1): 29–64.

Hareven, Tamara K. 1991. "The History of the Family and the Complexity of Social Change." *The American Historical Review* 96: 95–124.

Hays, Sharon. 1998. *The Cultural Contradictions of Motherhood.* New Haven: Yale University Press.

Henretta, John C. 2007. "Early Childbearing, Marital Status, and Women's Health and Mortality After Age 50." *Journal of Health and Social Behavior* 48 (3): 254–66.

Hertz, Rosanna. 2008. *Single by Chance, Mothers by Choice: How Women Are Choosing Motherhood without Marriage and Creating the New American Family.* Oxford: Oxford University Press.

Hochschild, Arlie, and Anne Machung. 1989. *The Second Shift: Working Families and the Revolution at Home.* New York: Penguin.

House, James, Ken R. Landis, and Debra Umberson. 1988. "Social Relationships and Health." *Science* 241 (4865): 540–45.

Jacobs, Jerry, and Kathleen Gerson. 2005. *The Time Divide: Work, Family, and Gender Inequality.* Cambridge, MA: Harvard University Press.

Jacobson, Health. 2016. *Labor of Love: Gestational Surrogacy and the Work of Making Babies.* New Brunswick, NJ: Rutgers University Press.

Kahneman, Daniel, David Schkade, Claude Fischler, Alan Krueger, and Amy Krilla. 2010. "The Structure of Well-Being in Two Cities: Life Satisfaction and Experienced Well-Being in Columbus, Ohio; and Rennes, France." In *International Differences in Well-Being*, edited by Ed Diener, John F. Helliwell, and Daniel Kahneman, 16–33. Oxford.

Kessler, R. C., K. A. McGonagle, S. Zhao, C. B. Nelson, M. Hughes, S. Eshleman, Hu Wittchen, and K.S. Kendler. 1994. "Lifetime and 12-Month Prevalence of DSM-III R Psychiatric Disorders in the United States: Results from the National Comorbidity Survey." *Archives of General Psychiatry* 51: 8–19.

Kessler, Ronald C., and James A. McRae Jr. 1982. "The Effect of Wives' Employment on the Mental Health of Married Men and Women." *American Sociological Review* 47: 216–27.

Knoester, Chris. 2003. "Transitions in Young Adulthood and the Relationship Between Parent and Offspring Well-Being." *Social Forces* 81 (4): 1431–57.

Kohler, Hans-Peter, Francesco C. Billari, and José A. Ortega. 2006. "Low Fertility in Europe: Causes, Implications and Policy Options." In *The Baby*

Bust: Who Will Do the Work? Who Will Pay the Taxes? edited by Fred R. Harris, 48–109. Lanham, MD: Rowman & Littlefield.

Koropeckyj-Cox, Tanya. 2002. "Beyond Parental Status: Psychological Well-Being in Middle and Old Age." *Journal of Marriage and Family* 64 (4): 957–71.

Koropeckyj-Cox, Tanya, and Gretchen Pendell. 2007. "The Gender Gap in Attitudes About Childlessness in the United States." *Journal of Marriage and Family* 69 (4): 899–915.

Koropeckyj-Cox, Tanya, Amy Mehraban Pienta, and Tyson H. Brown. 2007. "Women of the 1950s and the 'Normative' Life Course: The Implications of Childlessness, Fertility Timing, and Martial Status for Psychological Well-being in Late Midlife." *The International Journal of Aging and Human Development* 64 (4): 299–330.

Kreider, Rose M., and Renee Ellis. 2011. "Living Arrangements of Children: 2009." *Current Population Reports,* 70–126.Lareau, Annettte. 2002. "Invisible Inequality: Social Class and Childrearing in Black Families and White Families." *American Sociological Review* 67: 747–76.

Lareau, Annette. 2011. *Unequal Childhoods: Class, Race and Family Life.* Berkeley: University of California Press.

Lasch, Christopher. 1995. *Haven in a Heartless World: The Family Besieged.* New York: Norton.

Lennon, Mary Clare, and Sarah Rosenfield. 1994. "Relative Fairness and the Division of Housework: The Importance of Options." *American Journal of Sociology* 100 (2): 506–31.

Lesthaeghe, Ron. 2010. "The Unfolding Story of the Second Demographic Transition." *Population and Development Review* 36: 211–51.

Lewin, Ellen. 2009. *Gay Fatherhood: Narratives of Family and Citizenship in America.* Chicago: University of Chicago Press.

Liefbroer, Aart C. 2005. "The Impact of Perceived Costs and Rewards of Childbearing on Entry into Parenthood: Evidence from a Panel Study." *European Journal of Population* 21: 367–91.

Lois, Jennifer. 2012. *Home Is Where the School Is: The Logic of Homeschooling and the Emotional Labor of Mothering.* New York: NYU Press.

Mandel, Hadas, and Moshe Semyonov. 2005. "Family Policies, Wage Structures, and Gender Gaps: Sources of Earnings Inequality." *American Sociological Review* 70: 949–67.

Margolis, Rachel, and Mikko Myrskyla. 2011. "A Global Perspective on Happiness and Fertility." *Population and Development Review* 37: 29–56.

McLanahan, Sara, and Julia Adams. 1987. "Parenthood and Psychological Well-Being." *Annual Review of Sociology* 13: 237–57.

McLanahan, Sara S. 1983. "Family Structure and Stress: A Longitudinal Comparison of Two-Parent and Female-Headed Families." *Journal of Marriage and the Family* 45 (2): 347–57.

McLanahan, Sara S., and Erin L. Kelly. 1999. "The Feminization of Poverty: Past and Future." In *Handbook of the Sociology of Gender,* edited by Janet Chafetz, 127–45. New York: Plenum.

Meadows, Sarah O., Sara S. McLanahan, and Jeanne Brooks-Gunn. 2008. "Stability and Change in Family Structure and Maternal Health Trajectories." *American Sociological Review* 73 (2): 314–34.

Milkie, Melissa, Alex Bierman, and Scott Schieman. 2008. "How Adult Children Influence Older Parents' Mental Health: Integrating Stress-Process and Life-Course Perspectives." *Social Psychology Quarterly* 71 (1): 86–105.

Milkie, Melissa A., and Catharine H. Warner 2014. "Status Safeguarding: Mothering Work to Secure Children's Place in the Status Hierarchy." In *Intensive Mothering: The Cultural Contradictions of Modern Motherhood*, edited by Linda Ennis. 66–85. Bradford, ON: Demeter.

Mintz, Steven. 2006. *Huck's Raft: A History of American Childhood*. Cambridge, MA: Harvard University Press.

Mirowsky, John. 2002. "Parenthood and Health: The Pivotal and Optimal Age at First Birth." *Social Forces* 81 (1): 315–49.

Misra, Joya, Michelle Budig, and Irene Boeckmann. 2011. "Work-Family Policies and the Effects of Children on Women's Employment Hours and Wages." *Community, Work and Family* 14: 139–57.

Moore, Mignon. 2011. *Invisible Families: Gay Identities, Relationships, and Motherhood among Black Women*. Berkeley: University of California Press.

National Center for Health Statistics. 2015. *Health, United States, 2015*. Centers for Disease Control. https://www.cdc.gov/nchs/data/hus/hus15.pdf.

Nomaguchi, Kei M., and Melissa Milkie. 2003. "Costs and Rewards of Children: The Effects of Becoming a Parent on Adults' Lives." *Journal of Marriage and Family* 65 (2): 413–30.

Nomaguchi, Kei M., Melissa Milkie, and Suzanne M. Bianchi. 2005. "Time Strains and Psychological Well-Being: Do Dual-Earner Mothers and Fathers Differ?" *Journal of Family Issues* 26 (6): 756–92.

OECD Factbook 2015–2016. http://www.oecd-ilibrary.org/economics/oecd-factbook-2015-2016/total-fertility-rates_factbook-2015-table3-en.

Offer, Shira, and Barbara Schneider. 2011. "Revisiting the Gender Gap in Time-Use Patterns: Multitasking and Well-Being among Mothers and Fathers in Dual-Earner Families." *American Sociological Review* 76 (6): 809–33.

Ono, Hiroshi, and Kristen Schultz Lee. 2013. "Welfare States and the Redistribution of Happiness." *Social Forces* 92: 789–814.

Pearlin, Leonard I. 1989. "The Sociological Study of Stress." *Journal of Health and Social Behavior* 30 (3): 241–56.

Pearlin, Leonard I., and Joyce S. Johnson. 1977. "Marital Status, Life-Strains and Depression." *American Sociological Review* 42 (5): 704–15.

Pickett, Kate E., and Richard G. Wilkinson. 2015. "Income Inequality and Health: A Causal Review." *Social Science & Medicine* 128: 316–326.

Pollman-Schult, Matthias. 2014. "Parenthood and Life Satisfaction: Why Don't Children Make People Happy?" *Journal of Marriage and Family* 76 (2): 319–36.

Pudrovska, Tatyana. 2009. "Parenthood, Stress, and Mental Health in Late Midlife and Early Old Age." *International Journal of Aging and Human Development* 68 (2): 127–47.

Ross, Catherine E., and John Mirowsky. 1988. "Childcare and Emotional Adjustment to Wives' Employment." *Journal of Health and Social Behavior* 29 (2): 127–38.

Ross, Catherine E., John Mirowsky, and Joan Huber. 1983. "Dividing Work, Sharing Work, and In-Between: Marriage Patterns and Depression." *American Sociological Review* 48 (6): 809–23.

Ross, Catherine E., and Marieke Van Willigen. 1996. "Gender, Parenthood, and Anger." *Journal of Marriage and the Family* 58 (3): 572–84.

Samuel, Lawrence. 2015. *American Fatherhood: A Cultural History.* Lanham, MD: Rowman and Littlefield.

Savolainen, Jukka, Eero Lahelma, Karri Silventionen, Anne Hélène Gauthier, and Karri Silventoinen. 2001. "Parenthood and Psychological Well-Being in Finland: Does Public Policy Make a Difference?" *Journal of Comparative Family Studies* 32: 61–74.

Schnittker, Jason, and Jane McLeod. 2005. "The Social Psychology of Health Disparities." *Annual Review of Sociology* 31: 75–103.

Senior, Jennifer. 2010. "All Joy and No Fun: Why Parents Hate Parenting." *New York Magazine.*

Shorter, Edward. 1975. *The Making of the Modern Family.* New York: Basic Books.

Simon, Robin W. 1992. "Parental Role Strains, Salience of Parental Identity and Gender Differences in Psychological Distress." *Journal of Health and Social Behavior* 33: 25–35.

Simon, Robin W. 1995. "Gender, Multiple Roles, Role Meaning, and Mental Health." *Journal of Health and Social Behavior* 36 (2): 182–94.

Simon, Robin W. 1998. "Assessing Sex Differences in Vulnerability among Employed Parents: The Importance of Marital Status." *Journal of Health and Social Behavior* 39 (1): 38–54.

Simon, Robin W. 2002. "Revisiting the Relationships among Gender, Marital Status, and Mental Health." *American Journal of Sociology* 107: 1065–96.

Simon, Robin W. 2008. "The Joys of Parenthood, Reconsidered." *Contexts* 7: 40–45.

Simon, Robin W. 2017. *A Perfect Storm: The Culture of Intensive Parenting and Parents' Mental Health.* (Unpublished manuscript).

Simon, Robin W., and Jennifer Caputo. 2018. "The Costs and Benefits of Parenthood for Mental and Physical Health in the U.S.: The Importance of Parenting Stage." *Society and Mental Health.* https://doi.org/10.1177/2156869318786760

Spence, Naomi J. 2008. "The Long-Term Consequences of Childbearing." *Research on Aging* 30 (6): 722–51.

Stone, Pamela. 2007. *Opting Out: Why Women Really Quit Careers and Head Home.* Berkeley: University of California Press.

Tausig, M. 2013. "The Sociology of Work and Well-Being." In *Handbook of the Sociology of Mental Health*, second edition, edited by Carol A. Aneshensel, Jo Phelan, and Alex Bierman, 433–55. New York: Springer.

Thévenon, Oliver, and Anne H. Gauthier. 2011. "Family Policies in Developed Countries: A Fertility Booster with Side Effects." *Community, Work and Family* 14: 198–216.

Thoits, Peggy A. 1986. "Multiple Identities: Examining Gender and Marital Status Differences in Distress." *American Sociological Review* 51 (2): 259–72.

Thompson, Warren S. 1949. "Population." *American Journal of Sociology* 34 (6): 959–75.

Thornton, Arland, and Linda Young DeMarco. 2001. "Decades of Trends in Attitudes Toward Family Issues in the United States: The 1960's Through the 1990's." *Journal of Marriage and Family* 63 (4): 1009–37.

Turner, R. Jay, Donald Lloyd, and Blair Wheaton. 1995. "The Epidemiology of Social Stress." *American Sociological Review* 60: 104–25.

Umberson, Debra. 1987. "Family Status and Health Behaviors: Social Control as a Dimension of Social Integration." *Journal of Health and Social Behavior* 28 (3): 306–19.

Umberson, Debra, Meichu D. Chen, James S. House, Kristen Hopkins, and Ellen Slater. 1996. "The Effect of Social Relationships on Psychological Well-Being: Are Men and Women Really So Different?" *American Sociological Review* 61 (5): 837–57.

Umberson, Debra, and Walter R. Gove. 1989. "Parenthood and Psychological Well-Being: Theory, Measurement, and Stage in the Family Life Course." *Journal of Family Issues* 10 (4): 440–62.

Umberson, Debra, Tetyana Pudrovska, and Corine Reczek. 2010. "Parenthood, Childlessness, and Well-Being: A Life Course Perspective." *Journal of Marriage and Family* 72 (3): 612–29.

Umberson, Debra, Mieke Thomeer, and Kristi Williams. 2013. "Family Status and Health: Recent Advances and Future Directions." In *Handbook of the Sociology of Mental Health*, edited by Carol S. Aneshensel, Jo Phelan, and Alex Bierman, 405–31. Dordrecht: Springer.

Vandenberg-Daves, Jodi. 2014. *Modern Motherhood: An American History*. New Brunswick, NJ: Rutgers University Press.

Veenhoven, Ruut. 2010. "How Universal Is Happiness?" In *International Differences in Well-Being*, edited by Ed Diener, John F. Helliwell, and Daniel Kahneman, 328–50. New York: Oxford.

Warner, Judith. 2006. *Perfect Madness: Motherhood in the Age of Anxiety*. New York: Riverhead Books.

Welter, Barbara. 1966. "The Cult of True Womanhood: 1820–1860." *American Quarterly* 18: 151–74.

Wickrama, K. A. S., Frederick O. Lorenz, Laura Ebert Wallace, Laknath Peiris, Rand D. Conger, and Glen H. Elder. 2001. "Family Influence on Physical Health During the Middle-Years: The Case of Onset Hypertension." *Journal of Marriage and Family* 63 (2): 527–39.

Williams, David R., and Morgan M. Medlock. 2017. "The Effects of Dramatic Societal Events—Ramifications of the Recent Presidential Election." *New England Journal of Medicine* 376: 2295–99.

Williams, David R., and S. A. Mohammed. 2009. "Discrimination and Racial Disparities in Health: Evidence and Needed Research." *Journal of Health and Social Behavior* 32: 20–47.

Williams, Kristi, Sharon Sassler, Adrienne Frech, Feneba Addo, and Elizabeth Cooksey. 2011. "Nonmarital Childrearing, Union History, and Women's Health at Midlife." *American Sociological Review* 76: 465–86.

Wolfe, Joseph D. 2009. "Age at First Birth and Alcohol Use." *Journal of Health and Social Behavior* 50 (4): 395–409.

Woo, Hyeyoung, and R. Kelly Raley. 2005. "A Small Extension to 'Costs and Rewards of Children: The Effects of Becoming a Parent on Adults' Lives.'" *Journal of Marriage and Family* 67 (1): 216–21.

Zelizer, Viviana. 1994. *Pricing the Priceless Child: The Changing Social Value of Children*. Princeton, NJ: Princeton University Press.

Zhang, Zhenmei, and Mark D. Hayward. 2001. "Childlessness and the Psychological Well-being of Older Persons." *Journal of Gerontology Series B* 56 (5): S311–S320.

PART 2

Work, Family, and Leisure for Parents

Introduction: Work, Family, and Leisure for Parents

One thing that family scholars are good at pointing out is the relationship between policies that are supposed to help families and what families are actually able to do. For example, just because a policy allows leave time upon the birth or adoption of a baby does not mean that people are able to take the time, afford it financially, or operate in social networks that support the decision to take advantage of a leave policy. Separate from the availability of policies that may help parents, time and support from other people are resources that are not evenly distributed across different types of parents. The chapters in this section capture what's going on with policies that affect working parents, these parents' likelihood to take advantage of policies in light of cultural values (especially those that relate to gender roles), and patterns in time spent doing leisure activities alongside work and family responsibilities.

Focusing on what happens with paid work when a child enters the picture, economist Ankita Patnaik provides a much-needed concise overview of what is going on with today's parental leave policies in chapter 6. In addition to comparing the United States to certain other countries (all of which have more progressive leave policies), Patnaik delves into how different groups have differential access to leave policies, resulting in short- and long-term strains and challenges that may exacerbate existing inequalities in families.

Sociologist Caitlyn Collins weaves together policy, cultural values, and practice in chapter 7 as she reveals how women in Germany have navigated the difficult terrain of work and family life as the country has enacted more progressive family-leave policies. As it turns out, there are strong cultural forces at play, such as gendered expectations for mothers that make parental leave benefits more difficult to take without penalty. U.S. sociologists today suggest an overhaul of United States' current political and legal system for organizing paid work and unpaid caregiving, because it is failing mothers and families. This chapter uncovers the complex answer to the question: What are the daily lived experiences and barriers of working mothers in a sociopolitical environment undergoing this sort of legal transformation?

Chapter 8, by sociologist Liana Sayer, offers a quantitative analysis of time use surveys and insight into how mothers and fathers of differing education levels spend their leisure time. We find out that, in addition to differences in the amounts of leisure time among parents, the type of leisure (and whether it is done with or without children) matters. Watching TV while a child is in another room, after all, is a different experience for parents compared to taking that child to a museum. And both of these activities need to be situated in a cultural context where job types and education levels affect choices in leisure activities and parents' ability to take time away from work and family responsibilities to participate in them.

CHAPTER SIX

Parental Leave Programs: What Do We Know about Designing Good Policies?

Ankita Patnaik

In late 2017, news reports noted that at city and state levels, paid parental leave policies were being enacted to meet the needs of working parents. But even this progress was incomplete, as a *New York Times* article entitled "Paid Parental Leave, Except for Most Who Need It" suggests. In this article, the author (Bellafante 2017) notes that although the city of New York introduced a generous six weeks of fully paid parental leave for public sector workers in 2016, only about 20,000 employees in the managerial class were eligible for this benefit while over 300,000 other public sector workers such as teachers, police officers, park rangers, paramedics, and child welfare case workers were not eligible. Beginning in 2018, these excluded public sector workers may be covered by New York State's Paid Family Leave program if their employer chooses to offer it; however, this program only compensates workers at 50 percent of their average weekly wages—a pay cut some workers simply cannot afford. So, even when seemingly progressive parental leave provisions are enacted, there are often restrictions about who is entitled to receive them and limitations on who is able to use them.

Parental Leave Policies around the World

What about paid parental leave at the national level? In the vast majority of countries, working women have a right to some kind of paid leave after childbirth (International Labor Organization 2014). In addition to paid maternity leave, many developed nations also provide access to other kinds of paid leave, such as paternity leave for fathers, parental leave for parents of either gender, or family leave for workers to care for an ill relative. Parental leave policies worldwide vary in their key features: eligibility requirements, funding mechanisms, coverage, duration, and benefit amounts and structure. In some countries, eligibility is conditional on one's recent work status, whereas in other countries, those who are not employed are also entitled to paid leave. Paid leave programs are often funded through employer mandates, direct government expenditures, or social insurance systems that all workers pay into. Usually, parental leave must be taken shortly after the birth of a child or in the first year of the child's life, but not always—for example, in Sweden, parents can use their leave at any time until a child is eight years old. The programs vary considerably in the financial compensation they provide: some pay a flat cash benefit, some pay a percentage of parents' earnings (usually up to a cap), and some provide higher benefits at first but gradually reduce benefits later in the leave period. There is also considerable variation in the duration of leave that programs cover. For example, while Mexico provides three months of maternity and parental leave to mothers, Estonia provides mothers with over three years of leave. Irrespective of these differences in policy designs, paid leave is provided to mothers after childbirth in almost every country in the world.

The United States is therefore an outlier when it comes to parental leave. The United States and Papua New Guinea are the only two members of the club of countries that do not offer women a statutory national entitlement to paid maternity leave. The situation in the United States seems particularly stark when we compare it to its economic peers: every other nation in the Organisation for Economic Co-operation and Development (OECD) offers mothers at least three months of paid maternity leave (see Figure 6.1)—and over half also grant fathers paid paternity leave (OECD 2017). In contrast, the United States does not guarantee any paid paternity, parental, or family leave at the national level. So, what provisions are made for new parents in the United States?

Parental Leave in the United States

The only national mandate for any kind of parental leave in the United States exists via the 1993 Family and Medical Leave Act (FMLA), which provides 12 weeks of unpaid job-protected leave to eligible workers. The FMLA

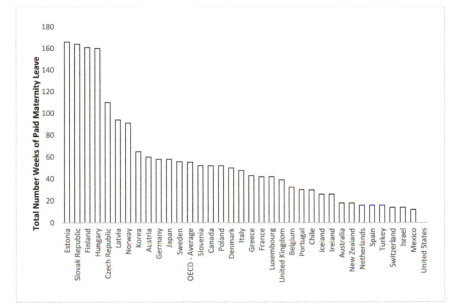

Figure 6.1 Weeks of Paid Maternity and Parental Leave Available to Mothers (Graph constructed by author using data for 2016 from http://stats.oecd.org. Notes: Data reflect the total number of weeks which a woman can be on paid leave after the birth of a child combining both maternity and parental leave. Data reflect entitlements at the national/federal level only, and do not reflect regional differences within countries.)

provisions can be used by workers for the birth of a child or to bond with a newborn, newly adopted child, newly placed foster child, or care for an ill family member. During FMLA leave, the worker receives no financial compensation, but the employer is required to guarantee his or her job and to continue to provide health insurance (if such coverage was already provided). To be eligible for FMLA, a worker must (i) work for a firm with 50 employees within 75 miles of the employee's worksite, (ii) have at least 12 months of tenure with the current employer, and (iii) have worked at least 1250 hours in the prior year. Partly as a result of these requirements, less than 60 percent of private sector workers are eligible for leave through the FMLA (Klerman, Daley, and Pozniak 2012). Further, FMLA coverage is unequally distributed, with low-income workers being more likely to be shut out since they are more likely to change employers frequently and cobble together multiple part-time jobs. Moreover, even if a worker is eligible for FMLA, the fact that the leave is unpaid makes it unaffordable for some families, particularly those with a single breadwinner or those with limited assets and savings.

In five states, women who give birth have access to some weeks of paid leave through Temporary Disability Insurance (TDI) programs.[1] However, TDI is inflexible and limited in duration, as it must be taken in the six weeks surrounding childbirth. Further, since TDI is premised on the idea of pregnancy and childbirth as a temporary disability, it offers narrow coverage: it covers leave for women who are about to give birth or have just given birth, but it does not cover leave for fathers, parents who adopt a child, or parents who wish to take time off at a different period than that immediately surrounding the birth.

Paid family leave (PFL) under a broader definition has only been introduced more recently in a handful of states. In July 2004, California began its Paid Family Leave program, becoming the first in the United States to provide paid benefits to workers of either gender to take time off from work to bond with a newborn, newly adopted child, newly placed foster child, or care for an ill family member. Since then, New Jersey, Rhode Island, and New York have also implemented such programs, while Washington and the District of Columbia have passed legislation for paid family leave but have not begun implementation yet.

Studies of states' existing PFL programs report mostly positive effects thus far. Studies have found that California's PFL program led to not only an increase of three to six weeks in mothers' average leave duration but also higher employment probabilities for mothers 9 to 12 months after birth (Baum and Ruhm 2016) and increased usual weekly work hours and wage income of employed mothers of one- to three-year-old children (Rossin-Slater, Ruhm and Waldfogel 2013). Byker (2016) studied the California and New Jersey PFL programs using panel data and found that the PFL programs increased women's labor-force participation in the months surrounding their births, particularly for less educated women who tend to have more limited access to paid leave in the absence of these laws. Fathers' leave-taking also increased under California's PFL program (Baum and Ruhm 2016; Bartel et al. 2018). Further, while critics of PFL programs cite concerns about increased costs for employers and the burden on small businesses, there is little evidence of such negative effects on employers. Surveys of firms of varying sizes in California and New Jersey have found that employers reported either a "positive effect" or "no noticeable effect" of PFL programs on productivity or profitability/performance (Appelbaum and Milkman 2011; Milkman and Appelbaum 2013; Lerner and Appelbaum 2014; Bartel et al. 2016). Bedard and Rossin-Slater (2016) examined data on nearly all California employers between 2000 and 2014 and found no evidence that firms with higher rates of paid family leave take-up were burdened with significantly higher wage costs or employee turnover.

Nevertheless, the state PFL programs are far from perfect. For one thing, there is limited awareness about the programs (Houser and White 2012;

Tisinger et al. 2016). For example, one field poll found that only 36 percent of voters were aware of California's PFL 11 years after the program began (DiCamillo and Field 2015). This suggests that education or information campaigns are important complements to PFL programs in order to promote utilization. Another serious concern with the PFL programs arises from the asymmetry in eligibility requirements between state and federal policy. State PFL programs provide financial compensation to nearly all workers, while the FMLA mandates job protection and continued health insurance but is not available to a significant proportion of workers. Therefore, workers may find that they qualify for PFL but not FMLA, meaning that they can access financial compensation for leave, but that they might not have their health insurance while they are on leave or that they might return from leave to find their jobs have been given away to others. In their survey of employees in California, Appelbaum and Milkman (2011) found that fear of repercussions at work was the main reason cited by survey respondents who were aware of PFL but did not apply for the program when they needed a family leave. About 37 percent of such respondents reported being worried that their employer would be unhappy, their career advancement would be stunted, or they would lose their jobs for using PFL.

What about the workers who live in the other 46 states that do not currently provide PFL? The lack of a national mandate for paid job-protected leave in the United States is problematic since over three-quarters of the U.S. population lives in states without PFL programs. Workers in these states must rely on their employers for paid family leave, which is by no means a standard job benefit. According to the Bureau of Labor Statistics, only 14 percent of civilian workers had access to paid family leave through their employer as of 2013 (Bureau of Labor Statistics 2016). One survey found that only 17.6 percent of worksites provided paid maternity leave to all their employees (Klerman et al. 2012). This means that in states without PFL, the vast majority of new parents must use unpaid leave, vacation days, or sick days to care for their newborns.

It is important to note that the dependency of U.S. workers on employer-provided paid leave leads to inequalities in access to leave. When employers have more resources or are more invested in the careers and well-being of their employees, they are more likely to provide their employees with paid family leave or paid vacation days or sick days. The data accordingly show significant differences in workers' access to employer-provided paid family leave: employees in the top 10th percentile of the wage distribution are nearly four times as likely to have access to paid family leave as those in the lowest quartile (Bureau of Labor Statistics 2016).[2] This disparity was thrust into the news in 2015 when Netflix announced a two-tier system of benefits for workers within the same firm: 12 months of paid leave for employees within the company's fast-growing streaming business but just 12 weeks for the lower-paid, hourly workers in the DVD division. The Netflix story is a rather dramatic case, of course, but it reflects the wider reality that, in a capitalist nation without a national paid leave program, taking time off to care for one's newborn is largely a privilege reserved for the elite professional class. In the meantime, the low-income workers who are least likely to have access to paid leave through their employers are also less able to make do without it, since they cannot afford the high costs of daycare if they return to their jobs; nor can they afford to take unpaid leave or quit and risk their family's health insurance and financial stability. Ultimately, since paid family leave enables workers to make crucial investments in their family's health and well-being, inequalities in access to parental leave can only exacerbate income inequalities in American society.

Fortunately, it seems like paid parental leave is an issue whose time has finally come. There is a great deal of interest and support among the American public for paid leave to be provided to new mothers and fathers. A survey conducted by the Pew Research Center in 2016 found that 82 percent of people felt that mothers should get paid leave following the birth or adoption of a child, and 69 percent felt that fathers should too (Horowitz et al. 2017). The issue is also gaining some political traction, with both presidential candidates in the 2016 election putting forward a proposal for some kind of paid family leave. The United States is certainly lagging behind its economic peers in developing a comprehensive plan to provide paid parental leave to workers. However, an optimist would choose to focus on the valuable opportunity that this presents to learn from the policy experiences of other nations and design an effective parental leave policy that can secure the best outcomes for families, workers, and the economy. What's at stake with parental leave policy?

A key first step to designing a good parental leave program is understanding the outcomes that it can impact in the short run and long run, and the mechanisms through which those effects work. I focus my discussion on the three topic areas that are of policy interest and have been found to be impacted by parental leave: children's health, mothers' health and careers, and gender equality. For the first two areas, I will describe the effects of policies enabling mothers to take leave, as that is what the vast majority of research has focused on. For the sake of brevity, wherever possible, I will focus on rigorous studies that help us get at cause and effect.

Children's Health and Development

There are three mechanisms through which we expect that children's long-run outcomes may be impacted by parental leave policies. First, maternal stress may be reduced by enabling mothers to take some antenatal leave—in fact, even the prospect of postnatal leave may lower a mother's stress levels during pregnancy. Maternal stress is in turn negatively associated with child health at birth and later in life (Talge, Neal, and Glover 2007; Mennes et al. 2009; Buss et al. 2010; Currie and Rossin-Slater 2013; Black, Devereux, and Salvanes 2016; Aizer, Stroud and Buka 2016; Persson and Rossin-Slater 2016). Second, parental leave may facilitate investments in a child's health such as by enabling parents to keep regular doctors' appointments, stick to an immunization and vaccination schedule, and breastfeed the child. Third, paid parental leave can improve children's outcomes by supporting family finances in the period around birth, which can facilitate access to, for example, higher-quality nutrition and medical care.

Rigorous studies of the relationship between maternity leave and child outcomes have found mixed results—some report positive effects, while others report no effects. In the United States, perhaps because the baseline level of parental leave provisions has been low, policies providing even a little bit of leave (unpaid or paid) have been found to result in improved outcomes for children. For example, the introduction of the FMLA in 1993 was the first time that maternity leave became available to mothers at a national level. Rossin-Slater (2011) examined the causal effects of this law by exploiting the fact that some states had enacted maternity leave policies prior to FMLA, and that FMLA eligibility rules only applied to parents who worked in firms with 50 or more employees. She found that the FMLA led to increased birth weight, decreased likelihood of a premature birth, and reduced infant mortality for children. However, since the leave offered by FMLA was unpaid, it is unsurprising that Rossin-Slater (2011) also found these effects to be concentrated among college-educated and married mothers, who were more likely to be able to afford unpaid leave. In contrast, the introduction of paid leave through state TDI programs was found to have particularly large positive impacts on birth weight and early births of children born to unmarried and black mothers, who are on average less likely to be able to take unpaid time off from work (Stearns 2015). These two studies suggest that while the introduction of some parental leave has had an impact on children's health, the provision of paid leave might be needed to battle inequalities in children's health outcomes.

The literature on European leave reforms also suggests that policies improving leave entitlements can have a positive impact on child outcomes, but the effects are smaller or nonexistent when maternity leave is expanded from a baseline level that is already generous. This pattern is apparent in two rigorous studies of Norway. Paid maternity leave was introduced for the first time in Norway in 1977. Previously, mothers had been entitled to 12 weeks of unpaid leave (similar to that currently provided by the FMLA in the United States), but after this reform, mothers could access 18 weeks of paid leave and 1 year of unpaid leave. Carneiro, Løken, and Salvanes (2015) studied this reform and found significant positive impacts on children's long-term outcomes. The reform led to a two-percentage-point decrease in children's high school dropout rates and a 5 percent increase in their earnings at age 30, with impacts concentrated among children whose mothers would have taken very low levels of leave in the absence of the reform. However, Dahl et al. (2016) studied a series of subsequent extensions to Norway's maternity leave and found no impacts on children's academic achievement or graduation from high school. Similarly, studies from Canada, Sweden, Denmark, Austria, and Germany that examined extensions in mothers' leave entitlements have found little impact on long-run outcomes such as children's cognitive or behavioral development, test scores, and educational attainment (Baker and Milligan 2008, 2010; Liu and Skans 2010; Rasmussen 2010; Danzer and Lavy 2016). Interestingly, one study found that a Norwegian policy that introduced paid paternity leave reserved for fathers—and led to a dramatic increase in fathers' leave-taking—was associated with children's improved school performance at age 16 in families where the father was more highly educated than the mother (Cools et al. 2015).

One possibility is that a leave policy has larger impacts on child outcomes when it provides parents access to unpaid or paid leave for the first time rather than extending the amount of leave a mother can access. However, the institutional context of a parental leave policy is likely to also matter greatly. The studies that found no effects of paid leave extensions were all conducted in developed nations with high public spending, universal healthcare, and government-funded child care supports.[3] When we consider the wider context of these studies, it is perhaps unsurprising that, for example, extending paid leave from 6 to 12 months had no long-term impact on child outcomes in Canada, where parents enjoy universal health care and publicly subsidized child care, whereas the introduction of 6 weeks of unpaid FMLA leave had positive impacts for children in the United States since it facilitated child care and health insurance that are otherwise expensive in the United States. Ultimately, the impact of a maternity leave policy on child outcomes is likely to depend on not only the marginal change offered by the reform but also the circumstances surrounding the utilization of the policy.

Mothers' Health and Careers

In theory, taking a break from work could also improve mothers' own health, but less research has been conducted in this area. Longer leave duration is associated with reduced depressive symptoms (Chatterji and Markowitz 2005; Chatterji and Markowitz 2012; Dagher, McGovern, and Dowd 2014). Researchers have found a positive correlation between length of maternity leave and mothers' mental and physical health in two studies that exploit variation in the timing of leave policy reforms (Avendano et al. 2015; Hewitt, Strazdins, and Martin 2017). However, a rigorous study by Baker and

Milligan (2008) that examined an increase in maternity leave entitlements in Canada found no causal impact on mothers' self-reported measures of health. In order to better understand how maternity leave can improve maternal health, we need not only more studies that can identify causal impacts but also studies that examine a broader range of maternal health outcomes, such as the incidence of caesarean deliveries and maternal mortality rates.

In contrast, there exists an extensive literature examining the impact of maternity leave policies on women's labor market outcomes. Klerman and Leibowitz (1997) present a helpful framework for thinking about how parental leave policies are likely to affect employment and leave-taking. Their model shows that leave entitlements are expected to increase mothers' leave-taking, but the overall effects on employment are ambiguous. The net effect depends on how women would have behaved in the counterfactual world where no leave entitlement was available. For women who would have quit their jobs to take time off to be with their children in the counterfactual, the leave entitlement might have induced them to take leave from their jobs instead of quitting. In addition, some women may increase their labor supply prior to childbirth in order to qualify for leave. Such women may experience improvements in their long-term labor market outcomes as a result of the policy due to increased work experience, mitigation in human capital depreciation, and greater job continuity. For women who would have taken little or no time off in the counterfactual, a leave policy might have induced them to take a break for the full duration of their entitlement, and these women might have experienced negative impacts on their careers because they spent a longer period away from work as a result of the policy. There may also be larger effects of such policies on the female work force— for example, employers who find leave-taking costly may engage in statistical discrimination against female employees of childbearing age by being less likely to hire them, offering them lower wages, or stunting their career advancement.[4]

Comparing across countries, several studies have found that paid maternity leave provisions of up to one year typically increase the likelihood of women's short-term employment after childbirth, but also that significantly longer leave provisions can negatively affect women's employment and relative wages (Ruhm 1998; Thévenon and Solaz 2013; Olivetti and Petrongolo 2017). However, such cross-country studies cannot prove causal links between policies and outcomes, since the assignment of countries to policies is not random. For example, some countries may have cultures that highly value women working outside the home, which contributes to policies that support working families (such as maternity leave) and also high levels of women's labor force participation—but this does not mean that the maternity leave policy causes high rates of female employment. Therefore, these studies show informative correlations but cannot prove that these are the causal effects of maternity leave policies on women's labor market outcomes.

Nevertheless, studies that examine the causal impact of a single policy change within one nation find results similar to these cross-sectional studies. Leave provisions of up to one year have been found to have either positive or zero effect on women's employment rates (Waldfogel 1999; Han, Ruhm, and Waldfogel 2009; Baker and Milligan 2008; Dahl et al. 2016). Studies of modest leave entitlements have also found increases in women's job continuity—that is, the probability that a mother returns to her prebirth employer—which would enable her to reap the benefits of her tenure and job-specific human capital (Baum 2003; Baker and Milligan 2008). However, significantly longer paid leave durations may negatively impact women's careers. Extended maternity leave was found to be linked to reduced employment and earnings for mothers in the first three years after birth in both France (Lequien 2012) and Austria (Lalive and Zweimüller 2009).

This pattern is particularly apparent in the research on parental leave in Germany. Schönberg and Ludsteck (2014) conducted a rigorous examination of several expansions of paid parental leave in Germany between 1979 and 1993 and found that each expansion reduced mothers' postbirth employment rates in the short run, with limited effects on their long-term labor market outcomes. However, in 2007, Germany's means-tested parental leave transfer program that had paid benefits for up to two years was replaced by a more generous earnings-based transfer that only paid benefits for up to 12 months, and this significantly increased mothers' employment at the one-year mark as well as three to five years after the birth (Kluve and Tamm 2013; Kluve and Schmitz 2014; Bergemann and Riphahn 2015). Therefore, those who wish to design a good parental leave program should keep in mind that the research suggests that providing some parental leave may benefit both mothers and children, but that very lengthy leave entitlements may undermine women's careers.

Gender Equality

You may have noticed that while the title of this chapter refers to "parental leave," we are more than halfway through it and have been talking mostly about maternity leave. Until very recently, the policy and research discussions around how to care for babies has frequently overlooked male parents of these babies. This can be ascribed to not only social conventions regarding gender roles in earlier times but also the purpose of early parental leave policies. Certainly, in previous generations, male involvement in caregiving for infants was more limited, but, equally important, the purpose of many early parental leave provisions was to enable mothers to recover from the physical ordeal of childbirth, which men, naturally, don't undergo. In recent decades, the notions of parental leave in both policy and research discussions have been broadened to include men for three reasons. First, changing social norms have led to more egalitarian beliefs about gender roles in many societies. Second, there is mounting evidence that fathers' involvement in child care is positively associated with children's social, emotional, physical, and cognitive development (Allen and Daly 2007) provide a useful summary) as well as fathers' psychological well-being and life satisfaction (Eggebeen and Knoester 2001; Knoester, Petts, and Eggebeen 2007; Schindler 2010, Kotila and Dush 2013). Third, parental leave is now commonly believed to be important not only for women to recover from childbirth but also for gender-neutral purposes such as bonding with the child and making investments in child health. As a result, more nations have begun to offer men access to time off after the birth or adoption of a child. In 27 of the 35 OECD member nations, some paid leave is set aside specifically for fathers, with the average duration of reserved leave being eight weeks (OECD 2017).

Even though parental leave programs are increasingly designed with both parents in mind, the leave participation rates of fathers worldwide remain much lower than those of mothers. When family leave is provided for the mother and father to share, it is often considered de facto maternity leave, with mothers using nearly all the leave in most families. When paid leave is offered as an individual, nontransferable entitlement to workers, men still make considerably less use of it than women. For example, California's PFL program led to an increase of five weeks for mothers but of only two to three days for fathers (Baum and Ruhm 2016). Japan offers one of the world's most generous paternity programs, reserving a year of paid leave for fathers, and yet less than 3 percent of fathers utilize it (Japanese Cabinet Office 2015).

Fathers' reluctance to take parental leave can be understood via many lenses. First, there is a strong economic disincentive for men to take parental leave. Men continue to earn higher average wages than their female counterparts and get promoted more often. In heterosexual couples, the loss of the bigger paycheck from the higher-earning parent can be an important factor in fathers' decisions not to take parental leave. Fathers also commonly cite workplace attitudes as a barrier to utilizing parental leave even when they are entitled to it, as they fear it could damage their careers or workplace relationships (Bygren and Duvander 2006). For example, a survey of U.S. workers in 2016 found that 57 percent of men felt that taking parental leave would be perceived as a lack of commitment to the job, and 54 percent of all respondents said that their colleagues would judge a man more than a woman for taking the same amount of parental leave (Deloitte 2016). Social and psychological factors also may play a role: it is possible that men have a lower taste for caregiving work, that social mores pressure men to prioritize paid work and their role as breadwinners, and/or that there are few role models in the form of men who engage in care work.

Early research on men's leave-taking tended to use cross-country comparisons to explore how easing these barriers could improve fathers' participation. Fathers' leave take-up was found to be higher in countries with generous compensation rates (Moss and O'Brien 2006). In a comparative study of 24 nations, O'Brien (2009) finds that fathers' use of statutory leave provisions is greatest when the programs provide fathers with high income replacement (50 percent or more of earnings) along with extended duration (more than 14 days). Fathers also respond more to policies providing them an individual and nontransferable right to leave compared to policies where fathers are given access to "family leave" that may be used by either parent. Several cross-country comparisons have shown that fathers are more likely to utilize parental leave in the form of a "daddy quota"—that is, a period of nontransferable leave reserved for the father on a "use it or lose it" basis (Bruning and Plantenga 1999; O'Brien 2009; Haas and Rostgaard 2011). These findings provide suggestive associations between different kinds of leave entitlements and fathers' take-up but should be not interpreted as causal links, since countries don't usually happen upon policy designs by accident. That is, a country may offer a generous paternity leave program precisely because its citizens are highly motivated—or perhaps highly concerned—about men's participation in family life.

In recent years, more researchers have attempted to identify the causal impacts of paternity leave by studying sudden policy "shocks" where leave policy was changed suddenly, and comparing births just before and just after the shocks. Dahl, Løken, and Mogstad (2014) study Norway's introduction of a daddy quota and find that it increased fathers' take-up by 32 percentage points. Studies of Sweden find a strong effect on parental leave use resulting from the reservation of the first "daddy month" and a smaller but still significant effect from the second "daddy month" (Duvander and Johansson 2012; Ekberg, Eriksson, and Friebel 2013). My own research has examined a parental leave reform in Quebec that improved financial compensation for all parents and added five weeks of "daddy-only" leave to the family's total entitlement (Patnaik 2019). I found that it led to an immediate jump in fathers' participation rates of over 250 percent and increased their leave duration by over three weeks. Thus, there is strong evidence that earmarking some well-compensated leave for fathers and making it nontransferable can significantly incentivize men to take parental leave. I also found evidence that Quebec's daddy quota did not owe its success to "forcing" fathers to use the leave in order not to waste it, but rather that the "framing effect" of labeling of some weeks as daddy-only helped elicit participation from fathers.[5]

Another mechanism that is sometimes used to incentivize men to take leave is an "equality bonus" wherein a family that shares leave equally between mother and father is rewarded with either additional leave or a financial reward. In Sweden, a bonus was introduced in 2008 such that parents that split leave equally between the mother and father were given a tax credit. Duvander and Johansson (2012) found it had no impact on fathers' take-up, but their finding should be considered within the context that Sweden already offered pretty generous paternity leave incentives—over one year of paid leave offered to fathers, with two months reserved specifically for them. Moreover, since the reward was in the form of a tax credit, the rules to claim it were complicated, and the money was not paid out during the leave period but instead a year later. More recently, Japan also introduced a bonus whereby parents could receive an extra two months of leave if they shared some of the leave—but this policy has not been rigorously evaluated. At this point, a strong body of research does not exist on the effectiveness of equality bonuses.

We know that some kinds of policies aimed at getting men to take leave are successful in their aims—but what are the implications of more men taking leave? Father's time in child care is higher in countries with generous paternity leave policies (Fuwa and Cohen 2007; Sullivan et al. 2009; del Carmen Huerta et al. 2013; Boll, Lepin, and Reich 2014), and fathers who take leave are more involved in child care (Haas 1990; Brandth and Kvande 2003; Haas and Hwang 1999; Tanaka and Waldfogel 2007; Nepomnyaschy and Waldfogel 2007; Brandth and Kvande 2009). A handful of cross-sectional studies finds that men taking parental leave is associated with their increased participation in time-inflexible and typically female housework (Hook 2006, 2010; Brandth and Kvande 2017). Fathers' participation in parental leave has also been found to be correlated with shorter work hours for fathers (Haas and Hwang 1999; Duvander and Jans 2009; Bünning and Pollmann-Schult 2016) and shorter career breaks for mothers (Pylkkanen and Smith 2003). However, these cross-sectional studies are unable to control for differences in fathers' preferences, beliefs, motivation, and workplace constraints, which influence both the decision to take leave and future domestic responsibilities. For example, they cannot control for the fact that some men may have had particularly close relationships with their own fathers, which would motivate them not only to take parental leave but also to spend more time with their children when they are older.

Newer studies have sought rigorous evidence of causal links by comparing the behavior of parents before and after a "policy shock" that led to a sudden increase in fathers' leave-taking. Interestingly, these studies have found mixed results and are not consistent in their findings on the causal effect on parents' labor market outcomes. While two studies found that paternity leave reduced fathers' earnings (Johansson 2010; Rege and Solli 2013), another study reported no significant impacts on fathers' earnings or work hours (Cools, Fiva and Kirkebøen 2015). Similarly, some studies have found that paternity leave has no significant causal effects on mothers' labor supply or earnings (Kotsadam, Finseraas, and Ugreninov 2011; Rege and

Solli 2013), others have reported significant positive effects on maternal earnings (Johansson 2010) and labor supply (Patnaik 2019).

Multiple causal studies have failed to confirm a significant causal relationship between fathers' leave-taking and the sharing of child care between parents (Kluve and Tamm 2009; Rieck 2012; Ekberg et al. 2013; Ugreninov 2013). One study did find that paternity leave leads to more equal sharing of the chore of laundry (Kotsadam and Finseraas 2012). My own research, which used the 2006 Quebec reform to examine how parents' time-use patterns changed after the sudden jump in fathers' leave-taking, found that more paternal leave-taking led to more equal sharing of housework but not child care (Patnaik 2019).

Taken together, these studies do not provide a definitive verdict on the usefulness of paternity leave in promoting gender equality. More studies with high-quality data and rigorous methodology will be needed to fully understand how these policies impact relative earnings and the sharing of care work and paid work between parents. Because it is only in recent decades that parental leave policies have been designed to specifically target men, we know little about how they affect outcomes in the very long-term, such as mothers' and fathers' career trajectories and retirement savings. We also know very little about the intergenerational effects of paternity leave policies. Only one study has explored this: Kotsadam and Finseraas' (2013) study of Norway found that girls born immediately after the introduction of a father's quota were less likely to do household work in their teenage years. More research is needed on whether and how fathers taking leave can impact gender equality in the next generation—for example, by shaping children's attitudes about gendered work and providing role models of male caregivers.

Conclusion

In designing a paid family leave program, there are many lessons to be learned from the policy experiences of other countries. For one thing, it seems that the greatest gains to mothers and children appear from the first six months of leave provided to a mother. In comparison, leaves of significantly longer than one or two years can undermine women's careers without necessarily providing much benefit in terms of children's health and development. It is encouraging that policy makers and researchers have begun considering the idea of substituting very long maternity leaves with some sharing of leave between mothers and fathers, since this may end up being a win-win situation—though more rigorous and long-term research is needed on the effects of fathers' leave-taking. More generally, research is also needed on the effects of parental leave policies on other stakeholders; for example, on employers and on childless men and women. Last, while most studies and policy discussions in the past have assumed a traditional, married, heterosexual two-parent model, that model is not reflective of the average American family today, with fewer than half of U.S. children living in a home with two married heterosexual parents in their first marriage (Livingston 2014). Therefore, to design successful and inclusive paid family leave policies, we will need to consider the implications of any program design on the diverse family structures and circumstances that children are raised in today.

Notes

1. As of 2017, California, Hawaii, New Jersey, New York, and Rhode Island had TDI programs.

2. Low-income workers also have significantly less access to paid sick days, temporary disability benefits, paid vacation days, or paid personal leave, so they are less able to use such types of leave in place of parental leave.

3. Carneiro et al. (2015) note that access to childcare in Norway in 1977 was relatively limited, and therefore, their studies examine the introduction of maternity leave in a context where households had few alternative options but for the mother to care for the baby.

4. Statistical discrimination occurs when rational decision makers use (real or imagined) aggregate group characteristics to evaluate an individual in lieu of directly measuring or assessing the individual's characteristics. For example, this would occur if an employer chose not to hire a young woman because he assumed that young women as a group are more likely to take long career breaks and provide a poor return on investment in its human capital.

5. Framing effects are a concept from behavioral science that suggests that the way in which a choice is presented can influence how someone feels about the choice and the decision that he or she makes about it (Kahneman and Tversky 1979).

References

Aizer, Anna, Laura Stroud, and Stephen Buka. 2016. "Maternal Stress and Child Well-Being: Evidence from Siblings." *Journal of Human Resources* 51 (3): 523–55.

Allen, Sarah, and Kerry Daly. 2007. *The Effects of Father Involvement: An Updated Research Summary of the Evidence Inventory*. Report. University of Guelph: Centre for Families, Work Well-Being. Accessed December 18, 2017. http://www.fira.ca/cms/documents/29/Effects_of_Father_Involvement.pdf.

Appelbaum, Eileen, and Ruth Milkman. 2011. *Leaves That Pay: Employer and Worker Experiences with Paid Family Leave in California*. Washington, D.C.: Center for Economic and Policy Research. Accessed December 18, 2017. http://cepr.net/documents/publications/paid-family-leave-1-2011.pdf.

Appelbaum, Eileen, and Ruth Milkman. 2013. *Unfinished Business: Paid Family Leave in California and the Future of U.S. Work-Family Policy.* Ithaca, NY: ILR Press.

Avdic, D., and E. Karimi 2018. "Modern Family? Paternity Leave and Marital Stability." *American Economic Journal: Applied Economics.* Forthcoming.

Avendano, Mauricio, Lisa Berkman, Agar Brugiavini, and Giacomo Pasini. 2015. "The Long-Run Effect of Maternity Leave Benefits on Mental Health: Evidence from European countries." *Social Science & Medicine* 132: 45–53.

Baker, Michael, and Kevin Milligan. 2008. "How Does Job Protected Maternity Leave Affect Mothers' Employment?" *Journal of Labor Economics* 26 (4): 655–91.

Baker, Michael, and Kevin Milligan. 2008. "Maternal Employment, Breastfeeding, and Health: Evidence from Maternity Leave Mandates." *Journal of Health Economics* 27 (4): 871–87.

Bartel, Ann P., Maya Rossin-Slater, Christopher J. Ruhm, Jenna C. Stearns, and Jane Waldfogel. 2018. "Paid Family Leave, Fathers' Leave-Taking, and Leave-Sharing in Dual-Earner Households." *Journal of Policy Analysis and Management* 37 (1): 10–37.

Bartel, Ann P., Maya Rossin-Slater, Christopher J. Ruhm, and Jane Waldfogel. 2016. *Assessing Rhode Island's Temporary Caregiver Insurance Act: Insights from a Survey of Employers.* Washington, D.C.: U.S. Department of Labor. Accessed December 18, 2017. http://www.dol.gov/asp/evaluation/completedstudies/AssessingRhodeIslandTemporaryCaregiverInsurance Act_InsightsFromSurveyOfEmployers.pdf.

Baum, Charles. 2003. "The Effects of Maternity Leave Legislation on Mothers' Labor Supply after Childbirth." *Southern Economic Journal* 69 (4): 772–99.

Baum, Charles, and Christopher Ruhm. 2016. "The Effects of Paid Family Leave in California on Labor Market Outcomes." *Journal of Policy Analysis and Management* 35 (2): 333–56.

Bedard, Kelly, and Maya Rossin-Slater. 2016. "The Economic and Social Impacts of Paid Family Leave in California: Report for the California Employment Development Department." California Employment Development Department. Accessed July 31. https://www.edd.ca.gov/Disability/pdf/PFL_Economic_and_Social_Impact_Study.pdf

Bellafante, Ginia. 2017. "Paid Parental Leave, Except for Most Who Need It." *New York Times.* December 1. Accessed December 31. https://www.nytimes.com/2017/12/01/nyregion/paid-parental-leave-except-for-most-who-need-it.html. Bergemann, Annette, and Regina Riphahn. 2015. "Maternal Employment Effects of Paid Parental Leave" IZA working paper No. 9073.

Berger, Lawrence, Jennifer Hill, and Jane Waldfogel. 2005. "Maternity Leave, Early Maternal Employment and Child Health and Development in the US." *The Economic Journal* 115 (501): F29–F47.

Black, Sandra E., Paul J. Devereux, and Kjell G. Salvanes. 2016. "Does Grief Transfer Across Generations? Bereavements during Pregnancy and Child Outcomes." *American Economic Journal: Applied Economics* 8 (1): 193–223.

Blau, Francine D., and Lawrence M. Kahn. 2013. "Female Labor Supply: Why Is the United States Falling Behind?" *American Economic Review* 103 (3): 251–56.

Boll, Christina, Julian Leppin, and Nora Reich. 2014. "Paternal Childcare and Parental Leave Policies: Evidence from Industrialized Countries." *Review of Economics of the Household* 12 (1): 129–58.

Brandth, Berit, and Elin Kvande. 2003. "Father Presence in Child Care." In *Children and the Changing Family,* edited by A. M. Jensen and L. McKee, 61–75. London: RoutledgeFalmer.

Brandth, Berit, and Elin Kvande. 2009. "Gendered or Gender-Neutral Care Politics for Fathers?" *The Annals of the American Academy of Political and Social Science* 624: 177–89.

Brandth, Berit, and Elin Kvande. 2017. "Fathers on Leave Alone in Norway: Changes and Continuities." In *Comparative Perspectives on Work-Life Balance and Gender Equality. Life Course Research and Social Policies,* edited by M. O'Brien and K. Wall. 29–44. London: Springer.

Bruning, Gwennaële, and Janneke Plantenga. 1999. "Parental Leave and Equal Opportunities: Experiences in Eight European Countries." *Journal of European Social Policy* 9 (3): 195–209.

Bureau of Labor Statistics. 2016. *National Compensation Survey: Employee Benefits in the United States, March 2016.* Washington, D.C.: U.S. Department of Labor, Bureau of Labor Statistics. Accessed September 26, 2017. https://www.bls.gov/ncs/ebs/benefits/2016/ebbl0059.pdf.

Buss, Claudia, Elysia P. Davis, L. Tugan Muftuler, Kevin Head, and Curt A. Sandman. 2010. "High Pregnancy Anxiety during Mid Gestation Is Associated with Decreased Gray Matter Density in 6–9-Year Old Children." *Psychoneuroendocrinology* 35 (1): 141–53.

Bünning, Mareike, and Matthias Pollmann-Schult. 2016. "Family Policies and Fathers' Working Hours. Cross-National Differences in the Paternal Labor Supply." *Work, Employment and Society* 30 (2): 256–74.

Bygren, Magnus, and Ann-Zofie Duvander. 2006. "Parents Workplace Situation and Fathers Parental Leave Use." *Journal of Marriage and Family* 68 (2): 363–72.

Byker, Tanya S. 2016. "Paid Parental Leave Laws in the United States: Does Short-Duration Leave Affect Women's Labor-Force Attachment?" *American Economic Review* 106 (5): 242–46.

Carneiro, Pedro, Katrine V. Løken, and Kjell G. Salvanes. 2015. "A Flying Start? Maternity Leave Benefits and Long-Run Outcomes of Children." *Journal of Political Economy* 123 (2): 365–412.

Chatterji, Pinka, and Sara Markowitz. 2005. "Does the Length of Maternity Leave Affect Maternal Health?" *Southern Economic Journal* 72 (1): 16–41.

Chatterji, Pinka, and Sara Markowitz. 2012. "Family Leave after Childbirth and the Mental Health of New Mothers." *Journal of Mental Health Policy and Economics* 15 (2): 61–76.

Cools, Sara, Jon H. Fiva, and Lars J. Kirkebøen. 2015. "Causal Effects of Paternity Leave on Children and Parents." *Scandinavian Journal of Economics* 117 (3): 801–28.

Currie, Janet, and Maya Rossin-Slater. 2013. "Weathering the Storm: Hurricanes and Birth Outcomes." *Journal of Health Economics* 32 (3): 487–503.

Dagher, Rada K., Patricia M. McGovern, and Bryan E. Dowd. "Maternity Leave Duration and Postpartum Mental and Physical Health: Implications for Leave Policies." *Journal of Health Politics, Policy and Law* 39 (2): 369–416.

Dahl, Gordon B., Katrine V. Løken, and Magne Mogstad. 2014. "Peer Effects in Program Participation." *American Economic Review* 104 (7): 2049–74.

Dahl, Gordon B., Katrine V. Løken, Magne Mogstad, and Kari Vea Salvanes. 2016. "What Is the Case for Paid Maternity Leave?" *The Review of Economics and Statistics* 98 (4): 655–70. Danzer, Natalia, and Victor Lavy. 2017. "Paid Parental Leave and Children's Schooling Outcomes." *The Economic Journal*. Accessed December 10, 2017. http://onlinelibrary.wiley.com/doi /10.1111/ecoj.12493/full.

del Carmen Huerta, Maria, Willem Adema, Jennifer Baxter, Wen-Jui Han, Mette Lausten, RaeHyuck Lee, and Jane Waldfogel. 2013. "Fathers' Leave, Fathers' Involvement and Child Development: Are They Related? Evidence from Four OECD Countries." OECD Social, Employment and Migration Working Papers 140. Paris: OECD Publishing.

Deloitte. 2016. *Parental Leave Survey: Less Than Half of People Surveyed Feel Their Organization Helps Men Feel Comfortable Taking Parental Leave.* https:// www2.deloitte.com/us/en/pages/about-deloitte/articles/press-releases /deloitte-survey-parental-leave.html.

DiCamillo, M., and M. Field 2015. *Just 36% of Voters Aware of State's Paid Family Leave Program.* San Francisco, CA: California Center for Research on Women and Families. Accessed December 10, 2017. http://www.field .com/fieldpollonline/subscribers/Rls2494.pdf.

Duvander, Ann-Zofie, and Ann-Christin Jans. 2009. "Consequences of Father's Parental Leave Use: Evidence from Sweden." *Finnish Yearbook of Population Research* 44: 49–62. https://journal.fi/fypr/article/view/45044/11322.

Duvander, Ann-Zofie, and M. Mats Johansson. 2012. "What Are the Effects of Reforms Promoting Fathers' Parental Leave Use?" *Journal of European Social Policy* 22 (3): 319–30.

Eggebeen, David, and Chris Knoester. 2001. "Does Fatherhood Matter for Men?" *Journal of Marriage and Family* 63: 381–93.

Ekberg, John, Rickard Eriksson, and Guido Friebel. 2013. "Parental Leave: A Policy Evaluation of the Swedish Daddy-Month Reform." *Journal of Public Economics* 97: 131–43.

Fuwa, Makiko, and Philip N. Cohen. 2007. "Housework and Social Policy." *Social Science Research* 36 (2): 512–30.

Haas, Linda. 1990. "Gender Equality and Social Policy: Implications of a Study of Parental Leave in Sweden." *Journal of Family Issues* 11 (4): 401–23.

Haas, Linda, and C. Phillip Hwang. 2008. "The Impact of Taking Parental Leave on Fathers Participation in Childcare and Relationships with Children: Lessons from Sweden." *Community, Work and Family* 11 (1): 85–104.

Haas, Linda, and Tine Rostgaard. 2011. "Fathers' Rights to Paid Parental Leave in the Nordic Countries: Consequences for the Gendered Division of Leave." *Community, Work & Family* 14 (2): 177–95.

Han, Wen-Jui., Christopher J. Ruhm, and Jane Waldfogel. 2009. "Parental Leave Policies and Parents' Employment and Leave-Taking." *Journal of Policy Analysis Management* 28 (1): 29–54.

Hewitt, Belinda, Lyndall Strazdins, and Bill Martin. 2017. "The Benefits of Paid Maternity Leave." *Social Science and Medicine* 182: 97–105.

Hook, Jennifer. 2006. Care in Context: Men's Unpaid Work in 20 Countries, 1965–2003. *American Sociological Review* 71 (4): 639–660.

Hook, Jennifer. 2010. "Gender Inequality in the Welfare State: Sex Segregation in Housework, 1965–2003." *American Journal of Sociology* 115 (5): 1480–1523.

Horowitz, Juliana, Kim Parker, Niki Graf, and Gretchen Livingston. 2017. *Americans Widely Support Paid Family and Medical Leave, but Differ over Specific Policies.* Washington D.C.: Pew Research Center: Social and Demographic Trends. Accessed November 11, 2017. http://assets.pewresearch.org/wp-content/uploads/sites/3/2017/03/22152556/Paid-Leave-Report-3-17-17-FINAL.pdf.

Houser, Linda, and Karen White. 2012. *Awareness of New Jersey's Family Leave Insurance Program Is Low, Even as Public Support Remains High and Need Persists.* New Brunswick, NJ: The Center for Women and Work. Accessed December 10, 2017. http://njtimetocare.com/sites/default/files/03_New%20Jersey%20Family%20Leave%20Insurance-%20A%20CWW%20Issue%20Brief.pdf.

International Labour Organization. 2014. *Maternity and Paternity at Work: Law and Practice across the World.* Gender, Equality and Diversity Branch of the Conditions of Work and Equality Department. Accessed December 10, 2017. http://www.ilo.org/wcmsp5/groups/public/---dgreports/---dcomm/---publ/documents/publication/wcms_242615.pdf.

Japanese Cabinet Office. 2015. *Fourth Basic Plan for Gender Equality.* Accessed December 18, 2017. http://www.gender.go.jp/about_danjo/basic_plans/4th/.

Johansson, Elly-Ann. 2010. "The Effect of Own and Spousal Parental Leave on Earnings." Working Paper Series 2010:4. Institute for Evaluation of Labour Market and Education Policy.

Kahneman, Daniel, and Ariel Tversky. 1979. "Prospect Theory: An Analysis of Decision Under Risk." *Econometrica* 47: 263–91.

Klerman, Jacob, Kelly Daley, and Alyssa Pozniak. 2012. *Family and Medical Leave in 2012: Technical Report.* Prepared for the U.S. Department of Labor (Contract #GS10FOO86K). Cambridge, MA: Abt Associates.

Klerman, Jacob, and Arleen Leibowitz. 1997. "Labor Supply Effects of State Maternity Leave Legislation." In *Gender and Family Issues in the Workplace*, edited by F. Blau and R. Ehrenberg. 65–85. New York: Russell Sage Foundation.

Kluve, Jochen, and Sebastian Schmitz. 2014. "Social Norms and Mothers' Labor Market Attachment—The Medium-Run Effects of Parental Benefits," Ruhr Economic Papers 481, RWI—Leibniz-Institut für Wirtschaftsforschung, Ruhr-University Bochum, TU Dortmund University, University of Duisburg-Essen.

Kluve, Jochen, and Marcus Tamm. 2013. "Parental Leave Regulations, Mothers' Labor Force Attachment and Fathers' Childcare Involvement: Evidence from a Natural Experiment." *Journal of Population Economics* 26 (3): 983–1005.

Knoester, Chris, Richard J. Petts, and David J. Eggebeen. 2007. "Commitments to Fathering and the Well-Being and Social Participation of New, Disadvantaged Fathers." *Journal of Marriage and Family* 69: 991–1004.

Kotila, Letitia E., and Claire M. Kamp Dush. 2013. "Involvement with Children and Low-Income Fathers' Psychological Well-Being." *Fathering* 11 (3): 306–26.

Kotsadam, Andreas, and Henning Finseraas. 2012. "The State Intervenes in the Battle of the Sexes: Causal Effects of Paternity Leave." *Social Science Research* 40 (6):1611–22.

Kotsadam, Andreas, Henning Finseraas, and Elisabeth Ugreninov. "The Long-Term Effect of Parental Leave on Mothers' Earnings." PhD thesis, University of Gothenburg 2011.

Lalive, Rafael, and Josef Zweimüller. 2009. "How Does Parental Leave Affect Fertility and Return to Work? Evidence from Two Natural Experiments." *The Quarterly Journal of Economics* 124 (3): 1363–402.

Lequien, Laurent. 2012. "The Impact of Parental Leave Duration on Later Wages." *Annals of Economics and Statistics* 107/108: 267–85.

Lerner, Sharon, and Eileen Appelbaum. 2014. *Business as Usual: New Jersey Employers' Experiences with Family Leave Insurance*. Washington, D.C.: Center for Economic and Policy Research.

Liu, Qian, and Oskar Skans. 2010. "The Duration of Paid Parental Leave and Children's Scholastic Performance Children's Scholastic Performance." *The B. E. Journal of Economic Analysis & Policy* 10 (1): 1–33.

Livingston, Gretchen. 2014. *Less Than Half of U.S. Kids Today Live in a 'Traditional' Family*. Washington, D.C.: Pew Research Center. Accessed December 10, 2017. http://www.pewresearch.org/fact-tank/2014/12/22/less-than-half-of-u-s-kids-today-live-in-a-traditional-family/. Mennes, Maarten, Bea Van den Bergh, Lieven Lagae, and Peter Stiers. 2009. "Developmental Brain Alterations in 17 Year Old Boys Are Related to Antenatal Maternal Anxiety." *Clinical Neurophysiology* 120 (6): 1116–22.

Milkman, Ruth, and Eileen Appelbaum. 2013. *Unfinished Business: Paid Family Leave in California and the Future of U.S. Work-Family Policy*. Ithica, NY: ILR Press.

Moss, Peter, and Margaret O'Brien, eds. 2006. *Employment Relations Research Series 57. International Review of Leave Policies and Related Research 2006*. London: Department of Trade and Industry. Accessed November 12, 2017. http://www.leavenetwork.org/fileadmin/Leavenetwork/Annual_reviews/2006_annual_report.pdf.

Nepomnyaschy, Lenna, and Jane Waldfogel. 2007. "Paternity Leave and Fathers' Involvement with Their Young Children." *Community, Work and Family* 10 (4): 427–53.

O'Brien, Margaret. 2009. "Fathers, Parental Leave Policies, and Infant Quality of Life: International Perspectives and Policy Impact." *The Annals of the American Academy of Political and Social Science* 624 (1): 190–213.

OECD. 2017. *Key Characteristics of Parental Leave Systems*. OECD—Social Policy Division—Directorate of Employment, Labour and Social Affairs. Accessed December 10, 2017. https://www.oecd.org/els/soc/PF2_1_Parental_leave_systems.pdf.

Olivetti, Claudia, and Barbara Petrongolo. 2017. "The Economic Consequences of Family Policies: Lessons from a Century of Legislation in High-Income Countries." *The Journal of Economic Perspectives* 31 (1): 205–30.

Patnaik, Ankita. 2019. "Reserving Time for Daddy: The Consequences of Fathers' Quotas." *Journal of Labor Economics*. Forthcoming.

Persson, Petra, and Maya Rossin-Slater. 2016. "Family Ruptures, Stress, and the Mental Health of the Next Generation." National Bureau of Economic Research. Working Paper 22229. Accessed December 2, 2017. http://www.nber.org/papers/w22229.pdf.

Pylkkänen, Elina, and Nina Smith. 2003. "Career Interruptions Due to Parental Leave: A Comparative Study of Denmark and Sweden." *OECD Social, Employment and Migration Working Papers*. Paris: OECD. https://econpapers.repec.org/paper/oecelsaab/1-en.htm

Rasmussen, Astrid Wurtz. 2010. "Increasing the Length of Parents' Birth-Related Leave: The Effect on Children's Long-Term Educational Outcomes." *Labour Economics* 17 (1): 91–100.

Rege, Mari, and Ingeborg Solli. 2013. "The Impact of Paternity Leave on Fathers Future Earnings." *Demography* 50 (6): 2255–77.

Rieck, Karsten Marshall Elseth. 2012. "Does Child Care Affect Parents Sickness Absence? Evidence from a Norwegian Paternity Leave Reform." Working papers in Economics, University of Bergen, Department of Economics.

Rossin-Slater, Maya. 2011. "The Effects of Maternity Leave on Children's Birth and Infant Health Outcomes in the United States." *Journal of Health Economics* 30 (2): 221–39.

Rossin-Slater, Maya, Christopher J. Ruhm, and Jane Waldfogel. 2013. "The Effects of California's Paid Family Leave Program on Mothers' Leave-Taking and Subsequent Labor Market Outcomes." *Journal of Policy Analysis and Management* 32 (2): 224–45.

Ruhm, Christopher J. "The Economic Consequences of Parental Leave Mandates: Lessons from Europe." *The Quarterly Journal of Economics* 113 (1): 285–317.

Schindler, Holly S. 2010. "The Importance of Parenting and Financial Contributions in Promoting Fathers' Psychological Health." *Journal of Marriage and Family* 72 (2): 318–32.

Schönberg, Uta, and Johannes Ludsteck. 2014. "Expansions in Maternity Leave Coverage and Mothers' Labor Market Outcomes after Childbirth." *Journal of Labor Economics* 32 (3): 469–505.

Stearns, Jenna. 2015. "The Effects of Paid Maternity Leave: Evidence from Temporary Disability Insurance." *Journal of Health Economics* 43: 85–102.

Steingrimsdottir, Herdis, and Anna Vardardottir. 2014. "Domestic Equality and Marital Stability: Does More Equal Sharing of Childcare Affect Divorce Risk?" Paper presented at European Economic Association & Econometric Society 2014 Parallel Meetings, Toulouse, France.

Sullivan, O., S. Coltrane, L. Mcannally, and E. Altintas. 2009. "Father-Friendly Policies and Time-Use Data in a Cross-National Context: Potential and Prospects for Future Research." *The ANNALS of the American Academy of Political and Social Science* 624 (1): 234–54.

Talge, Nicole, Charles Neal, and Vivette Glover. 2007. "Antenatal Maternal Stress and Long-Term Effects on Child Neurodevelopment: How and Why?" *Journal of Child Psychology and Psychiatry* 48 (3–4): 245–61.

Tanaka, Sakiko, and Jane Waldfogel. 2007. "Effects of Parental Leave and Work Hours on Fathers' Involvement with Their Babies." *Community, Work and Family* 10 (4): 409–426.

Thévenon, Olivier, and Anne Solaz. 2013. "Labour Market Effects of Parental Leave Policies in OECD Countries." *OECD Social, Employment and Migration Working Papers* No. 141. Paris: OECD Publishing.

Tisinger, Russell, Margaret Johnson, Abby Hoffman, Caitlin Davis, Maya Jean-Baptiste, and Myra Tanamor. 2016. *Understanding Attitudes on Paid Family Leave: Discussions with Parents and Caregivers in California, New Jersey and Rhode Island.* Prepared for the U.S. Department of Labor. Washington, D.C.: L&M Policy Research.

Ugreninov, Elisabeth. 2013. "Can Family Policy Reduce Mothers' Sick Leave Absence? A Causal Analysis of the Norwegian Paternity Leave Reform." *Journal of Family and Economic Issues* 34 (4): 435–46.

Waldfogel, Jane. 1999. "The Impact of the Family and Medical Leave Act." *Journal of Policy Analysis and Management* 18 (2): 281–302.

CHAPTER SEVEN

The Promise and Limits of Work-Family Supports in a Shifting Policy Landscape: A Double Bind for Working Mothers in Western Germany

Caitlyn Collins

Today, two out of every three mothers work outside the home in industrialized countries (OECD 2016), yet they still complete the lion's share of child care and housework for their families (OECD 2017). This unequal division of labor constrains mothers' job success and is a source of profound inequality between women and men (Williams 2000). News headlines highlight the reality that the United States lags far behind other countries in offering the supportive work-family policies that women need:

> "The U.S. Ranks Last in Every Measure When It Comes to Family Policy, in 10 Charts"
>> — *The Washington Post* (June 23, 2014)

> "The Great Divide in Workplace Benefits"
>> — *New York Times* (September 23, 2015)

"Offering Paid Parental Leave is Just the Start"
                                                    — *USA Today* (April 19, 2016)

"On Your Mark, Give Birth, Go Back to Work"
                                                    — NPR (October 4, 2016)

"How to Close a Gender Gap: Let Employees Control Their Schedules"
                                                    — *New York Times* (February 7, 2017)

"Businesses Push Back On Paid-Sick-Leave Laws"
                                                    — NPR (May 6, 2017)

"Americans Love Families. American Policies Don't."
                                                    — *New York Times* (June 24, 2018)

Scholars of work and family are also in consensus: the current system for organizing paid work and unpaid caregiving is failing American mothers and families (Glass 2009). A recent study found that parents in the United States report the highest levels of unhappiness compared to nonparents across 22 European and English-speaking countries (Glass, Simon, and Andersson 2016). The researchers found that this "happiness gap" is entirely explained by the absence of a robust work-family policy infrastructure. Thus, sociologists endorse policy recommendations to replace the United States' "patchwork system" of supports (Damaske 2011) with comprehensive work-family policies. Their call is buoyed by recent experimental research providing causal evidence that: 1) young men and women today would prefer egalitarian, dual-earner/carer relationships if supportive work-family policies made it possible (Pedulla and Thébaud 2015), and 2) "family-friendly" legal mandates can best reduce the motherhood penalty by signaling a broad social consensus about women's right to participate in both paid work and child rearing (Albiston et al. 2012).

These appeals for an overhaul of American work-family policy beg the question: What are the daily lived experiences of working mothers in a sociopolitical environment undergoing this sort of legal transformation? A sea change in policies can have dramatic—and sometimes unintended—consequences for people in their day-to-day lives that policymakers do not necessarily anticipate. Policies interact with cultural ideologies in ways that scholars are still trying to puzzle out (Budig, Misra, and Boeckmann 2012, 2016; Kremer 2007; Padamsee 2009; Pettit and Hook 2009). So it is important to gain insight directly from policy recipients to get a clearer picture of how people perceive and experience policy transformations in everyday life.

In this chapter, I investigate work-family policy reforms using the case of working mothers in western Germany. Germany, like other economically developed countries, is "involved in a process of 'unlearning' old policies . . . and learning new ones" (Mahon 2006, 179). It has long been the archetype of a conservative welfare state (Esping-Andersen 1990, 2009) or "strong bread-winner state" (Adler and Brayfield 2006; Lewis 2009; Ostner 2010). How-ever, since the 2000s Germany has initiated a major shift toward a new model called *Nachhaltige Familienpolitik* ("sustainable family policy") (Ostner 2010; Ziefle and Gangl 2014) with more gender-egalitarian, dual-earner legal mandates from the European Union. Drawing on 26 in-depth interviews with middle-income working mothers, I investigate how mothers experience this fluid sociopolitical context—a vital perspective if the United States is to consider similar policy reforms. Are work-family policies the panacea they seem?

Germany is an ideal case with which to examine the impact of shifting work-family policies in the daily lives of working mothers, because the state has a long history of intervention in family life (Ostner 2010). Yet, as in the United States, competing political interests mean that there is no consensus about the best work-family policy (Lewis et al. 2008). This study is import-ant because policies have transformative potential to help reduce women's work-family conflict, yet sociologists know very little about how women themselves conceptualize their options for combining motherhood and employment in a context undergoing significant legal changes from one wel-fare state model to another. In this chapter, I identify the opportunities and barriers that women perceive to attaining successful careers and contented family lives in the face of this shifting policy landscape. My goal is to explore both the promise and the limits of work-family policy for helping women reconcile motherhood and employment given its interplay with a country's cultural context.

Employment, Motherhood, and the German Policy Context

We can understand a welfare state as interventions by the state in civil society to alter social and market forces (Orloff 1993). Not all state social interventions are aimed at, or actually produce, greater equality among cit-izens (Orloff 1993). Western Germany's welfare state (Esping-Anderson 1990, 2009) has long sought to preserve and facilitate the traditional family as a core unit in society (Fleckenstein and Lee 2014) with a male breadwin-ner family model and traditional work-family policy constellation (Adler and Brayfield 2006; Ostner 2010). Dominant cultural ideologies presupposed that women were primarily caregivers and perhaps, secondarily, part-time income earners (Lewis 1993; Pfau-Effinger and Smidt 2011), assuming com-plementary, different-but-equal gender roles (Ostner 2010).

Until 2007, this family model was reinforced by laws that disincentivized full-time working motherhood: punitive tax rates for second earners within families, long and rigid parental leave, short school days, and very few public child care facilities (with short, inflexible opening hours) were long the standard (Adler and Brayfield 1997; Hummelsheim and Hirschle 2010; Pfau-Effinger and Smidt 2011).[1] Mothers' caring labor at home was further materially supported by three years' maternity leave and by public healthcare and pension systems that automatically granted insurance rights to an economically inactive wife of a working husband.

Germany has recently been forced to reconsider the conservative bread-winner model. The country grapples with a low fertility rate and a labor shortage. Its fertility rate stands at 1.4 births per woman of childbearing age, which is far below the replacement rate of 2.1 needed to sustain a country's population (Bacci 2013). Demographic research suggests that fertility will increase if a state resolves the incompatibility between work and family for women (McDonald 1997; Rindfuss et al. 2010). McDonald (1997) argues that governments can boost fertility by giving money and services to families with children and by encouraging a model of gender equity in the family. Germany embraced this argument and put it into practice in the past decade with sweeping structural reforms aimed at work-family balance. Germany is also required to meet mandates and legal directives established by the European Union and the United Nations to promote gender equality between women and men. These agreements have propelled the topics of work-family policy, gender equality, and antidiscrimination law to the forefront of current political debates (Ferree 2012). In Germany, as is the case across western industrialized countries ranging from Canada to Hungary, the policies offered are contested and in a state of flux (Lewis 2009).

Since the mid-2000s, Germany moved toward a new logic of work-family policy, called a "sustainable," "social investment," or "increasing returns" model (Esping-Andersen 2002; Ostner 2010). This approach addresses the goals of reducing maternal and childhood poverty and enhancing fertility and female labor supply. These policies are a striking break from the previous legal standard, seeking to support parents as workers in dual-earner families, promote mothers' continuous employment, increase the availability of preschool facilities, and enhance early childhood education (Ostner et al. 2003). These are precisely the policies called for by many U.S. scholars (Glass 2009; Gornick and Meyers 2003, 2004; Hochschild 1989, 1997; Jacobs and Gerson 2004; Pettit and Hook 2009; Pedulla and Thébaud 2015; Williams 2000).

Here I outline German work-family policy as of 2012, at the time of my interviews. Women were required to leave work six weeks before childbirth, and for eight weeks afterward, receiving full pay. They were entitled to a total of 12 months of paid leave (*Elterngeld*) at 67 percent of their salary (with a ceiling of €1,800 monthly [≈ $2,400]) and an additional two months were available provided that they were taken by the other parent. Parents were allowed to take a total of three years of parental leave (*Elternzeit*), and employers were legally required to keep a position open for the parent's eventual return to work. The German government also paid families a "children's allowance" (*Kindergeld*) of 184 € per month (≈ USD $240) per child until the child is 18, or until age 25 if she/he is still in school.

All full-time workers had a legal right to 24 days of fully paid vacation per year. Employees working less than full time got fewer days in proportion to how much they worked. Workers could take as many personal sick days as needed over the course of a year at full wages paid by one's health insurance. All employees received 10 days' leave per year to tend to a sick child at 70 percent pay. All of these benefits extended to couples registered in same-sex partnerships and for parents who adopt children.

Part-time work continues to be widely available across both white- and blue-collar job sectors and accounts for 27 percent of those in employment (Eurostat 2014). Of employed women in western Germany, 38 percent work part-time compared to 19 percent of American women (U.S. Bureau of Labor Statistics 2011). Part-time work is not associated with lower wages in Germany like it is in the United States (Gangl and Ziefle 2009). In 2012, 25.2 percent of mothers worked full time in western Germany. And 30.7 percent of two-parent households had a stay-at-home mother. In 1996, this figure was 44.8 percent, suggesting that many families have moved away from male breadwinner households (Holst and Wieber 2014). Additionally, flexible schedules, telecommuting, and job sharing are often available for white-collar workers. The government provides support through taxes for health care, child rearing, and education from preschool through graduate school (Ferree 2012).

State-sponsored child care is widely available for children over age three, but places for younger children have been difficult to find (Cooke 2007; Lewin-Epstein, Stier, and Braun 2006). The federal government has made it a political priority in the past several years to substantially expand child care for children under three (Fleckenstein and Lee 2014), in part because expanding child care is understood to increase birth rates (McDonald 1997).

Western German women's rates of labor force participation tend to be lower than that of U.S. women, and they tend to have higher rates of part-time employment, work interruptions, and long-term withdrawal from market work (Stier, Lewin-Epstein, and Braun 2001). However, the negative direct effects of lengthy work interruptions and part-time work such as wage penalties are smaller for mothers in western Germany than in the United States because of these protective policies (Gangl and Ziefle 2009).

Ilana Ostner (2010, 213) suggests that this new set of policies "altered the German family policy logic quite remarkably and also surprisingly [given that the previous] West German one can be summarized as marriage-based 'maternalism.'" The planned and enacted measures bring German policy much closer to a Scandinavian dual-earner model (Ostner 2010) and represents one of "the most radical series of changes in terms of policy goals . . . in taking steps to promote the adult worker model family, accompanied by significant reform of and changes in policy instruments" compared to other EU countries (Lewis et al. 2008, 270).

Despite these reforms, the laws available remain somewhat contradictory. Primary schools, for example, are still often open only part of the day regardless of encouragement on the federal level to expand their opening hours. Although the government is currently making great strides to expand child care for children under age three, Germany's two main Christian democratic conservative parties (the CDU and CSU) campaigned heavily to guarantee "freedom of choice" and pushed through a highly controversial bill in August 2013 that gives stay-at-home mothers financial compensation (*Betreuungsgeld*) since they do not benefit from public child care. Rønsen (2009) evaluated a similar bill in Norway and found that it had a large negative effect on women's labor supply.

In this chapter, I investigate German mothers' experiences and perceptions about motherhood and employment given this shifting policy landscape. Understanding how women grapple with work and family decisions in a context undergoing dramatic legal change helps uncover cultural, political, and economic assumptions embedded in these laws about the value of women in society—both where women feel they belong and what they deserve, and where they perceive the state feels they belong and what they deserve. This analysis provides new empirical and theoretical insights for American scholars calling for similar work-family policy transformations on this side of the Atlantic. I demonstrate how this reform process impacts middle-income mothers "on the ground" in their day-to-day lives.

Methods

The data for this chapter are based on semi-structured interviews with 26 working mothers conducted in 2011 and 2012 in the western German cities of Munich, Stuttgart, and Heilbronn. The data are part of a larger interview study on the experiences of 135 working mothers in Germany, Sweden, Italy, and the United States. I focus on mothers because across industrialized countries, they complete the majority of families' child care and housework and report greater work-family conflict than men. They also use work-family policies more often than fathers, and policies have long targeted women rather than men (Blair-Loy and Wharton 2002; Dilworth 2004; Gornick and Meyers 2003; Hill 2005; Hook 2006; Jacobs and Gerson 2004; Lewis 2009).

I interviewed middle-class mothers. I used a multidimensional evaluation to filter and classify respondents as middle-class using women's education, occupation, personal income, household income, lifestyle, and self-reported social class. My respondents were relatively privileged: most women had the sorts of resources that make work-family balance easier to achieve than for poorer women. Most cohabited with a partner, owned a car, and had a solid job with a stable wage. Their social networks generally possessed greater social and cultural capital—a feature lacking among the networks of the poor (Desmond 2012). The rationale to interview middle-class mothers was threefold. First, the majority of work and family research in the United States also examines white, middle-class couples in professional occupations (Perry-Jenkins, Repetti, and Crouter 2000), making this sample a parallel comparison. Second, studies of "elite" women allow researchers insight into what may be a sort of best-case scenario, given that mothers with high levels of privilege, skills, education, and resources can use this capital to their advantage in managing career success and involved parenthood (Blair-Loy 2003; Stone 2007). Finally, because German laws and policies apply to all citizens, the experiences of my respondents may resonate with other German women across racial/ethnic and class lines, though they likely differ in important ways given their varying social locations. Future research should investigate how women disadvantaged by race, class, sexuality, and migration status perceive these policies.

The mothers in my sample had at least one child currently living at home and were either employed or on maternity leave. Respondents were generally well educated, and they worked in a variety of occupations, including office and administrative support (three), media and communication (three), architecture (one), education (six), community and social services (two), social sciences (three), business/financial operations (two), personal care and service (four), and entertainment (two).

I used my social networks and snowball sampling to identify interview respondents. I began by reaching out to personal contacts in each of the three cities and then employed snowball sampling with multiple informants from different social networks to find additional respondents who met my criteria. Of the 26 respondents, 6 were personal contacts, 8 were organizational connections, and 12 were recruited and interviewed through referrals. This respondent-driven snowball approach attempts to reduce bias by tapping into multiple networks.

Interviews lasted from 40 to 70 minutes (with the average lasting one hour) and were conducted in women's offices and homes as well as in cafés, parks, and restaurants. I constructed the interview schedule to facilitate systematic comparisons among the participants. The schedule contained questions about balancing motherhood with a job, household division of labor, and general views on working mothers. Participants were given an opportunity to bring up other topics not previously discussed during interviews.

Interviews were conducted in English. Roughly 56 percent of Germans report speaking English well enough to have a conversation (European Commission 2006), and the country ranks seventh out of 27 European countries for English proficiency overall. Germany is considered a "high English proficiency workforce" and women generally have better English skills than do men (Education First 2017). As a result, it was not difficult to recruit participants who could speak English with me, particularly among women in middle-income jobs with relatively high levels of education. Again, future studies would benefit by capturing the breadth of experiences for non-English-speaking and low-income mothers, whose work-family conflict is likely magnified compared to that of the participants in my study.

Interviewees ranged in age from 21 to 52, with a median age of 38. Of the women, 18 were married, 1 divorced, 1 separated, 2 single, and 4 were cohabiting. Most mothers had 1 or 2 children (16 were age 5 or younger, 10 were ages 6 to 11, and 7 were age 12 or older). Twenty-three mothers were German. Three were from England, France, and the United States—they were married to German men (one later divorced, and one separated) and raised their children in Germany, lending a helpful perspective as cultural outsiders. The majority of respondents had a bachelor's degree or higher. The women's median annual salary was $31,000 USD.

Because the German state mandated that all mothers take eight weeks of maternity leave and offered paid leave for up to one year at the time interviewees gave birth, all mothers took off two or more months of work after childbirth. With the exception of one woman who left the workforce for 10 years to raise her sons, these mothers took an average leave of eight months. Eighteen women changed their working hours or jobs after returning to work. Of the 26 women, 14 worked flexible hours or had some flexibility in their work schedule. Six mothers used a home office or "flex location" for part of their workweek.

All interviews were digitally recorded and transcribed. They were coded and analyzed using the ATLAS.ti software package. I employed Emerson, Fretz, and Shaw's (2011) qualitative analytic coding strategy. This tactic approaches the analysis as a dialectical, reflexive interplay between theory and data. As unexpected patterns emerged from comparing my data across discrete observations during open coding, I developed new analytic themes and categories during the focused coding stage. Here I discuss the three most prominent themes that surfaced during the interviews and subsequent analyses: guilt as a "raven mother," lack of fulfillment at home, and marginalization at work.

Findings

My interviews detected a great deal of ambivalence on the part of working mothers about their experiences in navigating motherhood and employment. The first section briefly highlights an overarching sense of guilt women feel for defying German cultural ideals of the "good mother" by working outside the home while raising young children. The second and third sections highlight what I refer to as the "gendered double bind" that mothers experience when they try to use work-family policies in a shifting cultural and political landscape (for more on double binds in various gendered contexts, see Bart 1971; Benard and Correll 2010; Correll 2017; Hamilton and Armstrong 2009; Rudman 1998; Rudman et al. 2012; Webber and Williams 2008). I examine how women feel when they take advantage of policies that give them more time at home. Finally, I discuss women's perceptions of their treatment in the workplace amid these changing family policies.

Guilt as a "Raven Mother"

Despite the rise in maternal employment and presence of increasingly family-friendly and gender-egalitarian laws, the women I spoke with sensed substantial hostility directed toward them as working mothers. Western Germans have a special, disparaging word for women who work while their children are infants and toddlers: *Rabenmutter*, or "raven mother." These women "leave their children in an empty nest while they fly away to pursue a career" (Landler 2006). Anja, a mother of two who worked as a personal care aide, explained: "Women are asked to work, to have a career. But if they have children and they work, it's—I don't know if in any other language there is a word like that—they are *Rabenmütter*[2] . . . They are neglecting their children, they are no-good mothers."

All of the women I spoke with expressed familiarity with the term, and none felt free of its stigma. Respondents often raised the topic of raven mothers during interviews, asking, "Have you heard of this word, *Rabenmutter*?" Many reported being explicitly subjected to raven mother criticism by other women when they did not take the full duration of maternity leave time that the German government provided at the time they gave birth. Ilona, a university professor with 8- and 10-year-old sons, explained that she had been castigated for returning to work while her sons were young:

> It's culturally completely accepted that it's better to stay home as a mom, and it's completely culturally not accepted to go away [and work]. I experienced really many problems with other mothers. . . . Expressions like, "Do you really have to work?" "Do you think this is good for your children?" "Do you think that it's OK that they have to be in childcare for that long? Don't you see that they are not developed correctly?" "You are too competitive." . . . It's an open conflict.

Ilona felt stigmatized for working outside the home when she could be on leave. The question "Do you really have to work?" implies that as a woman, she should not work unless she is financially compelled to do so. She confronted the assumption that employment somehow damaged her children and meant that she was "too competitive," a stereotypically masculine trait. Ilona got the message that "good mothers" take the full maternity leave; having a job while raising young children made her a raven mother.

Like Anja and Ilona, Julia said that she confronted the *Rabenmutter* ideology when she enrolled her child in a daycare facility and went back to work as a teacher before the end of the allowable maternity leave:

> They think of you as a bad mother. A mother has to stay home with their kids until they are like 3 or 4 years old and go to the kindergarten. And if they don't, and spend a lot of time at work, in Germany, they are called *Rabenmütter.* . . . You always have to justify yourself. [. . .] "You cannot do this, you are selfish, you are a career whore," they say in Germany.

Julia loved her work: "It never actually occurred to me to leave the job because I liked it too much." Yet she still felt the need to justify to others why she worked outside the home.

The women I spoke with expressed dismay, anger, and guilt at being called raven mothers to their faces, primarily by other women who are stay-at-home mothers. Although nationally representative survey data demonstrate that western Germans report significantly more positive attitudes toward women's employment over the past two decades (Adler and Brayfield 2006; Lee, Alwin, and Tufiş 2007), the middle-income women I interviewed still felt strongly criticized by their peers for not living up to the cultural ideal of a "good mother" because they worked outside the home while their children were small.

This stigma has a cultural parallel in the United States, where middle-class mothers are also expected to devote their full time, energy, and attention to their children regardless of whether they work outside the home. Scholars refer to this ideal as the "family devotion schema" (Blair-Loy 2003) or the "cult of domesticity" (Williams 2000). Although public support for maternal employment is expanding in western Germany alongside policies that try to facilitate women's labor force participation, my interview data indicate that this support has not translated into more perceived respect in the day-to-day lives of working mothers. These middle-income mothers still felt obliged to live up to the ideal of the good mother and perceived that this unrealistic ideal had consequences for them in their home lives and on the job.

Lack of Fulfillment at Home

Several women reported feeling pressured to spend more time at home than they wanted after giving birth. Although some respondents welcomed the time away from work while on leave, others, like Erika, seemed desperate to return to their jobs. Erika was a single mother and high school teacher who took the full three years of maternity leave available to her at the time. During leave, she described feeling disconnected, lonely, and bored:

> I'm not very good with children, I think. I want to get ahead with things—learn things. And to just be forced to do nothing, this was terrible. I always told my sister the first three years was like living in a daze. You are not yourself; you don't have time for yourself. You are just like a machine. . . . It was just so boring and I felt all my brains you know, like not able to think anymore.

Erika did not enjoy her maternity leave and seemed to resent the necessity that she devote all her time and energy toward her child. These feelings spurred her to question her abilities as a mother. Erika told me she had never considered going back to work before the three years of leave were up because, as bad as she felt at home, the reproach she would face if she did return to work felt to her like a worse fate.

Several women explained that they enjoyed their parental leave for a time but found it untenable after a number of months. For Edith, an educational administrator and mother of two, this tipping point occurred after one year following both pregnancies:

> When I stayed at home for two years, in the end, I was very unhappy. And if you are unhappy, you can't listen to the children. You don't want to play with them. . . . After one year, I want to come out to meet other people, don't talk about children. Talking to grown-ups [laughs].

Edith believed that she was a better parent when she worked. The lack of adult talk and disproportionate time spent on domestic tasks made her stir-crazy. Many of my respondents discussed the lack of stimulation, challenge, and fulfillment they felt while on leave. My interviewees, ranging from a retail cashier to an architect, emphasized that the benefits they enjoyed from paid work outside the home were qualitatively different from the benefits they enjoyed from the unpaid work of caring for their young children at home. For this reason, they wanted both to work outside the home for pay and to raise their children.

Each woman's interpretation of how much time she wanted at home was different. Erika could likely have returned to work quite soon after childbirth and been satisfied, while Edith was satisfied at home for one year. The problem for mothers like Erika and Edith arose when they felt *obligated* to remain at home longer than they would have liked. Substantial paid leave may compel mothers to take longer leaves than they want in order to comply with traditional cultural ideologies about good mothering.

With one exception, all the women I spoke with took more parental leave time than their partners. They felt that this uneven division reinforced traditional gender roles in their families. As a result, mothers tended to feel frustrated about their home lives. For example, Ilona (mentioned above) and her husband were both professors and had two sons. When I asked how she and her husband divided family and household responsibilities after her children were born, she laughed: "After birth, everything changed." Ilona explained that they had been together for many years before having children and were emphatic about being equal partners. She and her husband had separate bank accounts, separate bedrooms in addition to their shared room, kept their own last names, and alternated paying for meals at restaurants. They regularly discussed equality and the importance of not having delineated gender roles in their household. Ilona took the bare legal minimum of two months' leave when she had her boys, and her husband did not take any official leave. During and after this short maternity leave, though, Ilona told me with exasperation in her voice, "We have a completely developed role system. I'm the one who's doing everything. I am the one who's cooking, washing clothes, buying clothes, buying shoes. He's the one who's doing the money, the house, the cars." She explained that both she and her husband noticed the drastic change when she began leave, and neither liked the new division of labor. But Ilona said that neither had any idea how this pattern had developed or why it persisted. She expressed irritation and distress at this unexpected pattern.

The unbalanced division of labor that women reported following leave echoes previous research: the birth of a baby affects how parents divide paid work and housework (Neilson and Stanfors 2014; Sayer 2005). Time diary data in the United States shows that even among dual-earner couples who report an egalitarian division of labor prior to having a child, women typically shoulder more of the unpaid work after becoming parents than do men (Yavorsky, Kamp Dush, and Schoppe-Sullivan 2015). Compared to their partners, the women I interviewed said they did more of the laundry, cooked more of the meals, cleaned a larger proportion of the house, did more of the grocery shopping, and completed more of the caring tasks for their children during and after their maternity leave. These mothers were aggravated by what they perceived as sliding backward from a more egalitarian relationship to a more conventional one.

As of 2012, Germany's available 12 months' paid parental leave is formally gender neutral: it can be split evenly between partners (with an extra 2 months available if the leave is shared between parents, totaling 14 months), but according to my respondents, this has rarely happened. While the proportion of children with fathers that use parental leave has increased dramatically in Germany (from 8.8 percent for children born in 2007 to 32 percent for children born in 2013) (OECD 2016), it remains quite uncommon for fathers to share leave time equally with mothers. In my study, one respondent—Birgit—shared the leave time equally with her spouse, while one father took four months, three took two months, and one took six weeks away from work. In two of these six cases, the men who took leave were unemployed when their child was born.

Birgit was a government adviser married to a public relations consultant. They had a two-year-old and six-month-old. Birgit frowned when explaining the logic that she often heard friends and colleagues use to justify their unequal division of leave time and reduced working hours:

> You could also split up seven months the man, seven months the woman. Here in reality, unfortunately, most people split it up 12 months the mother, and 2 months the father. Unfortunately, many fathers don't even take the two months because they say, "Yeah, it's a really good thing [for fathers to take leave] but in *my* job, of course, that's not possible that I stay at home because I'm a project leader. I would have to give away my project if I do that."

My respondents suggested that deference is paid to men's jobs over women's, although both careers can suffer from extended leaves. This dilemma isn't isolated to Germany. Even in countries like Sweden, where gender equality is a strong cultural ideal and an explicit national priority, mothers still take more parental leave than do fathers (though fathers' share is increasing; see Duvander and Johansson 2012; Ferrarini and Duvander 2010).

Fourteen of 26 respondents in western Germany worked fewer than 30 hours per week (two of these women were on maternity leave at the time of our interview, and three more worked longer part-time hours between 30 and 34 hours weekly). Working part time seemed to be a tactic to deter raven mother criticism and alleviate work-family conflict. Edith, who was unhappy after staying home for one year following the birth of her two children (now ages five and seven), had a master's in civil engineering and worked as an educational administrator part time when we spoke. Although Edith wanted to return to work after one year, she instead stayed at home for two years, returning to work part time afterward. She explained to me that mothers who worked long hours could not be good parents. This view may have shaped her own decisions about work and family life: Edith worked 20 hours per week and was overqualified for her job given her education, but her part-time schedule allowed her to fulfill the cultural definition of a "good mother" who can focus more time on her children.

The German government pays families both a children's allowance (*Kindergeld*) to defray the costs of child rearing, regardless of parents' work status, and a parents' allowance (*Elterngeld*), which funds their parental leave and is based on their previous average net income.

My respondents were critical of the financial offering called *Betreuungs-geld*. In 2013, the German government instituted this small stipend for parents who decide to stay home with their young children instead of enrolling them in publicly subsidized child care. While the money was useful, several interviewees believed that it incentivized women—especially low-income women—to take too much time off from work and stay at home, which disadvantaged them in the workplace and at home.

Nadine, a professor and mother of a three-year-old, explained that in western Germany, these incentives are referred to colloquially as a *Herdprä-mie*, or "stove premium"—the state pays women to stay in the kitchen:

> You should know about in Germany, we have the so-called *Herdprämie* [laughs]. That's not the technical term. . . . And I think that was the worst decision ever! . . . [Because] the people tend to stay at home this time and for me, one year out of a job is too long. I don't understand why they put that in place. Of course it's comfortable . . . and you are out of the game after a year. And the state has given an incentive to you that you do that. And that's something I don't really understand. . . . It is backwards.

This cash allowance encourages the "primary caregiver," almost always a woman, to stay at home. Parental allowance (*Elterngeld*) is meant to be a wage replacement, so it is only awarded if a parent takes leave time after childbirth.

Women also explained that because of *Elterngeld*, mothers who decided to work after the mandatory two months spent at home following childbirth could end up financially worse off than if they remained at home. Nadine lamented:

> But the *Elterngeld*, I didn't get it because I was back at work then, and I didn't get a lot more [money] at work. So I was working, paying for the childcare, paying for the commuting, but didn't get the money from the state when I would have stayed at home. I would have had *more* money not working. And that's counterproductive, in my perspective. . . . It was less money than if I would have stayed at home.

Research has found that cash allowance benefits depress women's labor force participation, while subsidies for child care increase it (OECD 2004). My respondents felt strongly that increasing the availability of high-quality affordable child care would be more effective at decreasing their stress than giving families cash allowances that seemed to encourage women to stay home with their young ones. The German government, taking up the call in an effort to increase women's employment, has worked to create hundreds of thousands of new child care spaces in the past decade. As of 2013, children under age three have a legal right to a spot in a daycare facility (Ziefle and Gangl 2014).

Women's comments suggest that the increase in child care availability is a necessary but insufficient solution to the raven mother stigma that mothers perceive for enrolling their young children in daycare. These spaces need to be not only *widely available* but also more *widely used*. Perhaps as cultural attitudes about "good mothers" catch up to the more progressive policy options, women who enroll their young children in daycare will feel less stigma attached to their decision. In an effort to avoid this ostracism, a number of my respondents stayed home longer than they would have liked and explained feeling unhappy as a result.

Marginalization at Work

Family policies can sometimes exacerbate gender inequality in the workplace (Mandel and Semyonov 2005). In this study, over half the women reported feeling that using maternity leave and job protection policies damaged their standing at work. Ilona is one example. Prior to becoming a professor, she had been a departmental director for a multimedia company and found out that the CEO was plotting to fire her after she announced her pregnancy. Although she expressed her intention of living up to the "ideal worker" image—one unencumbered by family commitments (Acker 1990)—at her highly demanding job by taking only the required two months' leave, her boss secretly consulted with a lawyer to find a legal loophole so she could be fired. An office secretary informed Ilona of this plan. When she angrily confronted her supervisor, he implored, "You have to understand us." He explained that Ilona was of little use to the company now and was a financial drain, given the legal mandates that the company subsidize her leave and keep her job secure.

Ilona's boss invoked maternity leave and job security policies meant to protect working mothers to make her feel guilty for getting pregnant. This event incited her to quit, and she eventually sought a position in academia, which she considered more welcoming to working mothers, albeit at half the salary. Julia similarly described her boss' reaction to her pregnancy:

> They put on a lot of stress and make you feel guilty sometimes because it's like, "We have to pay for you although you cannot work, and now we have to pay two people for the same job because of all these regulations." And it sometimes makes you feel a bit bad, even if it's not meant like that. Actually I was the one taking care of it because they didn't know anything about like, "What shall we do now?" . . . I proposed a plan and I got a replacement and I told my replacement how to do my job.

A number of women explained that their supervisors had expressed displeasure at what they perceived to be inconvenient, expensive accommodations resulting from women's legal right to paid maternity leave and job security.

Supervisors often seem displeased about having to accommodate respondents' absence or to find, hire, and train a temporary replacement. This burden often got displaced onto women in a kind of "you created the problem, so it's your job to solve it" mentality, particularly because men rarely used parental leave time. This dilemma was especially apparent in the experiences of 9 of the 26 women I interviewed, because they were the first women to become mothers in their departments—and sometimes their entire companies.

Birgit believed that her boss might have seen maternity leave as a useful way to rid the workplace of "incapable" pregnant women and mothers of young children:

> I heard from a colleague when I was pregnant again . . . that [my boss] said, "Frau Mezger is not so capable anymore now that she is pregnant." And that is a thing that irritated me a lot because I didn't miss work a single day because of my pregnancy. . . . I think sometimes he thought, "These women with their problems and their children. Why don't they just stay at home for three years? Then they wouldn't make me so much problems." . . . I think he thinks it's a little bit irritating that he has so many women there getting pregnant all the time.

Birgit's impressions from her boss's behavior and the conversation repeated to her by the receptionist shaped her understanding of how she was viewed at work. This theme of overcompensation came up frequently among the women I interviewed. They tried to counter prejudice and discrimination spurred by their leave time by demonstrating their proficiency at work by living up to the ideal worker model (Acker 1990) and work devotion schema (Blair-Loy 2003), the cultural dictate that demands that workers dedicate undivided attention to their jobs.

In addition to leave time, several respondents said they believed some employers interpreted a mother working part time as a sign of disinterest or lack of commitment or ability. Simone, a researcher and cohabiting mother of a one-year-old, perceived that women's part-time schedules factor into supervisors' decisions about whom to recruit and mentor along the career ladder:

> I think when you are in part time, they interpret this in terms of, "She does not want to develop further. She is not committed enough." . . . I think the tendency is that . . . when you step into the world of part-time jobs, that might be decisive for your future development. . . . I don't think it's right. I'm not supporting these ideas that are dominant as it seems to me in personal recruitment . . . where the decisions are taken about whom to foster and whom to put aside.

Simone's observation highlights another way that women can be disadvantaged at work compared to men: women may be more likely to be overlooked or dropped by supervisors because their reduced hours are interpreted as their primary devotion to their children rather than to their jobs. Unlike being a father, being a mother is viewed as incompatible with being an ideal worker, because a mother is presumed to be encumbered by family and unavailable to commit herself fully to work (Blair-Loy 2003).

Several women explained their decision to work full time by pointing to the disadvantages they saw for women with part-time schedules. Both Ilona and Annette recognized that it hindered women's job prospects, encouraged them to do more housework, and highlighted women's status as mothers and less desirable job candidates in the eyes of employers (Webber and Williams 2007, 2008). They were both professors and adamantly encouraged their women students to keep up their labor continuity and not reduce their hours, even though they admitted that the option to work part time could be appealing.

Adelheid was grateful that her boss allowed her a flexible schedule. She could select her own working hours and shift them weekly as needed after she gave birth to her daughter and returned from leave. However, Adelheid acknowledged regretfully that the fluctuations in her hours and intermittent time spent at the office had damaged her career prospects. While a flexible schedule enabled her to spend more time with her two-year-old, it hurt her career trajectory in the long run:

> You have to expect less from work and from the position you can get, and from the salary you can get. . . . It wasn't clear to me that it takes such a long time altogether [to raise children]—around 15 or 16 years that I have to work part time until I could change to full time again. But in my case it's far too late then, because then, I'm 55. Then I have to be happy if I can stay in this agency with all these young people and that they don't ask me to sit downstairs in the cellar where nobody can see me because I'm an old woman. It's really like that. So it's over. It sounds horrible, but that's the truth. It's over.

Adelheid seemed remorseful and frustrated that her job prospects were less promising after she had a child. The ability to adjust her hours meant that she could play a more active role in her daughter's life, but that meant that she played a less active role at work, too. This fluctuation in hours over the years might have meant that Adelheid was less able to keep up with new developments at work, especially because her consulting job is in the field of digital media, where innovation happens rapidly. She worried about getting passed by in knowledge and expertise by younger workers who could relegate her to the proverbial "cellar."

To counter this stigma associated with Adelheid's family status and use of a flexible schedule, she put considerable effort into managing others' impressions of her by demonstrating her proficiency and downplaying her status as a mother. Her company employed lots of women who were mothers, and her boss was firm in his support of them. Despite their numbers, Adelheid still believed that people view women who are mothers as less capable than other employees:

> We don't talk about children. . . . We want to be part of this agency, and we work there, and we want to do a good job. And if we talked about our children all the time, everybody will always say, "Ah, the mothers. We have just the mothers." I have a quite high position there, and I can't have this image as a mother all the time because I'm quite hard and quite tough. So it's not going together. We don't do that.

In spite of mothers' substantial numerical presence, Adelheid acknowledged that motherhood and expertise at work were considered incompatible. Implicit in her comment that she was "quite hard and quite tough" is the cultural belief that mothers are soft and weak: these are undesirable traits in the workplace. Therefore, Adelheid downplayed the fact that she was a mother in order to demonstrate to others that she possessed the masculine traits of someone deserving of "a quite high position." The fact that she sometimes worked full time—living up to the standard of the ideal worker—and sometimes part time meant that she had to perform additional labor to compensate for her use of a purportedly family-friendly policy.

While policies like telecommuting were available to many respondents, not all women used them, because they were aware of the consequences of putting in less face time in the office and worried about being put on the "mommy track." Birgit had a home office but used it only in unusual circumstances, because she feared that coworkers would think she was not committed even though she worked 30 hours a week:

> I didn't use it so much because for me . . . I felt more comfortable most often to go to the actual [office] because there I have my colleagues around, I can go for a coffee with them, I can be more "seen." Because it can be a problem if you work part time and then, three of these days, you sit at home. Then maybe people feel like, "Uh, is she really working? Is she really there?"

Similarly, Sonia (a married journalist and mother of two) realized that only after beginning a flexible schedule, her time in the office rarely overlapped with her supervisor's. He scheduled meetings when she had already gone home for the day and could not attend, which she worried sent the message to her colleagues that she was disengaged and unavailable.

My interviews show that despite women's hard work, commitment, and enthusiasm for their jobs, the presence of seemingly progressive work-family policies does not necessarily, or does not yet, advantage them in the workplace. Women reported feeling marked as inferior at work for being mothers, so women therefore felt ambivalent about using work-family policy because it was potentially fraught with trouble for them on the job.

Discussion

This study answers a neglected but important question: how women living in a country that recently implemented more progressive work-family policy supports experience these policies "on the ground" in their day-to-day lives at home and in the workplace. Are progressive work-family policies a panacea that we should import to the United States? Although popular media and many feminist scholars advocate for European-style social policies here, this article draws on interview data from western Germany in 2011–2012 to raise concerns about the promise and the limits of work-family policy given its interaction with cultural attitudes. By doing so, I underscore the need for more nuance in popular media accounts of these policies across European countries that considers the cultural context in which women use policies (Budig, Misra, and Boeckmann 2012, 2016).

Although today's legal framework in Germany tends to encourage women to work and have children and relies on their labor in the paid workforce and at home, the 26 middle-income mothers I interviewed felt devalued and criticized in both spheres. I attribute mothers' reported conflict to this debilitating gendered double bind. My findings indicate that on the one hand, working mothers felt stigmatized for their family status at work: women's policy use highlighted their inability to enact an ideal worker identity that remained implicitly coded as male. On the other hand, women also felt stigmatized for being employed outside the home while raising young children; returning to their jobs and shortening their maternity leave incurred the "raven mother" slur—someone who left her nest and deserted her offspring to pursue a career. The women I spoke with expressed little desire to stay at home for years on end and great interest in working for pay, yet working mothers also described barriers to their occupational success despite (and sometimes because of) the available policies. This gendered double bind is not a new finding, nor specific to Germany. In 1971, American feminist sociologist Pauline Bart wrote that women's "personal experiences are *data*. Because of sexism women are in a double bind—a no win situation . . . damned if she does and damned if she doesn't" (734–735).

Although a woman in western Germany may not lose her job for leaving work to care for a sick child, thanks to work-family policy, this fact does not disrupt the cultural assumption that it continues to be primarily women's job to tend to children (a cultural expectation that transcends national borders; see Gornick and Meyers 2003). My respondents explained how their marriages slid from a more egalitarian to a more traditional dynamic once they gave birth and took maternity leave (Neilson and Stanfors 2014; Sayer 2005; Yavorsky, Kamp Dush, and Schoppe-Sullivan 2015). Women recounted their use of flexible hours or a home office as helpful but realized that they rarely saw their bosses. Mothers occasionally took advantage of the legal right to reduce their working hours after returning from maternity leave and, as we've seen, later learned that their bosses saw them as less capable and committed to their jobs. Some women decided to take longer leave instead of returning to work, because the cash allowance matched their normal salaries. In these regards, the western German mothers I interviewed expressed frustration at their inability to harmonize their careers with their domestic commitments using the work-family policies available to them, even with more recent policies that seem progressive in supporting women's dual responsibilities. The stories of my research participants make clear that the unintended consequences that scholars have identified with policies such as lengthy maternity leaves and part-time work schedules, as well as the lag time between policy implementation and attitudinal change, have real, negative consequences in western German mothers' day-to-day lives.

As American work-family scholars have argued for decades, the case remains that the right to job security as a parent, paid time to care for a newborn, the availability of high-quality affordable child care, the ability to take paid time off when a worker or her/his child is sick, and the guarantee of paid vacation are crucial, necessary entitlements to both women and men who are parents. The frequent media reports about American mothers suffering without these policies ring true in this regard. However, my findings suggest that work-family policies are limited in their ability to help women achieve successful careers and contented home lives if they are offered to and used disproportionately by women and not men. In other words, these policies need to be enacted in a cultural environment supportive of gender equality.

In the daily lives of my respondents, German policies do not yet disrupt the gender hierarchy between women and men. The current system maintains the power and privileges afforded to men across the home and work spheres. Indeed, scholars have documented the reality that Germany's policy goals have transformed more explicitly to stimulate changes in women's behavior but not men's (Lewis et al. 2008). Yet previous research shows that national context influences fathers' unpaid work behaviors (Hook 2006). Thus, I argue that a renewed conversation focusing on gender equality policy and policy instruments aimed at behavioral change on the part of men must go hand in hand with work-family policy debates in order to improve the social and economic climate for women.

The western German mothers in my study expressed dissatisfaction with the state's available laws and their ability to use them without fear of stigma. I suggest that this dissatisfaction stems from the German state's enforcement of a gender regime through its legal structure that is still pro-mother but not yet pro-equality. As in the United States, competing political groups in Germany have all shaped the current work-family policy landscape. The disparate voices around the table (European Union mandates, feminist groups, conservative parties, progressive parties, and religious groups, among others) seem to have led to a policy tug-of-war, with working mothers stuck in the middle.

Although German work-family policies seem to be mostly forging ahead toward a more social democratic model of gender equality and dual-earner families like in Scandinavia, this shift has not created consistent positive changes for working mothers on the ground in the decade or so since their inception. My interviews suggest that these tectonic shifts in the policy landscape leave working mothers with little stable ground upon which to stand: although motherhood and employment are ostensibly compatible in this new model (as the EU, feminist groups, and progressive political parties have pushed for), this study makes clear that this change on the policy level has not trickled down into consistent, widespread acceptance and support of women's dual work and family responsibilities in western Germany's cultural landscape. Furthermore, mixed signals evident in contradictory policy innovations do not create the sort of resounding, fundamental, positive change for which many sociologists might hope for mothers.

The "cultural lag" (Ogburn 1957; Swidler 1986) that occurs when implementing progressive, gender-egalitarian work-family policies in a traditional cultural environment where attitudes are resistant to change helps explain my respondents' guilt and stress. Cultural transformation tends to happen more slowly than changes to material conditions such as policy reforms. This period of incongruence may be inevitable. Nevertheless, a one-size-fits-all policy package (e.g., primarily supporting male breadwinner families; primarily supporting dual-earner families) is unlikely to suit all mothers and families, as evidenced in my interviews. Better would be a varied mix of work-family policies that allows individuals more agency in choosing the arrangement of their work and family lives. With more heterogeneity in policy offerings at the structural level, we may see less rigid gender expectations and more expansive cultural support of a variety of women's decisions about combining employment and motherhood at the interactional level. Indeed, feminist theories of social change suggest that structural changes to oppressive gender systems through policy may promote changes at the interactional level (Chafetz 1990; Deutsch 2007; Ridgeway and Correll 2000) that can, over time, "accumulate to produce gender equality" (Deutsch 2007, 118).

Much U.S. scholarship posits work-family policy innovation as the most promising tool to promote work-family reconciliation and gender equality (e.g., Albiston et al. 2012), but I suggest that realistically, the lack of consensus among competing political factions means that whatever policy innovations are achieved will have to be a compromise. Feminist voices are likely to compete heavily against other political interests that also shape the policy landscape, meaning that modest innovations are most plausible in an American context. The process of "'unlearning' old policies . . . and learning new ones" (Mahon 2006, 179), as Germany is currently undergoing, can be a rocky road for mothers as legal changes take time to become culturally embedded.

Notes

1. Former East Germany has a very different history. Mothers' employment was quasi-compulsory during the country's time as a socialist welfare state from 1949 to 1990 (Matysiak and Steinmetz 2008). The GDR was explicitly pronatalist, with universal childcare and generous labor-oriented maternity benefits. After reunification, the GDR had to adopt West Germany's legal infrastructure. Although their policies converged, remnants of the GDR's socialist legacy live on: women work at higher rates in former East Germany than in western Germany (especially mothers of young children), gendered cultural norms are more egalitarian, and there are still more public daycares (Lee, Alwin, and Tufiş 2007; Rosenfeld, Trappe, and Gornick 2004). See Collins (forthcoming) for an investigation of mothers' daily lived experiences with work-family policy in former East Germany.

2. In the plural form, *u* changes to *ü*.

References

Acker, Joan. 1990. "Hierarchies, Jobs, Bodies: A Theory of Gendered Organizations." *Gender & Society* 4: 139–58.

Adler, Marina A., and April Brayfield. 1997. "Women's Work Values in Unified Germany: Regional Differences as Remnants of the Past." *Work and Occupations* 24: 245–66.

Adler, Marina A., and April Brayfield. 2006. "Gender Regimes and Cultures of Care: Public Support for Maternal Employment in Germany and the United States." *Marriage & Family Review* 39 (3–4): 229–53.

Albiston, Catherine, Shelley Correll, Traci Tucker, and Christina Stevens. 2012. "Laws, Norms, and the Caretaker Penalty." Presented at the European Group for Organizational Studies, Helsinki, Finals, July 2–7, 2012.

Bacci, Massimo Livi. 2013. "Low Fertility in Historical Perspective." *Population and Development Review* 38: 72–82.

Bart, Pauline B. 1971. "Sexism and Social Science: From the Gilded Cage to the Iron Cage, or, the Perils of Pauline." *Journal of Marriage and Family* 33 (4): 734–45.

Benard, Stephen, and Shelley J. Correll. 2010. "Normative Discrimination and the Motherhood Penalty." *Gender & Society* 24 (5): 616–46.

Blair-Loy, M. 2003. *Competing Devotions: Career and Family among Women Executives.* Cambridge, MA: Harvard University Press.

Blair-Loy, M., and A. S. Wharton. 2002. "Employees' Use of Work-Family Policies and the Workplace Social Context." *Social Forces* 80 (3): 813–45.

Budig, Michelle J., Joya Misra, and Irene Boeckmann. 2012. "The Motherhood Penalty in Cross-National Perspective: The Importance of Work-Family Policies and Cultural Attitudes. *Social Politics* 19: 163–93.

Budig, Michelle J., Joya Misra, and Irene Boeckmann. 2016. "Work-Family Policy Trade-Offs for Mothers? Unpacking the Cross-National Variation in Motherhood Earnings Penalties." *Work and Occupations* 43 (2): 119–77.

Chafetz, Janet. 1990. *Gender Equity: An Integrated Theory of Stability and Change.* Newbury Park, CA: Sage.

Collins, Caitlyn. 2019. *Making Motherhood Work: How Women Manage Careers and Caregiving.* Princeton, NJ: Princeton University Press.

Cooke, Lynn Prince. 2007. "Persistent Policy Effects on the Division of Domestic Tasks in Reunified Germany." *Journal of Marriage and Family* 69: 930–50.

Correll, Shelley J. 2017. "SWS 2016 Feminist Lecture: Reducing Gender Biases in Modern Workplaces: A Small Wins Approach to Organizational Change." *Gender & Society* 31 (6): 725–50.

Damaske, Sarah. 2011. *For the Family? How Class and Gender Shape Women's Work.* New York: Oxford University Press.

Desmond, Matthew. 2012. "Disposable Ties and the Urban Poor." *American Journal of Sociology* 117 (5): 1295–335.

Deutsch, Francine M. 2007. "Undoing Gender." *Gender & Society* 21 (1): 106–27.

Dilworth, Jennie E. Long. 2004. "Predictors of Negative Spillover from Family to Work." *Journal of Family Issues* 25 (2): 241–61.

Duvander, Ann-Zofie, and Mats Johansson. 2012. "What Are the Effects of Reforms Promoting Fathers' Parental Leave Use?" *Journal of European Social Policy* 22 (3): 319–30.

Education First. 2017. *English Proficiency Index.* Accessed December 3. http://www.ef.edu/epi.

Emerson, Robert M., Rachel I. Fretz, and Linda L. Shaw. 2011. *Writing Ethnographic Fieldnotes.* 2nd ed. Chicago: University of Chicago Press.

Esping-Andersen, Gøsta. 1990. *The Three Worlds of Welfare Capitalism.* Hoboken, NJ: John Wiley & Sons.

Esping-Andersen, Gøsta. 2002. *Why We Need a New Welfare State.* Oxford: Oxford University Press.

Esping-Andersen, Gøsta. 2009. *Incomplete Revolution: Adapting Welfare States to Women's New Roles.* Cambridge, UK: Polity Press.

European Commission. 2006. "Europeans and Their Languages." Special Eurobarometer. ec.europa.eu/public_opinion/archives/ebs/ebs_243_ en.pdf.

Eurostat. 2014. "Labour Market and Labour Force Survey [LFS] Statistics Explained." http://ec.europa.eu/eurostat/statistics-explained/index.php /Labour_market_and_Labour_force_survey_(LFS)_statistics.

Ferrarini, Tommy, and Ann-Zofie Duvander. 2010. "Earner-Carer Model at the Crossroads: Reforms and Outcomes of Sweden's Family Policy in Comparative Perspective." *International Journal of Health Services* 40 (3): 373–98.

Ferree, Myra Marx. 2012. *Varieties of Feminism: German Gender Politics in Global Perspective.* Stanford, CA: Stanford University Press.

Fleckenstein, Timo, and Soohyun Christine Lee. 2014. "The Politics of Postindustrial Social Policy: Family Policy Reforms in Britain, Germany, South Korea, and Sweden." *Comparative Political Studies* 47 (4): 601–30.

Gangl, Markus, and Andrea Ziefle. 2009. "Motherhood, Labor Force Behavior, and Women's Careers: An Empirical Assessment of the Wage Penalty for Motherhood in Britain, Germany, and the United States." *Demography* 46 (2): 341–69.

Glass, Jennifer. 2009. "Work-Life Policies: Future Directions for Research." In *Work Life Policies (Urban Institute),* edited by Ann C. Crouter and Alan Booth, 231–50. Washington, D.C.: The Urban Institute.

Glass, Jennifer L., Robin W. Simon, and Matthew A. Andersson. 2016. "Parenthood and Happiness: Effects of Work-Family Reconciliation Policies in 22 OECD Countries." *American Journal of Sociology* 122 (3): 886–929.

Gornick, Janet C., and Marcia K. Meyers. 2003. *Families That Work: Policies for Reconciling Parenthood and Employment.* New York: Russell Sage.

Gornick, Janet C., and Marcia K. Meyers. 2004. "More Alike Than Different: Revisiting the Long-Term Prospects for Developing 'European-Style' Work/Family Policies in the United States." *Journal of Comparative Policy Analysis: Research and Practice* 6 (3): 251–73.

Hamilton, Laura, and Elizabeth A. Armstrong. 2009. "Gendered Sexuality in Young Adulthood: Double Binds and Flawed Options." *Gender & Society* 23 (5): 589–616.

Hill, E. Jeffrey. 2005. "Work-Family Facilitation and Conflict, Working Fathers and Mothers, Work-Family Stressors and Support." *Journal of Family Issues* 26 (6): 793–819.

Hochschild, Arlie Russell. 1989. *The Second Shift.* New York: Viking.

Hochschild, Arlie Russell. 1997. *The Time Bind: When Work Becomes Home and Home Becomes Work.* New York: Metropolitan Books.

Holst, Elke, and Anna Wieber. 2014. "Eastern Germany Ahead in Employment of Women." *DIW Economic Bulletin* 11. https://www.diw.de/documents /publikationen/73/diw_01.c.491960.de/diw_econ_bull_2014-11-5.pdf.

Hook, Jennifer L. 2006. "Care in Context: Men's Unpaid Work in 20 Countries, 1965–2003." *American Sociological Review* 71 (4): 639–60.

Hummelsheim, Dina, and Jochen Hirschle. 2010. "Mothers' Employment: Cultural Imprint or Institutional Governance? Belgium, West and East Germany in Comparison." *European Societies* 12 (3): 339–66.

Jacobs, Jerry A., and Kathleen Gerson. 2004. *The Time Divide: Work, Family, and Gender Inequality.* Cambridge, MA: Harvard University Press.

Kremer, Monique. 2007. *How Welfare States Care: Culture, Gender and Parenting in Europe.* Amsterdam: Amsterdam University Press.

Landler, Mark. 2006. "Quoth the Raven: I Bake Cookies, Too." *The New York Times Online,* April 23.

Lee, Kristen S., Duane F. Alwin, and Paula A. Tufiş. 2007. "Beliefs about Women's Labour in the Reunified Germany, 1991–2004." *European Sociological Review* 23 (4): 487–503.

Lewin-Epstein, Noah, Haya Stier, and Michael Braun. 2006. "The Division of Household Labor in Germany and Israel." *Journal of Marriage and Family* 68 (5): 1147–64.

Lewis, Jane. 1993. *Women and Social Policies in Europe: Work, Family and the State.* Cheltenham, UK: Edward Elgar.

Lewis, Jane. 2009. *Work-Family Balance, Gender, and Policy.* Cheltenham, UK: Edward Elgar.

Lewis, Jane, Trudie Knijn, C. Martin, and Ilona Ostner. 2008. "Patterns of Development in Work/Family Reconciliation Policies for Parents in France, Germany, the Netherlands, and the UK in the 2000s." *Social Politics: International Studies in Gender, State & Society* 15 (3): 261–86.

Mahon, Rianne. 2006. "The OECD and the Work/Family Reconciliation Agenda: Competing Frames." In *Children, Changing Families, and Welfare States,* edited by Jane Lewis, 173–200. Cheltenham, UK: Edward Elgar.

Mandel, Hadas, and Moshe Semyonov. 2005. "Family Policies, Wage Structures, and Gender Gaps: Sources of Earnings Inequality in 20 Countries." *American Sociological Review* 70: 949–67.

Matysiak, Anna, and Stephanie Steinmetz. 2008. "Finding Their Way? Female Employment Patterns in West Germany, East Germany, and Poland." *European Sociological Review* 24 (3): 331–45.

McDonald, Peter. 1997. "Gender Equity, Social Institutions, and the Future of Fertility. UNESCO.

Neilson, Jeffrey, and Maria Stanfors. 2014. "It's about Time! Gender, Parenthood, and Household Divisions of Labor under Different Welfare Regimes." *Journal of Family Issues* 35 (8): 1066–88.

OECD. 2004. "Female Labour Force Participation: Past Trends and Main Determinants in OECD Countries." Paris: OECD. https://www.oecd.org/eco/labour/31743836.pdf.

OECD. 2016. "PF2.2: Use of Childbirth-Related Leave by Mothers and Fathers." Paris: OECD. https://www.oecd.org/els/family/PF2-2-Use-childbirth-leave.pdf.

OECD. 2017. *The Pursuit of Gender Equality: An Uphill Battle.* Paris: OECD. http://dx.doi.org/10.1787/9789264281318-en.

Ogburn, William F. 1922. *Social Change with Respect to Culture and Original Nature.* New York: BW Huebsch.

Ogburn, William F. 1957. "Cultural Lag as Theory." *Sociology and Social Research* 41: 167–74.

Orloff, Ann Shola. 1993. "Gender and the Social Rights of Citizenship: The Comparative Analysis of Gender Relations and Welfare States." *American Sociological Review* 58 (3): 308–23.

Ostner, Ilona. 2010. "Farewell to the Family as We Know It: Family Policy Change in Germany." *German Policy Studies* 6 (1): 211–44.

Ostner, Ilona, Michael Reif, Hannu Turba, and Christoff Schmitt. 2003. "Family Policies in Germany." Third report for the project Welfare Policy and Employment in the Context of Family Change. York, UK: Social Policy Research Unit.

Padamsee, Tasleem J. 2009. "Culture in Connection: Re-Contextualizing Ideational Processes in the Analysis of Policy Development." *Social Politics* 16 (4): 413–45.

Pedulla, David S., and Sarah Thébaud. 2015. "Can We Finish the Revolution? Gender, Work-Family Ideals, and Institutional Constraint." *American Sociological Review* 80 (1): 116–39.

Perry-Jenkins, Maureen, Rena L. Repetti, and Ann C. Crouter. 2000. "Work and Family in the 1990s." *Journal of Marriage and Family* 62 (4): 981–98.

Pettit, Becky, and Jennifer L. Hook. 2009. *Gendered Tradeoffs: Family, Social Policy, and Inequality in Twenty-One Countries.* New York: Russell Sage.

Pfau-Effinger, Birgit, and Maike Smidt. 2011. "Differences in Women's Employment Patterns and Family Policies: Eastern and Western Germany." *Community, Work & Family* 14 (2): 217–32.

Ridgeway, Cecilia L., and Shelley J. Correll. 2000. "Utopian Visions: Engaged Sociologies for the 21st Century." *Contemporary Sociology* 29: 110–20.

Rindfuss, Ronald R., David K. Guilkey, S. Philip Morgan, and Øystein Kravdal. 2010. "Child-Care Availability and Fertility in Norway." *Population and Development Review* 36 (4): 725–48.

Rønsen, Marit. 2009. "Long-Term Effects of Cash for Childcare on Mothers' Labour Supply." *Labour* 23 (3): 507 –33.

Rosenfeld, Rachel A., Heike Trappe, and Janet C. Gornick. 2004. "Gender and Work in Germany: Before and After Reunification." *Annual Review of Sociology* 30 (1): 103–24.

Rudman, Laurie A. 1998. "Self-Promotion as a Risk Factor for Women: The Costs and Benefits of Counterstereotypical Impression Management." *Journal of Personality and Social Psychology* 74 (3): 629.

Rudman, Laurie A., Corinne A. Moss-Racusin, Julie E. Phelan, and Sanne Nauts. 2012. "Status Incongruity and Backlash Effects: Defending the Gender Hierarchy Motivates Prejudice against Female Leaders." *Journal of Experimental Social Psychology* 48 (1): 165–79.

Sayer, Liana C. 2005. "Gender, Time and Inequality: Trends in Women's and Men's Paid Work, Unpaid Work and Free Time." *Social Forces* 84: 285–304.

Stier, Haya, Noah Lewin-Epstein, and Michael Braun. 2001. "Welfare Regimes, Family-Supportive Policies, and Women's Employment along the Life-Course." *American Journal of Sociology* 106: 1731–60.

Stone, Pamela. 2007. *Opting Out? Why Women Really Quit Careers and Head Home.* Berkeley, CA: University of California Press.

Swidler, Ann. 1986. "Culture in Action: Symbols and Strategies." *American Sociological Review* 51 (2): 273–86.

U.S. Bureau of Labor Statistics. 2011. "Charting International Labor Comparisons of Annual Labor Force Statistics, 2010," 1–11.

Webber, Gretchen, and Christine L. Williams. 2007. "Mothers in 'Good' and 'Bad' Part-Time Jobs: Different Problems, Same Results." *Gender and Society* 22: 752–77.

Webber, Gretchen, and Christine L. Williams. 2008. "Part-Time Work and the Gender Division of Labor." *Qualitative Sociology* 31: 15–36.

Williams, Joan C. 2000. *Unbending Gender: Why Family and Work Conflict and What to Do about It.* Oxford, UK: Oxford University Press.

Yavorsky, Jill E., Claire M. Kamp Dush, and Sarah J. Schoppe-Sullivan. 2015. "The Production of Inequality: The Gender Division of Labor across the Transition to Parenthood." *Journal of Marriage and the Family* 77 (3): 662–79.

Ziefle, Andra, and Markus Gangl. 2014. "Do Women Respond to Changes in Family Policy? A Quasi-Experimental Study of the Duration of Mothers' Employment Interruptions in Germany. *European Sociological Review* 30: 562–81.

CHAPTER EIGHT

Parenthood and Leisure Time Disparities

Liana Sayer

A Google search on "time-crunched parents" returns about 129,000 results, with headlines with titles like "30 Life Tips for Time-Crunched Parents," "Meal Planning Tips for Time-Crunched Parents" and books named *Pressured Parents, Stressed-Out Kids.*[1] The conventional narrative about parents today presents them as desperately juggling the competing responsibilities of work and family while letting go any time for themselves.

Seismic changes in families since the 1960s, particularly the increase in single parent and dual-earner couples, have led to more similar work and family roles for mothers and fathers (Bianchi 2011). Cultural support for shared earning and caring is high, particularly among young adults (Gerson 2010). Although on average, women continue to do more housework and child care than men, and men more paid work than women, prior to parenthood, the gender division of labor is relatively equal (Sayer 2016). Transitions into parenthood, however, move couples toward more gendered roles, with mothers decreasing paid work and increasing housework and child care, and fathers doing the opposite (Grunow, Schulz, and Blossfeld 2012; Stone 2007). Parenting is a profoundly gendered and gendering experience. The "gendering" of parenting is based on cultural beliefs that parental roles are gender specialized: mothering involves tasks and characteristics that society frames as uniquely feminine—like nurturing, good communication, and family devotion—whereas fathering is thought to involve tasks and characteristics that are uniquely masculine, like breadwinning and protection. Over their life course, the specialization of mothers in housework and child care reduces labor force participation, earnings, and opportunities for career advancement, whereas fatherhood increases earnings and has positive influences on career trajectories (Budig and England 2001; Hodges and Budig 2010). Fathers experience other penalties associated with gendered division of labor. Those who take parental leave or prioritize care of children are evaluated less positively by supervisors and peers (Williams 2010). Those who prioritize breadwinning or caregiving have lower quality relationships with spouses and children (Elliott and Umberson 2008). Mothers and fathers still specialize based on gender despite increased similarity in their roles.

Specialized parental roles are associated with leisure inequalities. Since the 1960s, leisure time increased for all adults, including parents (Robinson and Godbey 1999). Today, though, parents have less leisure than nonparents, and mothers, particularly those who are employed full time and have young children, have less leisure than fathers (Bianchi, Robinson, and Milkie 2006; Milkie, Raley, and Bianchi 2009; Sayer 2005). American parents report lower levels of happiness compared with European parents and Americans without children, in part because of the limited support in the United States for work/family policies that would reduce the economic and social costs of parenting (Glass, Simon, and Andersson 2016). Concerns about losing time for oneself and activities with romantic partners and friends is part of the explanation for declines in marriage and increases in childlessness (Blackstone and Stewart 2012; Houseknecht 1978). Hence, parenting remains a persistent fault line in the tricky terrain of gender equality.

Defining leisure is more difficult than it might seem. Most studies define leisure as a residual category consisting of activities that are neither obligatory—like paid work, housework, and child care—nor biologically necessary, like sleep and eating. This definition is problematic, though, because some activities are both obligatory and discretionary. For example, going to a museum with friends is leisure, whereas viewing the same exhibit with young children is a mix of leisure and child care. Feminist leisure researchers have proposed using evaluations of enjoyment and free choice to define leisure, but this too is problematic because some obligatory activities are enjoyable. Hence, although not ideally, most studies measure leisure time as time left over after subtracting obligatory activity time—like paid work, housework, child care, sleeping, and eating.

Theoretically, time and money are the major determinants of leisure. The dominant theories that scholars who investigate parental leisure use are time availability and gender perspectives. Sociological and economic models of time use emphasize trade-offs between employment and leisure, theorizing that individuals with higher returns to paid work will allocate more time to employment, leaving less available for leisure (Coverman 1983; Kimmel and

Connelly 2007). Increased industry competition and job insecurity associated with globalization and downsizing toward the goal of nimble efficiency
have ratcheted up work hours among more highly educated women and men,
exacerbating time constraints and leading to an expanding leisure gap
according to education level (Aguiar and Hurst 2007; Sevilla, Gimenez-
Nadal, and Gershuny 2012). It is not clear, however, how economic changes
might have affected leisure differences between mothers and fathers or if
trends differ by education.

Work and family have long been characterized as greedy institutions that
have become more so due to emergence of the 24/7 economy, the bifurcation
of employment into "good" and "bad" jobs, and changes in context of childrearing (Bianchi et al. 2006; H. B. Presser 2003). The image of overworked
and stressed-out parents who focus most of their time and energy on their
jobs and their children is ubiquitous. This image, however, is partial and limited, because it masks how trends and gender differences in parents' leisure
time are affected by the widening inequality among families associated with
education-differentiated pathways into parenthood. The 1960s-style family
of a breadwinning father and a stay-at-home mother is waning, replaced by a
growing share of dual-earner, married parents and single-earner, single-
parent families (Cohen 2014). More parents today have a college education
compared with those in the 1960s, but over this same period, the timing and
sequencing of marriage and parenthood have diverged according to education. College-educated women and men are more likely to establish themselves in careers with good pay and benefits, and only afterward do they
transition into marriage and parenthood. In contrast, less educated women
and men are more likely to have children outside of marriage, to never marry,
and to experience more employment instability (McLanahan 2004; Musick,
Brand, and Davis 2012). College-educated mothers spend more time in child
care compared with less educated mothers, and some evidence suggests that
educational differences in mothers' child care time have widened since the
1960s (Gracia 2015; Hsin and Felfe 2014).

Cross-sectional studies (studies done with data from one moment in time
rather than longitudinally) document that gender, parental status, and education influence leisure because they affect time in employment, housework, and
child care. Prior to 1985, leisure time did not vary substantially by gender, but
a gender gap emerged in the 1980s. Education gaps in leisure have widened
over the same period. Yet, knowledge about how education affects trends in the
gender gap in parents' leisure is limited, despite the "diverging destinies" of
families by education (McLanahan 2004). To advance understanding of how
inequality among families and between parents is related to leisure time, it is
necessary to document if the gender leisure gap trend varies by education.

It is also necessary to know more about whether trends are dominated by
specific types of leisure and the extent to which leisure with children has

increased. Scholars have interpreted the gender gap in leisure as an emerging indicator of the evolving and resilient ways that the gender division of labor remained a linchpin of gender inequality (Sayer 2005). Disaggregating leisure into categories that reflect distinct opportunities and contexts for social integration and enhancement of physical and cognitive capabilities affords a more nuanced lens on whether the gender gap in leisure is disadvantageous to women. In other words, presenting a more complete picture of what *types* of leisure parents participate in, and how this differs by education, rather than just knowing whether there are group differences in the amount of time spent in leisure activities, will help us better understand contemporary family life.

This chapter provides new information about trends and gender differences in leisure time by examining the quantity and quality of parents' leisure. It considers how trends differ for mothers and fathers and whether the pattern is different for more or less educated parents. The chapter first reviews the dominant theoretical perspectives on gendered leisure before discussing the data and the analytic approach used to investigate parents' leisure trends. Gender differences at each point in time, and how gender gaps are conditioned by educational status, are the focus throughout the chapter.

Background

The time availability hypothesis posits that decisions about paid work affect how much time is "left over" for competing obligatory activities like housework and child care (Coverman and Sheley 1986). Employment status and, for married women and men, spouse employment hours, are typically used as measures of competing time demands. The time availability hypothesis is supported by much empirical research, but the same studies also document robust and persistent influences of ways in which gender exacerbates time constraints (Bianchi et al. 2012; Craig and Mullan 2013). Specifically, longer employment hours are negatively associated with women's and men's time in housework, child care, and leisure, net of other characteristics, but influences are stronger for women than for men (Sayer 2005).

The gender perspective points to the pervasive influence of cultural beliefs and norms about masculinity and femininity that operate throughout society, structuring identities, expectations, and institutions. Investing time in housework, and more so child care, reinforces women's femininity; time in paid work reinforces men's masculinity. Societal and organizational norms cast ideal workers as employees who prioritize their jobs over other responsibilities, with the preferred ideal worker being one who is free from family responsibilities (Acker 2009). Mothers experience a wage and career mobility penalty because of pernicious expectations among coworkers and managers that they are less devoted to their jobs than are fathers (Benard and Correll 2010). Men and women may both have a vested interest in maintaining gendered allocations of paid and unpaid work time because these naturalize and reinforce cultural beliefs about "essential" differences between women and men and also sustain men's greater societal resources and status (Charles and Bradley 2009). Although today younger women and men desire shared breadwinning and caregiving roles, men also continue to prioritize their jobs over their wives' jobs and think of their housework and child care as "helping out" (Gerson 2010). Despite mothers' increased employment and expectations of sustained labor force participation over the life course, mothers more than fathers remain responsible for housework and child care. Although mothers on average have fewer employment hours compared with fathers, they do the bulk of housework and child care and thus have longer combined work time when all obligatory activities are considered (Sayer et al. 2009). The scaffolding undergirding the gender division of paid and unpaid work theoretically should translate into a gender leisure gap favoring men.

Leisure differences between women and men support both time availability and gendered perspectives on time use. Mothers have less and lower-quality leisure than fathers, on average, because of their dual burden of paid work and household labor (Craig and Mullan 2010; Gornick and Meyers 2009; Mattingly and Bianchi 2003; Sayer 2005). Inadequate leisure resulting from mothers' second shift, as well as the third shift of managing complex familial emotional currents stirred up by the first and second shifts (Hochschild 1997), are linked with negative health outcomes, lower-quality relationships, and gender disparities in employment (e.g., Budig and England 2001).

Numerous studies also point to robust influences of education on leisure time and types of leisure. Having a college education is theorized to instill and reinforce characteristics like self-direction, ability to put off immediate gratification, and goal achievement. People with more education exhibit higher levels of self-efficacy, or sense of self control (Ross and Broh 2000). Education thus increases the ability to plan and organize activities and helps orient people toward future goals (C. E. Ross and Wu 1995; Sevilla, Gimenez-Nadal, and Gershuny 2012). Such an orientation has a positive effect on life chances (Mirowsky and Ross 2003; C. Ross and Mirowsky 2013). More educated women and men have less leisure time but devote more of that time to "higher quality" leisure, meaning leisure activities that enhance health (e.g., exercise) and social integration (e.g., socializing with others, volunteering) (Sevilla, Gimenez-Nadal, and Gershuny 2012). However, the research focuses on all women and men and does not examine if these patterns hold among parents. Parents have less leisure than nonparents, and children may constrain types of leisure because they require parents to be at home at specific times, making it more difficult to engage in leisure with others or when leisure facilities are open. Norms of intensive parenting require mothers, and to a lesser extent fathers, to orchestrate children's involvement in enriching extracurricular activities (Lareau and Weininger 2008). This likely imposes additional constraints on leisure time and types of activities that may likely affect the quality of parents' leisure.

Studies of gender leisure inequality have considered how children influence the quantity and quality of leisure. Mothers' leisure is more often interrupted by caregiving responsibilities than fathers, and mothers are more likely than fathers to do leisure activities with children (Craig and Mullan 2013). Fewer studies have examined gender and educational inequalities in leisure done alone, or in specific leisure activities, with most of this small literature limited to considering television time. This is due to the ubiquity of television and the theoretical links between more television time and poor health. Television makes up the majority of leisure time for all adults in the United States, but those with less education, the nonemployed, and racial/ethnic minorities report more television time (Passias, Sayer, and Pepin 2016).

Research that distinguishes types of leisure beyond television viewing is needed to advance understanding of ways in which gender- and education-differentiated leisure patterns may be one mechanism for gendered social and health disadvantage. More highly educated individuals have less leisure time but devote more of their leisure budgets to a diverse range of physically or mentally stimulating leisure experiences such as sports, cultural events like plays and concerts, and leisure socializing with others (Gershuny 2000; Gupta, Sayer, and Cohen 2009). Lower-income and less educated women spend less time in physically active leisure and more time watching television than other women (Crespo et al. 2000; Miller and Brown 2005). Economic constraints may affect time allocation through the financial cost of certain entertainment or cultural activities in public venues (Henderson 1991; Wearing and Wearing 1988). Hence, less educated or low-income individuals may spend more time in family- or home-oriented activities such as watching television. Because less educated mothers and fathers have less discretionary income than other parents, financial constraints likely limit leisure done with others and in public environments. Less educated mothers rely more on public transportation and are more likely to live in neighborhoods that are perceived as dangerous and with fewer recreational and social amenities (Bittman 2002). These factors heighten time and schedule constraints on activities that are done in public spaces. A gendered time availability perspective thus suggests that mothers will have less and lower quality leisure compared with fathers and less educated mothers may be more disadvantaged in access to leisure than more educated mothers.

Data and Measures

I use data from the American Heritage Time Use Study (AHTUS) to investigate trends in the quantity and quality of mothers' and fathers' leisure time. The AHTUS is an online archive and data extraction tool with harmonized data from five historical time diary studies done in 1965, 1975, 1985, 1995, and 1998 and two cross-sections of the American Time Use Study done in 2003 and 2012 (Fisher et al. 2017). The AHTUS is one of three integrated databases that make up the IPUMS Time Use project (see https://www.ipums .org/timeuse.shtml) that is designed to facilitate high-quality time use research by providing access to a broad array of harmonized data in a single system. Using IPUMS-Time Use, researchers can access and analyze time diary data through a web-based system that facilitates the creation of user-defined time use measures and data extracts.

This analysis is based on the five national studies in the AHTUS. The 1965 data are from the Americans' Use of Time Study collected by the Institute for Social Research at the University of Michigan (Converse and Robinson 1980). The study was one of 13 collected through the Multinational Study of Time Use, the first systematic attempt to collect comparable cross-national data on how people spend time (Szalai 1972). The 1975 data are from the first wave of the Time Use in Economic and Social Accounts Study collected by the Institute for Social Research at the University of Michigan (Juster et al. 1979). The 1985 and 1998 data were collected at the University of Maryland from a cross-section of the U.S. adult population (Bianchi, Robinson, and Sayer 2001; Robinson and Godbey 1999). The 2003 and 2012 surveys are from the American Time Use Survey, the first federally administered time diary survey in the United States (Statistics 2015). Respondents ages 15 and over are drawn from the outgoing rotation of the Current Population Survey (CPS) and are representative of the American population.[2]

The historical and contemporary time diary studies were fielded for similar reasons: to collect high-quality, nationally representative data on American adults' daily activities. Respondents in all studies provided a detailed accounting of all activities done over a 24-hour period (the time diary), and demographic and socioeconomic data. The studies differ in sample design and mode of administration, but evidence suggests that these are not associated with the reliability and validity of the data (Juster, Ono, and Stafford 2003; Robinson 1985). The AHTUS creates comparable indicators of individual and household characteristics and time use measures across the surveys to minimize the possibility that trends are affected by minor differences in how activities are coded across the surveys. The analytic sample used in this chapter consists of 9,322 mothers and 6,632 fathers (total n=15,954) ages 18 to 64 with coresidential children under age 18 in the household. All analyses presented are weighted to adjust for survey design, nonresponse, and the ATUS oversample of weekend days. Sample characteristics are shown in Appendix Table 8.3.

Time diary studies have been shown to provide accurate and reliable data on time in daily activities (Juster et al. 2003). Three other approaches are commonly used to collect data on men's and women's time allocations:

"stylized" questions that ask about the usual or typical amount of time spent in an activity over the course of a week or month; an experience sampling method (ESM) where respondents are contacted at predetermined intervals throughout the day and asked to report on activities; and direct observation. ESM and direct observation reduce bias from recall error but are infrequently used because of the large sample and relatively higher cost required for ESM studies and the intrusive, small-n design of direct observation (Juster et al. 2003). Stylized questions generate less accurate data than time diary studies because of bias from recall error, social desirability, and inconsistencies in respondent definition of activities (S. Presser and Stinson 1998; Stinson 1999).

Time diary studies, however, have three disadvantages. First, the U.S. time diary studies are cross-sectional and thus inappropriate for causal analyses. For example, the data can't be used to answer questions about how transitions into and out of relationships and employment influence daily time. Some of the U.S. time diary studies do not collect data on simultaneous activities (e.g., the ATUS) and thus prevent analyses of multitasking. Because women frequently combine leisure with housework or care of children (Bianchi, Robinson, and Milkie 2006), this means that the data presented here likely understate the extent of gender differences in leisure time. Last, although the IPUMS-Time Use data codes activities consistently, it is not possible to distinguish activities that respondents perceive as both obligatory and discretionary. For example, eating is both a physiologically necessary activity that is often a social activity when done with family and friends. Moreover, although coding is consistent across the surveys, it is possible that how mothers and fathers interpret what they are doing has changed over time. For example, parenting today requires investments of substantial time facilitating children's developmental abilities and exposing them to enriching environments, with some of this emphasis coming from ideologies of intensive parenting that emerged in the late 1970s (Lareau 2003). As a result, since 1985, mothers and fathers may be more likely to report children's copresence during an activity compared with parents in 1975 and 1965.

Measures

I analyze five mutually exclusive types of daily leisure, all measured in minutes per day. *Television* consists of time watching television shows and videos (including time watching on a computer, tablet, or phone in the ATUS data). *Cognitive leisure* consists of time reading books and magazines, using a computer for nonwork activities, writing, engaging in conversations, and listening to music. Cognitive leisure activities can take place either inside or outside the home. *Home leisure* consists of socializing with friends (either in own home or the friend's home), games, playing a musical instrument, singing, arts and crafts, hobbies, and relaxing. *Public leisure* includes attending sporting and entertainment events, going to museums or exhibitions, spending time at bars or restaurants and going to parties and receptions. *Active leisure* includes time in sports, exercise, and outdoor activities such as cycling, gardening, and walking dogs. Time in travel activities is excluded because of the ambiguous purpose and meaning of these activities (e.g., they may reflect a mix of social, care work, or household logistics). These categories are based on research that indicates that enjoyment and health and social benefits vary across these types of leisure. For example, respondents rate television lower in enjoyment relative to other types of leisure (Krueger et al. 2009). Television also has a negative correlation with mental health, although studies have not been able to determine if more television reduces mental health or if individuals in poor mental health report more time watching television (Berkman and Glass 2000; Singh-Manoux and Marmot 2005). In contrast, socializing with friends, exercising, and attending cultural or social events are rated as being more enjoyable and have positive correlations with health and social integration (Krueger et al. 2009; Schwarz, Kahneman, and Xu 2009).

To examine leisure quality, I disaggregate time in all leisure and in the five leisure activities by whether each is *done with children* or *alone*. Leisure activities done with children include time when children, but no other adults, are present. Leisure done alone, hereafter referred to as *solo leisure*, is time when no other adults or children are present. The "with whom" data are not available for the 1985 data archived in the AHTUS, and harmonization is not yet complete for the 1998 data; hence, the analyses of solo and with-children leisure compare trends in four years: 1965, 1975, 2003, and 2012. Leisure that is done alone is linked with lower life satisfaction and well-being in quantitative studies, but some qualitative research reports that mothers perceive some solo leisure as "time for themselves" with positive benefits (Craig and Mullan 2013; Krueger et al. 2009; Schwarz, Kahneman, and Xu 2009). Leisure that is shared with children is both enjoyable and more stressful than leisure experienced with adults, because this time blends child care with leisure (Craig and Mullan 2012).

The chapter first discusses trends in average minutes per day in total leisure and the five leisure types. Trends are evaluated for all mothers and fathers before a determination of whether education conditions the trends. The chapter then turns to trends in the average minutes per day in solo leisure and leisure with children. Education is coded into two categories: college degree and less than a college degree. The latter category applies to respondents who attended but did not graduate from high school, those with a high school diploma, and those who attended some college but did not graduate. Sensitivity analyses using education coded into three categories (college degree, high school diploma, and less than a high school education) showed that trends were similar to the two-category measure.

For ease of presentation, descriptive means that represent average minutes per day of the leisure measures are shown in the bar graphs (Figures 8.2 and 8.4) that display gender and education differences in the five leisure activities. The trends are similar using unadjusted and adjusted means. The estimates shown in the tables and remaining graphs (Figures 8.1, 8.3, and 8.5–8.6) are regression-adjusted means, calculated using Stata 15. The regression-adjusted means are the average minutes per day in all leisure, the types of leisure, solo leisure, and leisure with children, after accounting for variation due to mothers' and fathers' employment and marital status, age and number of children, race-ethnicity, and age. These covariates are correlated with time available for leisure. For example, because there are only 24 hours in a day, longer employment hours necessarily reduce leisure time, whereas being married and having younger or more children increases the demand for housework and child care, which also reduce leisure time. Mothers and fathers who are employed, married, and have young children have the longest workdays and the least amount of time for leisure (Milkie, Raley, and Bianchi 2009). Hence, it is necessary to adjust for these factors to have more confidence that associations of gender and education with leisure trends are "real" and not resulting from other characteristics of parents.

Results

Table 8.1 presents the regression-adjusted means of mothers' and fathers' total leisure and the five types of leisure from 1965 to 2012. The trend in total leisure is shown in Figure 8.1, and leisure activity trends are shown in Figure 8.2. Two key findings are notable from the table and figures. First, leisure increased for both mothers and fathers between 1965 and 1975, but the trend diverges by gender after 1975. Mothers' leisure increased by 40 minutes from 1965 to 1975 (from 3 hours and 40 minutes to about 4 hours 20 minutes in 1975), but in 1998 declined by about 20 minutes. Leisure time has been stable for mothers since 1998, clocking in at about 4 hours per day. In contrast, fathers' leisure increased by about 20 minutes between 1965 and 1975 (from 4 hours 30 minutes in 1965 to 4 hours 50 minutes in 1975) and has not changed significantly since 1975. Second, the gender leisure gap declined between 1965 and 1975 but then increased steadily—because of the gender divergence in the leisure trend. Fathers reported about 55 minutes more leisure than mothers in 1965, 35 minutes more in 1975, but 67 minutes more in 2012. Over a week, this difference means that fathers have an additional eight hours of leisure (comparable to a standard paid work shift).

Table 8.1 Adjusted Daily Minutes from OLS Regressions of Parents' Leisure and Leisure Type Trends

	Leisure			TV			Home		
	Mothers	Fathers	Gender Diff	Mothers	Fathers	Gender Diff	Mothers	Fathers	Gender Diff
1965	215.32	269.81	−54.49 ***	62.70	108.77	−46.07 ***	59.72	53.14	6.58
	(9.05)	(9.43)		(6.82)	(7.11)		(5.22)	(5.44)	
1975	254.97	290.30	−35.33 **	107.59	136.50	−28.91 **	62.72	50.29	12.43
	(8.54)	(9.15)		(6.43)	(6.89)		(4.92)	(5.28)	
1985	247.81	295.48	−47.67 ***	111.87	139.11	−27.24 ***	39.57	45.76	−6.19
	(7.30)	(7.78)		(5.50)	(5.86)		(4.21)	(4.48)	
1998	237.94	283.34	−45.4 **	93.96	107.16	−13.2	44.79	62.29	−17.5 ***
	(9.35)	(10.95)		(7.04)	(8.25)		(5.39)	(6.31)	
2003	238.60	294.13	−55.53 ***	110.35	133.14	−22.79 ***	56.09	67.07	−11 ***
	(2.56)	(2.81)		(1.93)	(2.11)		(1.47)	(1.62)	
2012	231.99	298.66	−66.67 ***	112.80	142.83	−30.03 ***	47.89	71.30	−23.4 ***
	(3.35)	(3.68)		(2.52)	(2.77)		(1.93)	(2.12)	

Table 8.1 (continued)

	Cognitive			Active			Public		
	Mothers	Fathers	Gender Diff	Mothers	Fathers	Gender Diff	Mothers	Fathers	Gender Diff
1965	53.36	61.34	−7.98 ^	8.29	17.68	−9.39 ^	31.25	28.87	2.38
	(3.16)	(3.29)		(3.65)	(3.81)		(3.51)	(3.66)	
1975	48.48	56.01	−7.53 ^	18.24	24.22	−5.98	17.93	23.29	−5.36
	(2.98)	(3.19)		(3.45)	(3.69)		(3.31)	(3.55)	
1985	57.27	45.25	12.02 ***	21.64	43.94	−22.3 ***	17.47	21.43	−3.96
	(2.55)	(2.71)		(2.95)	(3.14)		(2.83)	(3.02)	
1998	58.82	49.19	9.63 ^	23.65	39.95	−16.3 **	16.71	24.76	−8.05
	(3.26)	(3.82)		(3.78)	(4.42)		(3.63)	(4.25)	
2003	25.34	28.82	−3.48 *	19.46	37.17	−17.71 ***	27.36	27.93	−0.57
	(0.89)	(0.98)		(1.03)	(1.13)		(0.99)	(1.09)	
2012	24.77	25.76	−0.99	21.84	35.07	−13.23 ***	24.68	23.70	0.98
	(1.17)	(1.28)		(1.35)	(1.49)		(1.30)	(1.43)	

Note: Models include main effects of year and gender and interaction terms of year and gender. Models control for education, employment status, marital status, number of children, presence of children ages four and younger, age, race/ethnicity, and a weekend diary day

^p<.10; *p<.05; **p<.01; ***p<.001

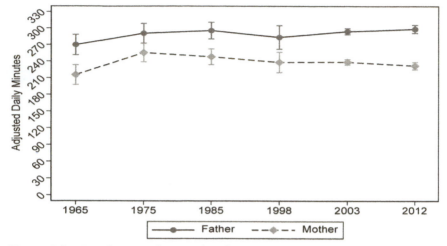

Figure 8.1   Trends in Mothers' and Fathers' Leisure

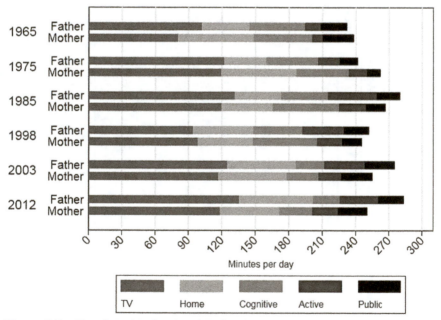

Figure 8.2   Trends in Mothers' and Fathers' Leisure Types

In addition, the mix of leisure activities has shifted, with television consuming a larger share and cognitive leisure a lower share of leisure among all parents. In 1965, mothers' and fathers' leisure time was more evenly distributed across the types of leisure. For example, mothers reported about one hour per day of television, cognitive and in-home leisure (socializing, hobbies, general relaxing), 30 minutes of public leisure (attending events), and less than 10 minutes of active leisure. Fathers reported significantly more TV time, about 1 hour 50 minutes per day, and about twice as much active leisure (18 minutes per day) as mothers. Like mothers, though, fathers also reported about an hour daily in cognitive and in-home leisure, and 30 minutes in public leisure. By 2012, both mothers and fathers reported an increase in television time (about 50 minutes for mothers and 30 minutes for fathers) and a 30-minute decrease in cognitive leisure. Trends from 1965 to 2012 differ by gender for home, public, and active leisure. Mothers' home and public leisure declined significantly, although changes are small (e.g., 12 and 7 minutes respectively), whereas active leisure increased from 8 to 22 minutes. In contrast, fathers' home leisure increased by about 18 minutes, whereas active leisure declined by 17 minutes. Fathers' public leisure time fluctuated around 20 to 30 minutes between 1965 and 2012, but differences are not significant.

In 2012, gender gaps in leisure time were significant for TV, home, and active leisure, but not for cognitive or public leisure. Fathers report about 30 minutes more TV, 23 minutes more home, and 13 minutes more active leisure than mothers. Gender gaps in leisure activities have also changed over time. For example, the gender gap in TV has decreased by about 16 minutes per day since 1965, because the increase in mothers' TV time was greater than the increase among fathers.

Figure 8.3 presents the adjusted trend in mothers' and fathers' total daily leisure by education. Three findings are revealed by the figure. First, regardless of education, fathers have more daily leisure than mothers. Less educated fathers reported between 4.5 hours of leisure in 1965 and 5 hours 15 minutes in 2012; in comparison, less educated mothers reported 3 hours 40 minutes of leisure in 1965 and about 4 hours in 2012. College-educated fathers reported about 4 hours 20 minutes of leisure in 1965 and 4 hours 40 minutes in 2012; in comparison, college-educated mothers reported 3 hours 30 minutes in 1965 and about 3 hours 45 minutes in 2012.

Second, although all fathers enjoy more leisure than mothers, the leisure gender gap has increased more among less educated parents compared with their college-educated counterparts. In 1965, high-school-educated fathers had about an hour more leisure per day than high-school-educated mothers; the gap was also about an hour when comparing college-educated fathers and mothers. Among less educated parents, the gender leisure gap hovered around an hour until 2012, when it increased to 1 hour 23 minutes. In contrast, the leisure gender gap among college-educated parents fluctuated between 1 hour and 30 minutes between 1965 and 2012; the gap of 46 minutes in 2012 is not statistically different from the gap of 56 minutes in 1965.

Third, the association of education with leisure trends differs by gender. For fathers, the data shown in Figure 8.3 confirm findings that leisure trends

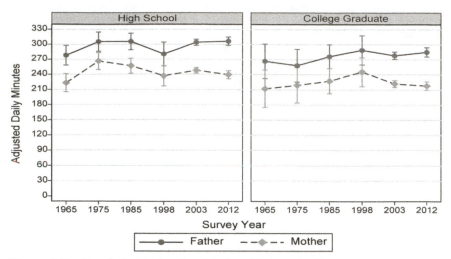

Figure 8.3 Trends in Mothers' and Fathers' Leisure by Education

have diverged according to college education (Sevilla, Giminez-Nadal, and Gershuny 2012). In 1965, fathers' leisure did not vary significantly by education: fathers with a high school degree and those with a college degree reported around 4 hours 30 minutes of leisure per day. By 1975, however, less educated fathers had around 1 hour more leisure per day compared with college-educated fathers; the gap narrowed in the 1980s and 1990s (differences are not statistically significant), but the gap widened in the 2000s. By 2012, fathers with less education reported 5 hours 15 minutes of leisure per day, 37 minutes more than in 1965, and about 42 minutes higher than the 4 hours 30 minutes of leisure reported by college-educated fathers. The growing education gap is due to different trends by education in fathers' leisure. Among less educated fathers, the leisure trend is nonlinear, with leisure increasing between 1965 to 1985, then dropping back to 1975 levels in 1998 before increasing in 2003 and 2012. In contrast, among college-educated fathers, the leisure trend is relatively stable after a dip of about 50 minutes between 1965 and 1975 before rising to about 4 hours 30 minutes in 1985, where it has held steady. Hence, since the 1980s, leisure has increased substantially among fathers with less education and remained roughly comparable for those with a college degree. This trend is notable because the 1980s were also when work hours began to differ substantially by education, with less educated fathers working less than full-time hours and college-educated fathers on average working 50 or more hours per week (Jacobs and Gerson 2004).

In contrast, there is an education leisure gap among mothers only in 2003. Gaps are not significant in other years. The trend in less educated and college-educated mothers' leisure is nonlinear. Among those with a high school education, leisure increased by about 40 minutes between 1965 and 1975, to about 4 hours 20 minutes, then declined to around 4 hours. Among college-educated mothers, leisure increased by about 20 minutes between 1965 and 1975, with an additional 30-minute increase in 1998, before falling 30 minutes. The fluctuation in 1998 from the 1965–2012 trend may reflect a lower precision of the 1998 estimates due to the relatively small sample or differences due to slight variations in question wording or survey administration. It may also reflect the actual trend. But because it is not possible to determine the cause conclusively, this analysis adopts a cautious interpretation that the trend in college-educated mothers' leisure has been relatively stable since 1975.

Education may also condition gender differences in leisure activities. These differences are explored in Figure 8.4, which shows the unadjusted trend in mothers' and fathers' leisure activities by education. The stacked bars show minutes per day in television, home, cognitive, active, and public leisure, with the overall bar indicating the total minutes per day of leisure time from 1965 to 2012. Mothers and fathers with high school or less education are shown on the left, and those with a college degree are shown on the right.

Figure 8.4 indicates that the trend in types of leisure is similar to the trend shown in Figure 8.2 for all women and men. Both less educated and more educated mothers and fathers increased time watching television and reduced time in cognitive leisure. College-educated mothers and fathers, as well as high-school-educated mothers, also reduced time in home leisure, whereas less educated fathers saw an increase in home leisure. The increase in

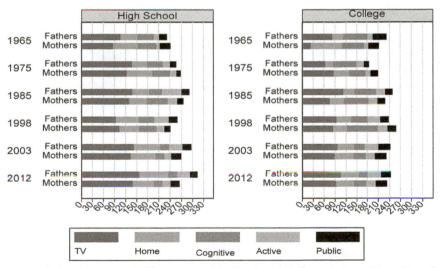

Figure 8.4 Education Differences in Mothers' and Fathers' Leisure Type Trends

television time was particularly sharp for college-educated mothers, rising from around 20 minutes in 1965 to 88 minutes in 2012. This has caused the education difference in television time to narrow among mothers—from 57 minutes in 1965 to 38 minutes in 2012. Additionally, the one-hour increase in television time among college-educated mothers is greater than the overall increase in leisure. In contrast, because television time increased more for high-school-educated fathers than college educated, the education gap in television increased among fathers—from 26 minutes in 1965 to 42 minutes in 2012. In-home leisure and cognitive leisure have declined among college-educated mothers by about 40 and 25 minutes respectively, suggesting that mothers today may substitute television for socializing with friends or reading. Cognitive leisure also declined among college-educated fathers, from about 1 hour 20 minutes in 1965 to only 30 minutes in 2012. Differences by education and gender are modest for active and public leisure, in part because most parents report little time in these activities at each time point. Fathers report about 15 to 20 minutes more active leisure than mothers, and the difference has increased among college-educated parents but not less educated. College-educated mothers and fathers report about 30 minutes of public leisure in 1965 and 2012, about 10 minutes more than less educated mothers and fathers. In general, then, education influences leisure activity time in similar ways for mothers and fathers. College-educated parents devote a smaller share of their leisure time to television and in-home leisure and more to cognitive, active, and public leisure compared with less educated parents. Gender differences in leisure activities result more from mothers having less overall leisure than fathers.

The more interesting intersectional influence of gender and education on leisure time is revealed in Table 8.2 and Figures 8.5 and 8.6 on trends in solo leisure and leisure shared with children. Data are shown for 1965, 1975, 2003, and 2012 because leisure time with others is not available in 1985 and 1998. The big story here is that leisure time with children has increased among mothers and fathers, and the shift away from solo leisure to more leisure with children is more pronounced among mothers. Mothers reported about 1 hour 50 minutes of solo leisure in 1965, only about 10 minutes less than the 2 hours reported by fathers. Leisure time shared with children was relatively modest for mothers and fathers—only 6 minutes for mothers and 20 minutes for fathers. Mothers' solo leisure increased about 30 minutes, about twice the increase among fathers, between 1965 and 1975, but then dropped by about one hour, to about 1 hour 10 minutes in 2003 and 2012. At the same time, leisure shared with children increased by 50 minutes, to just over one hour in 2003 and 2012. In contrast, fathers' solo leisure time has remained around 2 hours 15 minutes since 1975, and time with children increased by only 20 minutes. Trends in television watched with children shown in Table 8.2 indicate that it accounts for about one-half of leisure

Table 8.2 Adjusted Daily Minutes from OLS Regressions of Solo and with Children Leisure Trends

	Leisure				Television			
	Solo		With Children		Solo		With Children	
	Mothers	Fathers	Mothers	Fathers	Mothers	Fathers	Mothers	Fathers
1965	112.74	123.99	6.18	19.68 ^	29.11	45.54 *	1.03	8.53
	(7.15)	(7.46)	(5.06)	(5.28)	(4.78)	(4.99)	(3.51)	(3.66)
1975	138.46	138.62	7.32	21.58 ***	56.29	55.69	-0.34	11.65 ***
	(6.74)	(7.23)	(4.77)	(5.12)	(4.51)	(4.84)	(3.31)	(3.55)
2003	76.54 ***	127.47	63.85	42.08 ***	32.80	53.91 ***	32.59	22.35 ***
	(2.02)	(2.22)	(1.43)	(1.57)	(1.35)	(1.49)	(0.99)	(1.09)
2012	71.76 ***	134.81	60.34	41.51 ***	31.33	54.69 ***	32.43	22.93 ***
	(2.65)	(2.91)	(1.87)	(2.06)	(1.77)	(1.94)	(1.30)	(1.43)

^p<.10; *p<.05; **p<.01; ***p<.001

shared with children. Data not shown indicate that the remaining leisure with children is divided between in-home leisure (e.g., socializing with friends) and public leisure, like attending sporting or cultural events.

Figures 8.5 and 8.6 present solo leisure and leisure with children trends by gender and education. The shift out of leisure done alone to leisure shared with children is more pronounced among high-school-educated mothers

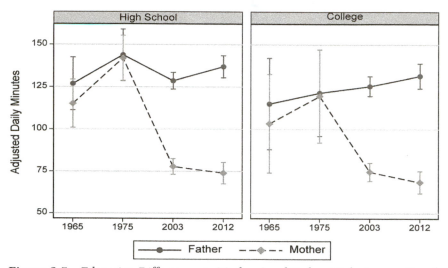

Figure 8.5 Education Differences in Mothers' and Fathers' Solo Leisure Trends

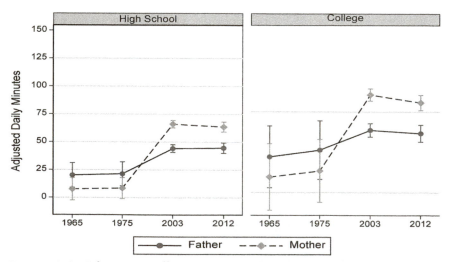

Figure 8.6 Education Differences in Mothers' and Fathers' Leisure with Children Trends

compared with college-educated mothers and all fathers. Solo leisure declined about 50 minutes among less educated mothers, whereas leisure with children increased by about one hour. In contrast, while college-educated mothers' solo leisure decreased by about 20 minutes (from about 1 hour 40 minutes to 1 hour 20 minutes), and leisure with children increased 40 minutes (from less than a quarter of an hour in 1965 to about one hour in 1965), only the latter difference is statistically significant. Additionally, whereas less educated mothers had more solo leisure in 1965 and 1975, they now have less solo and more leisure with children compared to college-educated mothers.

Gender differences in solo and shared leisure are also larger among less educated mothers and fathers, in part because less educated fathers have higher amounts of leisure compared to other fathers and all mothers. In 2012, less educated mothers have about 1 hour 20 minutes less solo leisure compared with less educated fathers, compared with a gap of only about 10 minutes in 1965. The solo leisure gap among college-educated parents is about 41 minutes in 2012, compared with around 20 minutes in 1965. In contrast, gender differences in leisure time with children do not vary by education. Regardless of education, mothers today report between 20 and 25 minutes more of leisure shared with children than comparable fathers.

Although coding is consistent across the surveys, it is possible that how mothers and fathers think about children's presence during leisure has changed over time. For example, parenting today requires investments of substantial time in facilitating children's developmental abilities and exposing them to enriching environments, with some of this emphasis coming from ideologies of intensive parenting that emerged in the late 1970s (Lareau 2003). As a result, since 1985, mothers and fathers may be more likely to report children's copresence during an activity compared with parents in 1975 and 1965. However, even if differential reporting accounts for the increase, the trend would still indicate that parents' experience of leisure has changed since the 1980s.

Conclusion

The analysis presented in this chapter underscores the importance of considering how trends in parents' leisure quantity and quality vary by gender and education. This lens reveals several new findings that add complexity to our knowledge about gender and class differences in parents' leisure and thus gender and family inequality. Although parents' leisure has increased, all of the increases were in earlier decades. Leisure time has not increased significantly since the mid-1970s for fathers and the mid-1990s for mothers. Fathers today have about 5 hours per day of leisure and mothers slightly below 4 hours per day. This translates over a week to about 35 hours for fathers, close to the standard 9-to-5 workweek. Fathers have slightly over an hour more leisure each day compared with mothers. This adds up over the week to an additional eight hours of leisure, comparable to a standard paid work shift.

This is initially hard to reconcile with popular depictions of parents who are time squeezed between work and family. Considering trends in types of leisure, and how these vary by education, helps address this seeming conundrum. Over the period when gender gaps in leisure widened, both mothers and fathers devoted more of their leisure to watching television and less to cognitive and home leisure. Fathers spend more time watching television than mothers. Parents rate television as one of the least enjoyable activities (Schwarz, Kahneman, and Xu 2009), indicating that the increase may be due more to constraints than preferences. Television is less expensive than some other types of leisure, and it doesn't require the coordination of schedules with other people or institutions. About 50 percent of the gender gap in leisure is accounted for by television. Gender gaps are larger for less educated parents, but again mainly due to more television watching among less educated fathers.

Further, the intersecting correlation of education and gender with leisure is adjusted for factors that affect leisure, like employment, marriage, and age and number of children, that reduce the hours in the 24-hour day that are available for leisure differences. This suggests that education and gender may reflect resource and spatial constraints. Lower incomes among less educated parents reduce their ability to outsource some housework or use more expensive convenience products to reduce the time necessary for activities like cooking. Because mothers are more socially "responsible" for housework and care work, any resource limitations constrain their leisure time more than they do that of fathers (Cooke and Baxter 2010). Compositional differences between more and less educated parents that are not "netted out" in regression models also play a role in the divergent trends in leisure. In 1965, parents with more and less education were more similar in employment, age, marital status, and race-ethnicity. By 2012, education increasingly differentiates parents, with the less educated having more precarious or no employment, below-median household incomes, and more likely to be younger, never married, and racial/ethnic minorities compared with married parents. Hence, the gender gap in leisure may signal social disadvantage as much as men's advantage over women.

Trends in solo leisure and leisure with children provide more support to arguments that gender gaps in leisure signal male privilege. Fathers' higher solo leisure time—and perhaps slightly higher time in active leisure—suggests that more men than women feel entitled to leisure that is relaxing and enjoyable (Craig and Mullan 2013). Leisure that is done with children may also be enjoyable, but interviews with parents indicate it is also

Appendix Table 8.3 Sample Characteristics by Survey Year & Gender

	Mothers											
	1965		1975		1985		1998		2003		2012	
	Mean	SD	Mean	SD	Mean	SD	Mean	SD	Mean	SD	Mean	SD
Married	0.86		0.72		0.75		0.60		0.67		0.61	0.49
Child <4	0.44		0.38		0.29		0.55		0.41		0.42	0.49
Number of Children	2.40	1.48	2.16	1.12	1.75	0.93	1.84	0.97	1.84	0.95	1.88	
< High School	0.28		0.26		0.12		0.07		0.13		0.12	
High School Graduate	0.62		0.64		0.70		0.66		0.49		0.43	
College Graduate	0.10		0.10		0.18		0.27		0.38		0.45	
Not Employed	0.66		0.55		0.41		0.21		0.31		0.34	
PT Employed	0.05		0.07		0.15		0.17		0.23		0.22	
FT Employed	0.29		0.38		0.44		0.62		0.46		0.45	
Age	35.56	9.53	34.42	9.79	35.12	9.39	33.58	10.16	36.05	9.80	36.31	10.51
Black	0.09		0.13		0.00		0.14		0.13		0.14	
Weeknd Diary Day	0.27		0.13		0.27		0.33		0.28		0.29	
N	401		378		530		290		4930		2793	

(continued)

Appendix Table 8.3 (*continued*)

	Fathers											
	1965		1975		1985		1998		2003		2012	
	Mean	SD	Mean	SD	Mean	SD	Mean	SD	Mean	SD	Mean	SD
Married	0.94	0.23	0.86	0.35	0.81		0.75		0.82	0.39	0.79	0.41
Child <4	0.47	0.50	0.38	0.49	0.30		0.51		0.40	0.49	0.40	0.49
Number of Children	2.27	1.40	2.33	1.36	1.70	0.89	1.96	1.11	1.85	0.93	1.86	0.95
< High School	0.33	0.47	0.29	0.46	0.12		0.06		0.14	0.35	0.12	0.33
High School Graduate	0.47	0.50	0.50	0.50	0.61		0.59		0.46	0.50	0.45	0.50
College Graduate	0.20	0.40	0.21	0.41	0.27		0.35		0.39	0.49	0.43	0.49
Not Employed	0.02	0.15	0.09	0.28	0.14		0.08		0.11	0.32	0.15	0.36
PT Employed	0.01	0.10	0.02	0.15	0.06		0.05		0.08	0.27	0.09	0.29
FT Employed	0.97	0.18	0.89	0.31	0.80		0.87		0.81	0.39	0.76	0.43
Age	37.58	10.07	35.53	10.37	35.89	10.22	36.29	10.97	37.03	10.16	37.96	11.11
Black	0.08	0.27	0.05	0.22	0.00		0.09		0.08	0.27	0.08	0.27
Weeknd Diary Day	0.29	0.45	0.12	0.33	0.28		0.25		0.29	0.45	0.29	0.45
N	326		269		460		177		3453		1947	

perceived as "work" and more stressful compared with leisure without children present (Musick, Meier, and Flood 2016). Mothers' solo leisure has declined partly because overall leisure has declined, and a larger share of their leisure time is now spent with children. This pattern fits a story of gendered leisure disadvantage among mothers. This interpretation is reinforced by studies indicating that one way in which mothers manage expectations of intensive mothering is by cutting back on leisure activities done with friends or done solely for personal benefit (Collins 2016). Taken together, results in this chapter highlight that leisure quality, more than quantity, is a powerful indicator of gender and family inequality.

Notes

1. https://www.google.com/search?biw=1536andbih=735andei=S2kgWvblE OSpggf-jquABgandq=time+crunched+parentsandoq=timeandgs_l=psy-ab.1.0.3 5i39k1l2j0i131i67k1l2j0i67k1j0i131i67k1j0i20i263k1j0i131k1j0j0i131k1.4050 1.41745.0.45557.6.5.1.0.0.0.100.426.4j1.5.0....0...1c.1.64.psy-ab..0.6.433...0i131i2 0i264k1j0i20i264k1j0i46i67k1j46i67k1.0.6OfhGOF_-p0.

2. Refer to the AHTUS website (https://www.ahtusdata.org/ahtus/) for detailed information on the studies.

References

Acker, Joan. 2009. "From Glass Ceiling to Inequality Regimes." *Sociologie du travail* 51 (2): 199–217.

Aguiar, Mark, and Erik Hurst. 2007. "Measuring Trends in Leisure: The Allocation of Time over Five Decades." *Quarterly Journal of Economics* 122 (3): 969–1006.

Benard, Stephen, and Shelley J. Correll. 2010. "Normative Discrimination and the Motherhood Penalty." *Gender and Society* 24 (5): 616–46. doi:10.1177 /0891243210383142.

Berkman, Lisa F., and Thomas A. Glass. 2000. "Social Integration, Social Networks, Social Support, and Health." *Social Epidemiology* 1: 137–73.

Bianchi, Suzanne M. 2011. "Family Change and Time Allocation in American Families." *The ANNALS of the American Academy of Political and Social Science* 638 (1): 21–44.

Bianchi, Suzanne M., John P. Robinson, and Melissa A. Milkie. 2006. *Changing Rhythms of American Family Life*. New York: Russell Sage Foundation.

Bianchi, Suzanne M., John P. Robinson, and Liana C. Sayer. 2001. *Family Interaction, Social Capital, and Trends in Time Use (FISCT), 1998-1999 (ICPSR 3191)*. Ann Arbor, MI: Inter-University Consortium for Political and Social Research.

Bittman, Michael. 2002. "Social Participation and Family Welfare: The Money and Time Costs of Leisure in Australia," *Social Policy & Administration* 36 (4): 408–425.

Blackstone, Amy, and Mahala D. Stewart. 2012. "Choosing to be Childfree: Research on the Decision Not to Parent." *Sociology Compass* 6 (9): 718–27.

Budig, Mchelle J., and Paula England. 2001. "The Wage Penalty for Motherhood." *American Sociological Review* 66 (April): 204–25.

Charles, Maria, and Karen Bradley. 2009. "Indulging Our Gendered Selves? Sex Segregation by Field of Study in 44 Countries." *American Journal of Sociology* 114 (4): 924–76.

Cohen, Philip N. 2014. *The Family: Diversity, Inequality, and Social Change.* New York: W. W. Norton.

Collins, Caitlyn M. 2016. *Work-Family Policy and Working Mothers: A Comparative Study of Germany, Sweden, Italy, and the United States.* University of Texas dissertation. Accessed August 1. https://repositories.lib.utexas.edu /handle/2152/40288

Converse, Philip E., and Robinson, John P. . 1980. *Americans' Use of Time, 1965-1966.* Ann Arbor, MI: Inter-university Consortium for Political and Social Research.

Cooke, Lynn Prince, and Janeen Baxter. 2010. "'Families' in International Context: Comparing Institutional Effects Across Western Societies." *Journal of Marriage and Family* 72 (3): 516–36.

Coverman, Shelley. (1983). "Gender, Domestic Labor Time, and Wage Inequality." *American Sociological Review* 48: 623–37.

Coverman, Shelley, and Joseph F. Sheley. (1986). "Change in Men's Housework and Child-Care Time, 1965-1975." *Journal of Marriage and the Family* 48 (2): 413–22.

Craig, Lyn, and Killian Mullan. 2012. "Shared Parent–Child Leisure Time in Four Countries." *Leisure Studies* 31 (2): 211–29. doi:10.1080/02614367.20 11.573570.

Craig, Lyn, and Killian Mullan. 2013. "Parental Leisure Time: A Gender Comparison in Five Countries." *Social Politics: International Studies in Gender, State and Society* 20 (3): 329–357.

Crespo, Carlos J., Ellen Smith, Ross E. Andersen, Olivia Carter-Pokras, and Barbara E. Ainsworth. 2000. "Race/Ethnicity, Social Class and Their Relation to Physical Inactivity during Leisure time: Results from the Third National Health and Nutrition Examination Survey, 1988-1994." *American Journal of Preventive Medicine* 18 (1): 46–53.

Elliott, Sinikka, and Debra Umberson. 2008. "The Performance of Desire: Gender and Sexual Negotiation in Long-Term Marriages." *Journal of Marriage and Family* 70 (2): 391–406.

Fisher, Kimberly, Jonathan Gershuny, Sarah M. Flood, Joan Garcia Roman, and Sandra L. Hofferth. 2017. *American Heritage Time Use Study Extract Builder: Version 1.1.* Accessed August 1. https://www.ahtusdata.org/ahtus/

Gershuny, Jonathan. 2000. *Changing Times: Work and Leisure in Postindustrial Society.* Oxford and New York: Oxford University Press.

Gerson, Kathleen. 2010. *The Unfinished Revolution: How a New Generation Is Reshaping Family, Work, and Gender in America.* New York: Oxford University Press.

Glass, Jennifer, Robing. W. Simon, and Matthew A. Andersson. 2016. "Parenthood and Happiness: Effects of Work-Family Reconciliation Policies in 22 OECD Countries." *American Journal of Sociology* 122 (3): 886–929. doi:10.1086/688892.

Gornick, Janet C., and Marcia K. Meyers, eds. *Gender Equality: Transforming Family Divisions of Labor (The Real Utopias Project, Vol. VI).* London: Verso Books.

Gracia, Pablo. 2015. "Parent–Child Leisure Activities and Cultural Capital in the United Kingdom: The Gendered Effects of Education and Social Class." *Social Science Research* 52: 290–302. doi:http://dx.doi.org/10.1016/j.ssresearch.2015.02.005.

Grunow, Daniela, Florian Schulz, and Hans-Peter Blossfeld. 2012. "What Determines Change in the Division of Housework Over the Course of Marriage?" *International Sociology* 27 (3): 289–307.

Gupta, Sanjiv, Liana C. Sayer, and Philip N. Cohen. 2009. "Earnings and the Stratification of Unpaid Time Among U.S. Women." *Social Indicators Research* 93 (1): 153–57.

Henderson, Karla A., 1991. *Dimensions of Choice: A Qualitative Approach to Recreation, Parks, and Leisure Research.* State College, PA: Venture Publishing.

Hochschild, Arlie. 1997. *The Time Bind: When Work Becomes Home and Home Becomes Work.* New York: Metropolitan Books.

Hodges, Melissa J., and Michelle J. Budig. 2010. "Who Gets the Daddy Bonus?" *Gender and Society,* 24 (6): 717–45.

Houseknecht, Sharon K. 1978. "Voluntary Childlessness." *Alternative Lifestyles* 1 (3): 379–402. doi:10.1007/bf01082080.

Hsin, Amy, and Christina Felfe. 2014. "When Does Time Matter? Maternal Employment, Children's Time With Parents, and Child Development." *Demography* 51 (5): 1867–94. doi:10.1007/s13524-014-0334-5.

Jacobs, Jerry A., and Kathleen Gerson. 2004. *The Time Divide: Work, Family, and Gender Inequality.* Cambridge, MA: Harvard University Press.

Juster, F. Thomas, Paul N. Courant, Greg J. Duncan, John P. Robinson, and Frank P. Stafford. 1979. *Time Use in Economic and Social Accounts, 1975–76.* Ann Arbor, MI: Inter-university Consortium for Political and Social Research.

Juster, F. Thomas, Hiromi Ono, and Frank P. Stafford. 2003. "An Assessment of Alternative Measures of Time Use." *Sociological Methodology* 33 (1): 19–54.

Kimmel, Jean, and Rachel Connelly. 2007. "Mothers' Time Choices: Caregiving, Leisure, Home Production, and Paid Work." *Journal of Human Resources* XLII (3): 643–81. doi:10.3368/jhr.XLII.3.643.

Krueger, Alan B., Daniel Kahneman, Claude Fischler, David Schkade, Norbert Schwarz, and Arthur A. Stone. 2009. "Time Use and Subjective Well-Being in France and the US." *Social Indicators Research* 93 (1): 7–18.

Lareau, Annette. (2003). *Unequal Childhoods: Race, Class and Family Life*. Berkeley: University of California Press.

Lareau, Annette, and Elliott. B. Weininger. 2008. "Time, Work, and Family Life: Reconceptualizing Gendered Time Patterns Through the Case of Children's Organized Activities." *Sociological Forum* 23 (3): 419–54.

Mattingly, Marybeth J., and Suzanne M. Bianchi. 2003. "Gender Differences in the Quantity and Quality of Free Time: The U.S. Experience." *Social Forces* 81 (3): 999–1030.

McLanahan, Sara. 2004. "Diverging Destinies: How Children Are Faring under the Second Demographic Transition." *Demography* 41 (4): 607–27.

Milkie, Melissa A., Sara B. Raley, and Suzanne M. Bianchi. 2009. "Taking on the Second Shift: Time Allocations and Time Pressures of U.S. Parents with Preschoolers." *Social Forces* 88 (2): 487–517.

Miller, Yvette D., and Wendy J. Brown. 2007. "Determinants of Active Leisure for Women with Young Children: An 'Ethic of Care' Prevails." *Leisure Sciences* 27 (5): 405–420.

Mirowsky, John, and Catherine E. Ross. 2003. *Education, Social Status, and Health*. New York: Aldine de Gruyter.

Musick, Kelley, Jennie E. Brand, and Dwight Davis. 2012. "Variation in the Relationship between Education and Marriage: Marriage Market Mismatch?" *Journal of Marriage and Family,* 74 (1): 53–69.

Musick, Kelley, Ann Meier, and Sarah Flood. 2016. "How Parents Fare." *American Sociological Review* 81 (5): 1069–95. doi:10.1177/0003122416663917.

Passias, Emily J., Liana Sayer, and Joanna R. Pepin. 2016. "Who Experiences Leisure Deficits? Mothers' Marital Status and Leisure Time." *Journal of Marriage and Family* 79 (4): 1001–22. doi:10.1111/jomf.12365.

Presser, Harriet B. 2003. *Working in the 24/7 Economy: Challenges for American Families*. New York: Russell Sage Foundation.

Presser, Stanley, and Linda Stinson. 1998. "Data Collection Mode and Social Desirability Bias in Self-Reported Religious Attendance." *American Sociological Review* 63 (1): 137–45.

Robinson, John P. 1985. "The Validity and Reliability of Diaries versus Alternative Time Use Measures." In *Time, Goods, and Well-Being*, edited by F. T. Juster and F. P. Stafford, 33–62. Ann Arbor: Survey Research Center, Institute for Social Research, The University of Michigan. (Reprinted from: IN FILE).

Robinson, John P., and Geoffrey Godbey. 1999. *Time for Life: The Surprising Ways Americans Use Their Time,* vol. 2. University Park: Pennsylvania State University Press.

Ross, Catherine, and John Mirowsky. 2013. "The Sense of Personal Control: Social Structural Causes and Emotional Consequences." In *Handbook of the Sociology of Mental Health*, edited by C. Aneshensel, J. Phelan, and A. Bierman, 379–402. Netherlands: Springer. (Reprinted from: NOT IN FILE).

Ross, Catherine E., and Beckett A. Broh. 2000. "The Roles of Self-Esteem and the Sense of Personal Control in the Academic Achievement Process." *Sociology of Education* 73 (4): 270–84.

Ross, CatherineE., and Chia-ling Wu. 1995. "The Links between Education and Health." *American Sociological Review* 60 (5): 719–45.

Sayer, Liana. C. 2005. "Gender, Time, and Inequality: Trends in Women's and Men's Paid Work, Unpaid Work, and Free Time." *Social Forces* 84 (1): 285–303.

Sayer, Liana. C. 2016. "Trends in Women's and Men's Time Use, 1965–2012: Back to the Future?" 43–77. In *Gender and Couple Relationships*, edited by S. M. McHale, V. King, J. van Hook, and A. Booth. New York: Springer. (Reprinted from: IN FILE).

Sayer, Liana C., Paula England, Michael Bittman, and Suzanne M. Bianchi. 2009. "How Long Is the Second (Plus First) Shift? Gender Differences in Paid, Unpaid, and Total Work Time in Australia and the United States." *Journal of Comparative Family Studies* 40 (4): 523–45.

Schwarz, Norbert, Daniel Kahneman, and Jing Xu. 2009. "Global and Episodic Reports of Hedonic Experience." In *Calendar and Time Diary Methods in Life Course Research*, edited by R. F. Belli, F. P. Stafford, and D. F. Alwin, 157–74. Los Angeles: Sage. (Reprinted from: IN FILE).

Sevilla, Almudena, Jose Ignacio Gimenez-Nadal, and Jonathan Gershuny. 2012. "Leisure Inequality in the United States: 1965–2003." *Demography* 49 (3): 939–64.

Singh-Manoux, Archana, and Michael Marmot. 2005. "Role of Socialization in Explaining Social Inequalities in Health." *Social Science and Medicine* 60 (9): 2129–33.

Stinson, Linda L. 1999. "Measuring How People Spend Their Time: A Time-Use Survey Design." *Monthly Labor Review* 122 (8): 12–19.

Stone, Pamela. 2007. *Opting Out? Why Women Really Quit Careers and Head Home.* Berkeley: University of California Press.

Szalai, Alexander. 1972. *The Use of Time: Daily Activities of Urban and Suburban Populations in Twelve Countries.* The Hague: Mouton and Co.

U.S. Bureau of Labor Statistics. 2015. *American Time Use Survey User's Guide.* Retrieved from Washington, D.C. Accessed August 1. https://www.bls.gov/tus/atususersguide.pdf

Wearing, Betsy, and Stephen Wearing. 2006. "'All in a Day's Leisure': Gender and the Concept of Leisure." *Leisure Studies* 7 (2): 111-123.

Williams, Joan C. 2010. *Reshaping the Work-Family Debate : Why Men and Class Matter.* Cambridge, MA.: Harvard University Press.

PART 3

Inequalities

Introduction: Inequalities

From the digital divide to differential access to parental leave policies and leisure time, unequal access for parents and children to valuable resources is featured throughout this book. This section highlights particular categories of experience for parents, including socioeconomic status, citizenship, race, gender, and sexuality. While parents' experiences are marked by intersections of identities, and while inequality among groups is featured in all chapters in this volume, focusing a section on particular named locations of inequality can help us understand the breadth of ways that the joys and challenges of parenthood are experienced unequally in different groups.

Sociologist Allison Pugh, in chapter 9, weaves together ethnographic research from the United States and Australia to investigate how parents and their children come to understand inequality. Parenting advice media sometimes suggests that children need to be protected from "too much" information about topics such as poverty, but poor children often do not get that choice. Instead, children confront inequality every day as they navigate consumer culture, facing questions of who has what and what that means socially. This chapter critiques and adds to what consumer culture scholarship says about parenting inequality in an unequal world, especially as it may relate to children's understandings of empathy.

In chapter 10, psychologist Erin Pahlke shows how parents' races may impact how and whether they talk to their children about race itself. The research findings presented in this chapter show how the specific type of parental ethnic-racial socialization (cultural socialization, egalitarianism, preparation for bias, promotion of mistrust, and colorblind socialization) that parents employ can relate to their children's attitudes about other racial groups, including how the tendency among European American parents to ignore race may promote negative attitudes about racial out-group members for their children.

In chapter 11, sociologist Pallavi Banerjee brings us into the world of parents who hold dependent visas. By introducing her middle-class immigrant interviewees' parenting style—transcultural cultivation—Banerjee complicates past categories of parenting style by suggesting that immigrant status and gender (in addition to race and class) intersect. This chapter includes qualitative interview and observation data that show how and why mothers and fathers from India living in the United States on dependent visas create a more nuanced and intersectional form of "concerted cultivation" of their immigrant children than previous parenting style research has shown.

A book on parenting necessarily covers adoption, but, as sociologist Pamela Anne Quiroz discusses in chapter 12, adoption itself is a complicated matter. The nature of transracial and transnational adoption in particular has changed dramatically in the last decades, in part due to the blurring of the categories of domestic and transnational adoption due to deportations and policies that separate families. Through analysis of online adoption communities and interview data uncovering how parents practice and experience transracial adoption, this chapter tells the story of how the building of family on one end occurs, at times, with the loss of family on the other end. Conversations about transnational adoption must now include emphasis on what happens domestically as children stay in their new country but the parents are sent away.

Chapter 13, from sociologists Marshal Fettro and Wendy Manning, efficiently and thoroughly discusses current debates about same-gender parenthood, with particular emphasis on research findings uncovering the impact on children. Since the topic has been hotly debated within social scientific communities in recent years, this chapter relates what the initial findings have been as well as responses to them, and what new research is telling us—all of which dispel the myth that same-gender parenting is bad for children. The chapter combines an overview of legal cases, social scientific research, and how both have been portrayed in the news media.

Finally, in chapter 14, sociologist Taylor Field Quiroga shares interview findings from parents of lesbian, gay, and bisexual children. When parents first find out that their children are LGB, one common reaction is concern that they will never settle down with one partner or that they'll never get married or have children of their own. These concerns, as well as their subsequent relief, show the importance of seeing the next generation reproduce a "good" family. This chapter investigates how acceptance of gay families hinges on them looking like straight families, and how coming out is intimately connected to the reproduction of sexuality, gender, and family.

CHAPTER NINE

Understanding Inequality: Children, Consumer Culture, and the Empathy Framework

Allison J. Pugh

A recent post on a health blog regularly visited by 17 million people advised readers "how to talk to kids about poverty" (Morin 2017).[1] Keep it short and simple, and assure them you'll always be there, the author counseled, urging parents to be careful not to give kids "too much for them to handle." But with U.S. inequality yawning ever wider (Piketty, Saez and Zucman 2016), children absorb messages about poverty from more than just parents' talk. Recent research with kids in Oakland, California, and near Melbourne, Australia, shows how schools and neighborhoods, as well as parents, can convey different "empathy frameworks" that shape how kids come to think about the social inequalities around them.

In the mid-2000s, I had occasion to spend three years with low-income families of color in Oakland, California. My stated task was to investigate how low-income children thought about consumer goods and experiences, how their parents handled their consumer desires, and how those practices varied by class and race in the United States, in the hopes of decoding the commercialization of childhood beyond common explanations—the push of materialism or the pull of advertising.

As I was conducting research for my first book, *Longing and Belonging: Parents, Children and Consumer Culture* (Pugh 2009), among the families generous enough to welcome me into their homes were the Roas.[2] Theresa Roa was the friendly, confident 8-year-old daughter of Margaret, a Filipina American, and an African American man who still gave her a little money for Theresa but was no longer living with them. Margaret had since partnered with Rick, another African American man, who had been laid off from his job three months before Margaret had given birth to their new baby boy. The family was struggling. Margaret reported $888 in monthly "official" income, including food stamps, while their rent alone was $985. Dribs and drabs came in from a grandfather, an ex-husband's drug dealing, and some gambling winnings, but they were living hand to mouth, waiting for better times.

Theresa liked to play with her friend Jacquette at Sojourner Truth, the low-income after-school program where I did my research. They joked, told stories about their families, and sang the latest rap songs. A smart girl, Theresa had received several achievement awards at elementary school over the three years that I was at Sojourner Truth. She was knowledgeable about the goods that mattered in her social world—the music, the sneakers, the Poké-mon cards, the toys—and her talk helped her to belong in it, acting as her entrée to what I term the school's "economy of dignity": the system of social meaning whereby children navigate their belonging through material goods and experiences. Theresa and her mother, Margaret, had a warm, loving relationship, and they delighted in being together, chatting about, say, the tiniest details of current sneaker design ("On the top, they're like high-tops up here, but they're all open like this, over here. And they come out like little collars.")

One day, I visited with Theresa at her home in Oakland, talking to her about inequality while the street sounds filtered through the bars on the window. She sat with me in her tiny living room—which doubled as the bedroom where Margaret, Rick, and her baby brother slept at night—while her mother listened and the infant boy napped nearby.

Here's a record of one of our conversations.

Allison:	Are there people you know who have a lot less than you?
Theresa:	Yeah. The people in that house over there. People I see on the streets, carrying carts. People that have signs, that lay on the street because they don't have any money.
Allison:	And why do you think they have less than you?
Theresa:	Because they didn't do good in school, so they didn't get their education to get a job or to pass college. So they have to live on the streets, because they didn't get no money.

Theresa speaks confidently here, because she knows this answer. This is the answer that the teachers at school give her. This is the way that the school curriculum in the United States answers the question of inequality: if you do not do well in school, you will not be able to go to college or possibly even get a job, and you will have to live on the street. This is what Sennett and Cobb (1972) called *The Hidden Injuries of Class*: the persistent ideology of a meritocracy that rationalizes the inequality—indeed, the deep poverty—that Theresa walks by every day.

But today, Theresa's mother, Margaret, is listening. And she knows that she is desperately poor in the United States—maybe not homeless, but very close to it, and that her own daughter is unwittingly talking about her. So she interrupts:

Margaret: Theresa?

Theresa: Yeah?

Margaret: You don't think something else could have happened to them?

Theresa: Or their house could have burned down. That did happen to Juanita. They couldn't afford another one. Or the family could have died. Or they couldn't stay with them.

The mother is not satisfied with this explanation, coming as it does after Theresa's first reflexive response. "What about me and Rick?" she asks. "Don't you see me and Rick trying? There's people that have had a hard life—they've lost their job, and they felt they couldn't do something else." We're trying to get ahead, she says, but sometimes it is very hard to do, because there are not any jobs that pay enough or that last long enough—even if you are willing to work hard and even if you are smart enough in school. Theresa notices her mother's intensity, and it stops her in her tracks. But the exchange brings to light something powerful about inequality and the clash between home and school for low-income families.

Aspirations are part of youths' navigation of an adult-made world, and they are a crucial part of social mobility, which Americans view as a social good. Yet aspirations also require a particular view of adults on the part of low-income children with promise. As currently imagined in the United States, in exchange for its promise of financial independence and happiness, the American Dream asks low-income children to reject not just where they came from, but also on some level to turn away from the people who cared for them. That rejection can cause alienation from self and from their identities, as well as from their connections.

Structural causes shape the Roas' poverty. Margaret left Theresa's father because he went to prison, as will an estimated one in three black men in this country, according to Bureau of Justice statistics. Married to a convicted felon, Margaret had lost her eligibility for subsidized housing. Margaret had tried to ask her son's grandfather for money to help them, but he stopped, saying that Margaret's current partner had to step up. "Rick needs to support you. He needs to get a job." Rick had been looking for work, but work opportunities for men without college educations have evaporated over the past 25 years, while women without college degrees have seen some growth in such feminized occupations as retail cashier or health paraprofessional (licensed practical nurse, for example). The work opportunities that were plentiful for men were in the *informal* economy, and this bare fact found its way into the Roas' talk as well.

When Theresa mentioned Gloria, a girl "who had a lot" at Sojourner Truth, she meant that Gloria had access to the latest sneakers and Gap clothing. But on the side, Margaret kept up a steady but oblique commentary to me about what Gloria's parents did to keep her flush with fashion. "Oh," she said, "her father has a good job. I'm not going to go into it with Theresa here right now, but he make fast money. He just works on cars and he does paint jobs, and—" She then continued meaningfully, looking at me to see if I got it: "He's a deliveryman. Delivers stuff. Cars and things. Parts."

A year after our conversation in her living room, I saw Margaret at a school fair. She told me the family had had to move from the apartment where we had sat together in the living room with the bars on its windows, because a known local pimp had started to eye Theresa and make comments. Margaret had had no choice but to ask her ex-husband, the drug dealer, for the money to make the move possible. Rick was trying not to work illegally, Margaret was trying to stay with Rick; they were trying to prioritize their children's care, and they were trying not to reach out to Margaret's ex and his ill-gotten gains. But we can see the various pieces of race and class and gender—as enacted by the state, the penal system, and the cultural environment—closing in on them.

So, let's return to Theresa's comment about why people are poor—which she made innocently but with which her mother took issue. When we start from these multiple intersections, we can ascertain the complexity of what Theresa learns at school and at home about aspirations and performance. We might call this an "empathy framework," and Theresa's teachers have a particular one on offer. Its curriculum encourages bright low-income children to surpass their origins while asking them to ignore the contexts that complicate social mobility, to downplay parental labor and maternal care, and to deny their communities of origin.

I never published these conversations in *Longing and Belonging*, and yet they have stuck with me ever since. I found it profoundly moving, even haunting, as this smart young girl tried to come up with an understanding of poverty that somehow reconciles two competing, irreconcilable worldviews: that of her mother, struggling to make a life for her family among the frayed threads of what it is like to live poor in the United States, and that of

her teachers, who are trying to reinforce the myth of the American meritocracy and doing what they think will help Theresa get out of the poverty that
afflicts her family—to inspire Theresa's hard work with the notion of the
just reward. Theresa is stuck between love and a hard place: between a perspective that allows for empathy and compassion for the suffering she sees
in her neighborhood but also threatens to keep her there, and one that
frames deprivation as reasonable and inevitable—that reduces obligation
and curtails emotional connection as it dangles before her a bright and shiny
future.

Empathy frameworks are narratives that organize inequality, mobility,
and moral worth. And if parenting advice media sometimes suggests that
children need to be protected from "too much" information about poverty,
children confront inequality every day as they navigate consumer culture,
confronting questions of who has what and what that means socially. Consumer culture is the terrain on which parents and other adults in children's
lives enact their empathy frameworks to make sense, often implicitly, of the
inequality all around them. Consumer culture figures strongly in the everyday struggle that Theresa and Margaret enact to negotiate the competing
interpretations that these frameworks offer.

What We Know about Kids' Consumer Culture and Empathy

What is children's consumer culture doing for and to children? Thanks to
extensive scholarship, we have a number of different answers. First, a definition: children's consumer culture includes their knowledge and use of
branded goods and services, their access to money, their influence on spending, and their media use. Of course, talking about children's consumer culture and its "effects" on children does not mean that children and childhoods
are somehow distinct from consumer culture, as if there is a pristine, non-
commercial childhood that is then distorted by consumerism. At the same
time, we must also be able to think about various iterations of that culture as
having particular impacts, just as we can see that most childhoods are not
separable from inequality or parenting or play, and yet we can still be interested in how these various experiences affect it.

On the one hand, we have a significant body of work that we could say
looks at the impact of consumer culture upon children as *individuals*. In this
group, I would put the voluminous work investigating the links between
children's consumer culture and materialism, depression, obesity, and other
physical and mental health outcomes, such as work by Deborah Roeder
John (e.g., Chaplin and John 2005; 2007) and Juliet Schor (2004). I would
also group here research that investigates the benefits of children's participation in consumer culture—work finding that children's media use is not
occasion for panic but instead associated with positive school performance

and self-esteem (Anderson et al. 2001). Here also would go the scholarship arguing that children's participation in consumer culture reflects and contributes to children's empowerment or exploitation or both (e.g., Linn 2004; McNeal 1999).

However, I want to draw your attention to scholarship that focuses on how children's consumer culture constitutes and reflects *social relations* (Martens, Southerton, and Scott 2004). Foremost among this research has been that which views consumption as a sorting mechanism for inequality, a means by which people distinguish among themselves. Indeed, in the Bourdieusian tradition, scholars argue that children's consumption helps to establish and cultivate the habits they have later, habits that can serve to generate and reproduce social stratification of great consequence (Berhau 2000). This stratification also extends beyond class—to gender, race, and other axes of inequality, including age: scholars have demonstrated that children's tastes are often framed by adults as naive or unsophisticated and thus used to reinscribe the boundary line between children and adults (Buckingham 2011; Seiter 1993).

Despite the dominance of the Bourdieusian tradition in consumer studies generally, however, research with children has enabled new insights that sometimes challenge the emphasis on class distinction. In my own research with three communities of five- to nine-year-old children of varied income levels in Oakland, California (Pugh 2009), I found that children appeared not so much to be signaling their class through appropriate markers as they were pursuing at least four other discernible discursive goals: asserting 1) their relative autonomy from adult control, 2) their access to popular culture, 3) their claims to be somewhat older than they are (yet not adult), and 4) their status as the focal point of someone's dedicated caregiving. That is, children worked to present themselves as relatively autonomous subjects instead of passive objects; as knowing and aware of popular culture as opposed to innocent or naive; as older than their biological age (and developmentalist assumptions about that age) would peg them; and as loved and cared for.

In fact, the alternative distinctions that children make with each other suggest that, perhaps, people's symbolic work addresses their most deeply felt inequalities, whatever those may be, and that for children, their oppression by age can sometimes be most profound—more profound sometimes than class, race, or gender. Conversely, it suggests that as a stigmatized minority, children do not always get to choose when certain boundaries are more salient than others. Here we might look to the pathbreaking research of Mary Waters, who, in her book *Ethnic Options* (1990), demonstrated that nonblacks in the United States got to choose when and how to invoke their ethnicities, while African Americans often had their racial identities—and the various meanings attached to them—invoked for them regardless of their own will. Similarly, then, we might see that for children, downplaying—or invoking, but on their own terms—the axis upon which they are defined as lesser is not always an option (Pugh 2014). Thus, while Bourdieu emphasized the childhood roots of class reproduction, research with children suggests that they can be less focused on class than other markers of inequality that feel more powerfully salient.

Still others suggest that children are not always pursuing distinction through their consumer practices, urging us to view children's consumer culture instead as a common language among kids, a kind of lingua franca that functions to bind them together, to forge friendships and communities. Childhood research demonstrates that children in developed countries can actually evince similar tastes across race, class, gender, and other categories—signaled by, for example, the near-universal appeal of particular electronic game systems, Pokémon cards or other game fads, or even Beanie Babies (Allison 2006). Children often like all sorts of goods that might signal different kinds of identities. Similarly, some adults like opera, pop music, *and* rap or hip-hop, a phenomenon that scholars have called "omnivorous taste," through which they have found that people make connections rather than distinctions (Pugh 2011; Lizardo 2006; DiMaggio 1987).

Of course, we might understand these views of consumption-that-connects as the flip side of distinction: bonding creates boundaries that include some and exclude others (Pugh 2011). But some researchers explore how children build their social worlds through consumer culture (Buckingham 2011). As Barrie Thorne (2008) showed us in her sensitive ethnographic work with immigrant kids in California, for example, consumer culture intersects with preexisting social categories—in her research "Chinese girls" and the "Pokémon kids"—to reinscribe social identities (although Thorne also demonstrated the durability of some identities; in her research in one multicultural public school, the Chinese girls were so stigmatized by their white, black, and Latino peers that even "cool" clothing could not redeem them). My own work (2009) talks about consumption as central to visibility/citizenship: In contemporary advanced industrialized nations, children's participation in consumer culture is part of that which makes them fully visible in their social worlds. Through talk and trading, they actively negotiate the meanings and value of consumer products and experiences that make up part of their economy of dignity, even as such goods are not equally available to all children.

Other scholars investigating consumption-as-connection have argued that children's consumer culture works as a signal of or conduit for care, a means by which both adults and children communicate the intimate knowledge and recognition that convey relationship. Here one would include Elizabeth Chin's (2001) groundbreaking ethnographic "shopping trips," in which she reported that her inner-city informants spent some of their windfall on mothers, siblings, and others. Children also read adult spending as a statement of how well they are seen and recognized, a reflection of their visibility to adults, and also of how caregivers interpret their desires—how small or large those desires loom in their households.

Despite the focus of this body of work on how consumption figures in social relations, most work on consumer culture does not address empathy. For our purposes here, I define empathy as the fellow feeling that stems from the capacity to share another's perspective, whether that person is experiencing positive or negative emotions, versus compassion, which is more like the empathy we might feel for someone who is specifically suffering (and we might juxtapose both of these with sympathy, which is an external, distancing feeling more akin to pity). Studies of empathy and compassion comprise a burgeoning field right now, with investigators from many different fields weighing in, most frequently philosophers, religious scholars, cognitive scientists, and psychologists. Much of this research investigates the universals of empathy—its biological bases, early family dynamics that seed its development, or neurological triggers. This is partly because sociologists have viewed compassion with suspicion, viewing most social action as animated by ulterior motives or material interests, leaving compassion and empathy to those fields that embrace a normative vision of individual health or thriving. Perhaps this explains why, in the near absence of sociological theorizing, much scholarship considers empathy and compassion as individual attributes—developed and expressed by some people more than others. Like research about consumption, studies of empathy can overemphasize the single actor as someone who operates in a social vacuum. Yet what if we were to conceive of empathy and compassion as profoundly social and cultural emotions—ones that reflect and shape social relations, and thus ones that are enacted through consumption? Empathy brings together the two major ways in which scholars have considered the social impact of consumer culture: inequality and connection/care.

We can look to anthropologists for terrific work on how empathy frameworks (although they do not use that phrase) serve to shape flows of money that mark off moral obligations among social relations. In noncapitalist societies, people feel obligation to intimate others—close relatives and neighbors with whom they have long histories of exchange (Berdahl 1999). Yet, studies show that advanced capitalism enables more abstract, less parochial relations—governed less by reciprocity norms with our neighbors than fellow feeling for the (global) stranger. For example, China is experiencing a clash between the moral visions of young, wealthier beneficiaries of market reforms, who send money to the victims of distant earthquakes or help elderly people who fall in the street, and older villagers who view such acts of unbidden altruism with suspicion. The anthropologist Yunxiang Yan (2009) has studied a phenomenon of those who extort these young Good Samaritans: elderly villagers who insist to credulous police officers and witnesses that there would be no reason for the young people's sacrifice if they were not in fact responsible for the misfortune in the first place, if they did not somehow trip them and then feel guilty about it. The very notion of helping someone you do not know, according to the village worldview, is unfathomable. Thus, in contrast to the nostalgic story line that capitalism replaces a warm communality with a cold rationality and inequality, Yan tells us that we instead veer from a thick reciprocity to a thin compassion as we simultaneously enlarge but efface our communities. We might care more about the tsunami victim than we once would have, but we might care less now about the neighbor.

Fairness, Empathy, and Children's Consumer Culture

In Theresa Roa's life, consumer culture actually plays many roles. When she and her mother take so much pleasure in knowing about and sharing the details of the Melissa "Bee-Fly" shoe, it works as a bridge to connect them, just as when Theresa points out that the shoes her mom bought her are "still in style." When Theresa quickly identifies her classmate Gloria as the one who has "more" and who has it first, this is consumer culture as a vector of distinction and inequality, even in this relatively homogeneous world—where those who have more do so because, as Margaret points out, her father makes "fast money."

We might view the empathy framework that Theresa gets at school as an acutely neoliberal one, reflected in the topography of poverty and plenty around her, a topography shaped by those well-worn characteristics of neoliberalism: the withdrawal of the state, structural adjustments, the evisceration of stable low-income work, and the devolution of risk and responsibility to the individual.

What happens in a different cultural context, one where cultural narratives make inequality less acceptable, less apparently "inevitable"? For the answer to this, I refer to some excellent work being done in Australia by anthropologist Rose Butler (2017). Butler spent 18 months conducting ethnographic observations with children between the ages of 8 and 13 in a small regional city in the southern state of Victoria. The research site was one with mostly low-income Australian children, but it also included some refugees and immigrant kids. Australia is an interesting comparison to Oakland, California, because it shares many characteristics with the United States—advanced capitalism, English-speaking, a celebration of the rugged individual, and on the more unequal end of the OECD countries, although of course the United States is an extreme outlier here.[3] Australia is unusual, however, in that it has a strong cultural emphasis on "fairness," or what the Australians call "a fair go." Fairness plays an important role in political discourse, invoked by government policymakers and news media alike. For example, the Australian Labor government's 2013 national disability insurance scheme, DisabilityCare Australia, promoted the policy as being "Stronger. Smarter. Fairer" while asserting that "Labor is for fairness." Debates over fairness sit at the forefront of contemporary economic policies, Butler observes, while fairness persists in Australian cultural narratives. And, as her ethnographic data show, the culture of "fairness" is enforced at home and in school by adults and peers alike, ironically posing particular challenges for immigrant kids struggling to belong.

Butler observed that many parents went to extensive efforts to instill in their children an appreciation of money as the key to life's opportunities. This was a significant theme among both working-class and lower-middle-class parents and was anchored in a strong "work and save" ethic, which, they hoped, would serve children well in adulthood. As one Anglo Australian single mother of three boys under 13 explained, "I tell them how much money I make each week, how much the bills and food and stuff costs, then how much what they're asking for costs, and then I say, 'Add it up, see for yourself,' and then they see I just can't afford it" (Butler 2017, 102). But the children also enacted another set of discourses around consumer culture to manage those occasions when they were faced with economic deprivation.

Butler identifies three strategies by which kids handled economic uncertainty: "going without," "cutting down," and "staying within." For going without, children often seemed to use their families' economic hardship to connect with their friends and position themselves against others, including the school as institution. One day, Butler (2017, 102) observes, the teacher handed out netbooks to 6 of 24 students, explaining "Only the ones who've paid all the money get to take a netbook home. You can't pay just for the netbook and not the school fees, you have to pay both." Evan, an Anglo Australian 10-year-old boy who lived in a single-parent household, called out loudly, "My mum can't afford a hundred and twenty-five dollars!" This was followed by murmurs of agreement from two classmates.

Yet only that morning, Evan had described to Butler a new dirt bike he wanted his mother to buy him. She contrasts the two comments usefully: "In private, Evan boasted of his hope to acquire the 'right' things and projected a future desired self," while in the public classroom, he laid claim to "fairness discourse" in order "to connect with his friends while detaching himself from the school as the cause of this unfairness." Butler notes that the strength of "fairness" as a pervading cultural narrative meant that "there was something else out there—the threads of a deeper and more powerful story—on which children could draw in such moments when financial disparity threatened to exclude them from an immediate social context."

"Cutting down" was another strategy, akin to the "patrolling" strategy I identified in *Longing and Belonging*, in which kids made sure their peers were accurate when making claims and "cut them down" when they were not. In

Australia, this is linked to what is termed the "tall poppy syndrome," in which people who are seen as reaching too far are summarily discouraged—like cutting the head off of a proverbial tall poppy. Butler witnessed teachers "cutting down," as "when 9-year-old Mitchell, who was wearing a new pair of Nikes, spoke rudely to a classmate, and Mrs. Allen announced 'Mitchell's new shoes have gone to his head!' Her students laughed loudly, and Mitchell looked down at his page subdued" (Butler 2017, 104). But children also participated. For example, Butler reported:

> Another morning before school at Inner North, Dakota divulged excitedly that her family had a new car. She described its "soft seats, automatic windows and air-conditioning." We were standing in the playground, and her family car, a big blue shiny Commodore, was parked just beyond the school gates. Dakota then spoke of a second and much older car which her family still owned, but which they had had "for seven years." Her friend Tina, who was also with us and who regularly played at Dakota's house after school, replied coolly, "I can't see the difference between them." Dakota, subdued, said nothing in response. (Butler 2017, 104)

These strategies were far more available to native-born Australians, however, and proved challenging to master for the immigrant kids in the school. Furthermore, the dominance of the "fairness" narrative meant that the simple ploys to belong through commodified goods or services, or sheer knowledge about them, such as I observed in Oakland, California, were not as available to these kids. Thus, rather than going without or cutting down, these kids adopted a strategy of what Butler called "staying within," essentially hiding the extent of their poverty from other children rather than trumpeting it or using it to their cultural advantage to generate solidarity. Butler tells the story of Aisha, a 12-year-old Afghani Australian girl, who told her privately that she was unable to play sports on the weekends, as they cost money. "Like other children from refugee backgrounds whose families faced severe economic disadvantage, Aisha remained silent or changed the subject when money was discussed among her peers" (Butler 2017, 105). As a result, she missed out on many extracurricular, nonschool-sponsored social activities. This work suggests that what was socially useful here, for these children, was not the experience of deprivation itself but the cultural know-how to deploy it effectively for forging solidarity—a know-how that was missing for the refugee children who were actually far more disadvantaged.

What sort of empathy frameworks are the children experiencing in these examples? On the one hand, just like in Oakland, California, consumer culture informs the children's desires—for the dirt bike, for the new car, for the weekend sports opportunity. Inequality puts these desires out of reach for some, generating a topography of poverty and plenty that the children must navigate, just like in Oakland. Parents actively shape children's access to consumer culture, as I've noted elsewhere (Pugh 2009)—sometimes indulging children's desires in an effort to make them feel normal or to communicate their own provisioning abilities, sometimes declining to so as not to appear materialistic. Yet in Australia, the explicit institutional and cultural support for "fairness" acts as a resource for the children, particularly those Anglo Australians who are disadvantaged or low income. In those cases, however, it is not clear that the fairness doctrine acts to nurture empathy for others. Instead, it appears to act as a clarion call to which those similarly disadvantaged (but sometimes advantaged by race and national origin) can respond; the cultural narrative generates no empathy for those who are worse off but only solidarity among relative equals.

Indeed, with regard to cutting down, the fairness discourse appears to be used by adults and children not as a source of emotional connection but as a powerful shaming device, isolating anyone who violates this strong cultural ethos. Finally, the careful secrecy of the refugee/immigrant kids who hide evidence of their own deprivation suggests that they do not perceive a lot of social safety with regard to their disadvantage. This is perhaps the most powerful evidence that the cultural narrative of fairness, while a useful resource for some low-income kids fighting their own consumer invisibility, does not promote greater empathy among those children trying to make sense of inequality or poverty. Australia demonstrates that simply having a different cultural narrative, even one that engages with questions of justice, is not enough to generate significant empathy or compassion among children.

This finding captures something about my own work with kids in Oakland, California. Thanks to the work of Bourdieu and others, I had expected children to do much more differentiating from each other with their consumer talk and practices. Instead, I saw them using consumer culture primarily to connect with others. Yet in that context, it was often a thin connection, a parallel one, of, fellow citizens, with rights to participate, and not a lot of obligation, nor one of deep reciprocity.

Empathy Frameworks

Empathy frameworks give meaning to inequality, they tell us how to feel about poverty and mobility, and they make sense of social action, telling us who owes what to whom. They offer guidance as to how we might view the haves (as "the cream of the crop," "no better than the rest of us," lucky, or worthy of suspicion) versus the have-nots (as lazy or unintelligent, unlucky, martyred, commendable, or wronged). We can look to the empirical examples I've elaborated above to think further about the multiple roles that consumer culture plays in the frameworks that people face: as signal, symptom, ticket, gate, and lure.

- *Signal*: When someone uses consumption to intentionally convey a particular capacity or identity. Buying the right things—and being able to in the first place—can signal a cultural fluency about what makes a good person (e.g., as in the example of Evan's bike);

- *Symptom*: When consumption conveys an inadvertent message about a stigmatized identity or practice. In Australia, for example, it can become a symptom of overreach, of laying claim to what is not rightfully owned or displayed;

- *Ticket*: When consumer practices—including withholding—are used to forge solidarity. Deprivation can, paradoxically, be a means of joining in (as when Evan marshaled peer support with his cry: "my mom can't afford $125");

- *Gate*: When deprivation, and the context that governs its use, serves as an impediment to kids' joining the economy of dignity. The immigrant kids in Australia could not use their poverty as a ticket and thus needed to suppress evidence of their own poverty; and

- *Lure*: When consumption is used to entice, a contingent promise particularly sonorous for low-income children. For Theresa, consumption was held out like a prize, the reward of future goods and the capacity to buy them if she would vault herself into the middle class.

In sum, "empathy frameworks" are embedded in consumer culture; they offer various ways of understanding inequality, poverty, and difference through which parents and other adults draw boundaries to include and exclude others, thereby creating social closeness and social distance. Second, consumer culture intersects with late-modern capitalism to shape and reflect a neoliberal perspective of individual risk and responsibility. Third, while capitalism can draw people into a common social fabric, allowing us to see others as human, nonetheless, such mutual recognition is spread wide and thin. Consumer culture can enable that recognition, as when cultural narratives of fairness work to forge a common solidarity—but even then, it can also serve to exclude.

The Limits of Empathy

One may be forgiven for thinking that consumer culture might impede or inhibit empathy as a matter of course. If empathy requires social closeness, then consumer culture can seem to widen the chasm between us. The competition at the core of consumer culture—the domain of brands, marketing, media, and capitalism—means hierarchy is almost inevitable, and with hierarchy comes social distance. Furthermore, evidence from postsocialist transitions in the ex-Soviet satellites suggests that the advent of capitalism transformed the collective into the aggregate, disembedding people from barter systems of reciprocity and making them into atomized, neoliberal individuals (Berdahl 1999).

To be sure, the example of another Oakland school suggests the complexities of teaching empathy in an environment of copious buying. Arrowhead was a mixed-income independent school that focused closely on developing children's capacity for empathy. The school staged entire weeks to address racial inequality and LGBT issues, its board of directors had multiple conversations about practices of inclusion, and it offered extensive financial aid. One teacher mock-complained to me that if a student called someone else a name at recess and he heard about it as they were filing in, he would just inwardly groan and say, "Well, there goes Math." One can be forgiven for thinking that if empathy was going to grow anywhere among children in the United States, it would be here. And, as I noted in *Longing and Belonging*, the ensuing warm emotional landscape there meant that most social difference—particularly in sexuality, racial/ethnic background, or in family structure—was celebrated rather than shunned. As one parent told me, with abashed pride:

> I just remember Cameron standing up. She got on the stool to get something out of the cabinet. [And then while she was up there,] she went like this [she raises her arm in a salute] and she goes, "I am an ally to gay and lesbian people!" You know, here is this kid! It made me laugh.

The school had helped Cameron, a straight kid, to empathize with the injustices experienced by lesbians and gays enough to proclaim it before her sympathetic mother.

Yet consumer culture, and the discrepancies it highlights in class status among children, proved more elusive for this school's empathy framework. I witnessed kids there, just like in other schools, talking about their birthday parties, their fancy vacations, their weekend plans—not necessarily to best each other but to lay claim to their social citizenship. I observed *some* sharing, to be sure, just as kids do everywhere—and maybe there was more. But it is hard to say that any difference was more than negligible. However, I did not see kids refrain from enjoying some vestige of consumer culture in deference to someone in their midst who couldn't afford to. I didn't see kids reject the valuing of commodified goods or experiences even amid disadvantaged peers, and no one ever got onto a stool to proclaim their allyship with the working class.

Conclusion

Different empathy frameworks are generated by children's social environments in fairly unequal settings—the neoliberal curriculum that Theresa experiences, the "fairness" doctrine that kids narrate in Australia, and the "ally culture" as proclaimed by Cameron. These different cultures give children different resources to use in their environments to interpret inequality, to manage disadvantage, and to understand their own relative fortune. Even as the "ally culture" seemed to enable greater fellow feeling for others, none of these frameworks ultimately was able to tackle the tough nut of class inequality in these advanced capitalist states.

These frameworks work to motivate action, make sense of poverty and mobility, and make difference meaningful not just for children but for adults as well. Consumer culture is thus deployed in these frameworks to offer images that tell children (and their parents) where they should feel shame, connectedness, defiance, hope, or obligation.

Parents interested in "how to talk to kids about poverty" should know that kids are already hearing about it, sometimes in subterranean tones at school, in neighborhoods, and at home. Choosing environments for kids entails not simply choosing the importance of academics or a friendly climate but also choosing the empathy frameworks that children learn from every day. The emotional terrain underlies a moral one whereby children learn the meaning of their place in the world and that of others who surround them.

Notes

1. This blog, verywell.com, reports 17 million unique visitors monthly here: https://mediakit.verywell.com/verywell-advertising/.

2. All names and some identifying details have been changed for confidentiality purposes.

3. The OECD, or the Organisation for Economic Co-operation and Development, is a collection of 35 more advanced countries, including Europe, Japan, and the Anglo American countries; its website, stats.oecd.org, offers continuously updated rankings of member countries' income, poverty, and inequality.

References

Allison, Anne. 2006. *Millennial Monsters: Japanese Toys and the Global Imagination.* Berkeley: University of California Press.

Anderson, Daniel R., Aletha C. Huston, Kelly L. Linebarger, and John C. Wright. 2001. *Early Childhood Television Viewing and Adolescent Behavior:*

Monographs of the Society for Research in Child Development. Hoboken, NJ: Wiley-Blackwell.

Berdahl, Daphne. 1999. *Where the World Ended: Re-Unification and Identity in the German Borderland*. Berkeley: University of California Press.

Berhau, Patricia. 2000. "Class and the Experience of Consumers: A Study of Practices of Acquisition." PhD diss. Temple University.

Buckingham, David. 2007. "Childhood in the Age of Global Media." *Children's Geographies* 5 (1–2): 43–54.

Buckingham, David. 2011. *The Material Child*. Malden, MA: Polity Press.

Butler, Rose. 2017. "Children Making Sense of Economic Insecurity: Facework, Fairness and Belonging." *Journal of Sociology* 53 (1): 94–109.

Chaplin, Lan Nguyen, and Deborah Roedder John. 2005. "The Development of Self-Brand Connections in Children and Adolescents." *Journal of Consumer Research* 32 (June): 119–29.

Chaplin, Lan Nguyen, and Deborah Roedder John. 2007. "Growing up in a Material World: Age Differences in Materialism in Children and Adolescents." *Journal of Consumer Research* 34 (4): 480–93.

Chin, Elizabeth. 2001. *Purchasing Power: Black Kids and American Consumer Culture*. Minneapolis: University of Minnesota Press.

DiMaggio, Paul. 1987. "Classification in Art." *American Sociological Review* 52: 440–55.

Linn, Susan. 2004. *Consuming Kids: Protecting Our Children from the Onslaught of Marketing and Advertising*. New York: Anchor.

Lizardo, Omar. 2006. "How Cultural Tastes Shape Personal Networks." *American Sociological Review* 71: 778–807.

Martens, Lydia, Dale Southerton, and Sue Scott. 2004. "Bringing Children (and Parents) into the Sociology of Consumption: Towards a Theoretical and Empirical Agenda." *Journal of Consumer Culture* 4 (2): 155–82.

McNeal, James U. 1999. *The Kids Market: Myths and Realities*. Ithaca, NY: Paramount Market.

Morin, Amy. 2017. "How to Talk to Your Kids About Poverty." *Verywell Blog*. July 18. Accessed November 29. https://www.verywell.com/how-to-talk-to-kids-about-poverty-4142890.

Piketty, Thomas, Emmanuel Saez, and Gabriel Zucman. 2016. "Distributional National Accounts: Methods and Estimates for the United States." No. w22945. National Bureau of Economic Research.

Pugh, Allison J. 2009. *Longing and Belonging: Parents, Children and Consumer Culture*. Berkeley: University of California Press.

Pugh, Allison J. 2011. "Distinction, Boundaries or Bridges?: Children, Inequality and the Uses of Culture." *Poetics* 39 (1): 1–18.

Pugh, Allison J. 2014. "The Theoretical Costs of Ignoring Childhood: Rethinking Independence, Insecurity and Inequality." *Theory and Society* 43 (1): 71–89.

Schor, Juliet B. 2004. *Born to Buy*. New York: Scribner.

Seiter, Ellen. 1993. *Sold Separately: Children and Parents in Consumer Culture.* New Brunswick, NJ: Rutgers University Press.

Sennett, Richard, and Jonathan Cobb. 1972. *The Hidden Injuries of Class.* New York: Knopf.

Thorne, Barrie. 2008. "The Chinese Girls and the 'Pokémon Kids': Children Constructing Difference in Urban California." In *Figuring the Future: Children, Youth, and Globalization,* edited by Jennifer Cole and Deborah Durham. 73–97. Santa Fe, NM: SAR Press.

Waters, M. 1990. *Ethnic Options: Choosing Identities in America.* Berkeley: University of California Press.

Yan, Y. 2009. "The Good Samaritan's New Trouble: A Study of the Changing Moral Landscape in Contemporary China." *Social Anthropology* 17: 9–24.

CHAPTER TEN

Do We Talk about Race/ Ethnicity with Our Children or Not? Variations in Parental Ethnic-Racial Socialization Strategies

Erin Pahlke

When Barack Obama became the first nonwhite president of the United States in 2008, many Americans believed it was a sign that the nation was post-racial (Debusmann 2016). However, subsequent events made race/ethnicity[1] seem even more salient. The Black Lives Matter Movement, launched in response to the 2012 shooting death of African American teenager Trayvon Martin, has brought renewed attention to cases of racial/ethnic injustice. The explicitly racial statements made during the 2016 presidential election by Donald Trump unearthed the anti-immigrant, and specifically anti-Muslim and anti-Mexican, sentiments that persist in the United States. The effect spread beyond campaign speeches, with teachers reporting a substantial increase in anti-Muslim and anti-immigrant sentiments within K-12 schools (Southern Poverty Law Center 2016), and the Ku Klux Klan held a victory march after Trump's election (e.g., Musumeci 2016). Around the world, readers have met with headlines like "Trump's Election Led to 'Barrage of Hate,' Report Finds," "Donald Trump's Rise has Coincided with an Explosion of Hate Groups," and "Chicago Police Department Plagued by Systemic Racism, Task Force Finds" (see Chen 2017; Davey and Smith 2016; Sidahmed 2016). The United States is, once again, very much a country focused on race/ethnicity. In this context, what—if anything—should parents say to their kids about race/ethnicity?

Social scientists have been studying parental approaches to topics of race/ethnicity with their children for the past three decades. This area of work was originally labeled as racial socialization and focused on the processes that African American parents engage in to raise physically and emotionally healthy African American children in a society in which being African American is perceived negatively (Peters 2002). However, as the field has developed, researchers have expanded the focus to all racial/ethnic groups. As such, ethnic-racial socialization is generally defined as race- or ethnicity-focused communications to children (Hughes et al. 2006). In the current environment, for example, ethnic-racial socialization may include talking to children about the white supremacy marches in Charlottesville, taking children to Black Lives Matter protests, or watching news programs as a family that include commentary about the role of race in U.S. politics.

The goal of this chapter is to highlight contemporary research and theorizing on ethnic-racial socialization. I emphasize examples from my own and other scholars' recent work to demonstrate current directions in the field. Ethnic-racial socialization can originate from a number of individuals in children's lives, including their extended families, peers, and teachers (see Priest et al. 2014 for a recent review); however, the vast majority of work has focused on parental messages and, given the theme of this volume, this is what this chapter will also do. Furthermore, the chapter will focus on parenting in the United States, both because the vast majority of research has been completed in that country and because ethnic-racial socialization approaches vary depending on country-level factors such as structural inequalities and norms surrounding intergroup contact. After providing a brief overview of ethnic-racial socialization, I explore five specific typologies of socialization. Within each typology, I highlight variations in the use of the socialization strategy both between and within racial/ethnic groups. Finally, I explore the impact of various ethnic-racial socialization strategies on children's outcomes.

Ethnic-Racial Socialization

Ethnic-racial socialization refers to ethnicity- or race-focused communications to children (Hughes et al. 2006). This communication can be either implicit or explicit and is generally communicated to children through a combination of family discussions, direct instruction about race/ethnicity, and observations that children make about their parents interacting with people of their own and other races (Murray and Mandara 2002; Thornton et al. 1990). Importantly, there is considerable variation in the content of these communications. In 2006 Hughes and colleagues reviewed the literature and identified four typologies of ethnic-racial socialization: cultural socialization, preparation for bias, promotion of mistrust, and egalitarianism. In recent years, as more information about white parents' socialization approaches has emerged, a fifth typology—colorblind socialization—has been proposed (Pahlke, Bigler, and Suizzo 2012; Vittrup 2017). These typologies sometimes overlap in practice; for example, parents often send preparation for bias and cultural socialization messages in tandem to promote the importance of being prepared for discrimination (negative behavior directed toward people based solely on their racial/ethnic group membership [Hughes et al. 2006]) while also having pride in one's race/ethnicity (Barr and Neville 2008; Suizzo, Robinson, and Pahlke 2008). However, examining the typologies separately allows for a clearer analysis of variations between and within racial/ethnic groups.[2]

Cultural Socialization

Cultural socialization is a typology of ethnic-racial socialization that includes messages about cultural beliefs, customs, and history, including rituals surrounding food, language, and holidays (Hughes et al. 2006). Regardless of whether they are verbal or nonverbal, these messages are generally designed to instill racial-ethnic pride in the child. Research suggests that almost all African American, Latino, and Asian American parents send cultural socialization messages to their children (Hughes et al. 2008; Huynh and Fuligni 2008; Phinney and Chavira 1995). In comparison, white parents who are not strongly identified with an ethnic group report sending cultural socialization messages relatively rarely. Indeed, many non-Jewish, white parents struggle to even identify what cultural socialization would look like in their families (Hughes et al. 2008).

Although many families participate in cultural socialization, the focus of the messages tends to differ based on racial/ethnic group membership. Within African American families, cultural socialization is often overt, with a focus on both teaching children about their heritage and beginning to prepare them for racial discrimination. Thus, although the content of cultural socialization messages does not explicitly address racism and discrimination, many African American parents hope that the racial/ethnic pride that cultural socialization is designed to promote can serve as a buffer against racism and inequality. As an African American mother explained to Hughes et al. (2008, 247), she displays African art and books with African American protagonists in her home for her son because "if he looks on TV, he doesn't see [himself]."

Within African American families, children's ages dictate the focus of socialization messages, with parents tending to focus particularly on cultural socialization and avoiding explicit messages about bias with their young preschool- and early-elementary-school-aged children (Caughy et al. 2002; Edwards and Few-Demo 2016; Hughes and Chen 1997; Suizzo, Robinson, and Pahlke 2008). In qualitative interviews, African American parents reported to Peters (2002) that they thought messages about racism were inappropriate for young children and worried that focusing on racism would negatively impact young children's self-esteem. By focusing on providing same-race/ethnicity dolls, attending cultural events, displaying ethnic art in the home, and reading books about culture and history, parents are able to promote their children's racial/ethnic pride while also laying the groundwork for future discrimination-focused ethnic-racial socialization. As one mother of a three-year-old girl explained during an interview, "I think [my daughter] needs to understand her heritage, where she comes from, and how society is going to react to her as a strong black female, because that's what we're raising her to be" (Suizzo et al. 2008, 298).

In comparison, within other racial/ethnic groups, cultural socialization tends to be covert, meaning that rather than being explicitly designed to teach children, it is deeply embedded in the family's everyday practices and traditions (Umaña-Taylor and Fine 2004). Compared to overt cultural socialization, during which children feel as though their families are trying to teach them about their racial/ethnic background, in covert cultural socialization, children feel as though their families are just going about their daily lives and, in the process, teaching them about their racial/ethnic group. In Latino families, for example, cultural socialization tends not to be focused around overt activities like buying books about the native culture that children are required to read (Umaña-Taylor et al. 2009). Instead, cultural socialization more frequently occurs as parents covertly teach their children about their heritage through everyday food preparation, native language use, and exposure to music and media from their home culture. This type of cultural socialization is often a method for ensuring that the children retain cultural values (Hughes et al. 2008).

Generational status is also sometimes related to families' cultural socialization practices, although the effect varies depending on racial/ethnic group (Hughes 2003; Phinney and Chavira 1995; Umaña-Taylor and Guimond 2012). Within Latino families, the frequency of cultural socialization in families is related to generational status, with more recent immigrants to the United States spending more time on cultural socialization (Umaña-Taylor et al. 2009). It may be that these more recent immigrants have closer ties to their cultural traditions and, as such, are more likely to emphasize cultural socialization. Interestingly, generational status has not been identified as a predictor of cultural socialization practices within Chinese families (Huynh and Fuligni 2008). More work is needed to understand why Latino—but not Chinese—parents who have recently immigrated to the United States may be more focused on ensuring that their histories are not forgotten.

Looking across racial/ethnic groups, other contextual factors influence parents' use of cultural socialization. For example, parents' own ethnic-racial identity has been positively related to the frequency of cultural socialization (Crouter et al. 2008; Hughes 2003); when race/ethnicity is a central and important part of parents' own conceptions of themselves, they are more likely to work to instill a similar sense of racial/ethnic centrality and pride in their children. Further highlighting the importance of considering context, researchers have found that wealthier racial-ethnic minority families tend to send more cultural socialization messages to their children (Crouter et al. 2008; Csizmadia, Rollins, and Kaneakua 2014). To explore why this may be, Crouter et al. (2008) looked at two-parent African American families. They found that the path between socioeconomic status and cultural socialization strategies was mediated by the mothers' sense of occupational self-direction and feelings of self-efficacy; in other words, control and power at work appear to lead African American mothers also to feel empowered to talk to their children more frequently about racial/ethnic pride and traditions. Wealth may also be related to cultural socialization practices because of differences in the racial/ethnic composition of neighborhoods; some scholars have found that families that live in more racially-ethnically diverse neighborhoods send more cultural socialization messages, perhaps out of a desire to ensure that their children are aware of their own culture (see Priest et al. 2014).

Research also suggests that gender plays a role in the frequency and impact of cultural socialization messages. In many families, traditional gender roles dictate the socialization that children receive. As such, females are viewed as the cultural keepers in many families (McHale et al. 2006; Phinney 1990), which may explain why African American, Mexican American, and Chinese American girls receive more cultural socialization messages than their male counterparts (Dunbar, Perry, and Leerkes 2015; Huynh and Fuligni 2008) and why African American and Latino mothers participate in more cultural socialization than fathers (Crouter et al. 2008; McHale et al. 2006; Thornton et al. 1990). Interestingly, in another recent study of Latino adolescents, Umaña-Taylor and Guimond (2012) did not find differences in the amount of cultural socialization that female and male adolescents reported receiving. They did, however, find that the link between cultural socialization and ethnic identity was stronger among female than male children. Furthermore, in a longitudinal study of Mexican American families, mothers' cultural socialization approaches impacted adolescents' ethnic identity, while fathers' cultural socialization practices did not (Knight et al. 2011). Although more work is needed on this topic, these findings suggest that gendered family experiences and expectations may impact the salience and impact of cultural socialization messages, with mothers disproportionately likely to do the work of cultural socialization and, further, with daughters disproportionately likely to review the cultural socialization messages.

Cultural socialization is positively associated with children's achievement and academic adjustment (Caughy et al. 2002; Cooper and Smalls 2010; Murry and Brody 2002). Recent work has reported that African American adolescents' experiences with cultural socialization positively affected their GPAs, educational aspirations, and cognitive engagement; further, cultural socialization attenuated the negative effects of teacher discrimination on adolescents' academic outcomes (Wang and Huguley 2012). Cultural socialization may lead children to focus on school out of a sense of family obligation, which is a consistent component of cultural socialization in many Latino and Asian American families (Huynh and Fuligni 2008). Cultural socialization may also promote academic achievement through its impact on children's own self-views (Neblett et al. 2006). Cultural socialization leads children to view race/ethnicity as a central part of their identity (Neblett et al. 2009; Rivas-Drake, Hughes, and Way 2009) and feel positively about their own racial/ethnic group (Tran and Lee 2010). And, consistent with the idea that changes in self-views may lead to increased academic outcomes, in a recent study of African American and white adolescents, the relation between cultural socialization and academic engagement was mediated by self-esteem (Hughes et al. 2009). In other words, cultural socialization impacted achievement through its influence on the youths' self-esteem. Cultural socialization, then, appears to have positive impacts on children's development. It does not, however, include messages about discrimination. For that, parents turn to socialization messages designed to prepare children for bias or promote mistrust.

Preparation for Bias and Promotion of Mistrust

The ethnic-racial socialization typology of preparation for bias refers to messages that are designed to prepare children to both identify and cope with discrimination (Hughes et al. 2006). In comparison, another typology—promotion of mistrust—socializes children to be wary of racial-ethnic out-groups' intentions (Hughes et al. 2006; Hughes and Johnson 2001). The distinction between these socialization typologies lies in their goals; while preparation-for-bias messages aims to advise children on ways to cope with and manage discrimination, promotion of mistrust messages merely aims to sow distrust about out-group interactions. Research suggests that the vast majority of parents do not promote mistrust of racial/ethnic out-groups (Hughes et al. 2008). For example, surveys have found that only between 3 and 10 percent of African American parents promote mistrust within their children (Hughes and Chen 1997, 1999; Thornton et al. 1990). In comparison, most African Americans do utilize preparation-for-bias socialization. Comparison studies suggest that African American parents send more frequent preparation-for-bias messages than Latino and Asian parents, who in turn send more messages than white parents (Hughes 2003; Hughes et al. 2008; Huynh and Fuligni 2008).

Differences in racial/ethnic groups' utilization of preparation-for-bias socialization messages may be related, in part, to differences in parents' concerns that their children will confront racial/ethnic bias in their lives. In a qualitative study of parents' perceptions of the barriers to education their children would confront, 67 percent of African American mothers spontaneously mentioned racial/ethnic discrimination compared to 14 percent of Mexican American and 0 percent of white American mothers (Suizzo et al. 2014). Although these trends may be changing in the wake of the anti-Mexican, anti-Muslim, and anti-immigrant sentiments surrounding the Trump presidential campaign in 2016 (Southern Poverty Law Center 2016), research suggests that in the past, it was African American parents, in particular, who were concerned about the racial/ethnic discrimination they believed their children would confront in the United States.

Parents who do focus on preparation-for-bias socialization tend to tailor their messages to their children's ages. In a cross-sectional study of African American, Dominican, and Puerto Rican parents, Hughes (2003) found that parents of older children (ages 10 to 17) were more likely to report sending preparation-for-bias messages than parents of younger children (ages 6 to 9). Other researchers have reported similar trends, with parents focusing on preparation for bias with increasing frequency as children move through adolescence toward adulthood (Barr and Neville 2008; Hughes and Johnson 2001). This shift in socialization strategies from a focus on cultural pride to preparation for bias may reflect parents' beliefs that children are cognitively capable of understanding racism (Hughes et al. 2008). Parents also may begin to focus more of their socialization on preparation for bias during adolescence because they believe that their children will have more personal experiences with racism as they age.

Indeed, children's reports of their own experiences with discrimination are related to the frequency of preparation-for-bias messages they report receiving (Crouter et al. 2008). There are several potential explanations for this relation. First, it may be that, consistent with bidirectional views of socialization, experiencing discrimination leads children to initiate discussions about bias with their parents (Crouter and Booth 2003). Second, it may be that the order of causation is reversed and that preparation-for-bias socialization leads children to be more aware of—and more likely to report—discrimination. Finally, it may be that when parents become aware of their children's experiences with discrimination, they communicate more preparation-for-bias messages to help their children cope with the discrimination. Consistent with this perspective, African American families are more likely to prepare their children for bias when they believe that their children have personally encountered racism (Hughes 2003; Hughes and Johnson 2001). Further, African American mothers who have themselves experienced racial discrimination at work are more likely to convey messages of preparation for bias to their children (Crouter et al. 2008). These findings are consistent with ecological models of development, which suggest that individuals' parenting decisions are impacted by their experiences within broader systems in society (Bronfenbrenner 1979).

Consistent with the hypothesis that parents use preparation-for-bias socialization approaches more frequently when they are concerned that their children will confront bias, African American boys receive more frequent preparation-for-bias messages than African American girls (Dunbar et al. 2015). This difference in part reflects the gender differences seen in cultural socialization; if girls are to be the cultural keepers, relatively more of the socialization they receive will be focused on cultural traditions and histories. However, this gender difference appears also to reflect differences in parents' beliefs about the amount and type of bias that their children will confront. A recent BBC News (2015) story titled "Why do U.S. Police Keep Killing Unarmed Black Men?" highlights this concern for many families. As an African American parent in a recent qualitative study explained, "Boys have historically been characterized as a threat more so than females" (Thomas and Blackmon 2015, 82). Many African American parents worry that society views African American boys as dangerous, and, as such, they are more likely to be unfairly targeted or hurt (Hill 2001). Thus, it is possible that parents focus on preparation-for-bias socialization with boys out of concern about the overt racial/ethnic discrimination they may experience (Dunbar et al. 2015).

In families that explicitly discuss discrimination, children have the opportunity to learn from their parents' experiences and ideas. Thus, African American parents' tendency to communicate preparation-for-bias messages may help to explain why African American children's understanding of racism tends to be more elaborate than that of their white peers (McKown 2004). We know relatively little about Latino and Asian American children's perceptions of racism, but a recent study of elementary-school-age children's views of the 2008 presidential election suggests that Latino children may adopt views similar to those of their African American peers. During one-on-one interviews, my collaborators and I asked black, Latino, and white children about their perceptions of how Obama's race might affect his chances of being elected president. Latino children were as likely as black children to attribute a hypothetical Obama loss to his race; white children, on the other hand, were less likely than their peers to think racism would influence the election outcome (Patterson, Pahlke, and Bigler 2013).

Messages about discrimination also appear to influence children's self-views and academic achievement. Preparation for bias, like cultural socialization, is positively related to racial-ethnic identity and self-esteem among African American adolescents (Murry et al. 2009), perhaps because the messages provide children a sense of belonging to a broader group as well as with a mechanism for understanding negative interactions or outcomes. Preparation-for-bias messages have also been related to increased academic achievement and persistence in some samples. For example, among African American samples, preparation for bias has been associated with higher grades (Bowman and Howard 1985) and increased academic engagement (Smalls 2009). It may be that learning about discrimination motivates children to overcome the barriers (Huynh and Fuligni 2008). However, in some samples, and particularly those that include young children, preparation-for-bias messages have been linked to negative academic outcomes, including poor school performance and decreased school engagement (Smalls 2009; Smith, Atkins, and Connell 2003). Furthermore, although promotion-of-mistrust messages are rare, they have been linked to lower levels of academic achievement and engagement (Hughes et al. 2006). An overemphasis on messages related to racial barriers and mistrust of more privileged groups seems to undermine youths' sense of well-being and achievement (Hughes et al. 2009). Furthermore, socialization emphasizing whites' biases appears to prompt students to withdraw from predominantly white activities or institutions out of a fear that they will be unfairly judged (Biafora et al. 1993). To avoid these potential negative consequences, many parents incorporate messages of egalitarianism in their socialization approach.

Egalitarianism

In comparison to messages that highlight differences between racial/ethnic groups, egalitarianism messages promote intergroup interaction. These messages, which are positive in valence, emphasize the similarities between racial-ethnic groups (Hughes et al. 2006). For example, adolescents have reported that their parents have said things like, "No race is better than the other," or, "I should treat everybody the same no matter what and respect that everyone has their own way of living, culture wise" (Barr and Neville 2008, 145). These messages do not encourage silence about race; instead, the focus is on encouraging children to value and respect all individuals regardless of their racial/ethnic group membership. Self-reports from parents and children suggest that parents from all racial/ethnic groups send egalitarianism messages regularly (Hughes et al. 2006). However, the focus of the socialization appears to differ between racial/ethnic groups. Particularly for African American and Latino parents, egalitarianism is often designed to instill the idea in their children that they are equal to all and that their racial/ethnic differences do not make them inferior to others (Hughes et al. 2008; Suizzo et al. 2008). In comparison, white parents often use egalitarianism to deemphasize the importance of race/ethnicity and encourage diversity (Hughes et al. 2008).

Although egalitarianism can—and does—happen through parents' explicit comments to their children (Priest et al. 2014), this type of ethnic-racial socialization is also particularly well suited for less explicit forms of socialization. In the tripartite model of parental socialization, Parke et al. (1994) propose that parents socialize their children through three mechanisms: direct instruction, personal interaction, and provision of opportunities. Egalitarianism messages, then, can be socialized in children through (a) parents' discussions and explicit directives about equality (direct instruction); (b) parents' interactions with their children and with other people of their own and other races and ethnicities (personal interaction); and (c) parents' decisions about the schools their children attend, the neighborhoods where they live, and the resources and people to which they are exposed (provision of opportunities).

In a recent study, colleagues and I examined white parents' use of egalitarianism socialization in the form of both direct instruction and provision of opportunities. In a sample of 139 white late adolescents, we found that the frequency of direct instruction of egalitarianism was positively related to the adolescents' warmth toward racial/ethnic out-groups (Hughes, Patterson, and Pahlke 2016). However, the racial/ethnic composition of the adolescents' high school classes moderated the relationship. The adolescents who experienced high levels of egalitarianism socialization had relatively high levels of out-group warmth regardless of the racial/ethnic composition of their classes. Among adolescents who experienced low levels of direct instruction promoting egalitarianism, though, having more racially/ethnically diverse classrooms in effect worked as a buffer; these students had more positive feelings about the racial/ethnic out-groups than their peers in less racially/ethnically diverse high school classes. These findings suggest that parents' provisions of opportunities—in this case, the schools they sent their children to—also serve as a form of egalitarianism socialization. Specifically, when white children receive direct verbal messages from their parents about the importance of egalitarianism, they have better attitudes about racial/ethnic out-groups. And even if they do not receive those messages, they have positive attitudes about racial/ethnic out-groups as long as they have racially/ethnically diverse classrooms. These findings can be framed as hopeful: when children attend diverse classes, white parents do not need to do much to promote positive attitudes among their children. However, as neighborhood segregation and academic tracking further segregate schools (see Orfield et al. 2016), parents may need to rely on direct instruction.

As in our study of white adolescents, researchers have found that direct instruction promoting egalitarianism leads to positive outcomes for youth. For example, in a longitudinal study, African American adolescents with parents who sent more messages that focused on encouraging cross-race friendships did better on tests of verbal performance (Banerjee, Harrell, and Johnson 2011). Furthermore, if egalitarianism socialization is thought to include the opportunities that parents provide for children to integrate with racial/ethnic out-groups, a large body of research suggests that intergroup contact reduces intergroup prejudice (Pettigrew and Tropp 2006). Future research is needed to explore whether the effects of provisions of opportunity-based egalitarianism socialization differs depending on parents' motivations. If parents choose to send their children to racially/ethnically diverse schools out of a desire to promote egalitarianism, are their children more positively impacted by the diversity? We do not currently know the answer, although emerging work on colorblind socialization suggests that it might.

Colorblind Socialization

When the typology of egalitarianism socialization was first proposed, researchers suggested that messages that deemphasized race should be included within it (Hughes et al. 2006). However, more recent work suggests that some parents utilize a form of socialization that is more closely tied to a colorblind ideology (Bonilla-Silva 2003). At its core, colorblind ideology holds that recognizing race is a precondition to racism, and thus, failing to recognize race reduces racism. Some proponents of colorblind ideology assert that racism is no longer a significant social problem and therefore, attention to race is inappropriate, whereas others acknowledge that racism persists but believe that it can be effectively eliminated via attention to individuals' individuating characteristics rather than their race (Neville et al. 2000). Regardless of the specific components driving a parent's ideology, colorblind socialization refers to messages that indicate that race/ethnicity should not be acknowledged or discussed (Pahlke, Bigler, and Suizzo 2012; Vittrup 2017).

Particularly within white families, at times, parents' socialization strategies involve a concerted effort *not* to address race/ethnicity with their children. In one of the first studies to investigate white mothers' ethnic-racial socialization strategies (Pahlke, Bigler, and Suizzo 2012), I videotaped white mothers reading to their four- to five-year-old children. One of the books, *What If the Zebras Lost Their Stripes?* (Reitano 1998), asks a series of questions about what would happen if some zebras were white and others were black.

Although the book makes obvious parallels to relations among black and white people (for example, one page asks, "Could black and white friends still hold hands?"), only 11 percent of the mothers said anything about inter-racial interactions among people while reading the book. One mother's discussion of the zebras in the book highlights the way in which many families approached the story. She asked, "Would there be two different kinds of zebras? Black zebras and white zebras? Would it be like dogs? Like dachshunds. There are different colors of dachshunds, but they're all dachshunds." This mother's choice to compare black and white zebras to black and white dogs rather than to people highlights the way in which many mothers ardently avoided any discussion of race with their children.

White parents' preference for colorblind socialization seems to arise, at least in part, out of concerns that their young children are not cognitively prepared to learn about race (Pahlke, Bigler, and Suizzo 2012; Vittrup 2017), and so, they are in some ways similar to nonwhite parents who avoid sending preparation-for-bias messages to children while they are young (Suizzo et al. 2008). However, unlike their nonwhite peers, many white parents continue to avoid discussions or race/ethnicity when their children are older, citing concerns that discussions will sensitize children to racial/ethnic differences and lead them to become prejudiced (Kofkin, Katz, and Downey 1995) or that they believe, consistent with trends among U.S. white adults, that race/ethnicity is no longer relevant (Fletcher and Cohen 2009). Further, many white adults living in the United States report being fearful of saying the wrong thing about race (Apfelbaum, Norton, and Sommers 2012), and so it may be that white parents avoid discussing race with their children out of a fear that they will misspeak and make a situation worse.

Researchers have only recently begun to focus on colorblind socialization, and so we still know relatively little about its effects. However, colorblind socialization does not—as parents often hope—lead children not to see race/ethnicity or to develop unbiased attitudes (Pahlke, Bigler, and Suizzo 2012). Colorblind socialization may, however, teach children that race/ethnicity should not be discussed. Recent studies suggest that as white children age, they become increasing hesitant to discuss race/ethnicity (Apfelbaum et al. 2008) and often distrust others' reports of racism (Kaiser and Miller 2001). Finally, when parents choose not to discuss race/ethnicity, children may look to their parents' nonverbal behavior toward racial/ethnic out-group members for guidance (Catelli, De Dea, and Nesdale 2008; Pahlke, Bigler, and Suizzo 2012). Given the persisting racial/ethnic segregation in the United States (see Logan and Stults 2011), parents who are interested in promoting unbiased attitudes in their children need to reflect on whether their personal interactions with racial/ethnic out-group members are sending the right messages to their children.

Conclusion

The United States is becoming increasingly racially/ethnically diverse. The U.S. Census Bureau projects that by 2020, children and adolescents of color will compose the majority; further, by 2060, just 26 percent of all children are projected to be single-race, non-Hispanic whites (Colby and Ortman 2015). And yet, this increasing diversity is not leading to a post-racial society; the 2016 presidential election highlighted the many ways in which race/ethnicity continues to impact people's experiences and attitudes within the country. Thus, parents will need to continue to struggle with the question of how to best teach their children about race/ethnicity.

The research reviewed in this chapter suggests that parents' approaches to ethnic-racial socialization vary greatly. The variations can be understood through the framework of ecological models of development (Bronfenbrenner 1979; Garcia Coll et al. 1996). These models emphasize that development is the result of interactions between individuals and their surrounding environments. Embedded in this perspective is the acknowledgment that social position variables influence the ways in which individuals are impacted by proximal and distal factors. Thus, it is not surprising that the research reviewed in this chapter highlights the ways in which factors such as race/ethnicity, gender, generational status, and class are related to variations in ethnic-racial socialization.

Although there are many contextual factors related to variations in ethnic-racial socialization approaches, the central factor appears to be racial/ethnic group membership. Many white families avoid discussing race/ethnicity and focus on egalitarianism and colorblind socialization. Going forward, some white families may continue to avoid discussions of race/ethnicity with their children; indeed, they have the privilege of seeing their own racial/ethnic group portrayed positively in mainstream media and public institutions and, further, of experiencing relatively low levels of racial/ethnic discrimination. Other white families, however, may be motivated to modify their ethnic-racial socialization strategies and begin to encourage their children to be aware of their own racial/ethnic privilege and to develop color consciousness (Vittrup 2017). In the coming years, researchers will need to explore the factors that affect white parents' socialization strategies, particularly in light of the increasing number of books and interventions aimed at increasing awareness of white privilege and addressing racial inequality.

Nonwhite parents, in comparison, tend to draw on a more diverse range of ethnic-racial socialization strategies, with Latino and Asian American families often focusing relatively more of their efforts on cultural socialization and African American families, particularly as their children age, focusing relatively more on preparation for bias. These different ethnic-racial socialization approaches have different effects on children. Cultural socialization and preparation-for-bias messages appear to lead nonwhite children to develop more positive self-views and become further engaged in academics, as long as a promotion of mistrust of white institutions is not overemphasized. Colorblind socialization, in comparison, appears to be effective at teaching children not to mention race/ethnicity, although it does not teach children to develop unbiased racial attitudes effectively.

In the coming years, additional work is needed to better understand the ways in which variations in families' national identities impact ethnic-racial socialization strategies. Researchers are working to address these gaps, and I have attempted to highlight examples in this chapter. But, as the field of ethnic-racial socialization grows, it is important to continue to move beyond sweeping generalizations that suggest that all Latino or Asian American families, for example, are similar. Further, it is important to make sure that all groups are represented; currently, for example, the practices of Native Americans and Muslim Americans (among others) are largely left out of these discussions. Additional research focused on intersectionalities is also necessary. Recent work highlights the ways in which gender, socioeconomic status, generational status, and race/ethnicity intersect to impact ethnic-racial socialization strategies. Additional work highlighting these intersections will benefit the field. Future work is also needed to explore how the various typologies of ethnic-racial socialization interact with one another to impact children's outcomes. Finally, work that considers changes over time in parental socialization is important.

Recently, many Americans have felt as if issues of race/ethnicity are continually in the news. Researchers need to document the ways in which parents respond to these social events. Further studies of ethnic-racial socialization will hopefully provide parents with additional information on which to base their decisions about whether to talk to their kids about race/ethnicity—and, if they decide to talk, what to say.

Notes

1. In this chapter, I use the labels *racial/ethnic* and *race/ethnicity* to describe individuals' membership in groups that are commonly referred to as "white," "African American," "Latino," and so forth. I view race/ethnicity not as biologically but as socially created while also recognizing that the social construction of race/ethnicity impacts children and parents in the United States and around the world (see Smedley and Smedley 2005). I use the term *ethnic-racial socialization* both to acknowledge that the concepts of ethnicity and race often overlap in parental socialization and to remain consistent with other scholars in psychology (Hughes et al. 2006).

2. Although scholars recognize that the African American, Asian, Latino, and white populations in the United States are diverse in terms of national

origin, generation, immigration status, and socioeconomic status (e.g., Ramirez 2004)—and furthermore, do not include all individuals living in the United States (e.g., Native Americans, Muslim Americans)—research on ethnic-racial socialization tends to focus on these four broad groups. Whenever possible, within this chapter, I have noted variations within the racial/ethnic groups.

References

Apfelbaum, Evan P., Michael I. Norton, and Samuel R. Sommers. 2012. "Racial Color Blindness: Emergence, Practice, and Implications." *Current Directions in Psychological Science* 21 (3): 205–09.

Apfelbaum, Evan P., Kristin Pauker, Nalini Ambady, Samuel R. Sommers, and Michael I. Norton. 2008. "Learning (Not) to Talk About Race: When Older Children Underperform in Social Categorization." *Developmental Psychology* 44 (5): 1513–18.

Banerjee, Meeta, Zaje Harrell, and Deborah Johnson. 2011. "Racial/Ethnic Socialization and Parental Involvement in Education as Predictors of Cognitive Ability and Achievement in African American Children." *Journal of Youth and Adolescence* 40 (5): 595–605.

Barr, Simone, and Helen Neville. 2008. "Examination of the Link between Parental Racial Socialization Messages and Racial Ideology Among Black College Students." *Journal of Black Psychology* 34 (2): 131–55.

BBC News. 2015. "Why Do U.S. Police Keep Killing Unarmed Black Men?" http://www.bbc.com/news/world-us-canada-32740523.

Biafora, Frank A., George J. Warheit, Ric S. Zimmerman, Andres G. Gil, Eleni Apospori, Dorothy Taylor, and William A. Vega. 1993. "Racial Mistrust and Deviant Behaviors Among Ethnically Diverse Black Adolescent Boys." *Journal of Applied Social Psychology* 23 (11): 891–910.

Bonilla-Silva, Eduardo. 2003. *Racism Without Racists: Color-Blind Racism and the Persistence of Racial Inequality in the United States.* Lanham, MD: Rowman and Littlefield.

Bornstein, Marc H., and Robert H. Bradley. 2003. *Socioeconomic Status, Parenting, and Child Development: Monographs in Parenting.* Mahwah, NJ: Erlbaum.

Bowman, Phillip J., and Cleopatra Howard. 1985. "Race-Related Socialization, Motivation and Academic Achievement." *Journal of the American Academy of Child Psychiatry* 24 (2): 134–41.

Bronfenbrenner, Urie. 1979. *The Ecology of Human Development: Experiments by Nature and Design.* Cambridge, MA: Harvard University Press.

Catelli, Luigi, Cristina De Dea, and Drew Nesdale. 2008. "Learning Social Attitudes: Children's Sensitivity to the Nonverbal Behaviors of Adult Models During Interracial Interactions. *Personality and Social Psychology Bulletin* 34 (11): 1504–13.

Caughy, Margaret O'Brien, Patricia J. O'Campo, Suzanne M. Randolph, and Kim Nickerson. 2002. "The Influence of Racial Socialization Practices on the

Cognitive and Behavioral Competence of African American Preschoolers. *Child Development* 73 (5): 1611–25.

Chen, Michelle. 2016. "Donald Trump's Rise Has Coincided With an Explosion of Hate Groups." *The Nation.* https://www.thenation.com/article /donald-trumps-rise-has-coincided-with-an-explosion-of-hate-groups/.

Colby, Sandra, and Jennifer Ortman. 2015. "Projections of the Size and Composition of the U.S. Population: 2014 to 2060." *Current Population Reports.* U.S. Census Bureau. https://www.census.gov/content/dam/Census/library /publications/2015/demo/p25-1143.pdf.

Cooper, Shauna M., and Ciara Smalls. 2010. "Culturally Distinctive and Academic Socialization: Direct and Interactive Relationships with African American Adolescents' Academic Adjustment." *Journal of Youth and Adolescence* 39: 199–212.

Crouter, Ann C., Megan E. Baril, Kelly Davis, and Susan M. McHale. 2008. "Processes Linking Social Class and Racial Socialization in African American Dual-Earner Families." *Journal of Marriage and the Family* 70 (5): 1311–25.

Crouter, Ann C., and Alan Booth. 2003. *Children's Influence on Family Dynamics: The Neglected Side of Family Relationships.* Mahwah, NJ: Erlbaum.

Csizmadia, Annamaria, Alethea Rollins, and Jessica P. Kaneakua. 2014. "Ethnic-Racial Socialization and Its Correlations in Families of Black-White Biracial Children." *Family Relations* 63 (2): 259–70.

Davey, Monica, and Mitch Smith. 2016. "Chicago Police Dept. Plagued by Systemic Racism, Task Force Finds." *New York Times.* https://www.nytimes. com/2016/04/14/us/chicago-police-dept-plagued-by-systemic-racism-task-force-finds.html?_r=0.

Debusmann, Bernd. 2016. "After Two Terms of Obama, a Post-Racial America Is Elusive." *Newsweek.* http://www.newsweek.com/after-two-terms-obama -post-racial-america-still-elusive-506916.

Dunbar, Angel, Nicole Perry, and Esther Leerkes. 2015. "African American Parents' Racial and Emotion Socialization Profiles and Young Adults' Emotional Adaptation." *Cultural Diversity and Ethnic Minority Psychology* 21 (3): 409–19.

Edwards, Adrienne L., and April L. Few-Demo. 2016. "African American Maternal Power and the Racial Socialization of Preschool Children." *Sex Roles* 75 (1–2): 56–70.

Fletcher, Michael A., and Jon Cohen. 2009. "Far Fewer Consider Racism Big Problem." *Washington Post.* http://www.washingtonpost.com/wp-dyn /content/article/2009/01/18/AR2009011802538.html.

Garcia Coll, Cynthia, Gontran Lamberty, Renee Jenkins, Harriet Pipes McAdoo, Keith Crnic, Barbara Hanna Wasik, and Heidi Vazquez Garcia. 1996. "An Integrative Model for the Study of Developmental Competencies in Minority Children." *Child Development* 67 (5): 1891–914.

Hill, Nancy E. 2001. "Parenting and Academic Socialization as They Relate to School Readiness: The Roles of Ethnicity and Family Income." *Journal of Educational Psychology* 93 (4): 686–97.

Hughes, Diane. 2003. "Correlates of African American and Latino Parents' Messages to Children about Ethnicity and Race: A Comparative Study of Racial Socialization." *American Journal of Community Psychology* 31 (1–2): 15–33.

Hughes, Diane, and Lisa Chen. 1997. "When and What Parents Tell Children about Race: An Examination of Race-Related Socialization among African American Families." *Applied Developmental Science* 1 (4): 200–14.

Hughes, Diane, and Lisa Chen. 1999. "The Nature of Parents' Race-Related Communications to Children: A Developmental Perspective." In *Child Psychology: A Handbook of Contemporary Issues*, edited by L. Balter and C. S. Tamis-LeMonda, 467–90. Philadelphia, PA: Psychology Press/Taylor & Francis.

Hughes, Diane, and Deborah Johnson. 2001. "Correlates in Children's Experiences of Parents' Racial Socialization Behaviors." *Journal of Marriage and Family* 63 (4): 981–95.

Hughes, Diane, Deborah Rivas, Monica Foust, Carolin Hagelskamp, Sarah Gersick, and Niobe Way. 2008. "How to Catch a Moonbeam: A Mixed-Methods Approach to Understanding Ethnic Socialization Processes in Ethnically Diverse Families." In *Handbook of Race, Racism, and the Developing Child*, edited by Stephen M. Quintana and Clark McKown, 226–77. Hoboken, NJ: John Wiley and Sons.

Hughes, Diane, James Rodriguez, Emilie P. Smith, Deborah J. Johnson, Howard C. Stevenson, and Paul Spicer. 2006. "Parents' Ethnic-Racial Socialization Practices: A Review of Research and Directions for Future Study." *Developmental Psychology* 42 (5): 747–70.

Hughes, Diane, Dawn Witherspoon, Deborah Rivas-Drake, and Nia West-Bey. 2009. "Received Ethnic-Racial Socialization Messages and Youths' Academic and Behavioral Outcomes: Examining the Mediating Role of Ethnic Identity and Self-esteem." *Cultural Diversity and Ethnic Minority Psychology* 15 (2): 112–24.

Hughes, Julie, Meagan Patterson, and Erin Pahlke. 2016. "White Adolescents' Racial Attitudes: Exploring the Roles of Parental Racial Socialization, Intergroup Contact, and Motivation to Suppress Bias." Presented at the Association for Psychological Science meeting, Chicago, IL.

Huynh, Virginia W., and Andrew J. Fuligni. 2008. "Ethnic Socialization and the Academic Adjustment of Adolescents from Mexican, Chinese, and European Backgrounds." *Developmental Psychology* 44 (4):1202–08.

Kaiser, Cheryl R., and Carol T. Miller. 2001. "Stop Complaining! The Social Costs of Making Attributions to Discrimination." *Personality and Social Psychology Bulletin* 27 (2): 254–63.

Knight, George P., Cady Berkel, Adriana J. Umaña-Taylor, Nancy A. Gonzales, Idean Errekal, Maryanne Jaconis, and Brenna M. Boyd. 2011. "The Familial Socialization of Culturally Related Values in Mexican American Families." *Journal of Marriage and Family* 73 (5): 913–25.

Kofkin, Jennifer A., Phyllis Katz, and E. P. Downey. 1995. "Family Discourse about Race and the Development of Children's Racial Attitudes." Presented at the Society for Research in Child Development meeting, Indianapolis, IN.

Logan, John R., and Brian Stults. 2011. "The Persistence of Segregation in the Metropolis: New Findings from the 2010 Census." Census Brief prepared for Project US2010. http://www.s4.brown.edu/us2010.

McHale, Susan, Ann Crouter, Ji-Yeon Kim, Linda Burton, Kelly Davis, Aryn Dotterer, and Dena Swanson. 2006. "Mothers' and Fathers' Racial Socialization in African American Families: Implications for Youth." *Child Development* 77 (5): 1387–402.

McKown, Clark. 2004. "Age and Ethnic Variation in Children's Thinking about the Nature of Racism." *Journal of Applied Developmental Psychology* 25 (5): 597–617.

Murray, Carolyn Bennett, and Jelani Mandara. 2002. "Racial Identity Development in African American Children." In *Black Children: Social, Educational, and Parental Environments*, edited by H. P. McAdoo, 73–96. Thousand Oaks, CA: Sage.

Murry, Velma McBride, Cady Berkel, Gene H. Brody, Shannon J. Miller, and Yi-fu Chen. 2009. "Linking Parental Socialization to Interpersonal Protective Processes, Academic Self-Presentation, and Expectations Among Rural African American Youth." *Cultural Diversity and Ethnic Minority Psychology* 15 (1): 1–10.

Murry, V. M., and G. H. Brody 2002. "Racial Socialization Processes in Single-Mother Families: Linking Maternal Racial Identity, Parenting, and Racial Socialization in Rural, Single-Mother Families with Child Self-Worth and Self-Regulation." In *Black Children: Social, Educational, and Parental Environments*, edited by H. P. McAdoo, 97–115. Thousand Oaks, CA: Sage.

Musumeci, Natalie. 2016. "KKK Celebrating Trump's Election with Victory Parade." *New York Post.* http://nypost.com/2016/11/11/kkk-celebrating-trumps-election-with-victory-parade.

Neblett, Enrique W., Cheri L. Philip, Courtney D. Cogburn, and Robert M. Sellers. 2006. "African American Adolescents' Discrimination Experiences and Academic Achievement: Racial Socialization as a Cultural Compensatory and Protective Factor." *Journal of Black Psychology* 32 (2): 199–218.

Neblett, Enrique W., Ciara P. Smalls, Kahlil R. Ford, Hòa X. Nguyên, and Robert M. Sellers. 2009. "Racial Socialization and Racial Identity: African American Parents' Messages about Race as Precursors to Identity." *Journal of Youth and Adolescence* 38 (2): 189–203.

Neville, Helen A., Roderick L. Lilly, Georgia Duran, Richard M. Lee, and LaVonne Browne. 2000. "Construction and Initial Validation of the Color-Blind Racial Attitudes Scale." *Journal of Counseling Psychology* 47 (1): 59–70.

Orfield, Gary, Jongyeon Ee, Erica Frankenberg, and Genevieve Siegel-Hawley. 2016. *Brown at 62: School Segregation by Race, Poverty, and State.* Washington, D.C.: Civil Rights Project.

Pahlke, Erin, Rebecca S. Bigler, and Marie-Anne Suizzo. 2012. "Relations between Colorblind Socialization and Children's Racial Bias: Evidence from European American Mothers and Their Preschool Children." *Child Development* 83 (4): 1164–79.

Parke, R. D., V. M. Burks, J. L. Carson, B. Neville, and L. A. Boyum. 1994. "Family-Peer Relationships: A Tripartite Model." In *Exploring Family Relationships with Other Social Contexts*, edited by R. D. Parke and S. G. Kellam, 115–46. Hillsdale, NJ: Lawrence Erlbaum Associates.

Patterson, Meagan, Erin Pahlke, and Rebecca Bigler. 2013. "Witnesses to History: Children's Views of Race and the 2008 United States Presidential Election." *Analyses of Social Issues and Public Policy* 13 (1): 186–210.

Peters, Marie Ferguson. 2002. "Racial Socialization of Young Black Children." In *Black Children: Social, Educational, and Parental Environments*, 2nd edition, edited by H. P. McAdoo and J. L. McAdoo, 57–72. Thousand Oaks: Sage.

Pettigrew, Thomas F., and Linda R. Tropp. 2006. "Interpersonal Relations and Group Processes: A Meta-Analytic Test of Intergroup Contact Theory." *Journal of Personality and Social Psychology* 90 (5): 751–83.

Phinney, Jean S. 1990. "Ethnic Identity in Adolescents and Adults: Review of Research." *Psychological Bulletin* 108 (3): 499–514.

Phinney, Jean S., and Victor Chavira. 1995. "Parental Ethnic Socialization and Adolescent Coping with Problems Related to Ethnicity." *Journal of Research on Adolescence* 5 (1): 31–54.

Priest, Naomi, Jessica Walton, Fiona White, Emma Kowal, Alison Baker, and Yin Paradies. 2014. "Understanding the Complexities of Ethnic-Racial Socialization Processes for Both Minority and Majority Groups: A 30-Year Systematic Review." *International Journal of Intercultural Relations* 43: 139–55.

Ramirez, Roberto R. (2004). *We the People: Hispanics in the United States.* Washington, D.C.: U.S. Census Bureau, Department of Commerce.

Reitano, John. 1998. *What If the Zebras Lost Their Stripes?* New York, NY: Paulist Press.

Rivas-Drake, Deborah, Diane Hughes, and Niobe Way. 2009. A Preliminary Analysis of Associations among Ethnic-Racial Socialization, Ethnic Discrimination, and Ethnic Identity among Diverse Urban Sixth Graders." *Journal of Research on Adolescence* 19 (3): 558–84.

Sidahmed, Mazin. 2016. "Trump's Election Led to 'Barrage of Hate,' Report Finds." *The Guardian*. https://www.theguardian.com/society/2016/nov/29/trump-related-hate-crimes-report-southern-poverty-law-center.

Smalls, Ciara. 2009. "African American Adolescent Engagement in the Classroom and Beyond: The Roles of Mother's Racial Socialization and

Democratic-Involved Parenting." *Journal of Youth and Adolescence* 38 (2): 204–13.

Smedley, Audrey, and Brian D. Smedley. 2005. "Race as Biology Is Fiction, Racism as a Social Problem Is Real: Anthropological and Historical Perspectives on the Social Construction of Race." *American Psychologist* 60 (1): 16–26.

Smith, Emilie Phillips, Jacqueline Atkins, and Christian M. Connell. 2003. "Family, School, and Community Factors and Relationships to Racial-Ethnic Attitudes and Academic Achievement." *American Journal of Community Psychology* 32 (1): 159–73.

Southern Poverty Law Center. 2016. "The Trump Effect: The Impact of the 2016 Presidential Election on Our Nation's Schools." https://www.splcenter .org/20161128/trump-effect-impact-2016-presidential-election-our -nations-schools.

Suizzo, Marie-Anne, Erin Pahlke, Lisa Yarnell, Kuan-Yi Chen, and Sylvia Romero. 2014. "Home-Based Parental Involvement in Young Children's Learning Across U.S. Ethnic Groups: Cultural Models of Academic Socialization." *Journal of Family Issues* 35 (2): 254–87.

Suizzo, Marie-Anne, Courtney Robinson, and Erin Pahlke. 2008. "African American Mothers' Beliefs and Practices with Young Children: Relations between Academic and Racial Socialization." *Journal of Family Issues* 29 (3): 287–316.

Thomas, Anita Jones, and Sha'Kema M. Blackmon. 2015. "The Influence of the Trayvon Martin Shooting on Racial Socialization Practices of African American Parents." *Journal of Black Psychology* 41 (1): 75–89.

Thornton, Michael C., Linda M. Chatters, Robert Joseph Taylor, and Walter R. Allen. 1990. "Sociodemographic and Environmental Correlates of Racial Socialization by Black Parents." *Child Development* 61 (2): 401–09.

Tran, Alisia G., and Richard M. Lee. 2010. "Perceived Ethnic-Racial Socialization, Ethnic Identity, and Social Competence among Asian American Late Adolescents." *Cultural Diversity and Ethnic Minority Psychology* 16 (2): 169–78.

Umaña-Taylor, Adriana J., Edna C. Alfaro, Mayra Y. Bámaca, and Amy B. Guimond. 2009. "The Central Role of Familial Ethnic Socialization in Latino Adolescents' Cultural Orientation." *Journal of Marriage and Family* 71 (1): 46–60.

Umaña-Taylor, Adriana J., and Mark A. Fine. 2004. "Examining Ethnic Identity among Mexican-Origin Adolescents Living in the United States." *Hispanic Journal of Behavioral Sciences* 26 (1): 36–59.

Umaña-Taylor, Adriana J., and Amy B. Guimond. 2012. "A Longitudinal Examination of Parenting Behaviors and Perceived Discrimination Predicting Latino Adolescents' Ethnic Identity." *Developmental Psychology* 46: 636–50.

Vittrup, Brigitte. 2017. "Color Blind or Color Conscious? White American Mothers' Approaches to Racial Socialization." *Journal of Family Issues* 39 (3): 668–692.

Wang, Ming-Te, and James P. Huguley. 2012. "Parental Racial Socialization as a Moderator of the Effects of Racial Discrimination on Educational Success among African American Adolescence." *Child Development* 83 (5): 1716–31.

CHAPTER ELEVEN

What Do Visas Have to Do with Parenting? Middle-Class Dependent Visa Holders and Transcultural Parenting

Pallavi Banerjee

A Google search of "H-4 visa, dependent spouses, H-1B" yields approximately 12,700 news reports and op-eds published since 2009. Most of these pieces, a few of which I authored, feature the travails of women who come to the United States on a visa granted to the dependents of temporary skilled workers who work and live in the country on an H1-B visa. The "high-skilled" workers migrate for employment on skilled workers' temporary visas (H1-B), and their spouses migrate on dependent visas, otherwise known as H-4s. These prevent the spouses of skilled workers from finding legal employment in the United States unless the family has a permanent residency application in process—which itself can take anywhere between 6 and 10 years. Those on H-4 visas are also not allowed to obtain any kind of U.S. government-issued identification in the United States. This visa law creates what I call "state-imposed dependence" whereby the state creates a household structure that is highly gendered, with a sole breadwinner and a stay-at-home spouse/parent (Banerjee 2012).

Of the many news articles published on the plight of dependent spouses of H-1B visa holders, one in *The Guardian* entitled "Silicon Valley's Reluctant

Housewife: Immigration Law Bars Women from Working" (Long 2016) caught my attention because it focused on the conflicting emotions of these highly educated wives. On one hand, they recognized their middle-class privilege; on the other, they felt resentful and deeply distressed by their forced dependence. I had also found this in my research with the same population. But what stood out to me in this article was the picture that went with the article—it was of a woman holding a child. If they have children, dependent spouses spend an inordinate amount of time with them because they are forced to stay home (Banerjee 2012). Given that most of these families are transnational in nature, belong to middle- and upper-middle-class families in India, and are ensconced in middle-class lifestyles in the United States with a stay-at-home parent, how do these families parent? What are their parenting styles?

My research, in which I examine how U.S. visa policies affect Indian transnational "high-skilled" migrants and their families in the United States, can provide some answers to these questions. I focus on two family forms: a) male-led migrant families (families of Indian high-tech workers) and b) female-led migrant families (families of Indian nurses). Using extensive qualitative methods—in-depth interviews with 45 couples and 15 immigration experts, observations in the migrant Indian communities, and archival data—I argue that the visa regimes govern more than just the mobility of the transnational subject. Visa policies reconfigure gender identities and notions of the self for visa holders and impose constraints on relationships, family, belonging, and migration. They shape parenting styles, parenting expectations, and parenting practices.

In this chapter, I examine if and to what extent Annette Lareau's theory of middle-class parenting—"concerted cultivation"—might work in the context of Indian immigrant families where one parent holds a professional job in the United States and the other spouse is highly qualified but stays at home due to visa restrictions. Annette Lareau, in her groundbreaking work *Unequal Childhoods* (2003; 2011), made the class backgrounds of both white and black parents the central analytical category in defining their parenting styles and what might be the outcomes of such parenting for their children's life chances. She proposed two distinct parenting styles—"concerted cultivation" as the kind of parenting done by black and white middle-class parents, and the "accomplishment of natural growth" as the path of working-class parents.

In working-class households, the middle-school children she studied in the 1990s participated in very few organized activities and spent leisure time hanging out with kin and neighborhood friends. Their parents' work and economic lives did not afford them as much involvement in their children's lives. As a result, they parented by issuing directives to their children. Parents in these households were authoritarian, using directives when speaking to children and creating clear boundaries between adult and children's lives. The children were discouraged from questioning authority within and outside of the family. In the 2011 edition of *Unequal Childhoods*, follow-up study shows that most of these working-class kids dropped out of college and had limited life chances, and their parents were still less involved in their lives than were the middle-class parents in their children's lives.

In sharp contrast, the middle-class parents who engaged in concerted cultivation of their middle-school children invested a big portion of their daily lives in developing their children's talents, organizing both leisure and learning activities, talking with their children in more discursive language and allowing for development of negotiation skills in the children, and interacting actively with the institutions that their children were part of. Lareau shows the deep involvement of middle-class parents in the lives of their children to motivate them as well as organize for them their various leisure and extracurricular activities. The parents often sacrificed their own leisure time to be involved in the lives of their children and the institutions their children were part of. All of this effort on the part of the parents was so that their children would be successful in the future. Lareau's 2011 edition reveals that almost all of these children ended up finishing college, and many went to Ivy League schools. The parents were still involved in their children's lives and education, and if a child did not perform according to their parents' expectations, the parents often blamed themselves for not investing enough in the child's interests when he or she was younger.

For Lareau, these are distinct paths that don't overlap across class divisions; that is, working-class parents do not enact concerted cultivation, and middle-class parents do not parent according to the accomplishment of natural growth. When as a graduate student I first read Lareau's work, it revolutionized the way I thought about class and life chances. It allowed me to recognize that privilege and/or disadvantage begins with acts of parenting. And yet, later, when I assigned *Unequal Childhoods* to my classes, my white and black students emphatically nodded in agreement while my immigrant-identified students shook their heads. When asked, they would often tell me, "Parenting is not either/or." They alleged that they had experienced both kinds of parenting in their households as well as parental class mobility during their lifetimes. This persistent reaction from my students, along with the aforementioned *Guardian* article, pushed me to reanalyze my data on parents who are middle-class Indians on immigrant visas. In many ways, my analysis in this chapter affirms some of the doubts raised by my immigrant-identified students. This chapter is an exploration of how dependent visa laws for middle-class families influence parenting in those families. I further unpack the parenting styles in these middle-class immigrant homes using Lareau's lens.

For the purposes of this research, I derive the definition of parenting styles from Baumrind's models of parenting combined with Lareau's description of middle-class and working-class parenting. Baumrind (1967) described parenting as: a) permissive, where parents are nonpunitive and affirmative toward their children's actions and desires; b) authoritarian, where parents expect obedience and absolute standards of behavior and practice punitive action if those rules are not followed; and c) authoritative, where parents attempt to direct a child's activities but in a rational, issue-oriented manner. In my analysis, Lareau's middle-class parents combined permissive and authoritative parenting, while the working-class parents were mostly authoritarian but at times authoritative. The bottom line was that for Lareau, working-class parenting and middle-class parenting are two distinct types of parenting.

What I find is that the parenting done by my participants lies squarely between the styles of concerted cultivation and accomplishment of natural growth due to their evocation of transnational and transcultural parenting norms. I call this form of parenting "transcultural cultivation." In the rest of the chapter, I build on concerted cultivation and natural growth by theorizing transcultural cultivation.

Concerted Cultivation and Immigrant [Asian] Parenting

Yale Law School professor Amy Chua's 2011 memoir, *Battle Hymn of the Tiger Mother*, in which she alleged that Chinese mothers and parents are superior to their Western counterparts, sparked controversy, with critics saying that Chua's memoir fed stereotypes about Asian parents. In 2014, Stanford psychologists Fu and Markus conducted an experimental study on middle-class European American (EA) high school students and Asian American (AA) high school students to assess how the AA students perceived and processed their mothers' involvement in their lives. They concluded that while the two groups of students differed in their interdependence level on their mothers (AA students reporting more interdependence), both groups perceived their mothers' involvement as motivation toward academic achievement. AA students perceived academic achievement as a team effort with their mothers, whereas the EA students saw it as a personal project encouraged by their mothers. While the researchers did not allude to or cite Lareau, my reading of the Chua controversy and the Fu and Markus (2014) research connects deeply with Lareau's class-based parenting styles.

Lareau (2003, 2011) argues that class-based parenting reproduces the cycle of class inequality because it sets working-class children up for failure in the competitive labor market without the life skills necessary to succeed while equipping middle-class children with skills to reproduce their class privileges.

The wide range of social scientific research on intergenerational relationships between first- and second-generation immigrants has certified the prevalence of authoritarian parenting in immigrant households. Here I borrow Baumrind's (1967) typology of authoritarian parenting described earlier. Psychological studies of parenting in first-generation immigrant families, including Caribbean, Chinese, East Indian and Mexican, have all concluded the enactment of authoritarian and directive parenting in these families, where independence and individualism were discouraged (Cheah et al. 2009; Driscoll, Russell, and Crockett 2008; Farver et al. 2007; Roopnarine et al. 2006).

Research in sociology has shown that the key source of intergenerational conflict and resentment in immigrant households emerges from what children perceive as authoritarian and directive-oriented parenting. Pyke's (2000) study on second-generation Vietnamese and Korean college students spotlights the students' desire for a "normal American family" with more affective parent-child relationships that encouraged open communication, flexibility, forgiveness, independence, and respect for individualism. In contrast, they perceived their families and parents as authoritarian and valuing obedience, respect toward elders, and collective interest as opposed to individual interest. Foner and Dreby, in their 2011 review article on intergenerational relationships in immigrant families, also reaffirm the conflict highlighted by Pyke (2000) and several other researchers (Foner 2009; Foner and Kasinitz 2007; Manohar 2008; Portes and Fernández-Kelly 2008; Suárez-Orozco and Suárez-Orozco 2009; Zhou 2009). Foner and Dreby assert that "immigrant parents often expect a level of respect, deference, and obedience that their second-generation children view as authoritarian and domineering. The children have been raised in a U.S. cultural setting in which early independence is encouraged and childrearing norms are generally more permissive than in the parents' home country" (527). If we were to reanalyze these parenting styles through Lareau's lens, we can assume that these first-generation immigrant parents were, at least in some respects, engaged in the accomplishment of natural growth.

However, many studies that posit immigrant parenting as authoritarian also showcase its complexities. Emotional closeness, interdependence, and support for educational achievement are also presented as hallmarks of immigrant parent-child interactions (Lopez 2003; Manohar 2008; Smith 2006; Schwartz 2009; Zhou 2009). Farver et al. (2007) argue that Asian Indian parents become more permissive with time and generations of stay in host countries. Other researchers are of the opinion that what is interpreted as authoritarian is a warped view of parenting in other cultures through applying a Western lens (Mohanty 1988). Applying a Western lens automatically presents the modern European American kind of parenting as the gold standard against which all other parenting styles must be measured. For instance, Gorman (1998) contends that parenting by immigrant Chinese mothers in the United States is interpreted as authoritarian by researchers when they should instead be focusing on the social and cultural nuances and adjustments that these mothers are making while parenting in host societies. In her interview study with mostly middle-class Chinese mothers in the New York City area, she found that Chinese mothers were rarely confrontational or controlling of their children. Much of the parenting happened through discussions and conversations, but what was emphasized as important for children was culturally specific. For example, the Chinese mothers stressed to their children the importance of respect for elders, caring for others beyond the singular concern for one's own self, being self-sufficient, not being influenced by the perceived ills of American adolescence (like drugs and sex), and learning to be bilingual. While these mothers did harbor some preconceived notions about American societies, Gorman contends that their parenting should be seen as more nuanced than just authoritarian.

While Gorman's description of Chinese-American mothering does not fit the concerted cultivation model, there is a small body of scholarship that contends that immigrant parents, particularly Asian immigrant parents, engage in concerted cultivation (Archer 2010, Cross-Barnet and McDonald 2015; Lee and Zhou 2015; Manohar 2013). For instance, Manohar (2013) shows that Indian Tamil immigrant mothers in the United States engaged heavily in concerted cultivation much like the middle-class parents in Lareau's study. Archer (2010), in her interview-based study of 13 middle-class immigrant parents mostly of Asian descent in Britain,[1] contends that these parents undoubtedly engage in concerted cultivation. They do so by expressing the "desire for personalized education" for their children, engaging with schools and other institutions, climbing up the authority ladder in these institutions, and providing their children with various organized opportunities for skill development (465). Archer puts much more emphasis on race than Lareau did and argues that, due to the constancy of racism in British institutions, immigrant parents have to work extra hard so that their children can reach their full potential. Likewise, Lee and Zhou (2004), in their book investigating the achievement paradox of Asian Americans by focusing on 1.5-generation Chinese immigrants and Vietnamese refugees in the Los Angeles area, argue that Asian American immigrant children are saddled with a "success frame" in their lives. The success frame is really a cultural frame that is handed to Asian American children by their parents and often means doing well in school and preparing for white-collar, professional jobs. The racialized "model minority" framework that creates expectations in teachers and other institutional actors of Asian American success further feeds this success frame. The expectation leads to a pooling of resources and support in the schools, in the communities, and within families to help Asian American children succeed and often also allows Asian American working-class children to be successful. This study shows that parenting in immigrant households includes transnational cultural resources along with concerted cultivation that extends beyond just middle-class parenting and is worth exploring.

This literature seems to suggest that immigrant parenting includes elements of both authoritarian parenting and concerted cultivation. While the literature also suggests that cultural frames are important in shaping immigrant parenting, the complexity of parenting for those who are immigrants and middle-class is somewhat underanalyzed. The complexity is heightened when the question changes to how visa policies, particularly ones that force highly educated, middle-class, newly immigrant parents (women and men) to stay home, might affect parenting. How might the cultural context of the immigrant family further complicate parenting? In this chapter, I answer these questions based on in-depth interviews with Indian middle-class families and ethnography conducted in the family setting.

Methodology

This study primarily involved conducting ethnography and in-depth interviews in communities of Indian professionals in the Chicago area. I studied two very distinct communities. The first were the families of male Indian high-tech migrant workers who were the breadwinners and were living in the United States with their spouses and children, who were on dependent visas. The second community was of Indian immigrant nurses, all of whom were women and were the main wage earners in their families and were accompanied by their dependent husbands and children.

I conducted life course interviews with the couples, exploring their lives prior to migration, their experiences with the migration process, their understanding of their own visas, and their description of their everyday family lives—including parenting and caregiving after migration. Each of the spouses was interviewed separately, followed by joint interviews. A total of 45 couples (n=90) were interviewed: 20 high-tech workers and their wives, and 25 nurses and their husbands. All of the nurses and their husbands were from one state and region in India—the southern state of Kerala. All of the nurses' families identified with the Christian faith. The nurses and their families usually lived in suburban communities close to their ethnic churches. The high-tech workers, on the other hand, were mostly from northern parts of India. Most were Hindu by faith with a few exceptions, and almost half of these families lived in gentrified urban neighborhoods; the other half lived in suburban communities for access to better public schools.

I also conducted over 300 hours of ethnographic observation at various community and public events to observe family and gender dynamics. These events and spaces included religious services, social parties, religious and cultural festivals, potlucks, and children's birthday parties. I also attended gender-segregated events such as high-tech workers' amateur weekly cricket games, or church activities run solely by husbands of nurses as well as women-only gatherings and events attended by nurses and the wives of high-tech workers. In these settings, I observed families' division of labor, discussions that men and women had about their work and family lives, and interactions among the spouses.

All of the mothers in my sample in both types of family had at least a college degree, and most had 16-plus years of education. All the high-tech fathers had professional college degrees, and most of the husbands of the nurses had some college education. The mean income in the nurses' families was about $65,000 and in the high-tech families, about $75,000. Most high-tech families self-identified as middle-class in the United States and as belonging to upper-middle-class families in India. The nurses identified as middle-class both in the United States and at their families' origins in India. For the purposes of this paper, I have included only families that had children—36 families. The nurses' children ranged in age from 5 to 17. Most had children in middle school. Of the 20 families of high-tech workers I interviewed, 16 had children, and these ranged in age from two to eight years, averaging at five. Both the observational data as well as the interview data for this chapter zoom in on activities and narratives about parenting with particular attention to how parents talk with children, what kind of activities they engage in and organize for their children, and what affective discourse emerges from the parents about their children and about raising them in the United States.

In what follows, I build on Lareau's concepts of concerted cultivation and accomplishment of natural growth through a thematic analysis of the parenting styles of these middle-class-identified immigrant Indian parents whose lives are majorly shaped by the visa laws that govern them. Given what we know about Asian American families and parenting, I argue that we need a more nuanced understanding of parenting in immigrant families, because they do not neatly fit into the two distinct groundbreaking categories of class-based parenting that Lareau has provided us. I investigate how class, culture, visa laws, and transnational experiences also shape parenting in these families.

Cultural, Transnational Middle-Class Parenting: Transcultural Cultivation

A different kind of concerted cultivation
"All happy families look alike."
"Was it Tolstoy who said it?"

"Yes, Jaya," I responded to Jaya's (all names are pseudonyms) rhetorical question as we watched her seven-year-old daughter perform a combination of ballet, salsa, and bharatnatyam (Indian classical dance) to a peppy Hindi film song on Skype for her grandmother (Jaya's mother) in India. It was about 11 a.m. on a Tuesday in Chicago and 10:30 p.m. in Chennai, India, where Jaya's mother lived. Jaya's daughter had missed school that day because she had to perform a bharatnatyam recital in a temple that afternoon, and she needed to get ready for it.

Jaya continued as her daughter finished her short performance for her grandma and us:

> Nothing can be farther from truth. Not all happy families look alike. American parents don't have to constantly worry about their kids losing their culture. But, we immigrant parents do. That makes our work so much harder. We are never sure if we are doing right by our kid. Are we putting too much pressure on our little one by having her learn three kinds of dance or are we just allowing her to learn more? Who knows!

Jaya's dilemma about how to balance cultural expectations while providing all the developmental opportunities to her child was shared by all the parents I talked to. Like the middle-class parents in Lareau's study, the parents in my sample spent a lot of time thinking, researching, and organizing leisure and developmental activities for their children, but the difference was that the Indian parents in my study were also actively and creatively thinking how best to impart cultural knowledge to their children without alienating them from the host society.

A poignant example of this delicate dance that parents have to do came through in my interview with Mira, who had been a copywriter of English commercials in a reputable international advertising firm in India before moving to the United States. She laid out her struggles of raising a seven-year-old boy, who had been born in the States. She confessed to me that she was always afraid that her son, who spoke three Indian languages and was also learning Spanish in school, would be bullied and laughed at if he slipped into an Indian language because he was juggling so many linguistic complexities. Mira and her husband were from two different regions in India and spoke different languages. These did not include Hindi, the national language of India. Mira told me that when her son was younger, she and her husband had wanted to ensure that he learned both of their languages and spoke to him only in those. They figured that the child would learn English in kindergarten and so they didn't need to actively promote it at home. After he had been in daycare a year, they had sensed that their son was being laughed at and isolated there because of what one of the teachers had called "his wacky language skills." He had refused to speak any of the Indian languages and said he only wanted to use what he had learned in school: English and Spanish. Devastated, Mira and her husband complained and had several conversations with the daycare teachers on how best to accommodate their son's cultural needs. This entailed Mira volunteering in the daycare for three days a week. And, in consultation with other immigrant parents and kindergarten teachers, Mira had begun a course in Hindi (which she did not know) with her son so that he would learn to value Indian languages as much as English and Spanish. Mira also spent a considerable amount of time talking with her child about how to speak to his friends and his teachers in school about his own languages and culture without getting intimidated by their reactions.

This particular case reveals different aspects of immigrant parenting. The time and effort that Mira invested to ensure that her son learned the languages she felt were important for his bicultural existence do not exist in the lexicon of nonimmigrant middle-class parents. While Mira and her husband engage and interact with institutions and have negotiation-based conversations with their child much as the middle-class parents do in Lareau's study, in the case of Mira and other Indian parents, much of this effort was to protect their children from institutional and individual racism. The black parents in Lareau's study also dealt with everyday racism, but immigrant parents often are seen to balance both racism and cultural expectations as part of the class and ethnic reproduction effort. In the context of the immigrant families in my study, it was important for the parents to imbue cultural knowledge in the forms of language, food, art, and religion in their children. This was both part of the social expectation and a marker of class status for the immigrant parents in the transnational community. However, the children were subjected to everyday racism due to the performance of some of the cultural expectations; for instance, they were teased for having an accent or wearing certain clothing. The parents then had the additional task of strategizing how to counter the forms of everyday racism that their children faced while still emphasizing the importance of cultural learning.

For immigrant parents of means, it mattered that their children grew up bi- or multilingual, that they were well-adjusted in the cultures of the home and the host countries, and that they received all the support they needed to develop their talents and skills in and outside of school. This made the weekly schedules of both the children and the parents, particularly the parent responsible for the lion's share of the work, tighter than perhaps even a corporate CEO's.

I asked to look at the weekly schedules of most of the children in my study. On average, except for an hour or so per day and sleeping hours, every moment was scheduled for most children. I requested one of the parent couples—Mary and George—to allow me to shadow them for a day during the summer vacation of their 10-year-old daughter. Mary was a nurse, and George was her husband on dependent visa. On the day I shadowed them, Mary had a two-shift workday, so George was responsible for their daughter's schedule. I arrived at George and Mary's suburban home at about 7:00 a.m., when Mary was preparing breakfast. I ate with the family, and Mary gave me a rundown of what the day would look like. George would take their daughter to the local ethnic church of Kerala (Indian regional ethnic identity) right after breakfast for an 8:30 a.m. children's choir group, followed by piano lessons in the town center at 10:00 a.m. That would be followed by a quick snack. After the snack, all of us were to drive to Evanston, Illinois, which was about 30 minutes away: George was taking their daughter to Northwestern University for a science summer camp orientation. Child and parent were supposed to attend together. I offered to wait in a café while they were at the orientation. Afterward, the child was scheduled for an Indian classical dance lesson for an hour, followed by a playdate with her friends from dance class. Many of the parents and the children in my study had a similar schedule.

Church activities were a regular part of the children's organized schedules in the families of the nurses. Gina, also a nurse who had two children (8 and 10) told me why it was important for them to live near their church. She confirmed that having the children involved in church and its activities was the main way that the parents in her community imparted cultural knowledge. The church offered writing and reading classes in Malayalee (the regional language of the nurses), and the priest taught catechism classes to the children in the same way, according to Gina, that she had learned her "Bible with local stories in our village in India."

The families of the high-tech workers, most of whom were Hindu, were less attached to an organized religious institution. The parents imparted cultural knowledge largely through activities with other Indian families; through music, dance, and language classes; and by ensuring that the children were familiar with the rituals and customs of their parents' natal culture. However, the parents in both types of families guaranteed that the children did not fall behind in school or in developing skills like learning the piano or participating in sports like other American middle-class children. If that meant the children had to learn three different languages, two different dance forms, and Indian and Western musical instruments, then the parents in these households did it all. As is the nature of this type of cultivation, the parents engaged with their children in dialogues and negotiations, often defining reward structures for accomplishments and actively involving themselves with the institutions that their children were part of. These parents, however, did more than just enact concerted cultivation. They also did the kind of parenting that might resemble what Lareau calls "accomplishment of natural growth."

Accomplishment of Natural Growth? Or Just Transcultural Parenting?

I attended a community event organized by Shija and Mathew in their suburban home near Chicago with five other nurses and their husbands and children. The family had invited their priest to hold a moral lesson for the children, and the event had been organized as a potluck. It was a summer afternoon; the hosts had laid out the food and chairs in the backyard, and most invitees were lounging outdoors. Most of the chairs were occupied by the adults, including me, and the children were sitting on the lawn or on the raised beds around the house. I went into the kitchen to get myself some water, and when I went out again, I found that a child had taken my chair. So I sat down on the lawn with the children without thinking much about it. But, two minutes later, I heard a very stern voice of one the fathers asking the child to move from the chair and to let me sit. The child protested and I, a little shocked and embarrassed, jumped to the defense of the child, saying I was perfectly fine sitting on the grass. At this point, the mother came up to the chair and hovered over the child. She said in a calm but cold voice, "Did you not hear Dad? When you are asked to move, you move. No questions. Miss Pallavi should not be sitting on the ground while you sit on the chair." She then turned to me and, refusing my protests, said, "You know how this is. They need to learn to respect their elders. They are growing up in America, but they cannot forget the respectful and the valuable lessons of our culture. Would you ever dare to do this when you were his age? No, right? He needs to learn."

This interaction between the parents and this child can be seen as a solid example of Lareau's "natural growth"—authoritarian and directive-oriented parenting. In the course of my fieldwork, I noticed other such interactions in almost all of the families, along with other attributes of the natural growth style of parenting. For instance, the children were often encouraged to negotiate playdates and sleepovers as rewards for good performance on educational and learning activities, but on day-to-day goings-on and when talking to authority figures, they were expected to follow orders and take directions. The parents issued strict directives about eating, sleeping, studying, and talking back. These orders issued by the parents, however, almost always were followed with an explanation about cultural expectations. The phrase, "this is part of our culture" was repeated often to children when the parents issued directives in almost all families.

Additionally, the children were expected to spend time with their kin and extended families as part of their cultural training. If extended family, especially grandparents, were visiting from India (these visits were usually for about six months), they were given charge of the children, and the children were directed to spend time with them. This was a way for the parents to take a break from parenting and also to make sure that the children were in touch with their transnational families and culture.

Additionally, the families, especially the nonworking spouse and the children, often spent two to three months of summer in India. There, the children's time was mostly unorganized leisure time with their kin and cousins.

These long vacations in India meant that the children missed out on the summer camp activities that their middle-class American counterparts were participating in. But, for the parents in my study, this time was important for transcultural learning.

There is no denying that the reasons for the immigrant children's time with their kin were different from those for the working-class children in Lareau's study. Those working-class children spent time with kin in the neighborhood because their parents did not have the resources to organize other skill-developing activities for them. In the case of the immigrant children, the parents designed their time with the kin and extended families in India and in the United States. The fact remains, however, that the immigrant children were spending some unstructured time with kin and family, which might have had the same effect on the children predicted by Lareau. The children might not have been engaged at all times of the year in talent development, but they might have developed a sense of community with their kin and extended families by spending unstructured time with them, much in the same ways as the working-class children in Lareau's study.

Again, the major difference between the accomplishment of natural growth as presented by Lareau for the working-class parents in her sample and my participants was that Lareau's working-class participants engaged in this form of parenting because they did not have the time, the means, or the know-how to engage in concerted cultivation. In case of the middle-class parents in my study, it was more a matter of a specific behavioral transmission of culture, through directive-oriented parenting, that they feared would be lost in the United States.

Consequences of the Transcultural Cultivation Style of Parenting

My analysis reveals that the middle-class immigrant Indian parents are practicing both concerted cultivation and some forms of natural growth styles of parenting. But, what is at the heart of why and how they parent? I argue that these parents have a "success frame" for their children (Lee and Zhou 2004). This success frame also emerges from the cultural frame of the value of achievement handed down to children from their immigrant parents, but this frame is more hybrid in nature than that experienced by the Vietnamese and Chinese second-generation children in Lee and Zhou's research. This success frame includes a concerted effort toward development of talents, skills, and success in school, but keeping these within a transnational and transcultural context. It was very important for the parents that their children have a balanced upbringing with American as well as Indian middle-class material and cultural resources, such as excelling in school, growing up multilingual, developing transnational artistic and other talents, and so on. That meant many extra hours at bicultural skill and talent development activities as well as a healthy dose of directive-based parenting and time with kin and extended families. What these parents are doing is converging these parenting styles to fit a cultural frame.

The reason it is important to decipher and dissect these parenting styles is that they have material meaning for the lives of the children being parented. From Lareau's research, we know that these distinct parenting styles have widely divergent consequences for the children's life chances and social attributes. According to Lareau, middle-class children grow up to be more entitled and materially successful, while working-class children remain materially deprived but become more empathetic and relational people. What are the consequences for the Indian immigrant children? The children in my study definitely had a more communal upbringing that was ensconced in transcultural contexts. These children received even more organized talent and skill development activities than an average white or black, native-born American middle-class child. They grew up in multiple institutions and learned to negotiate with parents and teachers and fought institutional and individual racism with their parents as their advocates. At the same time, their parents impressed upon them the value of kin and extended family and the requirement to be respectful of elders. This intersection of transcultural parenting and concerted cultivation is what I label "transcultural cultivation."

Transcultural cultivation in the context of my research, however, does not happen in a vacuum. It has two strong influences—the gender of the parents doing the parenting and the visa status of the parents and the families. Complexities emerge when the analysis takes these into account, as I explore in the next section.

Visa Laws, Gender, and Transcultural Cultivation

The gender of parents and parenting is not decidedly present in Lareau's discussion of parenting. Yet, we know from a host of research on household division of labor that gender is central to parenting work and that the feminine/woman partner often takes on the major share of parenting duties (Banerjee 2015; Hochschild and Machung 2012; Moore 2001; Purkayastha 2004; Risman 1998). Gender becomes even more relevant to explore when the structure of the family is shaped by a breadwinner and stay-at-home parent model, as in the case of the families in my study. Is there a difference in the ways that middle-class, stay-at-home fathers and stay-home-mothers who are legally forced to parent, parent? My analysis shows that there is definitely some material difference. Specifically, stay-at-home mothers are involved in all aspects of their children's lives with little help from their husbands, whereas stay-at-home fathers share transcultural cultivation with their wives equally.

In a previous paper (Banerjee 2015), I show that in the families of the nurses, the dependent husbands took on most of the child care duties while the nurse breadwinners still did most of the other housework. Here, I delve more deeply into the nature of the child care and parenting that the dependent fathers do in comparison to dependent mothers. There are two identifiable patterns that are structured by the visa status of each of the parents: a) dependent mothers are solely responsible for the work involved in parenting while their husbands are heavily invested in managing the finances of parenting; b) in comparison, the nurses and the husbands shared the parenting work, but there was still a gendered division of the parenting.

In the families of the high-tech workers, the wives, who were legally dependent and disallowed from working, did the bulk of the parenting work. This included meeting the everyday emotional and material needs of the children, being involved in school and the children's activities there, identifying their talents, researching the range of activities available for the children, finding both leisure and developmental activities relevant to the specific ethnic culture of the family, planning events for the children, and carting the children to their activities. An additional task also entailed making calculations of expenses related to the activities and bringing a plan of the activities to the breadwinning husband, who then determined the budget and where corners could be cut so that the needs of the children could be fulfilled. A notable concern in these families was affordability. Despite the middle-class professional status and identity of the families, the fact remained that only one person was allowed to work. With a single income, the families struggled to fulfill all of their financial needs, including the transcultural cultivation of the children. It was the job of the wife to find affordable activities without compromising the quality of their service. This took quite an emotional toll on the mothers. Radhika ruefully shared her feeling with me regarding this:

> Sometimes it feels like my head will explode. You know, it's like asking someone who barely can swim to cross the ocean. I am still learning to live in this country and I can't work but, I have the responsibility to give my child the best possible upbringing while maintaining all sides. It's very very hard.

And yet, the mothers did all of this willingly, because the fathers were mostly unavailable due to their work demands. Additionally, the transcultural cultivation had become a part of the women's parental identity in the absence of a professional identity. It was a way for them to defy their dependent status. Anjali describes her role as a parent in United States as achieving the "herculean task of parenting in a new country. The country takes away your selfhood from you." Jaya best articulated what Anjali meant by this statement.

Jaya, who used to be the chief accountant of a multinational corporation in India before moving to the United States on a dependent visa, told me:

> It felt like I had lost everything when I came to America as a dependent and then I became A's [her son] mother and I found this new vocation. I have to give him the best despite all the constraints. And, that best includes, the best of India and America. For a long time I felt worthless but the challenge of being a mother, who most of the time feels like a single mother because Ravi [husband] has to work so much, makes me feel whole again, as paradoxical as it sounds. Some days, it's too much but, then I bring on my accountancy skills into this parenting thing and all is right with the world [laughs].

What Anjali calls a "herculean task" and Jaya calls her new identity was the emotional work (Hochschild 1979) plus the physical and mental labor required for the transcultural cultivation that mothers were putting in to cope with their legally dependent status. The structure of the visa laws and their work demands made it easy for the men not to be very involved in the parenting, thus making parenting an intensively gendered process.

In contrast, in the families of the nurses, on the surface, the men who were the dependents were involved in parenting. However, upon closer examination, I discovered that the men were doing only the physical labor of carting the children to their various activities and being engaged in their children's everyday lives and in the institutions they were part of. Most of the behind-the-scenes work—researching, scheduling, arranging activities, and managing the expenses of the activities—was still being done by the mothers, who were also the main breadwinners in these families. The mothers were also responsible for cooking and cleaning and maintaining all transnational communication and relationships for the family, including the children.

The children in these families, however, were often more attached to their fathers because the father was the more present parent, inducing maternal guilt in the mothers. The mothers in these families repeatedly told me that the children were "closer to the fathers" than to them. The fathers also confirmed this. One of the fathers told me that he was his children's "go-to person—not their mother." This forced the fathers in these families to do some of the emotional labor of parenting (Pfeffer 2017; Hochschild 1979). Shija, one of the mothers, expands on how exactly the attachment of children to fathers manifest. She said, "Whenever my daughter is upset, she runs to her dad. I am an afterthought. I think they forget that I am around because I am gone to work so much. It kills me. So I make sure that I do as much for them when I am around." This guilt propelled the mothers to do as much as they could of the transcultural cultivation.

Many of the nurses told me as much. "It's hard to be the only earner in the family, especially if you are a woman. My kids never see me because I am always at work. It's so hard. But as they grow they will know how much their mother actually did. It's also about me feeling involved in their lives," Rosy told me in describing how she views her parenting responsibilities. The mothers also viewed themselves as cultural agents for their children. "It's mother who passes on culture" was a common rhetoric among the nurses. This is an example of what Risman (1998) calls the internalized gendered cultural script that the mothers in these families used for justifying the transcultural cultivation style of parenting they took so seriously.

The dependent husbands took pride in being the main parent but escaped tasks such as cleaning, organizing schedules, and cooking, which were less rewarding. These fathers claimed a fathering identity at the same time that they downplayed their legal dependent status, in part because their role as head of the household had been taken away (Banerjee 2015). However, the mothers, who were also the main breadwinners in these families, equally bore the load of parenting with fathers—if not a heavier load when paid work and family demands are added together.

Parents in both sets of families thought that transcultural parenting was important because of the precariousness of their status in the United States. Naureen, one of the dependent mothers, told me that she and her husband, Aasman, wanted to make sure that their children were not entirely out of touch with their Indianness in case they had to return to India if Aasman lost his job and they lost their visa statuses. Many of the nurses expressed similar concerns.

In both family types, women perform much of the parenting labor, though in the families of nurses, we see men performing more child care tasks and even taking on some of the emotional labor. We see some of the same trends of parenting as gendered labor in studies done on nonimmigrant families in the United States (Bobel 2002; Coltrane 1989; Hochschild 2012; Pfeffer 2017; Wade 2013, 2016). What distinguishes the families in my research, however, is that for the men and women who were forced to be stay-at-home parents due to their visa status, parenting became their main vocation. They saw the kind of intensive parenting they performed as a way to redefine their identities—from being dependent parents to transcultural parents. Parenting then became an intersectional experience for the dependent men and women where they negotiated race, class, gender, culture, employment, and immigration status. Unlike the stay-at-home fathers in Rehel's (2013) study who transitioned seamlessly into a main caregiver role in the absence of workplace constraints, the stay-at-home fathers in my study resisted being seen as mothers. They emphasized a fathering identity, especially to preserve their head-of-household status and counteract the loss of their provider status.

The effects of the visa laws, therefore, are unmistakable in the shaping of gendered parenting in the households of Indian middle-class migrant workers, and yet, similar trends in both transcultural parenting and gendered parenting can be found in many immigrant families (Archer 2010; Banerjee 2012; Foner 2009). Perhaps it is time to do a more focused study of parenting in immigrant households and expand Lareau's theory of parenting.

Conclusion

Middle-class Indian immigrant parents parent at the intersection of concerted cultivation and natural growth with a strong emphasis on raising transcultural children. I have called this parenting "transcultural cultivation" because much of what the parents do in both forms of parenting is a particular form of cultivation that includes both aspects of Lareau's parenting styles. The immigrant parents are doing a kind of cultivation that demands balancing acts on various levels. The parents balance their visa statuses with their identities as immigrant parents, balance their children's activities by prioritizing the transnational context of their existences, and balance the gendered act of parenting. In effect, I have provided an intersectional analysis (Collins 2002) of how middle-class class status, the gender of parents, immigration status, the racialization of immigrants in the host society, and cultural practices shape parenting among Indian families in the United States.

The empirical examination of these intersections in the context of parenting helps us theorize parenting as a practice that is not just molded by the class location of parents. For immigrant parents, it negotiates multiple dimensions of their and their children's lives while parenting to produce a type of cultivation that includes various transcultural elements. Does this kind of parenting affect the futures of immigrant children and/or contribute to reproduction of class statuses? How does the application of intersectionality change the ways we think about parenting in minority households? These are some questions that arise from this research that can become the topic of future inquiry.

Given the material success of Indian Americans in the United States, one can assume that this style of parenting reproduces, and will reproduce, middle-class status for the children in keeping with Lareau's thesis. But there is no denying that these middle-class immigrant parents and children have to work much harder than their American white counterparts to achieve similar levels of success, as ascertained by Gorman (1998). There have, however, not been many studies of parenting in middle-class immigrant families or the consequences of such parenting. The concept of transcultural cultivation I have introduced here can propel further exploration among and between other groups (e.g., LatinX families, Asian families that are not middle-class, and rural families) on the topic. The possibilities are many.

Note

1. Despite the study being set in Britain, I find this relevant for the current paper for two reasons: (1) it is one of the few studies that uses Lareau's theory to explain parenting in immigrant Asian families, and (2) there are not many studies specifically addressing parenting in Asian immigrant families in the West. And, since the study is based on middle-class immigrants, the family context is not drastically different from that in the United States.

References

Archer, Louise. 2010. "'We Raised It with the Head': The Educational Practices of Minority Ethnic, Middle-Class Families." *British Journal of Sociology of Education* 31 (4): 449–69.

Banerjee, Pallavi. 2012. "Constructing Dependence: Visa Regimes and Gendered Migration in Families of Indian Professional Workers." PhD diss. University of Illinois at Chicago.

Banerjee, Pallavi. 2015. "When Men Stay Home: Household Labor and Parenthood in Female-Led Families of Indian Migrant Nurses." In *Families as They Really Are*, vol. 2, edited by Barbara J. Risman and Virginia Rutter. 500–517. New York: Norton.

Baumrind, Diane. 1967. "Child Care Practices Anteceding Three Patterns of Preschool Behavior." *Genetic Psychology Monographs* 75 (1): 43–88.

Bobel, Chris. 2002. *The Paradox of Natural Mothering.* Philadelphia: Temple University Press.

Cheah, Charissa S. L., Christy Y. Y. Leung, Madiha Tahseen, and David Schultz. 2009. "Authoritative Parenting among Immigrant Chinese Mothers of Preschoolers." *Journal of Family Psychology* 23 (3): 311.

Chua, Amy. 2011. *Battle Hymn of the Tiger Mother.* New York: Penguin.

Collins, Patricia Hill. 2002. *Black Feminist Thought: Knowledge, Consciousness, and the Politics of Empowerment.* New York: Routledge.

Coltrane, Scott. 1989. "Household Labor and the Routine Production of Gender." *Social Problems* 36: 473–90.

Cross-Barnet, Caitlin, and Katrina Bell McDonald. 2015. "It's All about the Children: An Intersectional Perspective on Parenting Values among Black Married Couples in the United States." *Societies* 5 (4): 855–71.

Driscoll, Anne K., Stephen T. Russell, and Lisa J. Crockett. 2008. "Parenting Styles and Youth Well-Being across Immigrant Generations." *Journal of Family Issues* 29 (2): 185–209.

Farver, JoAnn M., Yiyuan Xu, Bakhtawar R. Bhadha, Sonia Narang, and Eli Lieber. 2007. "Ethnic Identity, Acculturation, Parenting Beliefs, and Adolescent Adjustment: A Comparison of Asian Indian and European American families." *Merrill-Palmer Quarterly* 53 (2): 184–215.

Foner, Nancy. 2009. *Across Generations: Immigrant Families in America.* New York: NYU Press.

Foner, Nancy, and Joanna Dreby. 2001. "Relations between the Generations in Immigrant Families." *Annual Review of Sociology* 37: 545–64.

Foner, Nancy, and Phillip Kasinitz. 2007. "The Second Generation." In *The New Americans: A Guide to Immigration Since 1965*, edited by M. C. Waters and R. Ueda, 270–82. Cambridge, MA: Harvard University Press.

Fu, Alyssa S., and Hazel Rose Markus. 2014. "My Mother and Me: Why Tiger Mothers Motivate Asian Americans but Not European Americans." *Personality and Social Psychology Bulletin* 40 (6): 739–49.

Gorman, Jean Cheng. 1998. "Parenting Attitudes and Practices of Immigrant Chinese Mothers of Adolescents." *Family Relations* 47 (1): 73–80. doi:10.2307/584853.

Hochschild, Arlie, and Anne Machung. 2012. *The Second Shift: Working Families and the Revolution at Home*. New York: Penguin.

Hochschild, Arlie Russell. 1979. "Emotion Work, Feeling Rules and Social Structure." *American Journal of Sociology* 85 (3): 551–75.

Lareau, Annette. 2003. *Unequal Childhoods: Class, Race, and Family Life*. Berkeley: University of California Press.

Lareau, Annette. 2011. *Unequal Childhoods: Class, Race, and Family Life*, 2nd edition. Berkeley: University of California Press.

Lee, Jennifer, and Min Zhou. 2004. *Asian American Youth: Culture, Identity and Ethnicity*. New York: Routledge.

Long, Katy. 2016. "Silicon Valley's Reluctant Housewife: Immigration Law Bars Women from Working." *The Guardian*, May 19.

Lopez, Nancy. 2003. *Hopeful Girls, Troubled Boys: Race and Gender Disparity in Urban Education*. London: Psychology Press.

Manohar, Namita N. 2008. "Gender and Ethnicity in Union Formation: The Case of Second-Generation Patels." *International Journal of Sociology of the Family* 34 (2): 209–34.

Manohar, Namita N. 2013. "Mothering for Class and Ethnicity: The Case of Indian Professional Immigrants in the United States." In *Notions of Family: Intersectional Perspectives*, edited by Marla H. Kohlman, Dana B. Krieg, and Bette J. Dickerson, 159–85. Binley: Emerald Group Publishing Limited.

Mohanty, Chandra Talpade. 1988. "Under Western Eyes: Feminist Scholarship and Colonial Discourses." *Feminist Review* 30: 61–88.

Moore, Mignon. 2001. *Invisible Families: Gay Identities, Relationships, and Motherhood among Black Women*. Berkeley: University of California Press.

Pfeffer, Carla A. 2017. *Queering Families: The Postmodern Partnerships of Cisgender Women and Transgender Men*. Oxford: Oxford University Press.

Portes, Alejandro, and Patricia Fernández-Kelly. 2008. "No Margin for Error: Educational and Occupational Achievement among Disadvantaged Children of Immigrants." *The Annals of the American Academy of Political and Social Science* 620 (1): 12–36.

Purkayastha, Bandana. 2004. "Skilled Migration and Cumulative Disadvantage: The Case of Highly Qualified Asian Indian Immigrant Women in the U.S." *Geoforum*: 36: 181–196.

Pyke, Karen. 2000. "'The Normal American Family' as an Interpretive Structure of Family Life among Grown Children of Korean and Vietnamese Immigrants." *Journal of Marriage and Family* 62 (1): 240–55.

Rehel, Erin M. 2014. "When Dad Stays Home Too: Paternity Leave, Gender, and Parenting." *Gender & Society* 28 (1): 110–32.

Risman, Barbara. 1998. *Gender Vertigo: American Families in Transition.* New Haven, CT: Yale University Press.

Roopnarine, Jaipaul L., Ambika Krishnakumar, Aysegul Metindogan, and Melanie Evans. 2006. "Links between Parenting Styles, Parent–Child Academic Interaction, Parent–School Interaction, and Early Academic Skills and Social Behaviors in Young Children of English-Speaking Caribbean Immigrants." *Early Childhood Research Quarterly* 21 (2): 238–52.

Smith, Robert. 2006. *Mexican New York: Transnational Lives of New Immigrants.* Berkeley: University of California Press.

Suárez-Orozco, Carola, and Marcelo M. Suárez-Orozco. 2009. *Children of Immigration.* Cambridge, MA: Harvard University Press.

Swartz, Teresa Toguchi. 2009. "Intergenerational Family Relations in Adulthood: Patterns, Variations, and Implications in the Contemporary United States." *Annual Review of Sociology* 35: 191–212.

Wade, Lisa. 2013. "The Growing Cost of Having Kids Is Tipping More Women Towards Ambivalence about Motherhood." *Alternet*, May 6.

Wade, Lisa. 2016. "The Invisible Workload that Drags Women Down." *Money*, December 29.

Zhou, Min. 2009. "Conflict, Coping and Reconciliation: Intergenerational Relations in Chinese Immigrant Families." In *The New Americans: A Guide to Immigration Since 1965*, edited by M. C. Waters and R. Ueda, 21–47. Cambridge, MA: Harvard University Press.

CHAPTER TWELVE

Lost in Detention and Deportation—"Found" through Foster Care and Adoption: Reviewing the Tensions between Family Building and Human Rights in the United States

Pamela Anne Quiroz

Accepted as one way to build a family, adoption continues to attract media headlines, some inspiring and others troubling. In the newspaper article "Simone Biles: From Foster Care to the Olympics," we learn about the story of Olympian gymnast Simone Biles, whose journey from foster care to Olympic history serves as inspiration. As a young child, Biles had been shuttled between the home of her mother and multiple foster homes prior to being legally adopted by her grandparents and becoming one of the most decorated female Olympic gymnasts and a role model for young women. Popular media also tells the story of adoption, sometimes across national borders. The Oscar-nominated film *Lion* features the story of Saroo Brierley, accidentally separated from his family in India at age five and later adopted by an Australian couple. More than 20 years later, Brierley located his birth family using Google Earth. Saroo's experience features adoption as a poignant story of loss, love, and redemption as the definition of family is expanded when birth parents and adoptive parents bridge their cultural differences through their love of Saroo.

Headlines in newspapers and popular and social media have featured prominent and changing adoption issues relevant in certain places and historical contexts. Their topics include children from war-torn countries, the disproportionate placement of African American children in foster care, China's one-child policy and its implications for girls, race matching, transracial adoption, embryo adoption, and positive and negative outcomes of international adoptions. In our current political climate, adoption headlines now include stories of detention, deportation, and children suffering from posttraumatic stress syndrome as enforcement of U.S. immigration policy results in family separation and child placement. These stories offer a new mirror on the tensions between family building and human rights. Highlighting a current aspect of domestic adoption that stems from detention and deportation of (overwhelmingly) Latino parents, I revisit the complex political and sociological nature of adoptive parenting that is too often ignored—the building of family that occurs because of the loss of family. In this chapter, I analyze newspaper articles, social media, a domestic Hispanic adoption forum, and transcripts from interviews with parents that feature adoptive and foster parenting of the children of immigrants. As an adoptive parent of two sons, one domestically adopted and the other adopted from Ethiopia, I am situated as what anthropologist Ruth Behar (1997) called the "vulnerable observer"—an ethnographer who integrates the subjective and empathic into the process of research and writing. As such, I offer observation that is lived and written in a personal voice in the hope that it leads to greater understanding and feeling for those about whom we write. In other words, I am implicated in the dynamics of these processes.

As a prospective adoptive mother in Chicago who was interested in adopting a Mexican child, city agencies had told me that Latinos simply do not place their children and that mothers who did would not be likely to select me, as I was a single woman. I therefore looked to the Internet to pursue adoption. That was nearly 16 years ago. Two years after becoming an adoptive mother, I began to research adoption, and eight years ago, I began seeing articles in the newspaper and online that described children of undocumented immigrants who had come home to find that their parents had been deported. When the Applied Research Center's (2011) study on children of undocumented immigrants emerged, I became even more interested in what seemed certain to become a significant problem for mixed-status families. I recognized incremental changes in domestic adoption and the substantial changes in transnational adoption, and I was drawn to potential connections between these events and the increase of Latino children in foster care and adoption. This was the basis for my current examination of the domestic adoption forum on Latino adoption at Adoption.com. As an adoptive parent, I also became aware of attempts by a few Chicago agencies to place Latino children with foster parents and through adoption. I therefore sought access to interview participants to understand their perspectives on parenting "citizen-children" (i.e., children who were born in the United States but who have at least one parent who is undocumented).

Adoption research has expanded to include studies on: identity (Samuels 2009; McGinnis 2009; Tuan and Shiao 2011; Hearst 2010); changes in language and discursive processes (Anagnost 2000; Noonan 2007; Quiroz 2007, 2015); intersectionality, or the study of overlapping or intersecting identities and related systems of discrimination (Dorow 2006; Gailey 2009); cultural socialization (Leinaweaver 2013; Volkman 2005; Lee et al. 2010; Quiroz 2012); the impact of technology (Howard 2011); policy (Briggs 2006; Roberts 2002; Fonseca 2006; Williams 2003; Freundlich 2000); and human rights (Smolin 2005, 2010, 2013; Meier and Zhang 2008; Rotabi 2015; Leifson 2008). This chapter seeks to bridge some of these areas of inquiry by reviewing where we were and where we are now in this latest dilemma of family building and human rights that is occurring in our own backyard.

Following a brief review of U.S. adoption history, I compare my prior online research on adoptive parenting with current patterns of adoption. I then examine the shifts in adoption with analysis of a domestic Latino adoption forum and weave in patterns that I found in a small number of interviews with foster and adoptive parents (n=14) to explore how immigration policy and the building of family through adoption is accompanied and accomplished by the loss of family. These practices highlight the dilemmas raised by the United Nations Convention on the Rights of the Child, which guarantees each child a right to certain basic human needs, to be raised in a family, and to retain her/his identity. It also clarifies how few children placed for international adoption are true orphans, meaning that most children who are adopted transnationally have at least one parent who is still living.

Adoption Overview

Adoption has been practiced for centuries, formally and informally. However, it was in the late 20th century that the number of formalized U.S. adoptions substantially increased and the number of international adoptions exploded. Since 1989, more than 300,000 children from other countries have been adopted by U.S. parents, who are predominantly white in ethnicity, college educated, and middle-class. The peak of these adoptions was in 2004, when more than 22,000 children were adopted, predominantly from four countries: China, Russia, Guatemala, and South Korea.

Multiple explanations have been offered for the increase in transnational adoptions. Sending countries have reportedly been motivated by poverty, cultural proscriptions (e.g., norms about unwed motherhood), preferences for male children, and inertia (i.e., participation that continues after the necessity of participation ceases, as in the case of South Korea) (Selman 2015). The outsourcing of children has also been suggested as a means to alleviate stress on the social welfare systems of countries such as China and Russia as they transition from communist to a capitalist economies (Wang 2016). Cultural and demographic changes and decreases in fertility are seen as the motivation for receiving countries (e.g., acceptance of single mothers, legalized abortion, a desire to avoid open adoption, and humanitarian motivations) (Briggs 20061997; Selman 2015). The dynamic of supply and demand has been blamed for stimulating the growth of illegal activities and abuses of human rights (Leifson 2008; Cardello 2009; Rotabi 2015; Meier and Zhang 2008; Smolin 2005, 2010, 2013; Smerdon 2008). Both sending and receiving countries have raised issues about the commodification of children and child trafficking, erosion of national interests, and damaging children's identities. Stories of illegal adoption, child abductions, and child laundering have occurred in multiple countries. Even China, the most popular sending country to the United States over the past 30 years, has had to address the issue of child trafficking, as six orphanages in China placed nearly 1,000 trafficked babies with Western adoptive families (Meier and Zhang 2008). During this period, nearly half of all sending countries either completely abandoned or temporarily restricted their transnational adoptions.

Several people have written about the shifting marketplace of adoption and how changes inevitably shift prospective parents' attention to other places. For example, between 2003 and 2010, more than 35,000 children were adopted from African countries, with the majority of these adopted from Ethiopia (22,282). During this same period, adoptions from China decreased by 70 percent; those from Russia decreased by 34 percent (prior to Russia's exclusion of U.S. adoptions in 2012); and those from Ethiopia decreased by 50 percent (Selman 2015). By 2016, we had seen a 72 percent decrease in transnational adoptions. Though policies and numbers of adoptions have changed, Chuck Johnson, chief executive of the National Council for Adoption, argues that there is a continued interest in adoption by Americans, as transracial adoptions and adoptions from foster care have increased (*Boston Globe* 2017). Given this viewpoint, which mirrors that of other adoption organizations, recent events in the United States regarding child placement raise new concerns about the tensions between family building and human rights as families are literally being separated through deportation and detention and their children placed into foster care and adoption. This is the latest chapter in the history of U.S. adoption that underscores the involuntary nature of immigration for children (via adoption) and the various social and political factors that enter into these processes.

Immigration Terrorism

The Obama administration's deportation or detainment of more than 400,000 Latinos resulted in a group of children, predominantly Latino, who were impacted by foster care and adoption. In 2011, the Applied Research Center [ARC] (now Race Forward) found more than 5,000 Latino children in foster care or adopted because their parents had been detained or deported. The ARC projected that another 15,000 children would be in this situation within the next five years of the study. Though no studies comparable to the ARC's have since been done, other data on the number of U.S. Latino children with parents who have been deported supports the ARC's projections. For example, in 2014, Immigration and Customs Enforcement carried out more than 72,000 deportations of parents who said they had U.S.-born children, and estimates from various research institutes and state and government agencies suggest that parents of the 5 million U.S. citizen-children are among the hundreds of thousands of undocumented immigrants who are being expelled each year. In California it is estimated that more than 10,000 parents of U.S. citizen-children are detained each year, and half of these detainees had no criminal histories or records (Nicholson 2017). The state of Texas deports more unauthorized persons than any other state in the country—more than twice that of California and almost 10 times that of Illinois (22,041 last year alone) (U.S. Deportation 2017). Added to this is the Trump administration's prioritization of expanding immigration and security policies preceded by his campaign comments about Mexicans as rapists and criminals (Lee 2015). Though Mexicans are about 60 percent of the undocumented population in the United States, in 2010, Mexicans comprised 83 percent of the detained, 73 percent of those forcibly removed, and 77 percent of voluntary departures (Dreby 2012).

Health disparities research provides valuable insights into the mental and physiological outcomes for children who live in fear of loss of family (Migration Policy Institute 2017). Because this is a process, loss of even one parent does not automatically result in state control of the child. Rather, this occurs over time as the economic impacts hit the remaining parent or relatives and directly or indirectly impact children. Such was the case for Nathaly Perez's mother, who was deported in June 2008, leaving her three teenage daughters behind. Nathaly was 12 when her father was deported. Reitmayer (2010) describes the family decline experienced by Nathaly Perez, whose family was torn apart by deportation of first her father and then her mother:

> Although Perez' father immigrated legally, his status was revoked when and Perez' mother were both jailed for a domestic disturbance. He was subsequently deported in 2006, Perez's mother was given probation. Following her father's deportation, Perez recalls her mother struggling to support the family alone, sometimes working two or more jobs to care for her three young daughters. . . "Before this happened my mom had been doing really well. She was doing awesome," Nathaly recalls. "I don't know if anything was going on with my brothers. We didn't know about it." Perez's mother and two older brothers were arrested and deported in the following months, and all three girls were placed in public foster care. After losing so many close family members, Nathaly says she struggled to find stability. "Little by little I felt like everybody was getting taken away from me. To me, in my head, I was just ready for my sister Eralia to be deported," Nathaly said.

Like all adoptees, these children face the dilemmas of cultural socialization as they become what I call the newest "neoethnics"—involuntary migrants whose identities are literally recreated through foster care and adoption and who typically do not experience direct links to their culture or ethnicity of origin (Quiroz 2015). Like most adoptees, these children are not likely to visit their countries of origin, to speak their native language, to establish intimate relationships with members of their first family or country, or even to form close social ties to members who have migrated from their communities of origin. Added to the loss of identity is the literal loss of family that occurs through traumatizing events (coming home from school to discover parents have been taken or having a father removed in front of a child). We do not typically think of adopted children as immigrants, let alone involuntary; however, recent events have heightened awareness that this is the status of adopted citizen-children and that the traumas they experience in the United States place them in the position for others to build a family. In his report for Human Rights Watch, Michael Blunt offers an example on children of witnessing the arrest of an undocumented parent:

> U.S.: Detention Hazardous to Immigrants' Health
> On the morning of February 28, 2017 Romulo Avelica-Gonzalez pulled up to Academia Avance, a small charter academy in Highland Park, CA, to drop off two of his daughters at school. After dropping off one daughter, Romulo was pulled over by Immigration and Customs Enforcement (ICE) agents, who were unaware that 13 year old Fatima was still in the backseat. Over uncontrollable sobs, Fatima filmed the arrest of her father with her cellphone (The Detention and Deportation of Californian Parents, May 8, 2017).

In 2008, the United States finally ratified and implemented the Hague Convention Treaty on Intercountry Adoption, which was designed in 1993 to regulate intercountry adoption and promote the welfare of children. Undoubtedly, changes in the political economies of other countries, national movements against international adoption, and the U.S. implementation of the Hague treaty have combined to substantially reduce the numbers of transnational adoptions. Two years ago marks a 35 year low in U.S. transnational adoptions from 22,884 adoptions in 2004 to 5,648 in 2016. The latest figure is the lowest since 1981, when there were 4,868 intercountry adoptions (Jordan 2017). Americans lead the world in overseas adoptions. The marketing of children is not a new phenomenon, and these practices have taken place for decades in several countries. However, in the United States, we now face a situation where the terms "transnational" and "domestic" have blurred, as have the terms "legal" and "illegal." The implications are profound, as foreign-born unauthorized nationals and their U.S. citizen-children (mixed-status families) are under siege and increasingly subject to separation. Media coverage and human rights reports suggest that children of deported parents often find themselves staying with a relative, in foster care or adopted, or even homeless. Though no statistics are kept on the number of children who end up in foster care due to deportation or detention, the cost to foster each child is approximately $40,000 each year (ARC 2011). The emotional costs to children, families, and communities are infinite.

The Internet Is Transforming Adoption

I noted that my prior research on adoption began two years after I became an adoptive parent. It was during my journey to becoming an adoptive mother that I looked to the Internet, and because of what I found, I began to research adoption. I later wrote a book about the online examination of private adoption agencies and the racial reality of this mode of family building (Quiroz 2007). Private adoption Web sites and their presentations of how children were placed into programs, as well as the criteria and restrictions on adoption (e.g., age, marital status, number of children already in the household, average wait time, and costs of adoption), reflected a racial stratification of children. Online adoptive parent networks illustrated how prospective adoptive parents advertised themselves to birth mothers and presented their preferences regarding the traits of their desired child, with race still an important factor. Adoptive parent forums also presented different perspectives and practices expressed by adoptive (and prospective) parents. Together, these data revealed the ways we describe and value children based on their race/ethnicity and nationality.

The value of online data is that they provide the parameters of adoption and unscripted viewpoints and practices of adoptive parenting. As adoptive parenting in the United States adds a new chapter that revolves around shifting policies of immigration and international participation, detention and deportation serve as the backdrop for a set of parents who participate in these processes. I first provide a brief review of my prior research findings on the context of domestic adoption, along with updates from recent examinations of this work. Next, I present an analysis of a domestic adoption forum whose participants included prospective and adoptive parents of Latino children, weaving this data with interviews of 14 Chicago parents who participated in a Chicago initiative to place Latino children in 2014. Participants' online comments drive home how adoption is inherently loss and gain accomplished through a political process and via social inequalities. As adoptive parents, we must be aware of these processes if we are to truly address the welfare of children.

My original research included a detailed examination of the largest online directory of adoption agencies in 2006: the Open Directory (also called the DMOZ) (Quiroz 2007). As Table 12.1 shows, private agency Web sites presented a picture of two- and three-tiered adoption programs, with placement of children dependent upon their racial/ethnic mixes, and criteria and costs of adoption based on program placement. Placement of Latino and

Table 12.1   The Open Adoption Directory [DMOZ] 2006 (N=96 Private Adoption Agencies)

Types of Programs	Costs	Restrictions	Wait Time
Caucasian (37–48%)	$20,000–$50,000	No more than 1 child in home	9 month to 4 year wait
		Age range of parents no more than 50 yrs.	
"Fully" Hispanic (7–13%)	$16,000–$28,000	Same as Caucasian (except in the Southwest)	Same as Caucasian (except in the Southwest)
Asian (3–13%)	$16,000–$30,000	Same as Caucasian	Same as Caucasian
African American (0–5%)	$0–$10,000	Unlimited number of children in home	1 month to 9 months
		Age range of parents up to 60 yrs.	

Asian infants suggested a type of honorary white status for members of these groups, as these children were placed with and priced the same as white ethnic children except in one region in the Southwest of the country where Latinos occupied a middle tier. African American and biracial babies, defined by virtually every Web site as any child with mixed ancestry of any type with African American heritage, were placed into separate programs with substantially different costs, criteria, and wait times, with the minimal wait time for "Caucasian" children (nine months to four years) serving as the maximum wait time for African American and biracial children (one month to nine months). Web sites also assured prospective parents that African American and biracial children were "healthy" or not "drug addicted" (see Table 12.2).

When I examined the DMOZ again in 2015, the number of agencies in the directory had dropped by a third (from 96 to 65 agencies), and many were different agencies. Those agencies that had remained the same had modified their Web sites to include transnational adoption programs that were different from those offered in 2006, and less explicit language regarding race was often found in descriptions of domestic adoption programs (i.e., it was far less common to find explicit definitions of children with any ancestry mixed with African American heritage placed into Black and biracial programs). As Table 12.3 shows, what was consistent was the different domestic programs offered for adoption—namely white/Caucasian (with all ethnic groups placed into this category) and black/African American programs, cost differences, and criteria for parents. Wait times had increased for African American children, as had costs.

Another aspect of adoption that I revisited was adoptive parent preferences. The existence of online adoptive parent networks allows us to view the preference ordering of racial/ethnic children (in relation to each other) by

Table 12.2   Adoption Facts 2015

Foster Care	Private	Intercountry	
37%	38%	25%	
Married couples	**Single F**	**Single M**	
70.2%	22.7%	5.5%	
Costs			
	Foster Care	**Private**	**Intercountry**
None	56%	22%	2%
<$5,000	29%	33%	1%
$5,000–$10,000	6%	13%	5%
>$10,000	9%	33%	93%

Table 12.3   The Open Adoption Directory [DMOZ] 2015 (N=63 Private Adoption Agencies)

Types of Programs	Costs	Restrictions	Wait Time
Caucasian (40–50%)	$26,000-$60,000 (average $40,000)	No more than 1 child in home Age range of parents no more than 50 yrs.	2 to 5 year wait
Hispanic (5–6%)	$22,000–$45,000	Same as Caucasian	Same as Caucasian
Asian (1%)	$24,000–$40,000	Same as Caucasian	Same as Caucasian
African American (0–5%)	$0–$26,000	Unlimited number of children in home Age range of parents up to 60 yrs.	6 months to 1 year

what are overwhelmingly adoptive couples. As Table 12.4 shows, in 2006, prospective parents demonstrated clear preferences by race, with virtually no parents willing to adopt African American or biracial children and relatively few willing to adopt a "fully" Hispanic or Asian child. A comparison of one of these networks, Adoptionnetwork.com, in 2006 and 2016 shows modest but significant changes in acceptance of racially different children by predominantly white ethnic parents. Though percentages of parents who were willing to cross the racial divide by adopting children from other racial/ethnic groups was still less than half (less than 50 percent), the percentage of those parents who were willing to adopt racially/ethnically different children had increased significantly.

Finally, as Table 12.5 outlines, three adoption forums of the largest "sending" countries between 1989 and 2009 (China, Russia, and Guatemala) presented online spaces where U.S. adoptive parents looked to the Internet to create identity and a sense of community. In these virtual spaces, participants engaged in unscripted discussions that generated threads that could be analyzed for themes. Parents conveyed the guidelines for adoptees' racial subjectivity, choosing, distancing, keeping, and purchasing culture and identity. "Choosing" refers to the choice of which children adoptive parents were willing to adopt and how they arrived at their decisions. "Choosing" also refers to the variety of decisions that parents made that directly and indirectly affected identity. These decisions included minor and substantive decisions, such as where to live, which schools their children would attend,

Table 12.4   AdoptionNetwork.com Race/Ethnicity Preference of Children by Adoptive Couples

2006		2016**	
White	49%	White	98%
Hispanic	5%	Hispanic	28%
Asian	13%	Asian	37%
African American	0	African American	11%
White/Hispanic	27%	White/Hispanic	76%
White/Asian	15%	White/Asian	63%
White/AA	1%	White/AA	32%
Any Child	0	Any Child	11%

**Whereas percentages for 2006 provide the percentages of the total number of 350 requests for children, there was no preference ordering available for more than one category of child at that time. In 2016, prospective adoptive parents were allowed to provide preference order. The percentages offered in 2016 therefore provide the percentage of parents who were willing to adopt a child from each racial/ethnic category. 99 percent of participants on this Web site were adoptive couples as opposed to single parents.

Table 12.5   Analysis of Interactions in Adoption Forums 2006–2008

Forum	Searches	Total Posts	Total # Participants
China	2006–2008	2,186 posts	312
Russia	2006–2008	1,874 posts	378
Guatemala	2007–2008	3,194 posts	397

4 Modal Responses: Choosing, Avoiding/Cultural Distancing, Keeping, and Purchasing.

Choosing: The variety of decisions parents make that directly and indirectly affect identity. These decisions include minor and substantive decisions, such as where to live, which schools to attend, which languages to learn and how, and other practices, such as circumcision.

Avoiding: Cultural distancing and the silence surrounding children's birth origins, culture, and race. The majority of posts in each forum indicated that parents either did not address their child's origins or addressed them in a perfunctory manner.

Keeping: Engaged in activities to help adoptees retain a sense of native group identity.

Purchasing: Use of cultural symbols, activities, media, and artifacts as a means of providing the basis of racial/cultural identity for adopted children.

learning language, and other practices, such as circumcision. "Avoiding" refers to cultural distancing and the silence surrounding children's birth origins, culture, and race, as the majority of posts in each forum indicated that parents either did not address their child's origins or addressed them in a perfunctory manner. "Keeping" refers to the activities of parents who subscribed to and engaged in activities to help their children retain a sense of native group identity. "Purchasing" refers to the use of cultural symbols, activities, media, and artifacts as a means of providing the basis of racial/ cultural identity for adopted children.

Forum interactions illustrated how parents conveyed the guidelines for adoptees' racial subjectivity. Choosing, cultural distancing, keeping, and purchasing are the processes by which adoptees learn the scripts for their new social position within the adoptive family and society. A significant number of online parents indicated that socialization of children whose race and ethnicity were different from that of their adoptive parents often resulted in divorcing children from their cultures, and we can begin to see how families formed through transnational adoption may simultaneously reflect race-mixing while allowing the current racial hierarchy to remain firmly in place.

Domestic Transracial Adoptions and the Power of Language

Adoption statistics have changed over the years. When I wrote my book over ten years ago, fewer children from foster care were being adopted, and typically, such adoptions were by relatives. Domestic transracial adoptions were still a small proportion of private adoptions. What remains consistent are the differences in cost between adopting from foster care, private, and transnational sources; in the programs for different groups of children; and in the projections of an increasing number of Latino children in foster care. These data are by no means definitive, and they are based on only a sample of adoptive parents who used the Internet, but they are part of the mix of studies on transracial and transnational adoption and add some nuance regarding parents' perspectives and practices.

Drawn to the news stories of Latino children who were entering foster care and adoption, I explored a domestic Latino adoption forum between 2012 and 2014 and conducted interviews to see how participants engaged in this process. As an adoptive parent, I had been approached by one of four Chicago agencies that were using formal and informal means (adoption newsletters and advertisements) to place Latino children with foster parents and adoption. I later sought access to interview participants in this process through this same agency, which yielded a convenience sample of 14 participants. These Chicago agencies explicitly sought to place children with Spanish-speaking Latino families; however, ten of my interviews were of white ethnic parents and four of Latino parents (only one of the white ethnic parents spoke Spanish). Only four of the parents were adoptive, and the rest were foster parents. All interviews were with the foster or adoptive mother.

Layered onto the research question is a methodological debate about online research, as Internet communications are seen as data taken out of context. Credibility of interpretation relies on details of the analytic process and how the researcher positions her- or himself in the study, along with how the data ties to other studies and relevant information. I followed the patterns of analysis used in prior research by structuring virtual observations to occur at regular intervals with a focus exclusively on threads that discussed fostering and adoption of children of immigrant parents. In addition to interviews, I analyzed online content from the Domestic Latino Adoption forum from 2012 until 2014. Like personal narratives, forum interactions often consist of retrospective and sequential constructions of major life events or activities. However, interactions in forums can also include anecdotes, comments, real or hypothetical events, and intensive debates that present meaningful accounts of the social world of participants. I analyzed only those threads that directly related to fostering and adoption of Latino children of immigrants.

Forum threads on immigration, fostering, and adoption initially contained an average of 200 posts (per week). Once I acquired permission to "lurk" in the forum, observations of threads occurred intermittently throughout the first year as I informally followed participants' conversations on adoption. I conducted formal analysis of threads for one-week periods during four months in the second year. Messages in this forum averaged 200 posts per week at the beginning of the observations, and by the end of the second year, they ranged from 200 to 700 posts in an average week. The actual number of participants engaged in any given conversation was significantly smaller than the number of posts, because, like most conversations, certain topics generated greater involvement by a subset of participants. I downloaded the entire set of messages in the threads and analyzed these interactions using grounded theory and a more finely tuned examination of the discursive patterns that I found in the written text.

The elasticity of interactions on the Internet (the "playground of identity") merges the past and the present, with participants serving both as framers of identity and as audience for identities presented by others [many know this as a "performative analysis"] (Gubrium and Holstein 2000; Bamberg 2008; boyd 2014). The chapter treats interactions found in the Latino domestic adoption forum as "small stories" that narrate identity and help people to create a sense of who they are (Bamberg 2004, 2008). Threads include anecdotes—real and possibly imaginary stories that exemplify adoption as rooted in myriad perspectives and experiences that may or may not resonate with other adoptive or prospective parents. A performative analysis of these interactions challenges the perception that forum interactions are discrete practices or "quotes taken out of context" and instead substitutes the notion of "collapsed contexts," in which multiple identities, views, and negotiations of self, "other," and process encourage us to reexamine our views and interpretations of adoption and immigrants (boyd 2014). Participants engage in interactions that extend across time (hours and days), and performing identity (as would-be or current parent) is inexorably intersubjective as participants rely on their audience to "hear" their stories or comments and respond to them. Because small stories do not always adhere to a typical narrative structure, researchers often overlook or disregard them as insignificant or irrelevant to the "big" story that he or she is telling. These are the data that exist in the margins of ethnographic fieldwork. The small stories of participants in the Latino adoption forum, however, reveal how the process of fostering and adopting citizen-children (and their immigrant parents) is talked about, acted on, and elided (van Dijk 2001).

Language is particularly important because terminology can evoke positive (or negative) attitudes toward groups. Terms can soften harsher images of persons or generate images and responses to those images, such as posts that describe biological parents as "criminal" and "illegal." The language for race-based programs described in the prior tables (Quiroz 2007) is not merely a neutral descriptor; it operates to mark children (most often African American children) as "other." Additionally, program labels are juxtaposed in racially evocative ways. For example, in 2006, the Evangelical Child and Family Agency separated its infants into five programs: Healthy Newborn Adoption (white), Special Needs, African American Infants, Intercountry Adoption, and Agency-Assisted Adoption. When descriptors like "healthy" are used to describe one type of child but not another, a flag is implicitly raised in the minds of adoptive parents regarding the other programs without this descriptor. Thus, the communicative power of language and adoption discourse perpetuates myths about entire communities and allows identities to be constructed and sustained. When communication either does not occur between powerful (those who adopt) and subordinate groups (those whose children are adopted), the rules of interchange are set in favor of the powerful group's interpretation, making prejudices and behaviors not less devastating but simply less tangible.

I solicited interviews with the assistance of the agency that had originally contacted me, and I acquired a convenience sample of 14 participants. The interviews were relatively open-ended. I asked parents about the process of entry to fostering/adoption, how their child had entered the program, the challenges of fostering/adoption, and their perspectives about their activities. The following sections capture the dominant foci of parents' responses to the interview questions.

Whose Rights Matter?

A great deal of time in forum threads and interviews was spent discussing the logistics of fostering and adoption of citizen-children (and immigrant children). In the interviews, I asked participants to describe how they had entered this process, but forum discussions emerged spontaneously in threads. Parents who were interviewed described being approached by an agency (as opposed to responding to an ad or newsletter), and participants in forum threads asked about the logistics, legal challenges, and possible conflicts with "illegal" parents. A small sample of such thread titles included "Illegal immigrant bio parents," "Adopting illegal children," "Illegal aliens? Foster care and adoption," "Bio parent illegal," "Adopting an illegal immigrant," "Experiences with the undocumented," and "Deportation of Bios while children are in foster care." Though much of the discussion in these threads revolved around information seeking, the language use and focus was on how adoptive/foster parents could secure their rights. Forum interactions present foster, adoptive, and prospective parents of citizen-children as creating identities and justifying the act of adoption itself. This is done by minimizing and criminalizing the biological or "birth" parents of the children whom they wish to parent. Because discursive analyses assume that language can have social consequences, and language regarding immigration is a contentious issue, it is notable that the term "illegal" was used instead of "undocumented" or "unauthorized."

The following forum interaction is only one of many such exchanges among prospective and foster/adoptive parents:

Seeking: One of my friends who is a foster mom is dealing with this . . . The mom is an American but the dad is an illegal immigrant . . . The kids got removed from the mom and now the dad is coming for a visit, he has kept in contact with the case workers but this is his first visit. The kids have been in care since the end of May. How would his rights be affected by him being illegal?

Diane: He has all the rights as any legal citizen. If he should be deported or re country, it will not stop RU from happening. Believe me, we are up to our eyeballs in this mess. According to some of the international conferences regarding children's rights, (forget which ones exactly), the children are also considered dual citizens of the U.S. and biological dad's country. Therefore, should dad want to, he could get his home country's consulate involved, which could have some pull. Unless Biological dad is unfit to raise the children, honestly, there is nothing the illegal status will affect.

Mommy: Here is a link to a story here in Portland Oregon that I have been following that is along the same lines. I am disgusted with the state's decision to send the U.S. born child to Mexico.

Alice: We had friends who were trying to adopt a little boy in Oklahoma a couple of years ago. They had him for over six months, then his BF, an illegal immigrant, showed up and with the court's backing took him back to Mexico. They [?] felt that the BF was not a fit parent but that he had family in Mexico and they decided that there was no legal standing to keep the baby in the U.S. since his birth mom had terminated her rights. My friends were devastated, but there was nothing they could do except pray that he would be loved by BF's family.

Accompanying the reference to "illegal" parents is a sense of indignation on the part of participants and avoidance of addressing the broader social and economic realities of children and their families.

> Colorado: I'm in Denver and we had a newborn drug addicted girl whose mother wouldn't work her plan and her dad is an illegal alien. We were told by the first caseworker that he wouldn't get her because he's illegal . . . NOT TRUE. The case was transferred to the Spanish speaking division and everything changed. I will avoid the Spanish division as long as I can (long long story about another child). Luckily the only reason cases go there is if the parents do not speak English. DHS does not care about alien status for parents. They do not report to immigration and [our daughter] now lives with her dad. He speaks no English, we speak no Spanish, but we are lucky enough get her every weekend.
>
> peaceforall: One of my friends, is currently going through something similar. The Biological dad was deported. A home study was completed in Mexico for the grandma. The kid had lived with my friend on and off for years (failed RU). My friend said the home study in Mexico was a joke. The kid doesn't even know his grandmother. CPS told her the kid was illegal anyway and costing the state money. Nice. She was pretty broken up about it.

Interwoven with these perspectives are narratives that resonate with other examinations of parents' destinies with their (adopted/foster) children (see Anagnost 2000; Noonan 2007). Here we find similarities between foster and adoptive parents in forum interactions and interviews as participants in both groups describe their intuitive connection to the child they parent, even prior to meeting him/her. Some mothers in this study also referred to instantly recognizing the child as destined to be theirs. These discussions result in distancing foster and adoptive parents from the situations in which children find themselves and divorce children from their biological families. They also help validate rights to a child and mitigate guilt about the circumstances under which we become parents.

> Cali: I don't know if it varies from state to state but we are in Missouri and had our permanency hearing the last part of October when the judge gave the orders for TPR to be filed. Our regular Juvenile Officer was on maternity leave and just came back this week. She has told us that the actual TPR petition will be filed by the middle of January. At that point, the petition has to be served to all those involved in the case. The biological parents have a certain amount of time to appeal the termination. We have been told that we could have a TPR hearing within several months after filing. WE have a new judge in our country and he is moving TPR's rather quickly. If the parents contest, whether they're in jail or not, it can slow

things down. In Missouri, incarceration is not a valid reason to terminate rights...It is my understanding that after the TPR hearing, the Biological parents may still contest it for up to 30 days. Our county has heard contested TPR's past the 30 day period, however, most counties also will look for a relative placement once the child is free for adoption. If no suitable relative placement can be found, Foster parents usually have the first option to adopt the child, if the "team" is in agreement. Hope this helps. Hang in there. It can be a long process. Our case worker has a friend who filed last year to adopt their foster child and on the last day of the appeal time frame, the Biological Dad decided to appeal it, from jail. It has taken 11 months to go through. But keep your chin up. I know for us, it will be worth it once our little girl is finally ours! God knows your child's destiny and he knows where your child needs to be in order for His will to be accomplished in his/her life!

Interviews with foster and adoptive parents did not conform to forum posts. Participants who were interviewed, most of whom had already been foster parents, were approached by agency social workers and therefore may have had different profiles from forum participants. The most striking difference was their use of language and discussions about how their children had come to them. Interviewed parents referred to the biological families of children as "unauthorized" or "undocumented" rather than "biological" or "illegal." Also, interview participants did not offer stories about drug addiction, parental neglect or criminality, or an unfair system. Almost everyone characterized their "foster journey" as a careful deliberation about the responsibility of parenting a citizen-child and at least some awareness of the conditions that had brought that child to them. Though little can be inferred from such a small sample of self-selected participants, the differences in language and approaches/viewpoints were palpable.

It is difficult to address the differences between participants' comments online and those of the parents who were interviewed. Both were interested or engaged in fostering and adoption; however, their perspectives regarding the birth families of the children who had ended up in their care appeared to differ. Why did several online participants use what many Latinos regard as pejorative language (see Lopez, Gonzalez-Barrera, and Krogstad 2014) while interview participants characterized the process as a situation in which everyone suffered? Both were small, self-selected groups. Could the difference lie in the selection process and something about the parents themselves, or in the venue where they expressed themselves?

danah boyd (2014) once described communications on the Internet as private by intent but public in nature. Other communications experts who research the Internet argue that online platforms allow participants to express themselves in more authentic ways because of the anonymity and the non-face-to-face character of interactions. Whether this explains the differences between participants or selection processes, certainly, modalities of communication and comparisons between modalities of communication need to be researched more carefully.

What either set of participants did not understand or address is how the child welfare system and the immigration enforcement system do not communicate with one another. Often, parents who are detained are sent to centers distant from their families, and they may lack appropriate information and opportunities to maintain parental rights (e.g., they are often not notified of hearings they must attend to maintain parental rights; nor do they have the ability to get to these hearings) (ARC 2011). Additionally, data is difficult to compile, as child welfare systems and immigration enforcement do not typically or systematically document cases of families who enter their systems in this way, and opportunities to examine the conditions of those in detention centers are minimal.

Family Building/Family Dissolution

Adoption is truly an act of love and faith, but it is also an act of power and loss. The losses for children are not always located in some distant past or vague set of memories. It is paramount that we remember who has the right to adopt or foster and which groups end up being fostered and adopted, along with the profound impact of physical, legal, and social relocation on adoptees. Although adoptive/foster parents make choices to parent, children rarely have options regarding who parents them. Citizen-children, in particular, often experience the trauma of having their biological parents torn from them only to end up in state care or assigned to a stranger. Their biological parents do not feel as though they have choices either, particularly when they are under duress.

Another example of the limited choices and the social and psychological impact on biological families occurred in the aftermath of Haiti's massive earthquake in 2010, when 10 American missionaries were jailed after attempting to smuggle 33 Haitian children who were not orphans into the Dominican Republic without seeking proper paperwork or permission from the Haitian government. Their purpose was to place these children for adoption with American families. It was discovered that some of these children's parents, who were clearly under duress, had been persuaded by the missionaries to relinquish their children in hopes of helping them. Such stories are common for parents and children from many countries, including Ethiopia, Guatemala, and Nepal. Thus, adoption is inherently embedded in what some call "neocolonial practice." There is no denying that cultures of privilege allow those who can afford it to seek out other people's children with which to build their families. As UNICEF has pointed out, many children who are adopted are not true orphans. This is clearly the situation for children whose parents have been detained or deported. Even when adoptions are thought to benefit children who would otherwise languish in orphanages or foster care, the act of adoption and the discursive practices of adoptive parents illustrate how, among all the other decisions that parents exercise on behalf of their children, adoptive/foster parents navigate issues of culture, race/ethnicity, and nation on behalf of their adopted children.

More than 4 million Latino children in the United States face the possibility of having a parent deported, and already hundreds of thousands of children have had this experience (American Immigration Council 2017; ARC 2011; Foley 2014; DePillis 2015). Under President Trump's administration, the priority of deportation has been vastly heightened, and it is projected that even more children will know what it is like to become part of a foster or adoptive family. We know from both research and popular media stories that children of deported parents suffer economically, emotionally, and physically as they are forced into different family situations (Dreby 2012; Migration Policy Institute 2015; American Immigration Council 2017). The novelty of this phenomenon is that it is occurring within the United States. As prospective parents seek available children with which to build their families, it is important that they understand the social and political circumstances in which the children they adopt or foster are embedded.

There have been attempts to align work between the child welfare and immigration enforcement systems, to encourage ICE officials to consider parental responsibilities when enforcing immigration law, and to place children with relatives or Latino families when parent(s) are detained. However, participants in adoption forums, social workers and immigration lawyers, children of deported parents, and adoptive and foster care parents suggest a number of ways in which the system fails these children and their first or biological families, even as it facilitates the creation of new ones.

Adults Adopted Prior to 2000

Latino children are not the only ones to experience the negative impact of recent immigration policies; adult adoptee deportations have also occurred. Along with many others, adult adoptees like Christopher Clancy (48), Adam Crapser (39), Alejandro Ebron (49), Jess Mustanich (29), and Kairi Shepard (30) were deported from the United States as undocumented immigrants despite having come here as adopted infants and toddlers (Hegstrom 2002; Domonoske 2016; Rojas 2012; Berestein 2008; Singh 2012). Because of misinformation or parental neglect, these adoptees never had their paperwork for U.S. citizenship completed. Though the U.S. Congress approved the Child Citizenship Act of 2000 to eliminate these situations, to date, little has been done to assist those adopted prior to 2000. Thus, much like citizen-children of undocumented immigrants, these involuntary migrants are also subject to deportation. Many of them have families with children who are citizens, as described in this news story:

> "Abandoned" South Korean adoptee faces deportation from U.S.
>
> More than three decades ago, a three year old South Korean boy and his sister flew to the U.S. to become the adopted children of American citizens but their life together didn't last long. They were abandoned, sent into foster care and separated even though he was dependent upon her. A family adopted the girl, and got her citizenship. The boy, named Adam Crapser, was not as fortunate: The parents he had were abusive, and never sought the green card or citizenship for him that they should have. Now at 39, after a life struggling with joblessness because of a lack of immigration papers, homelessness and crime, Crapser, a married father of three is facing deportation because he's not a citizen. . . . (CBS News 2015)

Conclusion

Changes in who is available for adoption have always created new markets and shifted adoptive parent interest to different groups of children. For example, as birth control, single parenting, and abortion became more acceptable in the United States, we saw a decline in the number of white ethnic infants who were available for adoption and hence the shift in adoptive parent attention to international adoption and available young children from other countries. It is easy to wonder what impact that detention, deportation, and separation of families might have for prospective parents looking to adopt. Whereas the majority of transnational and private adoptions cost more than $40,000, foster care adoptions are typically free, at minimal cost, or subsidized (the type of adoption that occurs through detention and deportation). This may serve the interests of prospective parents, but it does little to reduce the trauma of children whose first families are torn apart. We must gain a more substantive understanding of the emotional, cultural, social, psychological, and health-related costs of adoption for these children. Is the answer to place children in foster care or process them as adoptees? Prospective and adoptive parents also need workshops that address the conditions of power and privilege in the formation of family, as those who adopt and those who are adopted occupy radically different cultural, economic, social, and racial spaces.

Most of our evidence about the impact of detention and deportation on adoption and fostering of citizen-children is anecdotal and qualitative, in part because it is difficult to acquire funding to research it. Nevertheless, the Trump administration's approach to immigration (increasing deportation and detention and prioritizing all undocumented persons, as opposed to the former administration's prioritizing of those undocumented persons convicted of a crime) indicates an increase in health care issues for children in mixed-status families (Collier 2015; Muller 2015; Migration Policy Institute 2015). Even attempts to coordinate the immigration enforcement and child welfare systems do not guarantee a positive judicial outcome, as courts can decide that someone simply being an undocumented parent requires a child to be placed elsewhere. Even if immigration policy were to shift, it is projected that planned tax cuts will result in spending reductions on child welfare and burden an already underfunded system (ARC 2011). Demanding caseloads may further reduce opportunities to address the special needs of citizen-children in the system. It has been widely speculated by researchers and professionals in the social welfare system that expanded deportations will increase the number of citizen-children who enter the foster care and adoption process and exacerbate the mental health needs and development of children (ARC 2011; Migration Policy Institute 2015; American Immigration Council 2017).

How do adoptive parents address the tensions between the desire to parent with the reality that our role as parent is the outcome of family separation? Though the degree and circumstances vary, the loss is profound and cannot be ignored. I once attended an adoption workshop where adoptive parents were thanking the Latina birth mother for the "gift" she was giving to them (a son), at which point she became visibly upset and had tears in her eyes. She firmly responded, "Never misunderstand or believe that I am doing anything *for you*. I love my son. *You* are the gift I am giving to my son." As I struggle to be worthy of my sons' and their mothers' struggles, sacrifices, and loss, I am ever hopeful about the liminal space my children occupy between loss and opportunity, and I engage in the ongoing reflexive process to become a worthy "gift" to their children. And, as the years pass, I also hope to become part of the solutions required to assure that one family not be dissolved to form another.

References

American Immigration Council. 2017. "U.S. Citizen Children Impacted by Immigration Enforcement." Retrieved April 14, 2017. http://www.american immigrationcouncil.org/research/us-citizen-children-impacted-immigration-enforcement.

Anagnost, A. 2000. "Scenes of Misrecognition: Maternal Citizenship in the Age of Transnational Adoption." *Positions* 8: 389–421.

Applied Research Center. 2011. "Shattered Families: The Perilous Intersection of Immigration Enforcement and the Child Welfare System." Accessed July 31. https://www.raceforward.org/research/reports/shattered-families

Bamberg, Michael. 2004. "Talk, Small Stories, and Adolescent Identities." *Human Development* 47: 366–69.

Bamberg, Michael. 2008. "Twice-Told Tales: Small Story Analysis and the Process of Identity Formation." In *Meaning in Action*, edited by T. Sugiman, K. J. Gergen, W. Wagner, and Y. Yamada, 183–204. New York: Springer.

Behar, Ruth. 1997. *The Vulnerable Observer: Anthropology That Breaks Your Heart.* Boston, MA: Beacon Press.

Berestein, Leslie. 2008. "'Neither Here Nor There . . .'" Retrieved September 28, 2017. http://peachneitherherenorthere.blogspot.com/2008/07/us-adoptee -stranger-in-his-birthplace.html.

Berger Cardoso, J., E. R. Hamilton, N. Rodriguez, K. Eschbach, and J. M. Hagan, 2016. "Deporting Fathers: Involuntary Transnational Families and Intent to Remigrate among Salvadoran Deportees." *International Migration Review* 50 (1): 197–230.

Berger Cardoso, J., and Michael J. Zvolensky. Forthcoming. "Emotional Nonacceptance Within the Context of Traumatic Event Exposure: The Explanatory Role of Anxiety Sensitivity for Traumatic Stress Symptoms and Disability among Latinos in Primary Care Settings." *General Hospital Psychiatry.*

Boston Globe. 2017. "As Numbers of Adoptions Drop, Many U.S. Agencies Face Strains." Retrieved August 31, 2017. http://www.bostonglobe.com/news /nation/2017/04/30/number-adoptions-drops-many-agencies-face -strains/TxGI6mq1QaqyS92GlR5kcM/story.html.

boyd, danah. 2014. *It's Complicated: The Social Networked Life of Teens.* New Haven, CT: Yale University Press.

Briggs, Laura. 2006. "Making 'American' Families: Transnational Adoption and U.S. Latin America Policy." In *Haunted by Empire: Geographies of Intimacy in North American History*, edited by Ann Laura Stoler, 606–44. Durham, NC: Duke University Press.

Cardello, Andrea. 2009. "The Movement of the Mother of the Courthouse Square: Legal Child Trafficking, Adoption and Poverty in Brazil." *Journal of Latin American and Caribbean Anthropology* 14 (1): 140–61.

CBS News. "Abandoned" South Korean Adoptee Faces Deportation from U.S." Retrieved June, 05, 2017. http://wwww.cbsnews.com/news/abandoned -south-korean-adoptee-faces-deportation-from-us.xj.

Collier, Lorna. 2015. "Helping Immigrant Children Heal: Psychologists Are Working to Help Undocumented Immigrant Children Recover from Trauma and Deal with the Uncertainties of Their Lives." *American Psychological Association's Monitor on Psychology* 46 (3): 58.

DePillis, Lydia. 2015. "The U.S. Has Deported More Than Half a Million Parents Since 2009: Here's What Happens to Their Kids." Retrieved October, 31, 2017. https://www.washingtonpost.com/news/wonk/wp/2015/09/21/this -is-what-would-happen-to-the-children-of-11-million-illegal-immigrants -if-president-trump-deported-them/?utm_term=.4a307615ccc.

Domonoske, Camila. 2016. "South Korean Adopted at Age 3 Is to Be Deported Nearly 40 Years Later." Retrieved September 28, 2017. https://www.npr .org/sections/thetwo-way/2016/10/27/499573378/south-korean-adopted -at-age-3-is-to-be-deported-37-years-later.

Dorow, Sarah. 2006. *Transnational Adoption: A Cultural Economy of Race, Gender and Kinship.* New York: New York University Press.

Dreby, Joanna. 2010. *Divided by Borders: Mexican Migrants and Their Children.* Berkeley: University of California Press.

Dreby, Joanna. 2012. "How Today's Immigration Enforcement Policies Impact Children, Families and Communities: A View from the Ground." Retrieved September 09, 2017. https://www.americanprogress.org/wp -content/uploads/2012/08/DrebyImmigrationFamiliesFINAL.pdf.

Foley, Elise. 2014. "Deportation Separated Thousands of U.S.-Born Children from Parents in 2013." Retrieved November 11, 2017. https://www.huffington post.com/2014/06/25/parents-deportation_n_5531552.html.

Fonseca, Claudia. 2006. "Traditional Influences in the Social Production of Adoptable Children: The Case of Brazil." *International Journal of Sociology and Social Policy* 26 (3/4): 154–71.

Freundlich, Margaret. 2000. *The Market Forces in Adoption.* Washington, D.C.: Child Welfare League of America/The Evan B. Donaldson Adoption Institute.

Gailey, Christine. 2009. *Blue Ribbon Babies and Labors of Love: Race, Class, and Gender in U.S. Adoption Practice.* Austin: University of Texas Press.

Gubrium, Jaber F., and James A. Holstein. 2000. "The Self in a World of Going Concerns." *Symbolic Interaction* 23: 95–115.

Hearst, Alice. 2010. "Between Restavek and Relocation: Children and Communities in Transnational Adoption." *Journal of History of Childhood and Youth,* 3 (2): 273–92.

Hegstrom, Edward. 2002. "Adoption Snag Could Lead to Deportation." Retrieved September 28, 2017. http://www.chron.com/news/houston-texas/article /Adoption-snag-could-lead-to-deportation-2085286.php.

Howard, Jeanne. 2011. *Untangling the Web: The Internet's Transformative Impact on Adoption.* New York: Evan B. Donaldson Adoption Institute.

Jordan, Miriam. 2017. "Overseas Adoptions by Americans Continue to Decline." Retrieved May 13, 2017. https://www.nytimes.com/2017/04/13/us/overseas -adoptions-decline.html.

Lee, Michele. 2015. "Donald Trump's False Comments Connecting Mexican Immigrants and Crime." Retrieved August 23, 2017. https://www.washington post.com/news/fact-checker/wp/2015/07/08/donald-trumps-false -comments-connecting-mexican-immigrants-and-crime/?utm_term=.1d 660ec248c7.

Lee, Richard M., A. Bora Yun, H. Choi Yoog, and K. Park Nelson. 2010. "Comparing the Ethnic Identity and Well-Being of Adopted Korean Americans with Immigrant/U.S.-born Korean Americans and Korean International Students." *Adoption Quarterly* 13 (1): 2–17.

Leifson, Esben. 2008. "Child Trafficking and Formalization: The Case of International Adoption from Ecuador." *Children & Society* 22: 212–22.

Leinaweaver, Jessica B. 2013. *Adoptive Migration: Raising Latinos in Spain*. Durham, NC: Duke University Press.

Lopez, Mark Hugo, Ana Gonzalez-Barrera, and Jens Manuel Krogstad. 2014. "Hispanics and Their Views of Immigration Reform." PEW Research Center: Hispanic Trends. Retrieved November 14, 2016. http://www.pewhispanic.org/2014/10/29/chapter-5-hispanics-and-their-views-of-immigration-reform/

McGinnis, H., S. Livingston Smith, S. D. Ryan, and J. A. Howard. 2009. *Beyond Culture Camp: Promoting Healthy Identity Formation in Adoption*. New York: Evan B. Donaldson Adoption Institute.

Meier, P., and X. Zhang. 2008. "Sold Into Adoption: The Hunan Baby Trafficking Scandal Exposes Vulnerabilities in Chinese Adoptions to the United States." *Cumberland Law Review* 39 (1): 87–130.

Migration Policy Institute. 2015. "Deportation of a Parent Can Have Significant and Long-Lasting Harmful Effects on Child Well-Being, as a Pair of Reports from MPI and the Urban Institute Detail." Retrieved August 23, 2017. http://www.migrationpolicy.org/research/health-and-social-service-needs-us-citizen-children-detained-or-deported-immigrant-parents.

Muller, Robert. 2015. "The Traumatic Effects of Forced Deportation on Families: Children of Parents Who Face Deportation Often Face Psychological Difficulties." Retrieved September 23, 2017. https://www.psychologytoday.com/blog/talking-about-trauma/201305/the-traumatic-effects-forced-deportation-families.

Nicholson, Lucy. 2017. "The Detention and Deportation of California Parents." Retrieved May 17, 2017. https://www.hrw.org/report/2017/05/15/i-still-need-you/detention-and-deportation-californian-parents.

Noonan, Peggy. 2007. "Adoption and the Guatemalan Journey to American Parenthood." *Childhood* 13 (3): 301–18.

Quiroz, Pamela Anne. 2007. *Adoption in a Colorblind Society*. New York: Rowman and Littlefield.

Quiroz, Pamela Anne. 2012. "Cultural Tourism in Transnational Adoption: Staged Authenticity and Its Implications for Adopted Children." *Journal of Family Issues* 33 (4): 527–55.

Quiroz, Pamela Anne. 2015. "Adoptive Parents Raising Neoethnics." In *Families as They Really Are*, edited by Barbara Risman and Virginia Rutter. New York: W.W. Norton.

Reitmayer, Erynn Elizabeth. 2010. "When Parents Get Deported Children Fight to Survive." Latino America: Grappling with Immigration, Status, and Identity in 2010. http://asu.news21.com/2010/08/children-of-deported-parents/index.html.

Roberts, Dorothy. 2002. *Shattered Bonds: The Color of Welfare*. New York: Basic Books.

Rojas, Leslie Berestein. 2012. "How Does an Adoptee Get Deported? More Easily Than One Might Think." Retrieved September 28, 2017. http://www.scpr .org/blogs/multiamerican/2012/05/29/8304/how-does-an-adoptee -get-deported-more-easily-than-one-might-think.

Rotabi, Karen. 2015. "Fraud in Intercountry Adoption: Child Sales and Abduction in Vietnam, Cambodia and Guatemala." In *Intercountry Adoption: Policies, Practices and Outcomes*, edited by Judith Gibbons and Karen Rotabi. New York: Routledge.

Samuels, Gina. 2009. "Being Raised by White People: Navigating Racial Difference among Adopted Multiracial Adults." *Journal of Marriage and Family* 71: 80–94.

Selman, Peter. 2015. "The Rise and Fall of Intercountry Adoption in the 21st Century: Global Trends from 2001 to 2010." *International Social Work* 52 (5): 575–94.

Singh, Tejinder. 2012. "ICE Confirms Kairi Shepherd Deportation, Indian Embassy Plays Humanitarian Angle." Retrieved September 28, 2017. http://www.indiaamericatoday.com/article/ice-confirms-kairi-shepherd -deportation-indian-embassy-plays-humanitarian-angle/.

Smerdon, Usha Rengachary. "The Baby Market: Crossing Bodies, Crossing Borders: International Surrogacy Between the United States and India." *Cumberland Law Review* 39: 15–819.

Smolin, David. 2005. "Child Laundering: How the Intercountry Adoption System Legitimizes and Incentivizes the Practices of Buying, Trafficking, Kidnapping, and Stealing Children." *Legal Repository*. Retrieved December 05, 2016. http://law.bepress.com/expresso/eps/749.

Smolin, David. 2010. "Child Laundering and the Hague Convention on Intercountry Adoption: The Future and Past of Intercountry Adoption." *University of Louisville Law Review* 48: 441.

Smolin, David. 2013. "The Corrupting Influence of the United States on a Vulnerable Intercountry Adoption System: A Guide for Stakeholders, Hague and Non-Hague Nations, NGOs, and Concerned Parties." *Journal of Law & Family Studies & Utah Law Review* 15: 81–151 and 1065–135.

Tuan, Mia, and Jiannbin Lee Shiao. 2011. *Choosing Ethnicity, Negotiating Race: Korean Adoptees in America*. New York: Russell Sage Foundation.

U.S. Deportation Outcomes by Charge. 2017. Completed Cases in Immigration Courts. Retrieved September 12, 2017. http://trac.syr.edu/phptools /immigration/court.

van Dijk, T. A. 2001. "Critical Discourse Analysis." In *The Handbook of Discourse Analysis*, edited by Deborah Schiffrin Deborah Tannen, and Heidi E. Hamilton. 352–71. Oxford, UK: Blackwell.

Volkman, T. A. 2005. *Cultures of Transnational Adoption*. Durham, NC: Duke University Press.

Wang, Leslie K. 2016. *Outsourced Children: Orphanage Care and Adoption in Globalizing China*. Palo Alto: Stanford University Press.

Williams, Patricia. 2003. "Spare Parts, Family Values, Old Children, Cheap." In *Critical Race Feminism*, edited by A. D. Wing, 159–66. New York: New York University Press.

CHAPTER THIRTEEN

Child Well-Being in Same-Gender-Parent Families: Courts, Media, and Social Science Research

Marshal Neal Fettro and Wendy D. Manning

In recent years, children in same-gender[1]-parent families have received greater attention from the media, court systems, and researchers. Speaking of new research or the court battles surrounding the legality of marriages and adoptions for same-gender couples, the media has weighed in with such headlines as "The Kids Are All Right: Gay Parents Raising Children" in *The Huffington Post*, "Study Suggests Risks from Same-Sex Parenting" in *The Washington Times*, and "How Kids Became the Strongest Argument for Same-Sex Marriage" in *The Washington Post* (Drexler 2015; Somashekhar 2015; Wetzstein 2012). In light of several court cases, proponents and opponents of same-gender marriage presented numerous legal briefs, which primarily centered on child well-being.

Child well-being, although difficult to define, has often included the physical, psychological, academic, and social success of children. It has been seen as a metric of the efficacy of parenting, including in same-gender-parent families (Newland 2015; Manning, Fettro, and Lamidi 2014). Opponents of same-gender marriage highlighted a few studies that found poorer outcomes for children residing with same-gender couples. Yet, these findings were discordant with the bulk of the literature: children in families with parents of the same gender fare about the same as those in families with parents of different genders.

This chapter outlines trends in same-gender-parent families, the role of child well-being research in the media and in legal cases, current research on the well-being of children in same-gender-parent families, and implications for future research.

Trends in Acceptance and the Number of Same-Gender-Parent Families

During the past few decades, there have been radical shifts in the acceptance of lesbian, gay, bisexual, and transgender (LGBT) people and marriages of same-gender couples in the United States. Young adults aged 18 to 30 have voiced (and continue to voice) overwhelming support for LGBT rights, with 90 percent stating that they favor equal employment rights for LGBT individuals and 80 percent stating that they favor allowing gays and lesbians to legally adopt children (GenForward 2016). Americans' definitions of family have expanded to include same-gender couples with children (Powell et al. 2016). A majority (64 percent) of Americans voice support for same-gender marriage (McCarthy 2017), an unprecedented rise in support from 12 percent in 1988 (Gates 2015).

This shift in cultural acceptance has corresponded with changes in the legal rights of LGBT people and same-gender couples (Manning et al. 2014; Powell, Quadlin, and Pizmony-Levy 2015). While there have been many legal battles toward trying to ensure equal rights for LGBT people, major shifts in the legal climate did not occur until 2013. Initially, the Supreme Court of the United States (SCOTUS) ruled in June 2013 (*U.S. v. Windsor*) that the federal government must recognize the marriages of same-gender couples. This meant that federal institutions and agencies such the military, the Social Security Administration, Homeland Security, and the Internal Revenue Service were obligated to treat all married couples in the same manner. At this point, same-gender couples could only marry in 16 states, and only a third of Americans lived in a state that had legalized same-gender marriage (Payne and Manning 2014). The next major SCOTUS ruling in June 2015 (*Obergefell v. Hodges* 2015) ensured that marriage was legal for same-gender couples in every county and state in the country (Mason 2017). This has been considered a landmark case in LGBT rights. Since then, other LGBT rights (employment, adoption, bullying protections) have expanded and some contracted, forming a patchwork of LGBT rights across states (Ball 2016).

As there has been a rise in acceptance of LGBT rights and families, recent estimates from the Gallup poll have also shown considerable changes in the proportion of Americans who identify as LGBT. Compared to 2013, when 3.5 percent of Americans identified as LGBT, 4.1 percent did so in 2016 (Gates 2017; Gates and Newport 2013). These estimates parallel those produced by the General Social Survey, where the share of men and women identifying as LGB doubled from 2.8 percent to 5.4 percent between 2008 and 2016 (Bridges 2017; Gates 2010). While these proportions may seem relatively small, they represent 8.3 to 10.1 million Americans.

Estimates of the number of children being raised by gay or lesbian parents has been more difficult to assess. Nearly one in five same-gender couples lives with children (Payne and Manning 2014). Recent evidence has indicated that about a quarter of a million children in the United States live in a same-gender-couple family (Payne and Manning 2014). Given the recent legal recognition of same-gender marriage across the country, we do not know how many children live with married same-gender parents (Edwards and Lindstrom 2017). The rates of adoption by same-gender couples are three times higher than the rates among different-gender couples. Recent evidence from the U.S. Census Bureau indicates that 44,000 adopted children were being raised by 28,000 same-gender couples in 2015, which has doubled since 2011 (Gates 2013; Associated Press 2017b).

Most of what researchers know about LGBT couples and families has largely come from research examining same-gender *couples*. Thus, little is known about children living with single gay or lesbian parents. Since questions about sexual orientation have been scarce in national surveys, same-gender-couple families can be identified using the sex or gender of the respondent and their spouse or partner (Biblarz and Stacey 2010; Brewster, Tillman, and Jokinen-Gordon 2014). This strategy ignores many lesbian- and gay-parent families—such as those with adult children, same-gender parents with nonresidential children, and single gay or lesbian parents. An additional issue that has emerged is that LGBT couples and their families may be unwilling to respond to surveys—perhaps because they fear being harmed if their information is not kept confidential (Coffman, Coffman, and Marzilli Ericson 2016).

Same-Gender Parent Families in the News and Courts

Research examining child well-being in same-gender-parent families has garnered considerable media attention. Much of this attention coincided with legal challenges to state and federal restrictions on the marrying of same-gender couples. Proponents and opponents of these legal challenges have largely framed their arguments around the well-being of children raised by same-gender-parent families (Mason 2017). Scholars have consistently found that, when comparing children with similar life experiences, there are few differences between children from same-gender-parent families and those from different-gender-parent families across an array of well-being indicators, including academic performance, cognitive and social development, psychological health, early sexual activity, and substance abuse (Manning et al. 2014). This consensus is based on research drawing on a range of data sources, including both large convenience samples and nationally representative surveys in the United States.

Yet, a few studies appear to report poorer outcomes for children of same-gender-parent families. A research paper by Mark Regnerus (2012a) that was included in the legal briefs opposing marriage benefits to same-gender couples (Cohen 2012) ignited a flurry of media attention. Regnerus reported that adult children of "gay" and "lesbian" couples fared considerably worse than adult children of continuously married biological-parent families from the New Family Structures Study (NFSS). His study was reported and commented on by a host of news organizations (e.g., Ablow 2012). There were headlines that countered one another. For example, from *Fox News* came "Study Finds Host of Challenges for Kids of Gay Parents," and from *The Huffington Post*, "This 'Expert' Claims Gay Parents are Bad for Kids, But Here's Why You Shouldn't Listen" (Abbey-Lambertz 2014; Ablow 2012). Even late-night talk shows such as *The Daily Show with Jon Stewart* engaged in the discussion of the reputability of the evidence, saying that "there's some . . . guy who put out a thoroughly discredited study" (Cohen 2013).

Regnerus's study drew sharp criticism from the research community, including Gary Gates and some 200 other researchers—like Debra Umberson, who would later author her own critique with colleagues (Gates 2012; Umberson et al. 2012). Chief among their criticisms was that his study was "insufficiently capable," as Regnerus would himself later acknowledge in 2012, to measure the experiences of children raised in same-gender-parent families (Regnerus 2012b, 1376). Serious limitations of the study were that it was based on adult outcomes and that it compared adult children of continuously married biological-parent families with adult children who had reported a parent who had had, at some point, sex with someone of the same gender. This strategy provided an unorthodox measure of family structure and confused family stability and family structure. Where family structure tells us the type of family a child lives in (e.g., stepfamily or single parent), family (in)stability sheds light on a child's lived experiences, such as the number of parental romantic relationships or parental divorces. Reanalysis of the NFSS data has given weight to these concerns (Cheng and Powell 2015; Rosenfeld 2015). Cheng and Powell (2015) found that methodological choices and data quality account for many of the disadvantages reported by Regnerus. The authors argued that Regnerus's findings were "highly fragile and based in part on a couple of influential cases or outliers" (Cheng and Powell 2015, 624). Similarly, Rosenfeld (2015) reported that family transitions, rather than family structure, accounted for the bulk of differences that

Regnerus found. Other studies that reported poorer outcomes for children from same-gender-parent families (e.g., Sullins 2016) suffer from similar problems. Academic challenges to the Regnerus study have resulted in a broad questioning of his findings and showcase the importance of making data publicly available so that research can be replicated.

In 2012, after the SCOTUS agreed to hear *U.S. v. Windsor*, which challenged parts of the Defense of Marriage Act and federal limits on same-gender marriage, numerous legal briefs, or *amicus curiae*, drawing on social science research were filed. Among these was the American Sociological Association's assessment of a decade of scholarship, which concluded, "whether a child is raised by same-gender or opposite-sex parents has no bearing on a child's wellbeing" (Brief for the American Sociological Association 2013, 3). John Becker (2013) reported in *The Huffington Post* that, "in supreme court brief, American Sociological Association obliterates claim that same-gender couples are inferior parents." Regnerus was dominant in the reporting of *U.S. v. Windsor*. For example, *The Washington Post* reported in an article titled "Social Science Struggles with the Effects of Same-Sex Parenting on Children" that:

> Many opponents of same-sex marriage argue that the academy's [American Academy of Pediatrics] conclusions are premature. They point to some recent studies, including one from Mark Regnerus, a sociology professor from the University of Texas at Austin. (Somashekhar 2013)

Although the SCOTUS ruled in favor of *Windsor*, which handed the legality of marriages of same-gender couples to individual states, social science scholarship on the well-being of children from same-gender-parent families continued to dominate debates on the legality of same-gender marriage.

After the SCOTUS ruling on *U.S. v. Windsor*, numerous other legal cases were heard in state and federal courts (Mason 2017). Among these court cases was *DeBoer v. Snyder*, which challenged Michigan's ban on same-gender marriage. Social science scholarship played a pivotal role in this case. Erik Eckholm, in his *New York Times* article "Opponents of Same-Sex Marriage Take Bad-For-Children Argument to Court," reported that:

> In the first trial of its kind in years, the social science research on family structure and child progress will be openly debated, with expert testimony and cross-examination, offering an unusual public dissection of the methods of sociology and the intersection of science and politics. (Eckholm 2014)

Child well-being research by Mark Regnerus, Michael Rosenfeld (2010, 2013), and Douglas Allen (2013) was prominently featured in federal Judge Bernard Friedman's ruling against the marriage ban (*DeBoer v. Snyder* 2014).

Judge Friedman questioned the veracity of Regnerus's findings, stating that "the funder clearly wanted a certain result, and Regnerus obliged" (*DeBoer v. Snyder* 2014, 14). Following this decision, the issues surrounding child well-being were no longer the centerpiece of the opponents' arguments against the legalization of marriage for same-gender couples.

The 2015 SCOTUS ruling on *Obergefell v. Hodges* afforded full federal and state recognition of same-gender marriages—two years after their decision on *U.S. v. Windsor*. Coverage of *Obergefell v. Hodges* featured familiar narratives. As noted by Richard Wolf in *USA Today*, "it is perhaps the most controversial component of the national debate over same-sex marriage: who should raise children?" (2015). Justice Anthony Kennedy, in the majority opinion, stated in support of legal acceptance of same-gender marriage "that it safeguards children and families and thus draws meaning from related rights of childrearing, procreation, and education" (*Obergefell v. Hodges* 2015, 14). This decision received extensive coverage in all news outlets (Chappell 2015; Condon 2015; Liptak 2015).

The issues of the well-being of children in same-gender-parent families have more recently included reports based on shifts in adoption laws across states. Although adoption by same-gender couples is legal in the United States, and although the *Obergefell v. Hodges* decision afforded same-gender couples the right to marry in all states, same-gender couples have generally been viewed as being less preferred and have been met with greater scrutiny (Ball 2016). This was aptly highlighted in the title of an article in *The Atlantic*: "Equality in Marriage May Not Bring Equality in Adoption" (Giambrone 2015).

The landscape of same-gender adoption has been, and continues to be, a piecemeal set of limits and protections. The legalization of marriages to same-gender couples meant that in many states, adoptions by same-gender couples would be possible because they could meet the criteria of being legally married (e.g., Michigan). Several states, such as Mississippi and Florida, have included new language banning same-gender adoptions regardless of marital status (Reilly 2016; Schwartz 2010). Additional states have given agencies the right to refuse same-gender adoptions based on religious or moral convictions, including Alabama, Michigan, Mississippi, North Dakota, South Dakota, Texas, and Virginia. North Dakota, Virginia, and Michigan's laws predate *Obergefell v. Hodges* (Associated Press 2017a; Movement Advancement Project 2017; Sanchez 2017). Some states, such as New York and California, allowed adoptions by gay and lesbian couples well before the Obergefell case.

The legalization of marriage to same-gender couples provided a legal basis for adoption by lesbian women and gay men in many states. New legal challenges to adoption laws followed the Obergefell decision. Legal shifts in same-gender adoption run parallel with shifts in attitudes (Dotinga 2016). Former Governor of Mississippi Ronnie Musgrove, who signed the original ban on the adoption of children by same-gender couples in 2000, wrote in

The Huffington Post, "As I have gotten older, I came to understand that a person's sexual orientation has absolutely nothing to do with their ability to be a good parent" (Reilly 2016). When the Mississippi law was overturned by a federal judge in 2016, *The Huffington Post* proclaimed, "Same-Sex Couples Can Now Adopt Children in All 50 States" (Reilly 2016). Scholarship since the *Obergefell v. Hodges* decision has reiterated that children raised in same-gender- and different-gender-parent families experience similar levels of well-being (e.g., Bos et al. 2016; Cheng and Powell 2015; Reczek et al. 2016; Rosenfeld 2015). Some in the media have heralded that "The Scientific Debate Over Same-Sex Parenting Is Over" (Stern 2016). Despite this, Nanette Gartrell, a prominent researcher on this topic, has argued that "we still have so much to learn and find out about different types of families" (Kounang 2016).

Social Science Evidence on the Well-Being of Children Raised in Same-Gender Couples

Based on a wide range of outcomes, the majority of scholars have reported that children fare about the same regardless of whether they were raised in same-gender-parent families or different-gender-parent families. Our focus is on research using a large-scale convenience survey (National Longitudinal Lesbian Family Survey, NLFFS, which followed children from birth to adolescence), smaller samples of gay and lesbian parents, along with nationally representative survey data (US 2000 Census, Early Childhood Longitudinal Study-Kindergarten cohort, ECLS-K, National Health Interview Survey, NHIS, National Survey of Children's Health, NSCH, and National Longitudinal Study of Adolescent to Adult Health, Add Health). Variations in outcomes by family type are typically found to be the result of differences in family transitions or parental sociodemographic characteristics such as parental educational attainment or employment. For example, many children raised in single-parent families experience parental separation or divorce, and children from more disadvantaged backgrounds more often spend time in single-mother families. Accounting for these characteristics results in few differences. Below we outline current research on children's psychological and social well-being, academic achievement, delinquency and romantic outcomes, and physical well-being using nationally representative studies and large samples. Many of these results were reported by Manning et al. (2014), and here we update the results with more recently published research.

Psychological and Social Well-Being

Children residing in same-gender-parent families experience similar levels of psychological and social well-being as children in different-gender-parent families. Initial disparities in analyses found by some researchers in outcomes were largely the result of sociodemographic characteristics and family instability rather than family structure.

Examining children from kindergarten to fifth grade using data from the Early Childhood Longitudinal Study-Kindergarten cohort (ECLS-K), Potter and Potter (2016) found similar scores in terms of externalization behaviors, internalization behaviors, and interpersonal skills. In the analytic models without controls for family instability, children in same-gender-parent families displayed poorer outcomes compared to children in married two-biological-parent families. Indicators of family instability largely accounted for differences by family structure. In other words, it is the impact of changes in family life on children rather than the type of family a child lives with that influences his or her well-being. These findings are consistent with research that examined first graders' social adjustment for children living in same-gender- and different-gender-parent families during kindergarten, also using data from the ECLS-K (Fedewa and Clark 2009).

Similar results have been found among adolescents. Wainright and colleagues used data from the National Survey of Adolescent to Adult Health (Add Health) to examine both psychological and social well-being of adolescents by family type (Wainright, Russell, and Patterson 2004; Wainright and Patterson 2008). The authors found that adolescents in female same-gender-parent families had similar levels of depressive symptoms, self-esteem scores, number of friends, peer support, and quality of peer relationships compared to a matched sample of adolescents in different-gender-parent families. Although differences by family type were found in the number of friends adolescents reported, these differences faded after accounting for sociodemographic characteristics (Wainright and Patterson 2008).

Researchers examining children aged 6 to 17 in the National Survey of Children's Health (NSCH) have yielded similar results. Bos and colleagues (2016) found no difference in emotional difficulties, coping, and learning behaviors among children living in female same-gender-parent families and different-gender-parent families who have not experienced a parental divorce or family transition. By removing children who have experienced family transitions or disruptions, the researchers compared apples to apples— avoiding conflating family instability with family structure. Scholars drawing on large, but not nationally representative, convenience samples have reported consistent findings. Bos and colleagues (2004), using data from the NLFFS, find that children raised by lesbian mothers have similar levels of psychological well-being compared to a matched sample of children from heterosexual parents (Bos et al. 2004). Researchers examining school-aged children have similar results using nonrepresentative samples. Farr (2017) and Goldberg and Smith (2017) both found that children who were adopted by gay- and lesbian-parent families had similar scores of behavioral problems compared to children of heterosexual parents. Perrin and colleagues (2016) find similar levels of good behaviors, emotional concerns, and peer relationship problems when examining gay-father families.

Academic Achievement

Children living in same-gender-parent families are just as academically successful as children living in different-gender-parent families. Scholars using nationally representative data have examined grade retention and grade point average (GPA), math and reading proficiency, having trouble in school or school connectedness, and educational attainment (Manning et al. 2014). Sociodemographic characteristics and family instability, rather than family type, account for differences in children's academic success between same-gender- and different-gender-parent families.

Drawing on data from the 2000 Census, researchers have found that children from residentially stable families, regardless of family type, have similar progressions through school after accounting for parents' socioeconomic status (Allen, Pakaluk, and Price 2013; Rosenfeld 2010, 2012). Although Allen and his colleagues reported disparities in grade retention between children living with married different-gender parents and children in same-gender-parent families, these results are problematic, as the family circumstances in which children were held back are unknown. Children enter same-gender-parent families through a variety of other family types, and their experiences may hinder their academic success (Rosenfeld 2013).

Scholars focusing on either school-age children or adolescents have given consistent findings. Fedewa and Clark (2009) and Potter (2012) both used the ECLS-K to assess academic proficiency of school-age children. Fedewa and Clark (2009) found no significant differences in first graders' academic achievements, measured as the mean of reading and math scores, based on their family structure during kindergarten. Potter (2012) found that children's math and reading scores were about the same between those living in same-gender-parent families and married two-biological-parent families when examining children from kindergarten to eighth grade. Baseline differences in math and reading scores were largely explained by the number of family transitions children have experienced. Thus, it is family instability rather than family type that hinders children's academic proficiency. Adolescents living in female same-gender-parent families were found to have similar GPAs, trouble in school, and school connectedness scores compared to those in different-gender-parent families using the Add Health data (Wainright, Russell, and Patterson 2004). Although adolescents living in female same-gender-parent families were found to initially score higher on school connectedness, this relationship was accounted for by parents' socioeconomic status. Finally, Gartrell and others (2012), drawing on the NLFFS, found that 17-year-old adolescents raised by lesbian mothers have higher-than-average GPA scores (Gartrell et al. 2012).

Delinquency and Romantic Outcomes

Adolescents in female same-gender-parent families report similar levels of delinquency and romantic outcomes compared to different-gender-parent families in the Add Health data. Wainright and Patterson (2006) found that adolescents in female same-gender parent families reported similar use of tobacco, alcohol, and marijuana compared to their counterparts in different-gender-parent families. The authors also found similar levels of delinquent behaviors (e.g., damaging others' property, shoplifting, and getting into fights) and levels of victimization (i.e., being a victim of violence and witnessing violence) among teenagers in female same-gender- and different-gender-parent families. Patterson and Wainright (2012) also found that similar proportions of adolescents in female same-gender-parent families have had romantic relationships and sexual intercourse compared to those in different-gender-parent families. These findings are consistent with research that used data from the NLLFS, where adolescents from lesbian-parent families were found to have similar risks of sexually transmitted infection and getting or getting another pregnant, but they initiated sex later than a matched sample of children from heterosexual parents (Gartrell, Bos, and Goldberg 2012).

A concern expressed by same-gender parenting opponents is whether children raised by lesbian and gay parents are more likely to be lesbian or gay themselves. While this is not a negative child outcome, it is a popular query. This avenue of research has presented varied findings. Where some researchers have found that children of gay or lesbian parents are less likely to be exclusively heterosexual (e.g., Schumm 2010; Tasker and Golombok 1997), others have found no such relationships (e.g., Bailey et al. 1995; Fedewa, Black, and Ahn 2015; Gartrell, Bos, and Goldberg 2011). Children of gay and lesbian parents may face less stigma or consider it more acceptable to pursue a relationship with a person of the same gender. It is also important to consider the role of genetics in a person's sexual orientation. Researchers who have examined the sexual orientation of identical (monozygotic) and fraternal (dizygotic) twins have found that identical twins are more likely to share a sexual orientation than fraternal twins (e.g., Burri, Spector, and Rahman 2015; Kendler et al. 2000). These findings are suggestive that sexual orientation may be partly genetic.

Physical Health

Children living in same-gender-parent families have similar levels of physical health compared to those in different-gender-parent families.

Drawing on data from the NHIS, Reczek and colleagues (2016) found that children have similar levels of physical health among same-gender- and different-gender-parent families. Instead, differences in children's health exist between married and cohabiting families. Similarly, Bos and others (2016) find no differences in children's general health by family type when examining children in the NSCH who have not experienced a parental divorce or family transition.

Conclusions and Next Steps for Future Research

A sea change in Americans' acceptance of the LGBT community and same-gender relationships has occurred over the past decade. By and large, court case decisions have operated as a vehicle of change, affording same-gender couples new legal rights to marriage and adoption. Central to this debate has been the well-being of children raised in same-gender-parent families. Since the 1990s, researchers and reviewers have come to a clear consensus that scholarly research has found no significant differences across a variety of well-being indicators, including children's psychological, behavioral, and educational outcomes (Adams and Light 2015; Manning et al. 2014; Patterson 2017). Reports from the media have followed this "no differences" hypothesis.

Despite several studies that have found poorer outcomes for children of same-gender-parent families, scholars have cast serious doubts on their credibility based on methodological concerns. Researchers face many other challenges when studying same-gender-parent families. Schumm (2014), and other scholars have thoroughly discussed many of these challenges, including the issues surrounding the use of small sample sizes, cross-sectional studies, and nonprobability or convenience samples. These limitations may cloud statistical precision and applicability to a wide array of same-gender-parent families across the United States.

Although the share of children who have been raised by same-gender couples from birth is growing (that is to say, they were adopted or were conceived through IVF and surrogacy), the majority of children in same-gender-parent families are the offspring from one of the partner's failed previous heterosexual relationships (Gates 2015). Thus, children's pathways to a same-gender-parent family vary widely. However, relatively few empirical studies on child well-being in same-gender-parent families have been able to distinguish adopted children from children who are living with one biological parent and their partner or spouse. In much the same way, it is important to account for children's family disruptions and transitions. As families in general have become increasingly diverse because of larger demographic shifts in marriage and living arrangements, it is necessary to compare children who have similar life experiences. Powell and his colleagues (2015), along with other researchers, recommended that we move beyond the traditional approach of comparing children raised in same-gender-parent families with two-biological-married-parent families and instead include comparisons of children from other families with similar family transitions—e.g., adopted children or children living with one biological parent and their spouse or partner. Also, attention to variation within same-gender-parent families, such as transgender families and families of color, is warranted (Moore and Stambolis-Ruhstorfer 2013).

Research on child well-being in same-gender-parent families finds that parents' sexual orientation is not related to children's psychological and social well-being, academic achievement, delinquency and romantic outcomes, and physical well-being. Family instability rather than family structure is related to poorer outcomes for children. Landmark court decisions, such as those legalizing same-gender marriage, have elevated the discussion of child well-being in same-gender-parent families from solely academic circles to broad public interest through extensive media and news coverage. Although social science research has largely provided support for proponents of same-gender marriage, it has reemerged in recent legal debates surrounding same-gender-parent adoption. Yet, scholars have generally agreed that more research is needed to fully understand the experiences of children in same-gender-parent families in the United States. Media outlets will have a responsibility to report on new research findings, weighing in on the merits and reflecting on the nuance required to best understand child well-being. Given shifts in marriage and adoption laws as well as changing acceptance and support for LGBT families, it will become an increasingly complex, but important, endeavor to study, understand, and report on the well-being of American children.

Note

1. Although a person's sex and gender do not always align, we use the term "same-gender" rather than "same-sex" (except in direct quotations), following recent scholars in the field (e.g., Fedewa, Black, and Ahn 2015).

References

Abbey-Lambertz, Kate. 2014. "This 'Expert' Claims Gay Parents Are Bad for Kids, But Here's Why You Shouldn't Listen." *The Huffington Post*, March 5. Retrieved November 21, 2017. https://www.huffingtonpost.com/2014/03/05/mark-regnerus-michigan-gay-marriage_n_4904170.html.

Ablow, Keith. 2012. "Study Finds Host of Challenges for Kids of Gay Parents." *Fox News*, June 12. Retrieved November 21, 2017. http://www.foxnews.com/opinion/2012/06/12/study-finds-host-challenges-for-kids-gay-parents.html.

Adams, Jimi, and Ryan Light. 2015. "Scientific Consensus, the Law, and Same Sex Parenting Outcomes." *Social Science Research* 53: 300–10. doi:10.1016/j.ssresearch.2015.06.008.

Allen, Douglas W. 2013. "High School Graduation Rates among Children of Same-Sex Households." *Review of Economics of the Household* 11 (4): 635–58. doi:10.1007/s11150-013-9220-y.

Allen, Douglas W., Catherine Pakaluk, and Joseph Price. 2013. "Nontraditional Families and Childhood Progress Through School: A Comment on Rosenfeld." *Demography* 50 (3): 955–61. doi: 10.1007/s13524-012-0169-x.

Associated Press. 2017a. "New Alabama Law Lets Adoption Groups Turn Away Same-Sex Couples." *The New York Times,* May 4. Retrieved November 21, 2017. https://www.nytimes.com/aponline/2017/06/17/us/ap-us-gay-adoption-abridged.html.

Associated Press. 2017b. "For Advocates of Gay Adoption, Progress but also Obstacles." *The New York Times,* June 17. Retrieved November 21, 2017. https://www.nytimes.com/aponline/2017/06/17/us/ap-us-gay-adoption-abridged.html.

Bailey, J. Michael, David Bobrow, Marilyn Wolfe, and Sarah Mikach. 1995. "Sexual Orientation of Adult Sons of Gay Fathers." *Developmental Psychology* 31 (1): 124–29. doi:10.1037/0012-1649.31.1.124.

Ball, Carlos A., ed. 2016. *After Marriage Equality: The Future of LGBT Rights.* New York: NYU Press.

Becker, John. 2013. "In Supreme Court Brief, American Sociological Association Obliterates Claim That Same-Sex Couples Are Inferior Parents." *The Huffington Post*, February 28. Retrieved November 21, 2017. http://www.huffingtonpost.com/john-becker/supreme-court-american-sociological-association-gay-parents_b_2783523.html.

Biblarz, Timothy J., and Judith Stacey. 2010. "How Does the Gender of Parents Matter?" *Journal of Marriage and Family* 72 (1): 3–22.

Bos, Henny M. W., Justin R. Knox, Loes van Rijn-van Gelderen, and Nanette K. Gartrell. 2016. "Same-Sex and Different-Sex Parent Households and Child Health Outcomes: Findings from the National Survey of Children's Health." *Journal of Developmental & Behavioral Pediatrics* 37 (3): 179–87. doi:10.1097/DBP.0000000000000288.

Bos, Henny M. W., Frank van Balen, Dymphna C. van den Boom, and Th. G. M. Sandfort. "Minority Stress, Experience of Parenthood and Child Adjustment in Lesbian Families." *Journal of Reproductive and Infant Psychology* 22 (4): 291–304. doi:10.1080/02646830412331298350.

Brewster, Karin L., Kathryn Harker Tillman, and Hanna Jokinen-Gordon. 2014. "Demographic Characteristics of Lesbian Parents in the United States." *Population Research and Policy Review* 33 (4): 503–26. doi: 10.1007/s11113-013-9296-3.

Bridges, Tristan. 2017. "2016 GSS Update on the U.S. LGB Population." *Inequality by (Interior) Design,* April 4. Retrieved November 21, 2017. https://inequalitybyinteriordesign.wordpress.com/2017/04/04/2016-gss-update-on-the-u-s-lgb-population.

Brief for the American Sociological Association as Amicus Curiae Supporting Respondents, Kristin M. Perry and Respondent Edith Schlain Windsor, *Dennis Hollingsworth, et al. v. Kristin M. Perry, et al.*, 133 S.Ct. 2652 (2013) (no. 12–144), *United States v. Edith Schlain Windsor*, in her capacity as executor of the Estate of Thea Clara Spyer, et al. and Bipartisan Legal Advisory Group of The United States House of Representatives, 133 S.Ct. 2675 (2013) (no. 12–307), 2013 WL 840004.

Burri, Andrea, Tim Spector, and Qazi Rahman. 2015. "Common Genetic Factors among Sexual Orientation, Gender Nonconformity, and Number of Sex Partners in Female Twins: Implications for the Evolution of Homosexuality." *The Journal of Sexual Medicine* 12 (4):1004–11. doi:10.1111/jsm.12847.

Chappell, Bill. 2015. "Supreme Court Declares Same-Sex Marriage Legal in All 50 States." *NPR*, June 26. Retrieved November 21, 2017. http://www.npr.org/sections/thetwo-way/2015/06/26/417717613/supreme-court-rules-all-states-must-allow-same-sex-marriages.

Cheng, Simon, and Brian Powell. 2015. "Measurement, Methods, and Divergent Patterns: Reassessing the Effects of Same-Sex Parents." *Social Science Research* 52: 615–26.

Coffman, Katherine B., Lucas C. Coffman, and Keith M. Marzilli Ericson. 2016. "The Size of the LGBT Population and the Magnitude of Antigay Sentiment Are Substantially Underestimated." *Management Science* 63 (10): 3168–86. doi: 10.1287/mnsc.2016.2503.

Cohen, Philip. 2012. "Regnerus Study Controversy Guide." *Family Inequality Blog*. Retrieved November 21, 2017. https://familyinequality.wordpress.com/2012/08/15/regnerus-study-controversy-guide.

Cohen, Philip. 2013. "How the Response to Regnerus Homogenized LGBT Families." *Family Inequality Blog*. Retrieved November 21, 2017. https://familyinequality.wordpress.com/2013/08/17/how-the-response-to-regnerus-homogenized-lgbt-families/.

Condon, Stephanie. 2015. "Supreme Court: Marriage Is a Fundamental Right for Gay Couples." *CBS News*, June 26. Retrieved November 21, 2017. http://www.cbsnews.com/news/supreme-court-marriage-is-a-fundamental-right-for-gay-couples.

Crary, David. 2017. "For Advocates of Gay Adoption, Progress but also Obstacles." *Associated Press*, June 17. Retrieved November 21, 2017. https://www.usnews.com/news/best-states/new-york/articles/2017-06-17/for-advocates-of-gay-adoption-progress-but-also-obstacles.

DeBoer, et al. v. Snyder, et al., 12-10285, 18, 20 (E.D. Mich. March 21, 2014).

Dotinga, Randy. 2016. "Attitudes Shift on Gay Adoption." *CBS News*, March 17. Retrieved November 21, 2017. http://www.cbsnews.com/news/attitudes-shift-on-gay-adoption.

Drexler, Peggy. 2015. "The Kids Are All Right: Gay Parents Raising Children." *The Huffington Post*, May 23. Retrieved November 21, 2017. https://www.huffingtonpost.com/peggy-drexler/the-kids-are-alright-gay_b_1539166.html.

Eckholm, Erik. 2014. "Opponents of Same-Sex Marriage Take Bad-for-Children Argument to Court." *New York Times*, February 22. Retrieved November 21, 2017. https://www.nytimes.com/2014/02/23/us/opponents-of-same -sex-marriage-take-bad-for-children-argument-to-court.html.

Edwards, Ashley, and Rachel Lindstrom. 2017. "Measuring the Presence and Impact of Same-Sex Married Couples on Poverty Rates in the Current Population Survey." SEHSD Working Paper No. 2017-01. Prepared for the Applied Demography Conference, San Antonio, TX. Retrieved November 21, 2017. https://www.census.gov/content/dam/Census/library/working -papers/2017/demo/SEHSD-WP2017-01.pdf.

Farr, Rachel H. 2017. "Does Parental Sexual Orientation Matter? A Longitudinal Follow-Up of Adoptive Families with School-Age Children." *Developmental Psychology* 53 (2): 252–64. doi: 10.1037/dev0000228.

Fedewa, Alicia L., Whitney W. Black, and Soyeon Ahn. 2015. "Children and Adolescents with Same-Gender Parents: A Meta-Analytic Approach in Assessing Outcomes." *Journal of GLBT Family Studies* 11 (1): 1–34. doi: 10.1080/1550428X.2013.869486.

Fedewa, Alicia L., and Teresa P. Clark. 2009. "Parent Practices and Home-School Partnerships: A Differential Effect for Children with Same-Sex Coupled Parents?" *Journal of GLBT Family Studies* 5 (4): 312–39. doi:10.1080 /15504280903263736.

Gartrell, Nanette, Henny M. W. Bos, Heidi Peyser, Amalia Deck, and Carla Rodas. 2012. "Adolescents with Lesbian Mothers Describe Their Own Lives." *Journal of Homosexuality* 59 (9): 1211–29. doi: 10.1080/00918369 .2012.720499.

Gartrell, Nanette K., Henny M. W. Bos, and Naomi G. Goldberg. 2011. "Adolescents of the US National Longitudinal Lesbian Family Study: Sexual Orientation, Sexual Behavior, and Sexual Risk Exposure." *Archives of Sexual Behavior* 40 (6): 1199–209. doi:10.1007/s10508-010-9692-2.

Gartrell, Nanette K., Henny M. W. Bos, and Naomi G. Goldberg. 2012. "New Trends in Same-Sex Sexual Contact for American Adolescents?" *Archives of Sexual Behavior* 41 (1): 5–7. doi:10.1007/s10508-011-9883-5.

Gates, Gary J. 2010. *Sexual Minorities in the 2008 General Social Survey: Coming Out and Demographic Characteristics*. The Williams Institute. Los Angeles: University of California. Retrieved November 21, 2017. http://services .law.ucla.edu/williamsinstitute/pdf/Sexual-Minorities-2008-GSS.pdf.

Gates, Gary J. 2012. "200 Researchers Respond to Regnerus Paper." *Family Inequality Blog*, June 29. Retrieved November 21, 2017. https://family inequality.wordpress.com/2012/06/29/200-researchers-respond-to -regnerus-paper.

Gates, Gary J. 2013. *LGBT Parenting in the United States*. The Williams Institute. Los Angeles: University of California. Retrieved November 21, 2017. http:// williamsinstitute.law.ucla.edu/wp-content/uploads/LGBT-Parenting.pdf.

Gates, Gary J. 2015. "Marriage and Family: LGBT Individuals and Same-Sex Couples." *The Future of Children* 25 (2): 67–87. doi:10.1353/foc.2015.0013.

Gates, Gary J. 2017. "In US, More Adults Identifying as LGBT." *Gallup News*, January 11. Retrieved November 21, 2017. http://news.gallup.com/poll /201731/lgbt-identification-rises.aspx.

Gates, Gary J., and Frank Newport. 2013. "LGBT Percentage Highest in DC, Lowest in North Dakota." *Gallup News*, February 15. Retrieved November 21, 2017. http://news.gallup.com/poll/160517/lgbt-percentage-highest-lowest -north-dakota.aspx.

GenForward. 2016. *LGBT Policy Attitudes: Results from a Nationally Representative Survey of Young People Age 18–30 Taken July 9–20.* Black Youth Project. Center for the Study of Race, Politics, and Culture, University of Chicago. Retrieved November 21, 2017. http://genforwardsurvey.com/assets/uploads /2016/11/GenForward-July-2016_LGBT-factsheet.pdf.

Giambrone, Andrew. 2015. "Equality in Marriage May Not Bring Equality in Adoption." *The Atlantic*, May 26. Retrieved November 21, 2017. https:// www.theatlantic.com/politics/archive/2015/05/equality-in-marriage -may-not-bring-equality-in-adoption/393806.

Goldberg, Abbie E., and JuliAnna Z. Smith. 2017. "Parent-School Relationships and Young Adopted Children's Psychological Adjustment in Lesbian-, Gay-, and Heterosexual-Parent Families." *Early Childhood Research Quarterly* 40 (3): 174–87. doi:10.1016/j.ecresq.2017.04.001.

Kendler, Kenneth S., Laura M. Thornton, Stephen E. Gilman, and Ronald C. Kessler. 2000. "Sexual Orientation in a US National Sample of Twin and Nontwin Sibling Pairs." *American Journal of Psychiatry* 157 (11): 1843–46. doi:10.1176/appi.ajp.157.11.1843.

Kounang, Nadia. 2016. "'No Differences' between Children of Same-Sex and Opposite-Sex Parents." *CNN*, April 15. Retrieved November 21, 2017. http://www.cnn.com/2016/04/15/health/health-of-children-with-same -sex-parents.

Liptak, Adam. 2015. "Supreme Court Ruling Makes Same-Sex Marriage a Right Nationwide." *New York Times*, June 26. Retrieved November 21, 2017. https://www.nytimes.com/2015/06/27/us/supreme-court-same-sex -marriage.html.

Lofquist, Daphne. 2011. *Same-Sex Couple Households.* U.S. Census Bureau. Washington, D.C.: U.S. Department of Commerce. Retrieved November 21, 2017. https://www.census.gov/prod/2011pubs/acsbr10-03.pdf.

Manning, Wendy D., Marshal Neal Fettro, and Esther Lamidi. 2014. "Child Well-Being in Same-Sex Parent Families: Review of Research Prepared for American Sociological Association Amicus Brief." *Population Research and Policy Review* 33 (4): 485–502. doi:10.1007/s11113-014-9329-6.

Mason, Katherine. 2017. "'Won't Someone Think of the Children?': Reproductive Futurism and Same-Sex Marriage in US Courts, 2003–2015." *Sexuality Research and Social Policy* 15: 1–16. doi:10.1007/s13178-017-0279-8.

McCarthy, Justin. 2017. "U.S. Support for Gay Marriage Edges to New High." *Gallup News*, May 15. Retrieved November 21, 2017. http://www.gallup .com/poll/210566/support-gay-marriage-edges-new-high.aspx.

Moore, Mignon R., and Michael Stambolis-Ruhstorfer. 2013. "LGBT Sexuality and Families at the Start of the Twenty-First Century." *Annual Review of Sociology* 39: 491–507. doi:10.1146/annurev-soc-071312-145643.

Movement Advancement Project. 2017. *Foster and Adoption Laws.* Retrieved November 21, 2017. http://www.lgbtmap.org/equality-maps/foster_and_adoption _laws.

Newland, Lisa A. 2015. "Family Well-Being, Parenting, and Child Well-Being: Pathways to Healthy Adjustment." *Clinical Psychologist* 19 (1): 3–14.

Obergefell v. Hodges, 135 S. Ct. 2071, 576 U.S., 191 L. Ed. 2d 953 (2015).

Patterson, Charlotte J. 2017. "Parents' Sexual Orientation and Children's Development." *Child Development Perspectives* 11 (1): 45–49. doi:10.1111/cdep.12207.

Patterson, Charlotte J., and Jennifer L. Wainright. 2012. "Adolescents with Same-Sex Parents: Findings from the National Longitudinal Study of Adolescent Health." In *Adoption by Lesbians and Gay Men: A New Dimension in Family Diversity*, edited by David M. Brodzinsky and Adam Pertman, 85–111. New York: Oxford University Press.

Payne, Krista K. 2014. *Demographic Profile of Same-Sex Couple Households with Minor Children, 2012* (FP-14-03). National Center for Family and Marriage Research. Bowling Green, OH: Bowling Green State University. Retrieved November 21, 2017. http://www.bgsu.edu/content/dam/BGSU/college-of-arts-and -sciences/NCFMR/documents/FP/FP-14-03_DemoSSCoupleHH.pdf.

Payne, Krista K., and Wendy D. Manning. 2014. *Demographic Profile of Same-Sex Couple Households with Minor Children, 2012* (FP-14-03). National Center for Family and Marriage Research. Bowling Green, OH: Bowling Green State University. Retrieved November 21, 2017. http://www.bgsu.edu /content/dam/BGSU/college-of-arts-andsciences/NCFMR/documents /FP/FP-14-03_DemoSSCoupleHH.pdf.

Perrin, Ellen C., Ellen E. Pinderhughes, Kathryn Mattern, Sean M. Hurley, and Rachel A. Newman. 2016. "Experiences of Children with Gay Fathers." *Clinical Pediatrics* 55 (14): 1305–17. doi:10.1177/0009922816632346.

Potter, Daniel. 2012. "Same-Sex Parent Families and Children's Academic Achievement." *Journal of Marriage and Family* 74 (3): 556–71. doi:10.1111/j .1741-3737.2012.00966.x.

Potter, Daniel, and Emma C. Potter. 2016. "Psychosocial Well-Being in Children of Same-Sex Parents: A Longitudinal Analysis of Familial Transitions." *Journal of Family Issues* 38 (16): 2303–28. doi:10.1177/0192513X16646338.

Powell, Brian, Laura Hamilton, Bianca Manago, and Simon Cheng. 2016. "Implications of Changing Family Forms for Children." *Annual Review of Sociology* 42: 301–22. doi:10.1146/annurev-soc-081715-074444.

Powell, Brian, Natasha Yurk Quadlin, and Oren Pizmony-Levy. 2015. "Public Opinion, the Courts, and Same-Sex Marriage: Four Lessons Learned." *Social Currents* 2 (1): 3–12. doi:10.1177/2329496514562964.

Reczek, Corinne, Russell Spiker, Hui Liu, and Robert Crosnoe. 2016. "Family Structure and Child Health: Does the Sex Composition of Parents Matter?" *Demography* 53 (5): 1605–30. doi:10.1007/s13524-016-0501-y.

Regnerus, Mark. 2012a. "How Different Are the Adult Children of Parents Who Have Same-Sex Relationships? Findings from the New Family Structures Study." *Social Science Research* 41 (4): 752–70. doi:10.1016/j.ssresearch .2012.03.009.

Regnerus, Mark. 2012b. "Parental Same-Sex Relationships, Family Instability, and Subsequent Life Outcomes for Adult Children: Answering Critics of the New Family Structures Study with Additional Analyses." *Social Science Research* 41 (6): 1367–77. doi:10.1016/j.ssresearch.2012.08.015.

Reilly, Mollie. 2016. "Same-Sex Couples Can Now Adopt Children in All 50 States." *The Huffington Post*, March 31. Retrieved November 21, 2017. http://www.huffingtonpost.com/entry/mississippi-same-sex-adoption _us_56fdb1a3e4b083f5c607567f.

Rosenfeld, Michael. 2010. "Nontraditional Families and Childhood Progress through School." *Demography* 47 (3): 755–75. doi:10.1353/dem.0.0112.

Rosenfeld, Michael J. 2013. "Reply to Allen et al." *Demography* 50 (3): 963–69. doi:10.1007/s13524-012-0170-4.

Rosenfeld, Michael J. 2015. "Revisiting the Data from the New Family Structure Study: Taking Family Instability into Account." *Sociological Science* 2: 478–501. doi:10.15195/v2.a23.

Sanchez, Sam. 2017. "Gov. Abbott Signs Bill Allowing Adoption Agencies to Discriminate Against LGBT Parents." *San Antonio Current*, June 16. Retrieved November 21, 2017. http://www.sacurrent.com/the-daily/archives/2017 /06/16/gov-abbott-signs-bill-allowing-adoption-agencies-to-discriminate -against-lgbt-parents.

Schumm, Walter R. 2010. "Children of Homosexuals More Apt to Be Homosexuals? A Reply to Morrison and to Cameron Based on an Examination of Multiple Sources of Data." *Journal of Biosocial Science* 42 (6): 721–42. doi:10.1017/S0021932010000325.

Schumm, Walter R. 2014. "Challenges in Predicting Child Outcomes from Different Family Structures." *Comprehensive Psychology* 3 (10): 1–12. doi:10.2466/03.17.49.CP.3.10.

Schwartz, John. 2010. "Florida Court Calls Ban on Gay Adoptions Unlawful." *New York Times*, September 22. Retrieved November 21, 2017. http:// www.nytimes.com/2010/09/23/us/23adopt.html.

Somashekhar, Sandhya. 2013. "Social Science Struggles with the Effects of Same-Sex Parenting on Children." *The Washington Post*, March 26. Retrieved November 21, 2017. https://www.washingtonpost.com/national/health -science/social-science-struggles-with-the-effects-of-same-sex-parenting -on-children/2013/03/26/a6fa50ca-9655-11e2-8b4e-0b56f26f28de _story.html.

Somashekhar, Sandhya. 2015. "How Kids Became the Strongest Argument for Same-Sex Marriage." *The Washington Post*, June 24. Retrieved Nov. 21 2017. https://www.washingtonpost.com/politics/how-kids-became-the-strongest -argument-for-same-sex-marriage/2015/06/24/98955632-18fe-11e5-ab92 -c75ae6ab94b5_story.html.

Stern, Mark J. 2016. "The Scientific Debate Over Same-Sex Parenting Is Over."
    Slate, April 13. Retrieved November 21, 2017. http://www.slate.com/blogs
    /outward/2016/04/13/scientific_debate_over_same_sex_parenting_is
    _over.html.

Sullins, D. Paul. 2016. "Invisible Victims: Delayed Onset Depression among
    Adults with Same-Sex Parents." *Depression Research and Treatment* 2016:
    1–8. doi: 10.1155/2016/2410392.

Tasker, Fiona L., and Susan Golombok. 1997. *Growing Up in a Lesbian Family:
    Effects on Child Development.* London, UK: Guilford Press.

Umberson, Debra, Shannon Cavanagh, Jennifer Glass, and Kelly Raley. 2012.
    "Texas Professors Respond to New Research on Gay Parenting." *The Huff-
    ington Post*, June 26. Retrieved November 21, 2017. http://www.huffington
    post.com/debra-umberson/texas-professors-gay-research_b_1628988
    .html.

Wainright, Jennifer L., and Charlotte J. Patterson. 2006. "Delinquency, Victim-
    ization, and Substance Use among Adolescents with Female Same-Sex
    Parents." *Journal of Family Psychology* 20 (3): 526–30. doi:10.1037/0893
    -3200.20.3.526.

Wainright, Jennifer L., and Charlotte J. Patterson. 2008. "Peer Relations among
    Adolescents with Female Same-Sex Parents. *Developmental Psychology* 44
    (1): 117–26. doi: 10.1037/0012-1649.44.1.117.

Wainright, Jennifer L., Stephen T. Russell, and Charlotte J. Patterson. 2004.
    "Psychosocial Adjustment, School Outcomes, and Romantic Relation-
    ships of Adolescents with Same-Sex Parents." *Child Development* 75 (6):
    1886–98. doi:10.1111/j.1467-8624.2004.00823.x.

Wetzstein, Cheryl. 2012. "Study Suggests Risks from Same-Sex Parenting." *The
    Washington Times*, June 10. Retrieved November 21, 2017. http://www
    .washingtontimes.com/news/2012/jun/10/study-suggests-risks
    -from-same-sex-parenting.

CHAPTER FOURTEEN

Reproducing Family: How Parents Accept Their LGB Children's "Good" Families[1]

Taylor Field Quiroga

On June 26, 2015, the United States Supreme Court ruled on *Obergefell v. Hodges* in favor of same-sex couples' right to marry, legalizing same-sex marriage on a national level. Newspapers across the country were emblazoned with images of rainbow flags, same-sex couples kissing, and national monuments illuminated with rainbow lights. The next day, *The Washington Post*'s headline read, "Gays' Right to Wed Affirmed" (Somashekhar 2015). The front page of the *New York Times* displayed pictures of same-sex couples embracing, with the headline, "'Equal Dignity': 5–4 Ruling Makes Same-Sex Marriage a Right Nationwide" (Liptak 2015).

On June 27, *The Washington Post* gathered news headlines from a variety of sources and put them all in one place to capture the media's reporting of the historic U.S. Supreme Court ruling that legalized gay marriage. The title of the collection was "'Love Supreme': How Newspapers Played the Landmark Gay-Marriage Decision" (Freedom du Lac 2015).

As lesbian, gay, and bisexual (LGB) people celebrated across the country, this landmark decision also marked a victory for another group of same-sex marriage advocates—their parents. PFLAG, formerly Parents, Family and Friends of Lesbians and Gays, was founded as an organization for parents to find support and become activists advocating for their children on a national scale (Broad et al. 2008). But PFLAG parents don't always begin as activists when their children first come out as gay. PFLAG serves as a support group as well, where parents seek refuge and advice amid the confusion, loss, sadness, and fear that follow that disclosure.

In 2013, I conducted 60 interviews with PFLAG parents, asking them about those initial responses and their emotional journey to the acceptance and support they feel for their children now. I found that when their children first come out as LGB, many parents respond with feelings of fear or loss. They mourn the image they had dreamed of for their child, primarily the reproduction of a "normal" family in the form of marriage and grandchildren.[2] Respondents describe the stages of grief, including, ultimately, acceptance. Once they had come to terms with the new vision for their child, the parents proudly shared stories of marching in pride parades, writing op-eds, showing off family portraits, and fighting to repeal Prop 8, a ballot initiative in California opposing same-sex marriage.

This narrative mirrors findings from an abundant sociological literature on coming out. While research on coming out has primarily attended to LGB individuals themselves, there is a growing literature focused on parents' responses and reactions (Aveline 2006; Ben-Ari 1995; Broad 2011; Broad et al. 2004; Broad, Crawley, and Foley 2008; Connolly 2005; D'Augelli 2005; D'Augelli, Grossman, and Starks 2008; Field and Mattson 2016; Fields 2001; Grafsky 2014; Griffin, Wirth, and Wirth 1986; Herdt and Koff 2000; Johnson and Benson 2014; LaSala 2000; Lee and Lee 2006; Martin et al. 2010; Meadow 2011; Murray 2012; Pearlman 2012; Savin-Williams 2001; Savin-Williams and Dubé 1998; Sedgwick 1991; Solebello and Elliott 2011; Švab and Kuhar 2014; Reeves et al. 2010; Rothblum 2014; Whitley 2013). The process of grief and mourning I observed is well documented empirically among parents of LGB children (Ben-Ari 1995; Fields 2001; Griffin, Wirth, and Wirth 1986; Herdt and Koff 2000; LaSala 2000; Martin et al. 2010). Mahoney (1994, 24–25) notes that parents mourn "the loss of the heterosexual identity of their child and their hopes, dreams, and expectations for a traditional life for their lesbian or gay child [including] the lack of grandchildren."

Another common concept I found reflected in my own data was what Seidman, Meeks, and Traschen (1999) termed "normalization." In several studies, parents make an effort to prove to themselves and others that their children are normal and just like straight children (Broad, Crawley, and Foley 2004; Fields 2001; Martin et al. 2010). Fields (2001) explains how parents engage in normalizing identity work to mitigate the implications of their children's stigmatized sexual identities, using stories of proms and weddings to illustrate how their children are just like everyone else. Part of this concept rests on the argument that the child's identity reflects on and calls into question the parent's own identity, through what others call a "relational identity" model (Švab and Kuhar 2014; Whitley 2013; Connolly 2005). Coming out transforms not only the individual but also the family (Grafsky 2014; Roth-blum 2014). Through the coming out, parents come to understand and reenvision their own identities as parents of LGB children.

In sum, both the initial mourning of hetero family expectations and the subsequent parent activism celebrating their gay child as normal can be found echoed in previous research. Little work, however, has been done on the precise mechanisms through which parents are able to come to terms with their child's sexual identity. We know at first that they are upset because their view is "gay ≠ normal family," and when their narrative is fully accepting, they see (and say) that "gay = normal family." The question remains: How does queerness come to be understood as compatible with normative family ideals? And why is reproducing normative family so important to parents? The answers to these questions offer understandings of the continued contemporary salience of family norms as well as insight into the family unit as an essential cornerstone of capitalist society.

In this chapter, I use data from 49 interviews with parents of LGB children to explain how they come to terms with their child's sexual identity. I show that parents rely on three types of experiences to accept their LGB children as capable of reproducing a "good" family: (1) interacting with family-normative gay couples, (2) hearing their child's family-normative intentions, and (3) witnessing their children produce normative families of their own. I explore how parents understand their role as parents as well as the potential implications of legal and social change. Using these findings, I discuss the theoretical implications of the second research question: why does their children's sexual identity matter so much to parents? Theories of heteronormativity, repronormativity, and the family as a site of social control will address the significance of these findings and explain the importance of normative family for parents of LGB children and for modern U.S. society more broadly.

Methods

This chapter draws on a sample of 60 interviews I conducted with parents of LGBTQ (lesbian, gay, bisexual, transgender, and queer) children in 2013. Because I am specifically focusing on sexuality rather than gender identity, this chapter will only be based on the parents of LGB individuals (n=49).

Interviewees were recruited from the organization PFLAG, long a point of access for studies of families with LGBTQ members (e.g., Gray 2009; Broad 2011). Founded in 1972, PFLAG is the oldest and largest support group for parents of LGBTQ individuals and offers a form of "activist parenting," with PFLAG parents marching in pride parades and campaigning for LGB rights (Broad et al. 2008). When interviews were conducted beginning in January 2013, PFLAG reported over 350 autonomous local chapters.

Parents were recruited via respondent-driven sampling (RDS), a form of snowball sampling tailored for reaching "hidden" or "hard-to-reach" populations that has proven successful in researching LGBTQ families (Heckathorn 1997; see also Whitley 2013). Upon advice from the PFLAG national office, I sent e-mails to the chapter leaders with publicly available, functioning e-mail addresses (N=416), of which 65 confirmed they had forwarded the request to the parents in their chapter, producing a chapter response rate of 15.6 percent. Reasons that chapter leaders gave for refusing participation on behalf of their members included the inactivity of their organization, the overwhelming number of research inquiries they receive, and policies of limiting their listserv messages to meeting-related information. The 416 invitations yielded 107 potential respondents from 46 chapters, the first 58 of whom were selected for interviews over the telephone, or using Internet video chat software. The remaining two respondents were recruited through a visit to a PFLAG chapter and interviewed in person. All of the respondents lived near enough to PFLAG chapters to be on the mailing list, though participation ranged from nonattending nonmembers to chapter presidents.

I conducted semi-structured interviews using a schedule of open-ended questions mostly focusing on their experiences of their children coming out as LGBTQ. Interviewees were audio recorded, provided consent forms and confidentiality via pseudonyms, and were debriefed after the interview with information about local support services.

Interviews ranged from 20 minutes to two hours in length and lasted for 47 minutes on average. Almost all were conducted by telephone, as it is the most economical way to attain such extensive geographical diversity (Berg 2007). The use of the phone had unintended positive impacts on the interviews; parents were able to open up to me despite the age difference, and there was a deeper level of confidentiality because I would never be able to recognize any of the respondents in person.

I sought to immerse myself in my data, both through the compressed and intensive data-gathering timeline—more than 50 interviews in 40 days—and through the relistening, memoing, transcription, and coding of the data. Through extensive memos and fieldnotes by me and three research assistants, I noticed an emergent theme of marriage and grandchildren. I generated a codebook of related search terms with which I coded and compiled relevant excerpts using Dedoose, a Web-based application for mixed-methods research. These excerpts were organized and reviewed in memos that led to the dominant themes I explore in this chapter.

In 2013, I also presented my findings at four chapters of PFLAG in California. Attending these chapter meetings—as well as one in Ohio that served to inform my research design—allowed me to gather feedback from the community and face important critiques of my conclusions. This process allowed me to focus on my own accountability as a researcher and gain some critical insight from the lived experiences I seek to analyze. The meetings also allowed me to critically engage not only with PFLAG members but with the space and procedures of PFLAG meetings.

In this paper, I analyze 49 interviews with parents of LGB children from 23 states. The parents had an average age of 58 and included seven fathers. Of the children, 32 were gay sons, 20 were lesbian daughters, 1 was a bisexual son, and 3 were bisexual or pansexual daughters. I use the term "children" only to indicate the offspring of my respondents; these "children" ranged in age from 14 to 62, with an average age of 31. These parents' accounts vary greatly; some recounted events from decades earlier, while others shared more recent or even ongoing experiences. Additionally, the sample did not contain any parents who identified themselves as LGBTQ, who, if they were included, may have had additional conceptual resources to bring to bear on their child's experience (e.g., Meadow 2011). Given that PFLAG keeps no national membership roster, it is unclear the degree to which this sample resembles the population of PFLAG parents.[3]

Further demographic information about these respondents is listed in Table 14.1.

Table 14.1   Interview Demographics

Pseudonym	Parent			LGB Children	
	Age	Relation	State	Age	Identity
Amber	53	mother	Pennsylvania	30	gay son
Arthur	64	father	Arizona	36	lesbian daughter
Ben	58	father	Missouri	32	gay son
Bianca	67	mother	Michigan	39	gay son
Bonnie	51	mother	Missouri	17	gay son
Brianna	68	mother	New Hampshire	46	gay son
Bridget	50	mother	Oregon	28	gay son
Cassandra	45	mother	South Carolina	16	gay son
Chloe	45	mother	Missouri	24	gay son
Derek	73	father	Arizona	50	lesbian daughter
Emma	66	mother	Virginia	42	gay son
				39	lesbian daughter
Fiona	62	mother	Washington	32	lesbian daughter
				24	gay son
Grace	59	mother	Missouri	17	lesbian daughter

Table 14.1 *(continued)*

Pseudonym	Parent			LGB Children	
	Age	Relation	State	Age	Identity
Jolie	72	mother	Florida	48	lesbian daughter
				49	trans daughter
Justine	51	mother	Minnesota	17	pansexual daughter
Karen	46	mother	Illinois	16	gay son
Kate	45	mother	Texas	16	lesbian daughter
Katelyn	46	mother	Missouri	19	lesbian daughter
Kayla	56	mother	Illinois	21	gay son
Keira	62	mother	Louisiana	32	gay son
Kelly	68	mother	Wisconsin	35	gay son
Kelsey	59	mother	California	34	lesbian daughter
				31	bisexual daughter
Kendra	60	mother	New Jersey	34	bisexual son
				26	gay son
Leah	47	mother	New Hampshire	14	lesbian daughter
Leslie	56	mother	Michigan	27	lesbian daughter
Liam	59	father	New Mexico	30	gay son
Lindsay	51	mother	New Jersey	26	lesbian daughter
Liora	58	mother	New Hampshire	21	lesbian daughter
Liv	51	mother	Tennessee	29	lesbian daughter
Lola	53	mother	Texas	21	gay son
Lorelai	54	mother	Arizona	24	gay son
Lorena	49	mother	Illinois	21	lesbian daughter
Madeline	56	mother	Maryland	20	gay son
Miriam	43	mother	Illinois	16	gay son
Ned	57	father	California	23	lesbian daughter
Sara	51	mother	Washington	23	gay son
Scott	66	father	Maryland	36	bisexual daughter
Stephanie	59	mother	Florida	34	lesbian daughter
Wade	78	father	Indiana	52	lesbian daughter
Allison	60	mother	Mississippi	22	gay son
Jess	58	mother	Indiana	37	gay son

(continued)

Table 14.1   *(continued)*

Pseudonym	Parent			LGB Children	
	Age	Relation	State	Age	Identity
Joy	60	mother	North Carolina	26	gay son
Meghan	61	mother	Washington	35	gay son
				30	trans son
Molly	65	mother	Florida	26	gay son
Pam	70	mother	North Carolina	47	lesbian daughter
				49	gay son
Samantha	45	mother	Michigan	17	gay son
Sharon	52	mother	Louisiana	20	gay son
Flo	87	mother	California	53	gay son
Beatrice	87	mother	California	62	lesbian daughter
				51	gay son
				50	gay son

Findings

Much research has been conducted showing how parents of LGB children mourn the lost expectations of their child's "normal" hetero family life, and research has also demonstrated the normalization process that occurs after the coming out. However, little has been done to unpack the mechanisms through which parents come to accept their children. In this study, I find that parents use normative family ideals like marriage and biological reproduction as a means for accepting their child's nonnormative sexuality.

Just as previous research has found, more than half of the parents in this sample discussed the loss of heteronormative family ideals, responding with sadness that they wouldn't see a wedding or grandchildren. One respondent's story of her daughter coming out as gay follows this model perfectly. "It almost felt like there was a mourning process that I was going through," Lindsay, 51, told me. "There was my vision of the husband, and the wedding dress, and the children, and the white picket fence, and you just picture this for your family and you kind of go through a mourning where that's not actually going to ever happen." Others gestured at this sentiment as a larger theme they see commonly at PFLAG meetings.

All of the parents I interviewed described an accepting and supportive relationship with their children. In their narratives, I saw a path to acceptance that relied on their children approximating the normative family ideal. First, parents were relieved when their children assured them that they still wanted to marry and have kids of their own. Second, meeting other LGB individuals who were married with kids was comforting to parents. Finally, when their children fulfilled these dreams of marriage and family, the parents expressed pride and happiness. Through these three experiences, the process by which parents come to terms with their children's sexuality relies on the normative family ideal as a mechanism for acceptance, which is elaborated in the next section.

Toward Acceptance

Children share their family-normative dreams.

Even if there was no wedding ceremony or committed relationship yet, many parents found comfort in their child's assurances that family, marriage, and children were still part of their plan. Kayla, age 56,[4] was able to express the loss and mourning she was feeling about her son, and his response—"that he still expects to get married, he still expects to have grandchildren, and that part isn't going to change"—was very helpful for her to come to terms with his coming out. Kendra, a 60-year-old mother, explained that her son waited to come out until he knew he was in a committed relationship that wasn't casual.

When her daughter came out to her, Kate, age 45, immediately thought of flashy, flamboyant, and promiscuous stereotypes. She pictured "hot pants, a guy on roller skates, you know, waving around his rainbow flag, going to sex orgies."

One of Kate's friends asked her, "What does your daughter want?" Kate realized she didn't know, so she asked her daughter what being gay meant to her.

Her daughter said, "I just want to find one person to love and to love me back the rest of my life."

Kate responded, "Oh, well, you want the same thing I wanted you to have; it's just a girl now." This was enough reassurance for Kate that her dreams for her daughter were still intact, and "so from then on it's been no problem." Kate explained why hearing that helped her understand and accept her daughter: "I mean, she's always wanted to have children, it was just that she didn't want to have a husband; she wanted to have a wife, and I didn't get that. I just thought being gay means she's never going to get married, she's never going to have children."

Bridget, a 50-year-old mother, had a similar conversation with her 28-year-old gay son: "I expressed some of my fears to him . . . I thought he would never get married. I thought he would never have children. And he told me that he did want children and he would like to adopt sometime and someday."

Having conversations like this even at a young age reassured parents that their children's futures would still include marriage and children. One 47-year-old mother, Leah, recounted conversations with her daughter about her plans for the future. The 14-year-old talked about her future in a way that makes Leah feel closer to her. Leah told me that she asked questions like, "Mom, if I adopt a daughter would you go to China with me to, you know, when I would go?"

Leah reported telling her, "I'm so glad you can get married in New Hampshire," and asked questions like, "Do you think that you'd both be in wedding dresses?"

Her daughter started to think, "How would it be?" and, "What is it really going to be like when I XYZ?"

Leah shared, "It's questions like that where I think that for me it's like any family." By reinforcing the idea of marriage and children from a young age, Leah ensured that her daughter's sexuality wouldn't disrupt her normative family expectations.

When parents share their fears with their children, they are relieved to discover that their children still plan to have normative families with marriage and kids of their own in the future. This planned adherence to normative family expectations is the first step in their acceptance of their children.

Parents Meet Normative Gay Families

The idea that homosexuality is incompatible with marriage was disrupted for many parents through their experiences with same-sex couples who are in committed relationships or marriages. As parents see that their gay children can have a life nearly identical to the one they had envisioned, they become more comfortable.

When Ned's 23-year-old daughter came out in 2008, it was around the time that same-sex marriage became legal in California, and he began to see pictures of same-sex couples getting married. He said:

> As a father wondering how her sexuality, or her sexual identity, was gonna impact her life and mine, when I started seeing all these couples getting married, that was, to me, the big breakthrough. Like "Oh! Things are gonna be okay. Things are gonna be closer to what I expected. This is not a big deal." . . . You know, it was sort of the unknown, and so the event of seeing those pictures and saying "Oh! If she decides to get married someday, I could get to walk her down the aisle." . . . That was the transition. That was the critical breakthrough of, you know, things aren't gonna be as odd as one expects.

He quickly saw that he didn't have to lose the image of a wedding or the fatherly role of walking her down the aisle. Realizing that her sexuality didn't have to disrupt the reproduction of family that much enabled Ned to become more comfortable with his daughter's coming out. From seeing images of same-sex marriages, he was able to imagine a normative wedding. Ned added that hearing other PFLAG parents talking about having grandchildren also helped him come to terms with his daughter's identity.

One mother, Lorelai, explained that she was fortunate to know people who were gay, so she could envision her son's future. She described attending a friend's wedding and, seeing a same-sex couple in the wedding party, she saw in her mind, "Oh, that's what it would be like." She followed up with the comment, "I think parents need to see examples, need to talk about it."

This holds true in Cassandra's experience; a 35-year-old mother, she had never been around a gay couple before and found that that's really helped her since her son came out. She said, "Like we see other gay couples and we're, like, 'Wow, he could end up like one of these people'—you know, committed, in a relationship. Because you only hear really the bad stuff." Cassandra pointed out that the dominant narrative of homosexuality isn't of committed couples and seeing these "examples" helps her replace that narrative with a more palatable family-friendly alternative.

When Normative Family Dreams Come True

For many parents, the feeling that their gay child would never be married is dispelled only when they see their own child in a committed, monogamous, same-sex relationship. Liam, a 59-year-old father, was concerned about his son becoming sexually active and was so happy that the first person his son became involved with was a long-term partner who was older and had an established career. "I'm just really grateful for that," he told me. "I don't know how long it will last but it's lasted a lot longer than many gay male relationships do." Like Cassandra, Liam struggled to replace the stereotype of gay promiscuity with his real experience of his son's monogamy.

As a counterexample, Jolie, a 75-year-old mother of two LGBT children, was frustrated with her younger daughter's nonmonogamy. She said, "I would love to see her find a partner, instead of a revolving door. You know? That's what I wish for my kids at this point. I want them to have companionship. I don't want them to be alone. My older daughter has a friend, and they're living together, and, you know, I hope it's forever." She saw the "revolving door" as something that could not possibly make her daughter happy and that the only positive end goal was a committed monogamous relationship. Supporting this point, Liora, age 58, expressed that she's grateful and so happy that her daughter is in a monogamous relationship, that the couple is in love and shares promise rings and talk about marriage and children.

Reflecting on his initial fears, Scott, a 66-year-old father, proudly pointed out that none of them came true: he has a grandchild, and his daughter will likely get married soon. Derek, age 73, expressed that when his daughter came out, "there was a disappointment that she didn't have anybody, that she wouldn't have a husband. But that really passed quite quickly. She has found somebody and they've been together for 10 years and they're up in Seattle. And now that the elections are over up there, one of these days they're going to get married." Like Scott, Derek was accepting and happy to see that his fears had been disproven. Homosexuality means neither promiscuity nor loneliness, and for some, it can mirror the monogamous partnership of heterosexual marriages.

Kelsey, age 59, described her daughter's lakeside wedding ceremony in 2009 and the relief she felt. She said, "It just felt better to have things open and settled: 'Okay, you're in a relationship. And so it doesn't matter if you're a lesbian or bi or whatever; you've found someone you've made a commitment to.'" The commitment erases the perceived anti-family implications of homosexuality, and the wedding offers relief as a ritual of family reproduction used to equalize the disruptive perceived implications of homosexuality.

Another mother, Kelly, age 68, shared the story of a couple in PFLAG who were struggling with their daughter being a lesbian until she and her partner had triplets. She described how all of a sudden, they were more accepting and proud of their daughter's family, noting that "it was just the kids made them completely turn around." Not only did their daughter's situation mirror the normative commitment of a relationship, she was able to fulfill their family expectations and earn their acceptance by having children.

These three interactions—children sharing their family-normative dreams, meeting normative same-sex couples and families, and witnessing their children reproduce a normative family—allow parents to see their children as reproducing "good" normative family ideals of marriage and children. Through their children's reassurances, seeing other normative gay families and their own children fulfilling these expectations, parents see how the family structure can still be reproduced and become more accepting of their children's sexual identity.

Understanding the Parenting Relationship

In the previous three sections, I explored the mechanisms by which parents unpack their child's sexuality and repackage it in the normative family structure. This is vital to their acceptance of their children. But the question still stands: Why is this so important? For these parents, their children's reproduction of family is essential and coconstitutes their own identity and success as parents. Emma, a 66-year-old mother, expressed about her two gay children, "For me, they are a part of me."

Sara, age 51, questioned parenthood altogether and found the idea of reproduction at the heart of it. "I think that for parents who have a hard time, I think they are just probably heartbroken that what they wanted and what they decided when they chose to become parents isn't working out," she said, continuing:

> And I think most parents go into parenthood selfishly. They're going into it to have something that looks like them, that—I mean, really, what is it? What is parenthood? And I think it's really fascinating how we do have and claim this ownership somehow. There's not a day as a parent where you come to court and you go, "Well, really this was all about giving you the opportunity to have a life—go off and discover your life." No, as parents, we still think that what we expected for you is that. Right? You know what I mean? So I think that that's really tough for people to let go of.

When I asked how it was different to accept your own child as gay compared to accepting others as gay, Fiona, age 62, said that as a parent, you have "much more of an emotional tie to your child" and a "desire for your child to be like you." Being gay, she commented, is "just part of a million ways that your children could be different from you that you have to deal with." Sara went on to offer the advice to other parents to embrace the mystery of those differences. She cited the example of her grandchildren, who have blue eyes even though their parents have brown eyes—another of the "million ways" that children can be different.

Stephanie, a 59-year-old mother, explained that parents have these expectations because they're straight and it's the only life they've known. "And you kind of expected your kids are gonna follow that same path," she said. Stephanie shared Fiona's sentiment that it's different to accept her own daughter as gay, because "her life would have been entwined with ours no matter what." This interconnectedness means that a deviation in the child becomes a deviation in the family and a disruption to the parents' identities.

Leah summarized this finding succinctly: "It's not just one person in my family. Even though my husband and I are straight, we're a gay family. Because it's not just one of us." When a child comes out, the family is no longer a heteronormative family but becomes altogether a gay family affecting all members. This disruption to the normative family is intimately tied to parents' senses of self. The mental hurdle of fitting their gay children into normative families thus becomes a prerequisite of their acceptance.

Legal and Cultural Progress

Other parents noted the changing legal and cultural situation of LGB families. These interviews were conducted in 2013, before the nationwide same-sex marriage ruling in 2015. The immediate reaction that marriage is incompatible with homosexuality is being dispelled as same-sex marriages are more recognized, legally and culturally. Even when marriage or adoption was available to their children, however, it took a second for the parents to grasp that these options were not closed to them.

Katelyn, one of the younger mothers at age 45, explained that her feeling of loss or mourning wasn't directly about grandchildren or marriage, "because obviously she can have kids. She can do all the things that other people do for the most part, although hopefully it'll be recognized legally across the nation at one point in time, you know, marriage and things like that." Legal progress assured Katelyn that her child will someday be able to reproduce the same family structures. For Bonnie, there was a gap between her immediate reaction and what she knew to be true. She followed up her first response—that her only child wouldn't have a wedding—by saying, "And then once I thought about it a little further, I was like, 'Well, I hope so. There's no reason why we can't unless we're in a state where it's illegal, and then we'll just have to go to the next state over.'" Even while Bonnie knew that marriage is a legal option for her son, her immediate response to homo-sexuality was that marriage is impossible. Her emotional reaction to that response reflects how important the possibility of marriage is for parents to be able to accept their children.

Perhaps this gap can be addressed through more cultural change as the law reflects more and more how we understand same-sex couples. Brianna, a 68-year-old mother, spoke to both cultural and political progress, noting, "Today's parents absorb it because being gay is more out in our culture. And people aren't as fearful anymore. We know that gay people can get married in many states, we know that gay people can have children now. So there's a lot, so much has changed in 25 years. Sometimes it's hard to fathom it all." Not only are marriage and family legal for gay people now; parents are starting to know that. The diffusion of this knowledge through culture is an important point in changing how parents react to their children coming out. At the time I conducted these interviews in 2013, same-sex marriage was much less common. Legal changes since then have enabled more same-sex families, the cultural salience of which might help parents like Ned or Cassandra under-stand that their LGB children can still reproduce a normative family.

Discussion

Returning to the headlines of late June 2015, while many were celebrat-ing, it is important to note that not all LBGTQ people fully endorsed the fight for same-sex marriage. This subject has long been a site for contentious dis-cussion (Duggan 2002; Rothblum 2005; Seidman 2001; Stacey 1996; Stein and Plummer 1994; Warner 2003, 2014; Yep, Lovas, and Elia 2003).

Yep and colleagues (2003) explain the two primary opposing sexual ide-ologies on the topic as "assimilationist" and "radical." The assimilationist position argues that same-sex couples should be afforded the same rights to marriage and adoption as straight couples.[5] When Cassandra and Jolie, for instance, hope their children will end up married, they are attending to a conformist, homonormative model of family. They hope their child's family will be just like a heterosexual family.

The radical position, on the other hand, states that same-sex marriage serves only as an oppressive tool to regulate sexuality and that liberation should be sought instead through challenging normative social controls.[6] Aligned with the radical stance, Duggan (2002, 179) argues that the assimilationist position contributes to and enables the reproduction of the capitalist state, defining homonormativity as "a politics that does not contest dominant heteronormative assumptions and institutions but upholds and sustains them while promising the possibility of a demobilized gay constituency and a privatized, depoliticized gay culture anchored in domesticity and consumption." This theme of homonormativity policing sexual citizenship in service to the capitalist state comes up again at the end of this section.

First, however, I address the two hegemonic family ideals that construct the normative expectation that PFLAG parents described—heteronormativity and repronormativity. As Josephson (2016, 2) explains, "an ideal is hegemonic not because it is actually adhered to by a majority, but rather because it is the standard to which we all must respond. It is the standard by which less powerful groups are measured, and found wanting, and all of us are disciplined." Heteronormativity and repronormativity are the two standards to which PFLAG parents approximate their children's success and happiness.

Many scholars have urged that sexuality and heterosexuality be recognized as an institutionalized organizing social force beyond simply as a component of gender (Collins 2004; Gamson and Moon 2004; Ingraham 1994; Martin 2009; Rich 1980; Rubin 1994). Martin (2009, 190) explains that heterosexuality is upheld as a hegemonic standard not only through heterosexism and homophobia but also through heteronormativity:

> The mundane, everyday ways that heterosexuality is privileged and taken for granted as normal and natural [which] includes the institutions, practices, and norms that support heterosexuality (especially a particular form of heterosexuality—monogamous and reproductive) and subjugate other forms of sexuality, especially homosexuality.

Heteronormative expectations are apparent, for instance, in Ned's feelings of relief that he can still someday walk his daughter down the aisle at her wedding.

This "particular form" of heterosexuality connects to the second hegemonic ideal that structures the respondents' narratives. This organizing construct—repronormativity—was originally developed by Franke (2001) and Edelman (2004). Several of the parents explicitly link marriage and children together in their family expectations, illustrating the concept of repronormativity. Weissman (2016, 3) defines repronormativity as "a paradigm that is limited to legitimized, state-sanctioned heteronormative acts of reproduction specifically through the patriarchal heteronormative family, and service to this reproduction of the heteropatriarchal nation-state." And these hegemonic pillars of normative family come back to the reproduction of the capitalist state.

Family has long been a site for the constraint of sexuality. In *The History of Sexuality*, volume 1, Foucault (1978, 3) explains how sex was confined to the reproductive and utilitarian marriage bed. Cott (2000, 4) makes a similar argument: "By incriminating some marriages and encouraging others, marital regulations have drawn lines among the citizenry and defined what kinds of sexual relations and which families will be legitimate." Much research and theory contribute to the idea that the family operates as a form of social control (Josephson 2016; Morgan 1975; Weissman 2016; Zivi 2014). But to what end?

According to Althusser (2001), the family is an ideological state apparatus reinforcing the rule of the dominant class through ideology. The family maintains the state through the socialization and production of obedient subjects held accountable through a network of responsibility for kin (Morgan 1985, 74–75). The normative family ideal is so strongly ingrained in these parents by a capitalist system that reproduces itself through the structure of family.

Parents describe the deep interconnectedness of their own identities with their children's lives, evidenced by a desire to have their children follow in their footsteps. Parents seek to reproduce themselves. The normative family structure seeks to reproduce itself through parents' hetero- and repronormative expectations for their children. And the capitalist state seeks to reproduce itself through the normative family structure.

Now, the normative family structure is extending to incorporate homonormative family structures. According to the respondents in this study, government-sanctioned gay families mean that future parents will not struggle with their children not fitting into the family structure. Instead, their understanding of family will extend to match what the state deems permissible. These parents suspect that as the state changes its definition of normative family structure, so too will parents of LGB children.

Conclusion

One respondent told me that her daughter's sexual identity was "just another version of normal." For many parents, their initial fears that their child would not be "normal" and would not be able to have a "normal" family were disproven. They heard their children's assurances that they still dreamed of marriage and children, they encountered family-normative gay folks, and many saw their children realize those normative dreams. Respondents explained that a large part of parenting is the expectation that your child will be like you. Many hoped that cultural and legal shifts would change future parents' responses to their children coming out.

This study shows that parents have two expectations of their children: weddings and babies. Those expectations serve the hegemonic ideals of a normative family: heteronormativity and repronormativity respectively. These ideals, in turn, serve the capitalist nation-state. The concepts on which parents' acceptance is predicated reinforce multiple systems of inequality. Capitalism reproduces capitalism through families that reproduce families through parents who reproduce themselves.

Future research should investigate the ways in which other forms of nonnormative reproduction, like childlessness, affect families. The circumstances and responses of these parents should be attended to as legal and cultural acceptance of same-sex families becomes more widespread.

Notes

1. The author acknowledges financial support from the National Science Foundation Graduate Research Fellowship, the Rackham Graduate Student Research Grant, the Department of Sociology at the University of Michigan, the Jerome Davis Research Award, the Comfort Starr Award, and the Office of the Dean of Arts and Sciences at Oberlin College. I am grateful for the hard work of research assistants Sarah Fan, Lisa Rivoli, and Meredith Gillies. I am also grateful for advice from Professor Karin A. Martin, Samantha Hobson, Professor Elizabeth A. Armstrong, Professor Greggor Mattson, Professor Daphne John, and Miriam Gleckman-Krut.

2. Interestingly, recent studies have found that there is no "normal" or "typical" family and that the ideal that many espouse is achieved less and less frequently (Cohen 2014). Rather, the normative family I allude to here, which includes homeownership, a lifelong marriage, and children who reproduce all of this, is a hegemonic ideal, a concept to which I'll return later in the chapter.

3. PFLAG parents, like the ones I interviewed for this study, are not representative of all parents of LGB kids. They have all chosen to seek out the support of this advocacy organization, which affirms identities and behaviors that others may never accept.

4. Ages listed reflect age at the time of the interviews, which were conducted in January, February, and August 2013.

5. Terms affiliated with the assimilationist model include "normalization," "homonormativity," "civil rights model," "identity politics," "liberal argument," "sameness argument," and "conformity."

6. Terms associated with the radical model include "deconstruction," "transgression," "queer [rather than identity] politics," "anti-assimilationism," and "progressive [rather than liberal] argument."

References

Althusser, Louis. 2001. *Lenin and Philosophy and Other Essays*. New York: Monthly Review Press.

Aveline, David. 2006. "'Did I Have Blinders on or What?': Retrospective Sense Making by Parents of Gay Sons Recalling Their Sons' Earlier Years." *Journal of Family Issues* 27 (6): 777–802.

Ben-Ari, Adital. 1995. "The Discovery That an Offspring Is Gay: Parents', Gay Men's, and Lesbians' Perspectives." *Journal of Homosexuality* 30 (1): 89–111.

Berg, Bruce L. 2007. *Qualitative Research Methods for the Social Sciences*. New York: Pearson.

Broad, K. L. 2011. "Coming Out for Parents, Families and Friends of Lesbians and Gays: From Support Group Grieving to Love Advocacy." *Sexualities* 14 (4): 399–415.

Broad, K. L., Helena Alden, Dana Berkowitz, and Maura Ryan. 2008. "Activist Parenting and GLBTQ Families." *Journal of GLBT Family Studies* 4 (4): 499–520.

Broad, K. L., Sara L. Crawley, and Lara Foley. 2004. "Doing 'Real Family Values': The Interpretive Practice of Families in the GLBT Movement." *The Sociological Quarterly* 45 (3): 509–27.

Cohen, Philip N. 2014. *The Family: Diversity, Inequality, and Social Change*. New York: W. W. Norton.

Collins, Patricia Hill. 2004. *Black Sexual Politics: African Americans, Gender, and the New Racism*. New York: Routledge.

Connolly, Colleen M. 2005. "A Process of Change: The Intersection of the GLBT Individual and Their Family of Origin." *Journal of GLBT Family Studies* 1 (1): 5–20.

Cott, Nancy F. 2000. *Public Vows: A History of Marriage and the Nation*. Cambridge, MA: Harvard University Press.

D'Augelli, Anthony R. 2005. "Stress and Adaptation among Families of Lesbian, Gay, and Bisexual Youth: Research Challenges." *Journal of GLBT Family Studies* 1 (2): 115–35.

D'Augelli, Anthony R., Arnold H. Grossman, and Michael T. Starks. 2008. "Families of Gay, Lesbian, and Bisexual Youth." *Journal of GLBT Family Studies* 4 (1): 95–115.

Duggan, Lisa. 2002. *The Incredible Shrinking Public: Sexual Politics and the Decline of Democracy*. Boston: Beacon Press.

Edelman, Lee. 2004. *No Future: Queer Theory and the Death Drive*. Durham, NC: Duke University Press.

Field, Taylor L., and Greggor Mattson. 2016. "Parenting Transgender Children in PFLAG." *Journal of GLBT Family Studies* 12 (5): 413–29.

Fields, Jessica. 2001. "Normal Queers: Straight Parents Respond to Their Children's 'Coming Out.'" *Symbolic Interaction* 24 (2): 165–87.

Foucault, Michel. 1978. *The History of Sexuality*, vol. 1. New York: Pantheon Books.

Franke, Katherine M. 2001. "Theorizing Yes: An Essay on Feminism, Law, and Desire." *Columbia Law Review* 101 (1): 181–208.

Freedom du Lac, J. 2015. "Love Supreme: How Newspapers Played the Landmark Gay-Marriage Decision." *The Washington Post*, June 27. https://www.washingtonpost.com/news/post-nation/wp/2015/06/27/love-supreme-how-newspapers-played-the-landmark-decision/?utm_term=.dd580b8c77bc.

Gamson, Joshua, and Dawne Moon. 2004. "The Sociology of Sexualities: Queer and Beyond." *Annual Review of Sociology* 30 (1): 47–64.

Grafsky, Erika L. 2014. "Becoming the Parent of a GLB Son or Daughter." *Journal of GLBT Family Studies* 10 (1–2): 36–57.

Gray, Mary L. 2009. *Out in the Country: Youth, Media and Queer Visibility in Rural America*. New York: New York University Press.

Griffin, Carolyn Welch, Marian J. Wirth, and Arthur J. Wirth. 1986. *Beyond Acceptance: Parents of Lesbians and Gays Talk About Their Experiences*. Englewood Cliffs, NJ: Prentice-Hall.

Heckathorn, Douglas D. 1997. "Respondent-Driven Sampling: A New Approach to the Study of Hidden Populations." *Social Problems* 44 (2): 174–99.

Herdt, Gilbert, and Bruce Koff. 2000. *Something to Tell You: The Road Families Travel When a Child Is Gay*. New York: Columbia University Press.

Ingraham, Chrys. 1994. "The Heterosexual Imaginary : Feminist Sociology and Theories of Gender." *Sociological Theory* 12 (2): 203–19.

Johnson, Susan L., and Kristen E. Benson. 2014. "'It's Always the Mother's Fault': Secondary Stigma of Mothering a Transgender Child." *Journal of GLBT Family Studies* 10 (1–2): 124.

Josephson, Jyl J. 2016. *Rethinking Sexual Citizenship*. Albany: State University of New York Press.

LaSala, Michael C. 2000. "Lesbians, Gay Men, and Their Parents: Family Therapy for the Coming-Out Crisis." *Family Process* 39 (1): 67–81.

Lee, Michelle M., and Robert E. Lee. 2006. "The Voices of Accepting and Supportive Parents of Gay Sons: Towards an Ecosystemic Strengths Model." *Journal of GLBT Family Studies* 2 (2): 1–27.

Liptak, Adam. 2015. "'Equal Dignity': 5–4 Ruling Makes Same-Sex Marriage a Right Nationwide." *New York Times*, June 27: A1, A11.

Mahoney, Daniel. 1994. *Staying Connected: The Coming Out Stories of Parents with a Lesbian Daughter or Gay Son*. Master's thesis. University of Guelph.

Martin, Karin A. 2009. "Normalizing Heterosexuality: Mothers' Assumptions, Talk, and Strategies with Young Children." *American Sociological Review* 74 (2): 190–207.

Martin, Karin A., David J. Hutson, Emily Kazyak, and Kristin S. Scherrer. 2010. "Advice When Children Come Out: The Cultural 'Tool Kits' of Parents." *Journal of Family Issues* 31 (7): 960–91.

Meadow, Tey. 2011. "'Deep Down Where the Music Plays': How Parents Account for Childhood Gender Variance." *Sexualities* 14 (6): 725–47.

Morgan, D. H. J. 1975. *Social Theory and the Family.* Boston: Routledge & Kegan Paul.

Morgan, D. H. J. 1985. *The Family, Politics and Social Theory.* Boston: Routledge & Kegan Paul.

Murray, Heather. 2012. *Not in This Family: Gays and the Meaning of Kinship in Postwar North America.* Philadelphia: University of Pennsylvania Press.

Pearlman, Sarah F. 2012. *Mother-Talk: Conversations with Mothers of Lesbian Daughters and FTM Transgender Children.* Toronto: Demeter Press.

Reeves, Teresa, Sharon G. Horne, Sharon Scales Rostosky, Ellen B. Riggle, Linda R. Baggett, and Rebecca A. Aycock. 2010. "Family Members' Support for GLBT Issues: The Role of Family Adaptability and Cohesion." *Journal of GLBT Family Studies* 6 (1): 80–97.

Rich, Adrienne. 1980. "Compulsory Heterosexuality and Lesbian Existence." *Signs* 5 (4): 631–60.

Rothblum, Esther D. 2005. "Same-Sex Marriage and Legalized Relationships: I Do, or Do I?" *Journal of GLBT Family Studies* 1 (1): 21–31.

Rothblum, Esther D. 2014. "Mars to Venus or Earth to Earth? How Do Families of Origin Fit into GLBTQ Lives?" *Journal of GLBT Family Studies* 10 (1–2): 231–41.

Rubin, Gayle S. 1994. "Thinking Sex: Notes for a Radical Theory of the Politics of Sexuality." In *The Lesbian and Gay Studies Reader*, edited by Henry Abelove, Michele Aina Barale, and David M. Halperin, 3–44. New York: Routledge.

Savin-Williams, Ritch C. 2001. *Mom, Dad, I'm Gay.* Washington, D.C.: American Psychological Association.

Savin-Williams, Ritch C., and Eric M. Dubé. 1998. "Parental Reactions to Their Child's Disclosure of a Gay/Lesbian Identity." *Family Relations* 47 (1): 7–13.

Sedgwick, Eve Kosofsky. 1991. "How to Bring Your Kids up Gay." *Social Text* 29: 18–27.

Seidman, Steven. 2001. "From Identity to Queer Politics: Shifts in Normative Heterosexuality and the Meaning of Citizenship." *Citizenship Studies* 5 (3): 321–28.

Seidman, Steven, Chet Meeks, and Francie Traschen. 1999. "Beyond the Closet? The Changing Social Meaning of Homosexuality in the United States." *Sexualities* 2 (1): 9–34.

Solebello, Nicholas, and Sinikka Elliott. 2011. "'We Want Them to Be as Heterosexual as Possible': Fathers Talk about Their Teen Children's Sexuality." *Gender & Society* 25 (3): 293–315.

Somashekhar, Sandhya. 2015. "Gays' Right to Wed Affirmed." *The Washington Post*, June 27: A1, A10.

Stacey, Judith. 1996. "Gay and Lesbian Families Are Here; All Our Families Are Queer; Let's Get Used to It!" In *In the Name of the Family: Rethinking Family Values in the Postmodern Age*, 52–82. Boston: Beacon Press.

Stein, Arlene, and Ken Plummer. 1994. "'I Can't Even Think Straight': 'Queer' Theory and the Missing Revolution in Sociology." *Sociological Theory* 12 (2): 178–87.

Švab, Alenka, and Roman Kuhar. 2014. "The Transparent and Family Closets: Gay Men and Lesbians and Their Families of Origin." *Journal of GLBT Family Studies* 10 (1): 15–35.

Warner, Michael. 2003. *The Trouble with Normal*. Cambridge, MA: Harvard University Press.

Warner, Michael. 2014. *Publics and Counterpublics*. New York: Zone Books.

Weissman, Anna L. 2016. "Repronormativity and the Reproduction of the Nation-State: The State and Sexuality Collide." *Journal of GLBT Family Studies* 13 (3): 277–305.

Whitley, Cameron T. 2013. "Trans-Kin Undoing and Redoing Gender: Negotiating Relational Identity among Friends and Family of Transgender Persons." *Sociological Perspectives* 56 (4): 597–621.

Yep, Gust A., Karen E. Lovaas, and John P. Elia. 2003. "A Critical Appraisal of Assimilationist and Radical Ideologies Underlying Same-Sex Marriage in LGBT Communities in the United States." *Journal of Homosexuality* 45 (1): 45–64.

Zivi, Karen. 2014. "Performing the Nation: Contesting Same-Sex Marriage Rights in the United States." *Journal of Human Rights* 13 (3): 290–306.

Conclusion

The family is a social *institution*—a pattern or way of organizing parts of society in order to meet some kind of need, such as socializing the next generation in terms of collectively shared values. Families are made up of *individual* social actors who *interact* with each other, creating and changing rules and roles throughout the life course (including interacting with parents when the children are adults). Perhaps the greatest gift these chapters offer is a way to think of parents' and children's lives at many different levels—from individual to interactional to institutional—something that news stories usually don't have the column length to include. For example, we see various forms of "good parenting" analyzed and complicated in these chapters in terms of individual parents' experiences and fears about being labeled or judged by others. We read that parent-child interactions that may show signs of "helicoptering" are actually complicated by factors such as geography, social class, education level, age of the child, race, and family structure, among other things. At the institutional level, we include governmental regulations about visas and immigrant status in our understanding of how and whether parenting manifests in groups differentially affected by policy. Additionally, collective values are scrutinized by examining media representation of the moral dimensions of certain types of parenting.

Inequality among parents is shown at individual, interactional, and institutional levels in these chapters. Many decisions that seem as if they're located entirely within an individual family (e.g., the decision to watch television after kids go to bed or whether and how to talk to children about racial inequalities) actually demonstrate the impact of interactional and institutional factors. Watching TV depends on whether there are other household members who can participate in household labor, something that is limited for single parents or parents whose partners do not contribute in that way; this matters at the interactional level. Norms about who is supposed to perform certain household tasks—often cited by feminist scholars as a location where women are disproportionately charged to perform roles associated with household management and childcare—are powerful forces when it comes to even mundane tasks like being able to turn on the TV to relax for a while; this matters at the institutional level. Similarly, talking to a child about race depends not just on communication patterns within a parent-child relationship but also on larger structural inequalities that disadvantage minority groups; this matters at the institutional and collective level.

Parents want what's best for their children, but the way this is enacted, the definition of "best," and the resources available to achieve this are affected by factors beyond any individual parent's abilities or desires. If parents live in a country where leave time is plentiful, that will affect how much time they are able to spend with their child. The more generous the leave policy, the more time parents can spend with children after a birth or adoption (and the more likely parents may experience high levels of well-being and lower levels of stress). But the availability of a policy is not the only thing that matters, since cultural values about gender, parent-child bonding, privacy, and paid employment put varying degrees of pressure on parents to either take advantage of a policy or ignore it. More important, these factors affect whether parents have a choice to take or leave a policy in the first place.

The impact of factors beyond any individual parent cannot be overstated. This is true whether this impact pertains to a low-income parent's decision to buy his daughter an expensive video game system to maintain dignity among her more affluent friends, an immigrant parent's fear of being deported and leaving a U.S.-born child behind, a hopeful adoptive parent's desire to adopt a child, the desire of a parent whose child is gay to throw a wedding and have grandchildren, or the desire of that child to legally marry and adopt a child when he is an adult. Peer groups, structural inequality, immigration law, international relations, collective rituals, and marriage rights are all present in these examples that seem as if they are located entirely in individual families but are actually embedded in much larger systems. It is the important job of scholars such as those whose work is included in this book to capture how individual parents' experiences must be situated in these kinds of interactional and institutional contexts.

The research in this edited collection is presented using lenses from a variety of social science disciplines and research methods in order to examine parenting and parenthood in contemporary society. The authors connect issues ripped from news headlines to sound and sophisticated scholarship. The experiences of parents are examined using numeric demographic data, stories, texts, in-depth interviews, surveys, clinical composites, and ethnographic observations. The story of contemporary parenting and parenthood is complex, to say the least, which necessitates a wide variety of research methods to capture that complexity. Even within chapters, we see conflicting research findings, complications, and questions left unanswered. Such is the way of ongoing research, only a snapshot of which is captured in this book.

In addition to conducting research on parents' experiences at many levels, it is also the important job of researchers to communicate their findings so that the lives of parents and children can be understood and enhanced. One vehicle for the communication of research findings is via news stories. How do research and news intersect? Of course, this varies by discipline and topic. But it is safe to say that scholars who are interested in answering hard questions about parents and children look at news stories in a couple of ways. First, we are consumers of these stories just like everyone else, finding puzzles that may play out in our own lives, and finding inspiration for new research in unanswered questions present in the stories. When we read about parents who are faced with criminal charges for allowing their child to walk alone in an urban neighborhood, for example, we may wonder what steps may have led to that outcome, what the story says about how values shape expectations of parents and neighbors, and what different groups may say in response to the story. We may also worry that the story misrepresents the complexity of a situation or that it represents a reality that is troubling.

Not only are we consumers of the stories; we researchers are sometimes involved in the creation of news headlines. More than ever, academicians and practitioners offer their research and ideas to the public through news media outlets, blogs, and other media platforms. But we are constantly trying to figure out the best way to do this. On one hand, to have a piece of research be referenced in a captivating headline means that our work as public intellectuals is reaching a wide audience. We want our world to be an informed one, not one that is led by myths and misconceptions. So it's exciting when our research shows up in newsfeeds. On the other hand, any short-form writing or presentation of or about our findings may not capture the complex details that make our research so valuable. The crux and complications of our findings get missed in a short news article. To manage this, many researchers and practitioners are now devoting energy to offering the short-form versions of their research findings themselves. Platforms such as op-eds, blogs, or short-form research news stories on online sites devoted to sharing research findings in an accessible way allow the details to be selected by the researcher, and they allow researchers to write the pieces themselves. Indeed, entire branches of research organizations are devoted to narrating research findings to the public. In this way, scholars have had to add to their existing work. No longer is it enough to just produce the scholarship; the scholars are also expected to share their findings in an accessible way.

In addition to writing some pieces ourselves and dedicating writing energy to presenting research findings to a wide audience, we researchers also rely on the good work of journalists and other writers. But this, too, has changed. While it has always been the case that some academicians and journalists have maintained close relationships, the stories that reach our online newsfeeds have been widely dispersed. Now research findings are discussed in traditional news stories by sophisticated journalists, but they also show up in online "listicles," quizzes, and even clickbait. In other words, the "out there" of journalism is a wide field, and it is hard to control. For this reason, it is even more important to produce good research that can be presented accurately and accessibly.

About the Editor and Contributors

Editor

Michelle Y. Janning, PhD, is the Raymond and Elsie Gipson DeBurgh Chair of Social Sciences and a professor of sociology at Whitman College in Walla Walla, Washington. Her work focuses on the intersections between family life and material culture. She is the author of the books *The Stuff of Family Life: How Our Homes Reflect Our Lives* and *Love Letters: Saving Romance in the Digital Age*. She is a public speaker, award-winning teacher, blogger, and board member of the Council on Contemporary Families.

Contributors

Valerie Adrian, PhD, is a policy, performance, and research analyst for Clackamas County Community Corrections in Oregon City, Oregon. Her applied research focuses on the efficacy of alternatives to incarceration in a community justice setting. She blogs about life, family, and media through a sociological lens at kitchentablesociology.com.

Pallavi Banerjee, PhD, is an assistant professor of sociology at the University of Calgary, Canada. She is in the process of finishing her book entitled *Dismantling Dependence: Gendered Migrations, Indian High-Skilled Families and the Visa Regime*. She has published both academic and nonacademic pieces on gender, immigration, and families, and her research was cited by the Obama administration to reform visa laws for dependent spouses.

Joshua Coleman, PhD, is a psychologist in private practice in the San Francisco Bay Area. He is the author of numerous articles, chapters, and books. His most recent book, *When Parents Hurt: Compassionate Strategies When You and Your Grown Child Don't Get Along*, is published by HarperCollins. In addition to his private practice, he conducts weekly webinars for estranged parents and is also a board member of the Council on Contemporary Families.

Caitlyn Collins, PhD, is assistant professor of sociology at Washington University in St. Louis. She is the author of *Making Motherhood Work: How Women Manage Careers and Caregiving.* She is a Work and Family Researchers Network Early Career Fellow, and her research is supported by the National Science Foundation, the American Association of University Women, and the German Academic Exchange Service.

Marshal Neal Fettro, PhD, is a family demographer with research interests including families, gay and lesbian relationships, and the intersection of work and family. He has a doctorate in sociology from Bowling Green State University in Ohio. He currently examines variation in gender differences in time allocations in paid work, housework, and leisure between same-sex and different-sex couples.

Wendy D. Manning, PhD, is distinguished research professor in sociology and director of the Center for Family and Demographic Research at Bowling Green State University in Ohio. She was the lead researcher for the American Sociological Association's amicus briefs to the U.S. Supreme Court in support of marriage equality.

Margaret K. Nelson, PhD, is the A. Barton Hepburn Professor of Sociology emerita at Middlebury College in Vermont, where she taught for four decades. She is the author of *Parenting Out of Control: Anxious Parents in Uncertain Times,* and (with Rosanna Hertz) *Random Families: Genetic Strangers, Sperm Donor Siblings, and the Creation of New Kin.*

Erin Pahlke, PhD, is an associate professor of psychology at Whitman College in Walla Walla, Washington. She focuses on educational and developmental psychology, with recent publications investigating children's and adolescents' understandings of discrimination and experiences with racial and gender socialization.

Ankita Patnaik, PhD, is a labor economist and researcher at Mathematical Policy Research in Washington, D.C., where she leverages her expertise in designing quasi-experimental and nonexperimental studies to evaluate the impacts of various public programs. Her research on parental leave policies has been highlighted in the *New York Times, Washington Post, Atlantic,* and *Wall Street Journal,* and she presented her findings at a congressional Briefing in 2016.

Allison J. Pugh, PhD, is professor of sociology at the University of Virginia. She is the author of *Longing and Belonging: Parents, Children, and Consumer Culture*, which won the 2010 William J. Goode Award, and *The Tumbleweed Society: Working and Caring in an Age of Insecurity*. Her work has been funded by the National Science Foundation and the Alfred P. Sloan Foundation, and in 2016–2017, she was a fellow of the American Council of Learned Societies and the Center for Advanced Study in the Behavioral Sciences at Stanford.

Taylor Field Quiroga, BA, is a PhD student in sociology at the University of Michigan and a National Science Foundation Graduate Research Fellow. Her interests are in gender, sexuality, race, and parenting. She researches parents of LGBT children, as well as midlife divorce consequences, and has an article published in the *Journal of GLBT Family Studies*.

Pamela Anne Quiroz, PhD, is director of the Center for Mexican American Studies and professor of sociology at the University of Houston in Texas. She is also executive director of the Inter University Program on Latino Research. A researcher of children, youth, family, and identity, she is the author of *Adoption in a Color-Blind Society* and *Personal Advertising: Dating, Mating and Relating in Modern Society* (forthcoming). Professor Quiroz serves as editor of *Social Problems* and North American editor for *Children's Geographies*.

Liana Sayer, PhD, is professor of sociology, faculty affiliate of the Maryland Population Research Center, and director of the Maryland Time Use Laboratory at the University of Maryland. Her work documenting how time use is a fundamental mechanism that reinforces and reconfigures gender, race, and class inequality has been published in numerous journals, including *American Journal of Sociology*, *Demography*, and *Journal of Marriage and Family*.

Robin W. Simon, PhD, is professor of sociology at Wake Forest University in North Carolina. Her research examines the consequences of gender and other social inequalities for men's and women's social roles and relationships, identities, and emotions as well as mental and physical health in the United States. Dr. Simon has received several awards for her scholarship—including the 2018 Award for Contributions to the Understanding of Gender and Society from the Southern Sociological Society—and seven awards from the American Sociological Association and Society for the Study of Social Problems for articles that appeared in the *American Journal of Sociology*, *Social Forces*, the *Journal of Health and Social Behavior*, and *Social Psychological Quarterly*.

Index

Page numbers followed by "n." indicate notes, *t* indicate tables, and *f* indicate figures.

Shepard, Kairi, 276
"Silicon Valley's Reluctant Housewife"
    (Long), 237–238
Silva, Jennifer, 58–59
Silverstein, Merril, 54
Single parents: adult children,
    relations with, 56; community
    status of, 92; mental health, 98,
    100; socioeconomic status and, 92;
    statistics, 92
Slate, 17
Slovak Republic, parental leave, 121*t*
Slovenia, parental leave, 121*t*
Smartphones: digital divide, 72–73;
    family communications, 74; impact
    on children, 68–69; usage
    statistics, 71
Smith, JuliAnna Z., 290–291
Snowball sampling, 147, 305
Social class. *See* Socioeconomic status
Social media: adult children, parental
    relations with, 60–61;
    cyberbullying, 81–82; digital
    footprint and impact, 78; family
    communications, 73–74;
    introduction, xi; parental
    chronicling children's development,
    77–78, 84; parental monitoring of,
    73, 83–84; parental surveillance of
    children's lives, 77, 78, 83–84
Social policies: cultural lag, 161;
    parental mental health and,
    106–108; United States, calls for
    overhaul of, 142. *See also* Health
    insurance; Parental leave programs;
    Work-family supports, western
    Germany
Social relations, children's consumer
    culture and, 204–206, 207, 210
Social stratification, consumer culture
    and, 204
Social well-being of children. *See*
    Child well-being
Socioeconomic status (SES): class-
    based parenting styles, 34, 58,

238–240, 244, 250; definitions,
    difficulty of, 36; digital divide,
    72–73, 74; ethnic-racial
    socialization strategies, 220;
    fertility rates, 91–92; homework
    help and, 40, 40*f*; parental leave
    programs and, 121, 123–124, 125,
    133 n.2; parental mental health
    and, 100–102; parenting styles and,
    34; reproductive medicine, 92;
    school, parental intervention in,
    41–44, 42*t*–43*t*; single parenthood,
    92; text messaging disparities, 74;
    timing of parenthood, 91–92. *See
    also* Inequalities; Inequality,
    understanding of
Solo leisure, 176, 184, 185*f*, 186–187,
    186*f*, 191
South Dakota, same-gender-adoption
    laws, 288
South Korea: children adopted from,
    261, 277; parental leave, 121*t*
Spain, parental leave, 121*t*
Statistical discrimination, 127, 133
    n.4
Stewart, Jon, 286
Stress of parents: child health and,
    125; factors in, 96–98, 101; gender
    disparities, 99; intensive parenting,
    103; LGBT parents, 104–105;
    marital status and, 98; parental
    leave programs and, 124–125;
    racial/ethnic variations in, 101–102;
    socioeconomic factors in, 101;
    variations in, 98–100. *See also*
    Mental health and parenthood
The Stuff of Family Life (Janning),
    xiv–xv
Stuttgart, Germany, 146
Submarine parenting, 17
"Success frame," 242, 249
Sullivan, Orielle, 52
Supreme Court of the United States
    (SCOTUS): same-gender-marriage
    rulings, 284, 287, 288, 302